The Empire in the City

Arab Provincial Capitals in the Late Ottoman Empire

BEIRUTER TEXTE UND STUDIEN

HERAUSGEGEBEN VOM
ORIENT-INSTITUT
DER DEUTSCHEN MORGENLÄNDISCHEN GESELLSCHAFT

BAND 88

THE EMPIRE IN THE CITY

Arab Provincial Capitals in the Late Ottoman Empire

edited by

Jens Hanssen

Thomas Philipp

Stefan Weber

BEIRUT 2002

ERGON VERLAG WÜRZBURG
IN KOMMISSION

Umschlaggestaltung: Taline Yozgatian
Foto auf dem Umschlag: Abdulaly Bros. Baghdad, No 8, „The new bridge and old side of Baghdad" (Ansichtskarte aus der Sammlung Wolf-Dieter Lemke)

Die Deutsche Bibliothek — CIP-Einheitsaufnahme

Ein Titeldatensatz für diese Publikation ist bei
Der Deutschen Bibliothek erhältlich

ISBN 3-935556-89-6

 Gedruckt mit Unterstützung der Deutschen Forschungsgemeinschaft sowie des Orient-Instituts der Deutschen Morgenländischen Gesellschaft, aus Mitteln des Bundesministeriums für Bildung und Forschung.

Ergon-Verlag, Dr. H.-J. Dietrich
Grombühlstr. 7, D-97080 Würzburg

Druck: Dergham sarl
Gedruckt auf alterungsbeständigem Papier
Printed in Lebanon

PREFACE

The articles of this volume were presented at a five day conference on "Arab Provincial Capitals in the Late Ottoman Empire" held at the German Orient Institute in Beirut, the American University of Beirut and ESCWA in April 1999. It was held under the auspices of the Lebanese Ministry of Culture and Higher Education to mark Beirut as the cultural capital of the Arab World in1999. Both the conference and this publication were generously funded by the German Research Council (DFG) and the German Orient Institute in Beirut. To both institutions we would like to express our gratitude for bringing this ambitious project to fruition.

The preparation, organization and co-ordination could not have been possible without the generous help of many individuals. The preparation of the conference was carried out by Sybille Appelt and Philipp Stucki of the Program for Modern Middle Eastern Studies at Erlangen University. To them must also go credit for helping to prepare the manuscript, Stephen McPhillips for his language editing and Stefan Knost for additional proof reading. In Beirut, the former director of the German Orient Institute, Angelika Neuwirth, has been an inspiration throughout. The members of staff at the Orient Institute have provided all the necessary technical assistance and put in many an extra hour to guarantee the smooth running of the conference. The Director of the Orient Institute, Manfred Kropp, deserves special thanks for seeing this publication through and including the volume in the series of the Orient Institute, "Beiruter Texte und Studien". At the American University of Beirut, the director of the Center for Behavioral Research, Samir Khalaf, and his staff have facilitated the usage of AUB premises and infrastructure. Without these individuals and institutes the current publication would not have been possible. To all of them we extend our gratitude.

The book is intended to stimulate debate and offer a variety of historical perspectives, interpretations of sources and methodological approaches to the study of the modern Middle East. We do not attempt to forge one particular line of argument. The conclusions drawn by individual contributors may not necessarily be accepted by others. Many contributions attempt to reconstruct – as case studies embedded in the historical context of cities in the Middle East – particular aspects of urban life. In doing so, they are interdependent, while the different methodological approaches draw their strength from each other. Accounts seem contradictory only if we presuppose that 'history' has a unifying purpose that is external to the individuals and structures that produce it.

The present volume is divided into six parts. In the first part, Makdisi and Hanssen trace the "Discourses and Practices of Ottomanism" in order to capture both the imposition of a new state ideology on provincial societies on the one hand, and local participation and appropriation on the other. While Makdisi takes the view from the imperial center and argues that Ottoman imperialism created colonial differences, Hanssen argues that the new center-periphery relations during the *Tanẓīmāt* reforms took shape in the dialectic process of crisis management between Istanbul and the Ottoman provinces.

The second part, "The Foreign and the Ottoman in the Local Context," looks at regional dynamics in *Bilād al-Shām* prior to the *Tanẓīmāt*, the decades of intense European intervention in mid-century and the concoction of architectural styles and hybrid representations of identities and life-styles in late Ottoman Beirut. Philipp focuses on the first instances of European economic and cultural penetration in Acre at the beginning of the nineteenth century. At the same time, Philipp discerns in Aḥmad Pasha al-Jazzār and his successors in Acre a loyalty to Istanbul which was also expressed in building activity with distinctive Ottoman architectural features. Fawaz examines the period between 1840 and 1860 and shows how European diplomatic politics in Beirut were driven by the perception of Ottoman rule as inefficient and corrupt. European state rivalry in the Eastern Mediterranean turned Beirut into a battleground of conflicting models of rule and life-style that was to dominate urban politics and cultural production in the decades to come. Bodenstein's contribution picks up where Fawaz left off. He engages critically in the notion of 'westernization' in new cultural expressions and discerns a complex process of foreign and local Orientalization as both a form of art and hybrid identity. Drawing on the archeologist Sue West, Bodenstein maintains that "a house reflects the personality, the life style, the taste, the social standing, and the cultural background of its builder" and its residents. He reconstructs the relationship between the owners and residents of a particularly hybrid house in late Ottoman Beirut on the one hand, and its architectural vernaculars on the other.

The third part explores the modes of "participating in Empire, shaping the surroundings and challenging authority." Neumann focuses on eighteenth-century Anatolian towns and argues that even though there did not yet exist a centralized state structure, the local élites found ways to participate in the pre-*Tanẓīmāt* fiscal and administrative reforms of the Ottoman state. This process took place through "concerted action," particularly through petitions to the Sultan. Stefan Weber's contribution demonstrates the degree of internalization of Ottoman reforms among Damascene inhabitants. He introduces wall paintings of intramural residences as clues to understanding a new evidential paradigm for both wide-spread Ottoman loyalties to the imperial state and for the simultaneous discovery of a place for oneself in the modern world at large. Chalcraft examines the means of protection available to low-level artisans and providers of public services *vis à vis* encroaching British colonial rule and Egyptian state-building processes. Taking the cab drivers as a case study, he argues that far from constituting passive obstacles to 'modernization', urban professionals in the transport sector managed to challenge the Anglo-Egyptian authorities, again through petitions and, later, general strike, and rally public and intellectual support behind them.

The fourth part concentrates on benevolent endowments, the *waqf*, in order to trace an "urban institution between centralization and autonomy". The *waqf* was an omnipresent and long-standing urban institution which shaped urban politics across the Muslim worlds and stood at the center of Ottoman reform efforts. Indeed, as Meier argues in her contribution, the *waqf* "became one of the battlefields ... of reform in the name of progress and modernization." The imperial government recognized that the institution generated immense economic and fiscal revenues and sought to control and siphon off its output. Deguilhem argues that despite consistent efforts by the Ottoman government to centralize and streamline its structure, local urban élites – clerical or commercial, Muslim or Christian – continued to maintain a considerable autonomy over the everyday management and distribution of income of the *waqf*s.

In the fifth part, Lemke offers a visual introduction to the manifestations of a new Ottoman presence in the provinces. Through an analysis of photographs of government buildings, public squares and urban inhabitants he demonstrates the new dimensions of the production of space in Arab provincial capitals.

In the sixth part, the present volume examines the role of "Empire, patrons and domestic architecture" in different towns of the Eastern Mediterranean: Mersin, Aleppo, Beirut and al-Salṭ. All three contributions place architectural production within the new imperial frame of the Ottoman Empire. At the same time, specificities and communalities between the towns which serve their respective regions are given prime importance. Yenişehirlioğlu and Mollenhauer compare domestic architecture in Mersin and in al-Salt respectively to the building styles that began to develop in Beirut during the 1830s and 40s. As such Beirut emerges as a sub-center of cultural production in the late Ottoman Empire.

Like Yenişehirlioğlu in the case of the *waqf* of Bezm-i Alem Valide Sultan, and Mollenhauer in the case of the mansion ("*qaṣr*") of the local merchant Abū Jābir, Gonnella approaches new architectural production in Aleppo through the patronship of al-Sayyid Abū 'l-Hudā. At the point where biographical information on Abū-l Hudā becomes blurred or seemingly unreliable and, indeed, in itself contradictory in the haze of historiographical representations, she draws on an entirely different evidentiary paradigm – the architectural representations of his building complex in Aleppo. Like Weber, Mollenhauer and Bodenstein, she uses architectural styles as historical indicators of expressions of personal identity and self-perception.

The seventh and final part of the present volume takes up the question of Ottoman colonialism in the empire's most distant provinces, Baghdad and Yemen, as "the Ottoman civilizing mission". Both provinces share the fate of being latecomers to the family of *Tanẓīmāt* provinces. Baghdad was incorporated from the relative autonomy of Ottoman-Mamluk households in 1830, while Yemen was coerced back into the empire only in 1872, after a long period of local dynastic rule. Herzog examines the city of Baghdad through the eyes of Istanbul's literary élites. Travel books, proverbs and lexicons attest to an imperial discourse of cultural difference between the 'modern' center in Istanbul and the 'backward' periphery in Baghdad. Like Herzog, Thomas Kühn draws on Osterhammel's definition of colonialism when he traces the development of a discourse of the colonial 'other' in the city of Sanaʿa. Imperial bureaucrats operating in Yemen shared the urgency of an Ottoman civilizing mission comparable to European colonialists in North Africa and other colonies elsewhere in the world. Blumi warns us that the heuristic distinctions academics draw between tribes and urban dwellers, or between urban and rural spheres, are the categories with which imperial rulers try to make sense of the intricacies of local conflicts. Identification according to these distinctions are also ways in which local power groups present themselves in order to obtain their goals both *vis à vis* their local rivals and the Ottoman government. Instead, Blumi proposes to disentangle the macroscopic categories of analysis and examines the strategic utilization of the identitarian entities ('the tribe', 'the city', etc.) by different actors in Yemeni micropolitics.

TABLE OF CONTENTS

IV. URBAN INSTITUTIONS BETWEEN CENTRALIZATION AND AUTONOMY

V. PORTRAYING A NEW OTTOMAN PRESENCE

VI. EMPIRE, PATRONS AND DOMESTIC ARCHITECTURE

VII. THE OTTOMAN CIVILIZING MISSION

Abbreviations of Periodicals and Publishers

AAS: Asian and African Studies

AHA: Annales d'Histoire et Archéologie

AHR: American History Review

AHROS: Arab Historical Review for Ottoman Studies

AO: Archivum Ottomanicum

BJMES: British Journal of Middle East Studies

CSSH: Comparative Studies in Society and History

EI: Encyclopaedia of Islam

IHR: International History Review

IJMES: International Journal of Middle Eastern Studies

IJTS: International Journal for Turkish Studies

JAOS: Journal of the American Oriental Society

JESHO: Journal of Economic and Social History of the Orient

JUH: Journal for Urban History

MEJ: Middle East Journal

MES: Middle East Studies

NLR: New Left Review

NPT: New Perspectives on Turkey

REMMM: Revue des Etudes du Monde Musulman et Méditerranéen

ST: Studia Islamica

WI: Die Welt des Islams

ZDPV: Zeitschrift des Deutschen Palestina Verein

INTRODUCTION: TOWARDS A NEW URBAN PARADIGM

A Space of Socio-Economic Integration: the Eastern Mediterranean under Review

Cities in the Eastern Mediterranean region look back on a rich history encompassing thousands of years. During the long duration of Greek, Roman, Byzantine, Venetian, Caliphal and Ottoman rule, cities grew prosperous or were abandoned as economic cycles, the establishment of new settlements, trade and pilgrimage routes affected patterns of human transience and demographic change to constitute the coherence and vitality of an economic, social and cultural space that marks – as Fernand Braudel insists – the Mediterranean Sea until at least the seventeenth century. As we move into the eighteenth and nineteenth centuries we are presented with a Mediterranean economy that was fundamentally structured by the forces of an accelerating world-economy. Indeed, from the middle of the nineteenth century until today these cities were caught up in an intense process of profound changes, ruptures and new developments. This period is generally characterized by the impact of capital flow of global dimensions, by an evolving modernization of political, administrative and economic patterns and institutions, by enormous demographic and cultural changes and urban growth. The new transport and communication infrastructure and the expansion of European political dominance enhanced the region's geo-political and strategic position as a link between three continents and world seas.

Braudel's notion that the Mediterranean space exerts its own rhythm and, indeed, structural limits to individual and state agency was taken up enthusiastically, first by historians of demographic change in the Ottoman Empire,[1] and more recently by world-systems historians with an urban-centered perspective at the Fernand Braudel Center in Binghampton. They expound the idea that these cities began to share cultural similarities in the

1 Ömer L. Barkan, "La 'Méditerranée' de Fernand Braudel vue d'Istanbul," *Annales, E.S.C.* (1954), 189-200, and M. Cook, *Population Pressures in Rural Anatolia*, London 1972.

late eighteenth and nineteenth centuries due to their trade-based economies. They demonstrate how port cities were linked to each other on a number of levels through the agency of new urban-based, foreign and local merchant classes.[2] It is tacitly assumed that at the same time, these centers were therefore fundamentally different from inland cities of the Ottoman Empire. While we are offered the 'Mediterranean City' as a regional variation of the 'Colonial City' paradigm and as an alternative urban typology to the previously dominant paradigm of the 'Islamic City', Braudel's critique of the conventional historical view that "we historians of the west... glimpse the Turkish world from the outside only" still remains. The geographical boundaries of analysis are merely pushed to the Eastern Mediterranean shores where pockets of westernization form 'colonial bridgeheads', passively facilitating economic exploitation (or development, depending on one's political persuasion).

Despite the new understanding offered by Owen and Islamoğlu-Inan in *The Middle East in the World-Economy, 1800-1914*, and *The Ottoman Empire and the World-Economy* respectively, the 'west' uncomfortably remains the sole referent of social change. All individual or local activity is seen to develop in reaction to processes that originate in the 'west'. Those affected by the structural transformations of the world-economy are left, somewhat mechanically, to benefit (primarily 'minorities' – Jews, Greeks, Armenians, and other Christians) or suffer (members of a 'religio-traditional' economic order – the *qāḍī*, guilds, feudal lords, etc.) the consequences. In this view the historical subject can never quite step out of the objective and deterministic historical processes and acts merely in response to external influences and structures.

In the influential issue of the *Review* in 1993, the editors concluded that "[p]ort cities in the periphery emerge as the privileged locales of contact in the world capitalist economy."[3] The Eastern Mediterranean of the nineteenth century now emerges as "a sub-system of the world-economy" which was marked by liberal exchange ('liberal' because it was largely outside Ottoman state intervention and took place – as Kasaba put it – in the "nonstate arena"[4]). Thus this sub-system was also marked by the high

---

2 Donald Quataert, Raşat Kasaba, Elena Frangakis-Syrett, Basil Gounaris, Çağlar Keyder, Eyüp Özveren, "Port Cities in the Ottoman Empire," (Izmir, Patras, Salonica, Beirut, Alexandria), *Review* 16 (Autumn, 1993).

3 Ibid., 518.

4 Raşat Kasaba, "A time and a place for the nonstate: social change in the Ottoman Empire during the 'long nineteenth-century'," in *State Power and Social Forces: Domination and Transformation in the Third World*, edited by J. Migdal, A. Kohli and V. Shue, Cambridge 1994, 207-230.

degree of autonomy for a Levantine commercial bourgeoisie which – significantly – reinvested their income at home, in the ports, trading companies and land in and around their cities of origin.[5] As such the new consumption patterns and the ostentatious domestic architecture that emerged around the Eastern Mediterranean in the second half of the nineteenth-century was very much part of this locally produced Mediterranean subsystem.

Despite this paradigm's regional sensitivity to nineteenth-century urban history, *Empire in the City* intends to redress some of its theoretical assumptions and limitations of perspectives. Criticism from within the Binghampton School argued soon after, that work on port cities remained eurocentric and denied historical agency to the Ottoman state.[6] Moreover, methodologically the approach is unable – and indeed unwilling – to incorporate the discursive, semiotic or hermeneutic dimensions of social transformation.[7] All these aspects affected changes in social structures, shaped and 'domesticated' the world-economy and state-led modernization during the nineteenth century.

The present volume introduces the cultural dimension of change in the late Ottoman Empire. As we shall see in the course of this introduction and the book at large, the way we understand "the idea of culture" goes beyond the somewhat common sensical, all-embracing definition famously offered in the latter half of the nineteenth century by the founding father of British social anthropology, E. B. Tylor, as "that complex whole which includes knowledge, belief, art, morals, law, custom, and other capabilities and habits acquired by man as a member of society."[8]

As historians of the Ottoman Empire, the "Cultural Turn" offers us new perspectives and methodologies to deal with old and new archival material and interpret new sources as historical. The new sources introduced in this volume allow us to analyze symbolic and real-life struggles as well as everyday practices and experiences of modernity (see Chalcraft). In order to capture these struggles, practices and experiences, we rely on Stuart Hall's definition of culture as "'the lived practices' or practical ide-

---

5 Farouk Tabak, "Local Merchants in Peripheral Areas of the Empire: the Fertile Crescent during the Long Nineteenth Century," *Review* 11:2 (1988), 179-214.

6 W. G. Martin, "The World-Systems Perspective in Perspective: Assessing the Attempt to Move beyond Nineteenth-Century Eurocentric Conceptions," *Review* 17:2 (1994), 145-185.

7 Stuart Clarke, "The Annales Historians," in *The Return of Grand Theory in the Human Sciences*, edited by Quentin Skinner, Cambridge 1985, 196-198.

8 E. B. Tylor, *Primitive Cultures*, vol. 1, London 1871, 1.

ologies which enable a society, group or class to experience, define, interpret and make sense of its conditions of existence."[9]

Bringing the Ottoman State Back In

To consider nineteenth century Mediterranean history as operating in the "nonstate arena" is highly problematic (leaving aside Kasaba's assumed nexus of 'the liberal'), because it leaves out a whole empire metaphorically as well as literally – of signs, cultural expressions and societal articulations that gave meaning to the unfolding transformations. *Empire in the City* proposes to bring the Ottoman state (back) into the analysis of the (urban) culture of imperialism and center-periphery relations in the Middle East and Eastern Mediterranean. In doing so, we have to locate, as Makdisi has formulated so aptly in this volume, the "dynamic project that was worked on two fronts simultaneously and dialectically: the domestic and the foreign." Ottoman élites aspired to catch up with Europe and at the same time 'reform' the provinces. During the 'long nineteenth century', the Ottoman Empire was opened up to new influences from Europe but it was also a time of unprecedented integration of the empire, of strengthening the center, and of imperial power bearing upon the provinces – and not only the port cities.

The integration of the empire was pursued in many different ways: Government administration was reorganized on the imperial as well as the local level; establishing judiciary and executive councils in the provincial centers which gave certain local elements a voice in the management of local affairs but also enticed those elements to work closer with the central government. For the same purpose legislation and the law was reconstructed and canonized.[10] Legislation – enforced by the central administrative authorities – penetrated and shaped with a previsouly unknown intensity all aspects of life of provincial societies, such as building codes, regulations and laws concerning civil records, health and education. This constitutes – borrowing from Deringil – the administrative "fine-tuning" of the Ottoman Empire.[11] Finally, technological developments drew all parts of the empire together. Ships, railways, roads, and the telegraph brought

---

9 Stuart Hall, "Culture and the State," quoted in Eagleton, *The Idea of Culture*, 34.

10 Stéphane Yerasimos, "A propos des Reformes Urbaines des Tanzimat," in P. Dumont and F. Géorgeon (eds.), *Villes Ottomanes à la Fin de l'Empire*, Paris 1992, 17-32.

11 Selim Deringil, *The Well-Protected Domains; Ideology and the Legitimation of Power in the Ottoman Empire 1876-1909,* London 1998, 10.

Istanbul closer to the provinces than ever before. All administrative and legislative integration had its source and focus in Istanbul. At the same time, modern technological innovations also drew different Ottoman regions much closer to Europe.[12] The establishment of regular steamship services, the construction of ports and railways, as well as the promotion of European financial institutions in provincial capital, efficiently facilitated Europe's permanent quest for cheaper raw materials and new markets. Yet, particularly after the period of heightened and unprecedented European interventionism in the internal affairs of the Ottoman Empire between 1840 and 1864,[13] much European influence thereafter reached the provinces via Istanbul.

The present volume intends to overcome those notions of modernization that continue to inform the histories viewed from the center as normative-rational and enlightened imperial projects.[14] The provincial populations in the Ottoman Empire were deemed unwilling or even recalcitrant objects of modernization which had three primary sources of origin: the European economy, Christian missionaries and high, enlightened Ottoman bureaucrats. As will been demonstrated, the will to reform was not absorbed only by a small sector of Ottoman society; nor was the process of reform one of 'Westernization' and therefore alienating 'traditional identities'.

Against these views, the contributions of Hanssen, Chalcraft or Neumann demonstrate that these societies played a formative role in the process of modernization. Moreover, the contributions of Makdisi and Blumi demonstrate that the principle of political organization along the lines of 'traditional identities' only emerged as a product of the politics of modernization and the culture of modernity.[15] Finally, Mollenhauer and Weber show that the Ottoman reform process corresponded to a wide-spread experience of life in the Arab provinces. However, to emphasize greater social, economic and cultural congruence between imperial center and provincial periphery (than has been conceded by Marxian

---

12 This process has recently been discussed in T. Philipp, and B. Schaebler (eds.), *The Syrian Land in the 18th and 19th Century: Integration and Fragmentation,* Stuttgart 1998.

13 See Leila Fawaz' contribution.

14 For examples of this view, see J.S. Shaw, E. Shaw, *History of the Ottoman Empire and Modern Turkey*, 2 Vols., Cambridge 1977; or Carter Findley, "The Evolution of the System of Provincial Administration as Viewed from the Centre", in *Palestine in the Late Ottoman Period*, edited by D. Kushner, Leiden 1986, 3-29.

15 This notion follows a critical application of E. Hobsbawm, and T. Ranger (eds.), *The Invention of Tradition*, Cambridge 1994 (3rd ed.), to the Ottoman context.

and nationalist historiography) should not be read as imperialist nostalgia – a trend that has gained considerable currency in recent Ottoman historiography.[16] Nor – and this leads us to the next step of inquiry – does the attempt at bringing the Ottoman imperial state back into the framework of urban analysis succumb to what Ernest Gellner called – in a different context – "the sin of excessive charity" towards a floundering, non-Western empire that was itself under European military, political and economic pressures.[17]

Ottoman Imperialism and Discourses of Modernity

An underlying question of this volume is whether late Ottoman rule over its Arab provinces was comparable to imperialisms and colonialisms that characterized other parts of the world under European rule. More specifically, did the "benevolent" *Tanẓīmāt* reforms (*Tanẓīmāt-i ḥayriye*) turn the Ottoman Empire into a colonial empire? Is it time to 'mainstream' the Ottoman Empire and integrate it into academic debates on imperialism and colonialism elsewhere in the world, or would we abandon the specificities of the historical Ottoman context? This is not to provide a yes or no answer but to open up a new, multi-polar and complex line of inquiry that prioritizes everyday contact as well as practical and discursive interweaving between the imperial center and the provincial periphery. On the contrary, this line of inquiry rejects the notions that ethnic, racial or linguistic difference was congruent with state-society, ruler-ruled, Ottoman versus Arab divides.[18]

The Ottoman state was itself heavily indebted to European powers and banks. The Ottoman government was forced to abolish its long-standing, redistributive economy following the Anglo-Ottoman Trade Agreement of 1838. The Ottoman state gave up all remaining trade and industry mo-

---

16 For a critical – but somewhat reinforcing – engagement with the issue of Ottoman heritage, see L. Carl Brown (ed.), *Imperial Legacy: The Ottoman Imprint on the Balkans and the Middle East*, New York 1996.

17 Ernest Gellner, "Concepts and Society," in *Rationality*, edited by B. R. Wilson, Oxford 1970, 18-49.

18 On a timely critique of topographical notions of modern state-society, see Timothy Mitchell, "The Limits of the State, Beyond Statist Approaches and their Critics," *American Political Science Review* 85:1 (1991). Mitchell argues that the appearance of a state and society as separate entities should not be treated as natural givens but as discursively (but no less powerfully) produced.

nopolies.[19] This enabled European merchants to deal directly with port-city merchants and agricultural and sericultural producers in the hinterland. Indeed, we concur with Pamuk that in comparative perspective, the Ottoman Empire in the nineteenth century became itself peripheralized by world-economic forces neither as formal colony, nor as "belonging to the 'informal empire' of an imperialist power," but rather that the Ottoman Empire presented a case whereby

> the central bureaucracy was strong enough vis-à-vis imperialist powers and/or the rivalry among those powers was such that these countries never became part of a formal or informal empire. As a result of this particular constellation of power, greater integration into the world-economy could not readily proceed through an alliance between the dominant interests in the center countries and those social classes in the periphery whose interests lay in the same direction. Instead, this process advanced through an accommodation between the former and the [merchants and export-oriented landlords] and the central bureaucracy.[20]

Against this international perspective, *Empire in the City* explores the effect of Ottoman rule of Arab provinces through the prism of their capital cities during the *Tanẓīmāt* period. We propose to consider Ottoman imperialism as instantiating colonial situations rather than constituting a closed, coherent and clearly structured system of power. These situations occurred not only in French and British colonies but between so-called peripheral regions such as Chinese dynastic rule over Eastern Asia, pre-capitalist India or, less distantly, Meḥmet ʿAli Pasha's.[21] Indeed, we echo Herzog – who quotes Michael Adas in this volume – that one should not automatically "equate colonialism with European expansion and European domination of overseas peoples and cultures".[22]

Although each province of the Ottoman Empire had a particular geographical (Baghdad, Yemen) and discursive (Mount Lebanon) distance from the metropole, a typology of colonies – as offered by Moses Finley –

---

19 O. Okyar, "The Role of the State in the Economic Life of the 19th Century Ottoman Empire," in *AAS* 14 (1980), 143-164.

20 Şevket. Pamuk, "The Ottoman Empire in Comparative Perspective," *Review* 11:2 (1988), 131.

21 Khalid Fahmi, *All the Pasha's Men*, Cambridge 1998.

22 Michael Adas, "Imperialism and Colonialism in Comparative Perspective," *IHR* 20.2 (1998), 371.

is of little use.[23] During the four centuries of Ottoman rule over its Arab provinces, center and periphery were connected and intricately intertwined historically and culturally through career-paths, pilgrimage, marriage, political acculturation and religious networks to name but a few examples.[24] Long-standing elite- and everyday interaction throughout the realms of the Ottoman Empire defied the ethnic, racial, and geographic boundaries of exclusion that marked the violent and abrupt intervention of European imperialism in its colonies. *ʿUlamāʾ* from the Arab provinces had frequently been *Shaykh al-Islāms* in Istanbul throughout the Ottoman centuries. Right up to the end of Ottoman rule, grand veziers were born in the provinces or married the daughters of provincial notables. Christians and Jews held key ministries under Abdülhamid II and the Young Turks. Despite powerful *Tanẓīmāt* centralization efforts and later Young Turk unification projects, local institutions, such as the *waqf* administration described by Deguilhem and Meier in this volume, remained in local hands.

'Control' and 'resistance' are never as absolute as its exercisers pretend. Indeed, in the search for effective and equitable governance the imperial government in Istanbul modeled its provincial administration on the imperial interpretations of the demands of certain provincial representatives – i.e. on experiences drawn from the very provinces to which the new provincial rule came to be applied between 1864 and 1867. We cannot, therefore, speak of historical culture of political difference along (protonational) Turkish-Arab racial lines. Nor was the Ottoman state the prime – let alone the sole – beneficiary of the economic exploitation of 'indigenous' peoples or resources. We are dealing with an Ottoman imperialism without colonies but one which generated, in certain places and at certain times, colonial situations.

The provincial, urban experience of Ottoman modernity encompassed a variety of human sensibilities that reflected the specific and changing meanings of space, time and being. Ottoman modernization, constituted a process of societal restructuring that accelerated during the nineteenth century to produce a significant geographical recomposition of the time-space-being continuum in the concrete forms of state centralization. As an ambivalent and malleable concept of existence inside – and immanent to – the historical process, time acquired a distinct quality of political use in modern European and Ottoman imperial discourses alike. In the Arab

---

23 Moses Finley, "Colonies: An Attempt at a Typology," in *Transactions of the Royal Historical Society*, 5. Series, 26 (1976), 167-188.

24 Suraiya Faroqhi, *Kultur und Alltag in Osmanischen Reich: Vom Mittelalter bis zum Anfang des 20. Jahrhunderts*, München 1995.

provinces of the late Ottoman Empire, there evolved a dual cultural process. Certain individuals and groups in the provinces aspired to 'fit in' with the 'spirit of the age' while others appropriated the imperial policy of representative and equitable justice by imagining themselves in identitarian discourses of cultural authenticity and difference. This dual process found expression not only in central institutions and imperial bureaucracies but also in the writings of the *Nahḍa* intellectuals in Beirut and Cairo.[25] Moreover, as Stefan Weber shows in this volume, the consumption of – and the sense of belonging to – a self-consciously modern 'spirit of the age' gained far wider currency among the inhabitants of Damascus than has hitherto been credited in scholarship.

Late Ottoman imperialism emerged on the one hand as a dialectic and discursive process between imperial perceptions of the empire's own past and its provinces as backward on the one hand and of contemporary European states as models of progress and modernity to be aspired to on the other. It is the discourse of modernity (and not necessarily modernization per se) that set the *Tanẓīmāt* period apart from preceding modes of Ottoman provincial rule. The *Tanẓīmāt* reform fundamentally changed the political discourse in which some modes of social organization such as tribes in Yemen or institutions such as the guilds came to be viewed as remnants of the past that hindered 'enlightened' imperial reforms. Through the *Tanẓīmāt* reforms, the state attempted to assume a monopoly over the interpretation and implementation of 'modernity'. Yet, this attempt was constantly challenged by the pervasive presence of European missionaries, consuls and entrepreneurs in the Arab provinces. In his book *The Well-Protected Domain*, Deringil ably traces Ottomanism as a state ideology which at once tried to "minimize the exotic" within the empire, while 'othering' unincorporated groups of Ottoman provincial societies as 'traditional' and 'primitive' at world exhibitions, in the imperial museum, photo albums and travel literature. In fact, the metropolitan discourse of modernity employed the same attributes of culture discerned by E. B. Tylor: "knowledge, belief, art, morals, law, custom".[26] Drawing on Deringil's study, Herzog, Kühn, Blumi and Makdisi in this volume analyze how, in the cases of Mount Lebanon, Baghdad and Yemen, a discourse of the provincial, 'primordial other' informed the imperial perception of these three provinces. In the case of Mount Lebanon, this discourse becomes institutional reality through the implementation of imperial policy. In a similar

25 Jens Hanssen, "Public Morality and Marginality in *fin de siècle* Beirut," in *Outside In: On the Margins of the Modern Middle East*, edited by E. Rogan, London, 2002, 240-264.

26 See footnotes 8 and 9.

vein, Kühn and Blumi show in their work on Ottoman Yemen how the new institutional system of reference under centralized imperial rule was appropriated – "strategically utilized" – by certain local actors to advance their own social and political standing in the locality.

Center – Periphery Relations: 'Identifying 'the Ottoman'

In the nineteenth century, the image of the Muslim ruler governing the community of believers dealing with more or less obedient provinces receded into the background. Instead the idea developed of a center that was 'modern' and 'progressive' and which made it its mission to communicate and transfer this new condition to its provinces which had become by the same token 'traditional' and 'reactionary'. This view from the metropole was not necessarily shared by the urban societies in the provinces. Here, too, transitions were observed, changes initiated, and new world-views adopted. Did the total sum of these trends strengthen the integration of the empire or tear its social fabric apart? Did the center become a colonizer perceiving for itself a *mission civilisatrice* or did it become the pivot for a new kind of participant integration of the whole empire?

Given the historical transformations under the conditions of self-conscious modernity, the longstanding center-periphery relations in the late Ottoman Empire acquired new sets of reference through the *Tanẓīmāt* reforms. Based on efforts at population censuses, passports were issued and travel permits required by the 1840s in order to control population movement and make taxation more efficient. As a consequence, during the *Tanẓīmāt*, the passport became the official and exclusive marker of Ottoman subjecthood (or, indeed, citizenship). Yet, the passport was only a necessary but not a sufficient criterion for being Ottoman in the dynamic center-periphery relations.

Only two short works, by Şerif Mardin, and Metin Heper, explicitly deal with intra-Ottoman center-periphery relations in the nineteenth century. They are marked by the well-established prose of the passing of a traditional, feudal society into modernity through well-intended, state-led modernization initiated by a Weberian process of bureaucratization. To Mardin, Ottoman center-periphery relations were marked by constant "unidimensional" confrontation, and subversion ("rebellion" and "bribing") by the periphery.[27] Where compromises between the government and the local élites were achieved and where "localism [was] tolerated by the center" these only con-

[27] Şerif Mardin, "Centre-Periphery Relations: a Key to Turkish Politics?," *Daedalus* 102 (Winter 1973), 170-1.

tributed to an entrenchment of the 'primordial Oriental' structures that the enlightened program of reform attempted – in vain – to eradicate. "The provinces thus became centers of 'reaction'"[28], and by implication were to be blamed for Turkey's development failures in the 20th century. Heper argued in a similarly statist preconception:

> Two types of relationships existed between the center and the periphery: power politics and a degenerated form of patron-client relationship. The change that took place has been no more than a segregative change. Change in the periphery itself was not evolutionary, let alone revolutionary. At times it showed signs of involution; any weakening of the central control led to maximum legal irresponsibility.[29]

Heper's 1980 article defines the center as personified by those groups "who tried to uphold the state's autonomy and supremacy in the polity."[30] Indeed, "service in one of the central bureaucracies gradually inculcated a loyalty to the state," a process that was recently examined with regard to the graduates of the *Mülkiye Mektebi* in Istanbul in Corinne Blake's excellent study on "Training Arab-Ottoman Bureaucrats."[31] Yet, where we take issue with Mardin and Heper, is their mechanistic and state-centered typology of the relationship between the center and the periphery in the Ottoman Empire that, in fact, regurgitates the very perceptions of Ottoman imperial reformers.

Ottoman center-periphery relations cannot be explained by a zero-sum-game logic. Borrowed from the realist school of international relations there exists almost a knee-jerk assumption that – here in Heper's clumsy language – "[local] authority increased to the same proportion that the authority of the state in the localities became weakened. They [local notables?] filled a vacuum; they did not actively overcome authority."[32] Rather, as Hanssen argues in his essay, 'Ottomanization' and 'localization' took place simultaneously and conditioned each other. The focus is on the geographical and social differences in varied contexts.

Thus, on the one hand, Makdisi discerns colonial situations in the way Fuad Pasha dealt with the 1860 civil war in Mount Lebanon and the way

28 Mardin, "Centre-Periphery Relations," 179.

29 Metin Heper, "Center and Periphery in the Ottoman Empire, with special Reference to the 19th Century," *International Political Science Review* 1/1 (1980), 81.

30 Heper, "Center and Periphery in the Ottoman Empire".

31 Corinne Blake, *Training Arab-Ottoman Bureaucrats: Syrian Graduates of the Mülkiyye Mektebi, 1890-1920*, Princeton 1991.

32 Heper, "Center and Periphery in the Ottoman Empire," 87.

Osman Hamdi Bey and his brother represented Arabs as the backward 'other' in their ethnographic photo albums. Likewise, Herzog, examining Ottoman travel literature, discerns a recurrent trope of Baghdadi – and especially Iraqi – backwardness. On the other hand, Stefan Weber discerns a widespread internalization of being Ottoman in public and domestic spaces in Damascus by taking Ottoman motifs of wall-paintings in Damascene houses as clues to their owners' socio-political identity and affiliation. To simplify, Ottomanization as we understand it in this volume is the self-consciously Ottoman process of modernizing the provincial peripheries of empire. Localisation is the process of utilizing the new political and architectural field of Ottoman integration in order to carve out arenas of participation, negotiation and subversion.

As we shall see in Lemke's contribution, urban spaces became invested with a specific Ottoman meaning through commemorative architecture, flags, military marches and music as well as the repetitive ceremonials of awarding Ottoman medals to local notables-turned-bureaucrats.[33] In yet another turn of the identitarian processes of center-periphery relations in the late Ottoman Empire, Bodenstein discerns a degree of cultural hybridity, an auto-orientalization of style, decoration and dress, both amongst the local élites and foreign inhabitants of Beirut.

Under these circumstances it is clearly impossible, certainly undesirable, to arrive at a rigid, monolithic definition of who an Ottoman was, lest we take the normative categories of the Ottoman state at face value. We use the terms 'center' and 'periphery' to denote political, social and cultural relations *within* the realms of the Ottoman Empire. For clarity and to avoid world-economic connotations, we will add two adjectives and speak of 'imperial center' and 'provincial periphery'. As we shall see, these relations were determined by geography as much as by identity politics, political access and social hierarchy.

The appearance of a new centralized administrative grid exerted a powerful homogenizing quality after the Provincial Law of 1864.[34] Indeed

---

33 Selim Deringil, "Invention of Tradition as Public Image in the late Ottoman Empire, 1808-1908," *CSSH* 35:1 (1993): 3-29. For an example of commemorative Ottoman architecture in the province, see Jens Hanssen, "'Your Beirut is on my Desk', Ottomanizing Beirut under Sultan Abdülhamid II (1876-1909)," in *Projecting Beirut: Episodes of the Construction and Reconstruction of a Modern City*, edited by H. Sarkis and P. Rowe, London 1998, 41-67. Stefan Weber, "Der Marğa-Platz in Damaskus – Die Entstehung eines modernen Stadtzentrums unter den Osmanen als Ausdruck strukturellen Wandels (1808-1918)," *Damaszener Mitteilungen*, 10 (1998), 291-344, Taf. 77-88.

34 Following the *Idare ʿUmumi Vilayetler* of 1864, the administrative divisions were: *vilayet* (province), consisting of an average of 4-5 *sancaq*s or *liva*s (districts) which consisted of *kaẓa*s (subdistricts or townships) which consisted of *qariye*s. On all levels

– to borrow from Mitchell[35] – the appearance of a provincial order produced an order of appearance through an immense alignment of office hierarchies and bureaucratic competences, institutional atomization and proliferation of spatially separated locales of responsibility. The pervasiveness of this order and the regularity of its appearance represented an ideal state against which transgressions came to be measured and on the basis of which the Ottoman state carried out its 'fine-tuning' through "meticulous inculcation, indoctrination, enticing, frightening, flattering, forbidding, permitting, punishing or rewarding."[36] Within these evolving relations, provincial capitals were defined by their interstitial role between imperial center and provincial periphery. Despite the large-scale centralization and the totalising imperial discourse, different provincial capitals attracted different imperial perceptions and policies. Whereas before, Ottoman provinces referred fiscally, politically and legally to tax-farmers and *mutasallim*s resident in urban centers, under the new provincial laws of 1864 and 1867 the urban centers themselves became the referent points of provincial societies and the imperial government alike.

Towards an Alternative City Paradigm: Provincial Capitals in the Late Ottoman Empire

Cities are heterogeneous structures of social organization. The present volume is premised on Raymond's definition that "a city, that is to say a geographical concentration of a large population, can only subsist or develop within a system of coherent relations between its society and the space in which it expands."[37] It is significant here that Raymond employs a working hypothesis that is deliberately devoid of common references in Middle East urban studies, such as the 'Oriental'[38], the 'Muslim'[39] or the

---

there existed local councils which reported to the next higher authority. The provincial council reported to the governor and the Interior Ministry in Istanbul. See BBA, *Yildiz-Esas Evraki, 37/47/47-112.*

35 Timothy Mitchell, "An Appearance of Order," in his *Colonizing Egypt*, Cambridge 1988, 63-94.

36 Deringil, *The Well-protected Domains*, 10.

37 André Raymond, "Islamic City, Arab City: Orientalist myths and recent views," *BJMES* 21 (1994), 17.

38 Eugen Wirth, "Die Orientalische Stadt; Ein Überblick aufgrund jüngerer Forschungen zur materiellen Kultur," *Saeculum* 26:1 (1975), 45-94; Eugen Wirth, "Zur Konzeption der Islamischen Stadt; Privatheit im islamischen Orient versus Öffentlichkeit in Antike und Okzident," *WI* 31 (1991), 50-91.

39 Ira Lapidus, "Muslim Cities and Islamic Societies," in *Middle Eastern Cities*, edited by I. Lapidus, Los Angeles 1969, 47-79; for a subtle critique, see L. C. Brown, "The Uses

'Islamic'[40] city. The Orientalists' city paradigm has long been criticized for their evaluative perspective in comparison to Weberian ancient and medieval urban ideal-types ("essentially characterised *by what it is not*"[41]), their attribute-centered approach (a mosque, a *sūq*, and a *madrasa*), and their inability to account for the city's legal and administrative organization and regional particularities.[42] In this respect, Raymond's call to break down the units of analysis to 'Arab' in the Mediterranean domain and 'Turkish' and 'Irano-Afghan' elsewhere in the Islamic world is well taken. But what he does, in fact, is to replace one essentialist attribute with another – Islam with Arabo-Mediterranean, Oriental with Turko-Ottoman.

The 'Colonial City' is more than just a capitalist construction. Mitchell eloquently argues that it is a powerful, deliberate and constant representation of colonial truths on 'Oriental backwardness' and the cultural superiority of Western rationalism, progress and modernity:

> The identity of the modern city is created by what is kept out. Its modernity is something contingent upon the exclusion of its own opposite. In order to determine itself as the place of order, reason, propriety, cleanliness, civilization and power, it must represent outside itself what is irrational, disordered, dirty, libidinous, barbarian and crowded. The city requires this "outside" in order to present itself, in order to constitute its singular, uncorrupted identity.[43]

So compelling were these colonial representations that, according to Mitchell, they convinced the colonized themselves of their own deviation from that constructed truth. But here the colonial city approach becomes problematic. There exists a paradoxical continuity between certain assumptions of false consciousness about the local internalization of this colonial construct and the passivity and inescapable predeterminedness

---

of a Concept: The 'Muslim City,' in *Middle Eastern Cities in Comparison*, (eds.) K. Brown, M. Gilsenan & al., New Jersey, 1996, 73-82.

40 Gustave von Grunebaum, "Die Islamische Stadt," *Saeculum* 6 (1955), 138-153 and the contemporary critique by Claude Cahen, "Zur Geschichte der städtischen Gesellschaft im islamischen Orient des Mittelalters," *Saeculum* 9, (1958), 59-76; A. Hourani and S. M. Stern (eds.), *The Islamic City*, Oxford 1970; Halil Inalcik, "Istanbul: An Islamic City," *Journal of Islamic Studies* 1 (1990), 1-23.

41 Raymond, "Islamic City, Arab City," 7.

42 See for example Dale Eikelman, "Is there an Islamic City? The Making of a Quarter in a Moroccan Town," *IJMES* 5 (1974), 274-294, Janet Abu-Lughod, "The Islamic City: Historic Myth, Islamic Essence and Contemporary Relevance," *IJMES* 19 (1987), 155-176.

43 Mitchell, *Colonizing Egypt*, see fn. 35, 165.

in both the 'Islamic' and the 'Colonial City'. Despite the important contributions of the 'Colonial City' paradigm in deconstructing the 'Oriental City' as a colonial invention, there are similarities in the two approaches that tend to obfuscate local dynamics in any given city. In the 'Islamic City' the despotism of the rulers left no room for urban autonomy. Likewise, the powerful European armies, steamships, companies and banks nipped all nascent local initiative in the bud. By extension, then, there prevails a sense that both models share Max Weber's underlying assumption that cities in the Middle East are locales of illegitimate authority.[44] It is assumed that without colonial exploitation there would have been a more "authentic" and autonomous development towards modernization, and that whatever transformation was created at the hands of the colonizers or their local allies failed to ignite an essentially stagnant environment.

Mitchell is aware of these implications in the 'Colonial City' paradigm and explicitly states that he does not want to seem to be longing for a lost age of innocence prior to European intervention. He realizes that this perspective consciously or unconsciously falls into the false dichotomy of 'traditional' versus 'modern' he had demonstrated to have been constructed *a posteriori* by colonial rulers and academics. His way out of this methodological dilemma seems to lie in his presumption that the reforming Middle Eastern states-in-becoming, namely Khedival Egypt and the *Tanẓīmāt*-era Ottoman Empire, should be included in the mainstream of the colonial studies. But the 'Colonial City' paradigm developed by Mitchell falls into a conceptual trap by using images and theories of the state that employ assumptions given to us precisely by the language and practice of the later territorial nation state.

The recent study by Eldem, Goffman and Masters on *The Ottoman City between East and West* emphatically criticizes the false normativity that informs essentialist urban categories. Clearly drawing on Raymond's landmark study on the great Arab Cities[45], the authors deliberately chose Aleppo, Izmir and Istanbul, as borderland sites related to each other through commerce and religious networks on the one hand and to other civilizations (east-west), ethnicities (Turkish and Arab worlds), and historical periods (Byzantine to Ottoman) on the other. "They were also united, perhaps most significantly through the presence in each of an enclave of influential and at times dominant foreigners." At the same time "the three cities were each distinctly innovative and unique…they were

44 Max Weber, *The City*, New York 1958, 91ff.

45 André Raymond, *Grandes Villes Arabes á l'Epoque Ottomane*, Paris 1985.

transcultural, and as such served as intense intersections between peoples: cultural fusion as much as anything distinguished the sites."[46] Thus, Masters discusses Aleppo in terms of its function as overland trade center as "the Ottoman Empire's caravan city," Goffman traces Izmir's transformation "from village to colonial port city" while Eldem views the effects of world capitalist forces as turning Istanbul from an imperial to a peripheralized capital.

The conceptualization of a hybrid culture as a distinct feature of regional centres in the Ottoman Empire is an idea that also runs through the pages of *Empire in the City*. In many ways, the present volume represents a chronological and methodological continuation of *The Ottoman City between East and West*. However, before we return to the nineteenth century, a conceptual problem in our predecessors' study requires scrutiny. Though the authors insist that there does not exist a *typical* Ottoman, Arab, or Islamic city the authors continue by (inadvertently) adopting the evolutionary language of the Turko-Ottoman state-in-becoming and argue:

> If the fifteenth and sixteenth were formative centuries for the Ottoman state and society and the nineteenth was the century of decline, then the seventeenth and eighteenth centuries feature a mature stability. *Surely we should turn to this middle period in order to explore the nature and character of the Ottoman city.*[47]

Why should we turn to this middle period, unless the aim is not, as declared, to reconstruct the processes of change, but to eke out the essence of the 'Ottoman city'? Did the Ottoman Empire stop (or was it stopped) being its own self after the eighteenth century? What really distinguishes this golden age was a foreign-led "cosmopolitan, civic order of cohabitation". It is the kind that Goffman's nostalgically bemoans – in the case of Izmir – as having been wiped away by disease, natural disasters, rural immigration from the hinterland, and the ugly effects of industrialization and "singularly western (and ultimately fatal) notions such as nationalism, ethnicity and racism."[48] But are these processes not precisely the issues with whose validity and historical conjecture the critical historian should engage?

---

46 Edhem Eldem, Daniel Goffmann, Bruce Masters, *The Ottoman City between East and West: Aleppo, Izmir and Istanbul*, Cambridge 1999, 14.

47 *Ibid.*, 15, emphasis added.

48 *Ibid.*, 130-133.

Cities in the late Ottoman Empire have been considered to languish in a period of decay and disintegration and as such to be deviant from a constructed historical ideal-type. Only recently have we become aware of the cities' important urban heritage and architectural contribution in their own right, and of the political impact which these urban centers had in shaping the structures of today's societies in the Eastern Mediterranean and Middle East – often providing centers for future territorial nation-states. During this period, these provincial capitals were marked by a noticeable degree of political stability, an unprecedented construction boom and renewed economic prosperity. Indeed, in the second half of the nineteenth century we can observe profound transformations – indeed urban revolutions – in long-existing capital cities such as Istanbul, Aleppo, Damascus and Cairo as well as in the growing "new" port-cities such as Salonika, Izmir, Mersin, Beirut and Alexandria.

The present volume therefore concentrates thematically on the cities in the Arab provinces, their role as provincial capitals and/or port-cities and their functions as centers for regional, territorial integration. Arab provincial capitals were sites of new and enforced manifestations of state presence. Free-standing administrative buildings, monuments, wide boulevards and sumptuous squares created a vocabulary of a specifically Ottoman symmetry, regularity and order which enframed everyday conduct around markets, guilds, families and local, regional and international networks. At the same time, these cities functioned as bridgeheads for foreign interests in the region. Missions, schools, consulates, hotels, banks and insurance-, tourist- and development companies established head offices in provincial capitals and branches in secondary cities or district capitals, and local agencies in smaller towns.[49]

The specific locations of Ottoman and European institutions affected the regional, inter-urban structuration and city hierarchies in the Ottoman Empire.[50] In the Ottoman Empire, provincial capitals in the nineteenth century functioned as nodal points and relay stations of imperial state power that emanated from Istanbul to its provinces.[51] Despite Eldem's

---

49 The urban nomenclatura under the post 1864 provincial administrative system was: *ʿasimat Istanbul, vilayet merkezi* (Damascus, Aleppo, Baghdad, Mersin, after 1888, Beirut), *sancaq merkezi* (al-Salṭ, Nablus, Tripoli, Homs, Mersin, Beirut).

50 See the poineering work in this regard of Hans Bobek, "Die Hauptstufen der Gesellschafts-und Wirtschaftsentfaltung in geographischer Sicht," in *Die Erde* 90 (1959): 259-298 and Eugen Wirth, "Damascus - Aleppo - Beirut: Ein geographischer Vergleich dreier nahöstlicher Städte im Spiegel ihrer sozial und wirtschaftlich tonangebenden Schicht," in *Die Erde*, (1966) Heft 2, 96-137 and Heft 3,166-173.

51 Here we concentrate mostly on *vilayet merkezi*s, but *sancaq merkezi*s are also included (eg. al-Salṭ).

assessment of eighteenth-century Istanbul as a peripheralized capital – or, indeed, because of this world-economic process – Istanbul underwent a dramatic urban revolution in the nineteenth century in which urban spaces became increasingly differentiated economically and symbolically. Yet, while the causes of Istanbul's urban renewal and restructuring arguably lay in the city's incorporation into the world-economy, its physical manifestations had a plurality of indirect effects. The grand plans for Istanbul, the ostentatious architecture of new sultanic palaces, government buildings, huge apartment blocks and private villas along the shores of the Bosphorus gave the Ottoman capital a powerful appearance of political reinvigoration. Çelik's study on the remaking of Istanbul during the nineteenth century argues that "in their drive to modernize Istanbul, the Ottoman rulers sought to emulate the European scene. A capital city with a contemporary façade would have symbolized the rejuvenation of the empire."[52] Like the capitals of European state-empires – especially Paris[53], London[54] and Vienna[55] – Istanbul underwent a state-led, architectural development boom that reinforced its perception of metropolitan superiority *vis à vis* its provinces.

The inter-disciplinarian angle of the present volume aims to transcend the constructed dichotomy of architectural versus social urban history. The aim of conventional architectural history *à la* Mumford[56], Summerson[57] and Olson[58] is to capture urban form as the embodiment of social values embedded in architectural styles. Mumford's approach, for example, was driven by a desire to understand the gist of an epoch through the particularity of its dominant (and singular) architectural language. "Mind takes form in the city and in turn urban form conditions the mind."[59]

---

52 Zeynep Çelik, *The Remaking of Istanbul: Portrait of an Ottoman City in the 19th Century*, Los Angeles 1986, xvi.

53 See for example Walter Benjamin's influential study, "Paris, Capital of the Nineteenth Century," *in Reflections: Essays, Aphorisms, Autobiographical Writings*, edited by Peter Demetz, New York 1978.

54 See, for example, M. Port, *Imperial London: Civil Government Building in London, 1850-1915*, New Haven 1995.

55 See, for example, Carl E. Schorske, (1980), *Wien, Geist und Gesellschaft in Fin de Siècle*, München 1994 (2. ed.).

56 Lewis Mumford, *The City in History*, London 1961.

57 S. J. Summerson, "Urban Forms," in *The Historian and the City*, edited by O. Handlin and J. Burchard, Cambridge 1963.

58 Donald Olsen, "The City as a Work of Art, in *The Pursuit of Urban History*, edited by D. Fraser, A. Sutcliffe, London 1983, 264-285.

59 Lewis Mumford, *The Culture of the City*, London 1938, 3.

We share Mumford's conviction that archaeology, architecture and art history offer clues for historical investigation that potentially challenge and falsify historical truths based on textual evidence. These disciplines perform an important corrective function in history. However, Mumford's approach, in which diversity of urban meanings is reduced to different epochal forms of architecture, leaves out individual experience and the myriad levels of architectural meaning and interpretation, urban contestation and subversion of artistic and symbolic representations, and the myriad usages of urban space. If, as Rabinow proclaims, "representations are social facts,"[60] then the challenge of the present volume is "to link the discursive construction of the social to the social construction of the discourse."[61] The production of space in provincial capitals and its instrumentalization for Ottoman imperialism ushered in a process of acting, thinking and feeling urban modernity – a kind of 'internal urbanization' – that affected the inner life and mentality of every urban dweller in the late Ottoman Empire. In contrast to Çelik's Istanbul, then, our Arab provincial capitals were not merely a canvas on which political power was represented, their inhabitants also produced their own rhythms of change and adaptability within the pervasive and permeating power of Ottoman imperialism.

The contributions of Neumann, Philipp and Meier which cover the pre- and early *Tanẓīmāt* period argue that the process of cultural adaptation – or acculturation – did not take place *ad hoc* and *ex nihilo*. Rather, this process was built on – and integrated into – the historical, sociological and psychological experience of the individual. Beirut burst out of the confines of its walls in the 1840s, Mersin was only founded as a port town in the mid-nineteenth century. Even established cities like Damascus witnessed large-scale urban expansion out of its old city walls to administrative centers like Sāḥat Marja and residential quarters like Muhājirīn. According to Weber's estimate in this volume, Damascus underwent an annual house (re)construction at the rate of almost 15% in 30 years. Hence, the 'historic' Damascus of today is to a large extent the remnant of a *Tanẓīmāt* city. While provincial capitals grew relentlessly, the role of other former port cities declined, such as Acre and Ṣaydā – a potent reminder that being a historical port city was not sufficient to ensure a continuing dominant city position.

---

60 Paul Rabinow, "Representations are Social Facts: Modernity and Post-Modernity in Anthropology," *Writing Culture; the Poetics and Politics of Ethnography*, edited by G. Marcus and J. Clifford, Los Angeles 1986, 234-261.

61 Roger Chartier, *On the Edge of the Cliff; History, Language and Practices*, Baltimore 1997, 25.

Urban networks and Ottoman hierarchies of urban administration were not only critical for the development of urban prosperity and regional power that often determined the path of an overland road or the location of a railway *tête de la ligne* (as in Beirut), urban inhabitants were also critically aware of the importance of their city's central position within this unfolding infrastructural system. It is on this understanding that local municipalities and administrative council members supported and carried out the imperial projects of urban renewal, the reconstruction of city centers and the implementation of infrastructural development. Only by capturing this concurrence of imperial and local dynamics can we understand the mutual quest for modernization. The Arab provincial capital in the late nineteenth century became in many ways what Braudel called a 'dominant city'. While not strictly possessing a character of its own (because it is functionally part of a much greater spatial realm), it nevertheless imparts certain characteristics to its spheres of influence, or reflects in a distinctive manner the societal structures and the mentalities of the regions which it serves.[62]

Within these economic, social and political structures, thousands of men and women acted daily in this complex system and leave their mark on the city's rhythm and appearance. Cities were expressions of collective actions by their habitants corresponding to cultural traditions, self-perception and, indeed, self-staging.[63] It is in this dual process that individuals and social groups – or 'classes' – determine their sense of place in the world they inhabit. As Bourdieu argues:

> The perception of the social world is the product of a double social structuring: on the 'objective' side, this perception is socially structured because the properties attached to agents or institutions do not make themselves available to perception independently, but in combinations whose probability varies widely; on the subjective side, it is structured because the schemes of perception and evaluation susceptible of being brought into operation at a given moment, including all those which are laid down in language, are the product of previous symbolic struggles and express, in a more of less transformed form, the state of symbolic relations of power.[64]

An integrated structure-agency approach allows us to transcend the essentializing urban typologies that have marred discussions of cities in the Middle East ever since the inception of this sub-discipline. Here, the pro-

---

62 Fernand Braudel, *Afterthoughts on Material Civilisation*, Baltimore 1977, 78.

63 See Erving Goffman, *The Presentation of the Self in Everyday Life*, New York 1958.

64 Pierre Bourdieu, "Social Space and the Genesis of 'Classes'," in his *Language and Symbolic Power*, Cambridge 1991, 234.

vincial capital is a lieu of delegation and expression of imperial power while it uses this power centripetally to draw in its administrative hinterland. Some cites had been provincial capitals or administrative centers throughout Ottoman rule (Damascus, Aleppo, Baghdad), others were granted this status as a consequence of recent economic booms (Beirut, Mersin, al-Salṭ). Yet, provincial cities had to constantly legitimate their status with the Sublime Porte and others – such as Beirut – had to petition with the government in Istanbul in order to acquire this lucrative status.

In sum, four qualities of the provincial capital emerge: it was invested with a function and a political size; it was marked by relational capacities, both towards Istanbul and the province between which it mediated power, meaning and culture; it was both contextual because of its own historical space and the long-standing relations with its natural environment, and it was conjectural because of the dependence on the politico-administrative system of which it was part; finally, it was maintained by a population that was conscious of its urbanity.

Reading Material Culture and the Question of Sources

How can we reconstruct the history of these cities and their societies? For a kind of archaeology of late Ottoman societies in urban space we propose many different sources. 'Classical' archive material, like consular reports or economic statistics from the British Foreign Office, the German Auswärtige Amt or the French Quais d'Orsay are often cited. In other foreign archives in Europe or elsewhere much remains to be discovered. For some three decades now local archives have been used. Not only the Basbakanlik in Istanbul also the National Archives in Jordan, Syria, Lebanon, Egypt or Iraq bear rich documentation. But systematic research in these archives is only just beginning. Court records give insight into legal transactions of private property or pious foundations (*waqf*). The *Awāmir Sulṭāniyya* of Damascus reveal the central state's input, and the minutes of administrative councils about how cities were administrated. Other written sources like travel accounts, guide-books, prosopographic, biographic, and auto-biographic reports, have provided much information on urban life and involved individuals.

Non-written sources such as historical photographs and maps represent very important 'snapshots' which are still not sufficiently analyzed. Individual and collective memory are the focus of most interesting recent studies. Urban legends, oral information or sources of individual identification often deal with one or the other form of memory, transmitted in different forms through many decades. Material culture itself bears witness to human action as much as to social memory. Architectural design, inscriptions, decoration, furniture and wall-paintings allow a spatial analysis through ground- or access plans and an examination of construction material. Thus, building measures themselves may be used as sources for historical research. New conceptions of urban structure or planning have become directly visible on the urban surface. Expanding personal horizons and demands through new media like telegraphs, newspapers, or changing flexibility via steamboats or railways, became evident in residential houses – the smallest and most private section of planned urban spaces. As we will see in the contributions of Bodenstein, Gonnella, Mollenhauer or Weber, the understanding of principles of shaping private worlds will illuminate some aspects of life of Ottoman urban subjects. Moreover, the history of the foundation of public buildings, like schools and hospitals, furnish examples of urban change influenced by individual patrons. The compilation and utilization of these different sources help to create a more detailed picture of these urban societies.

The complex structure of a city cannot be captured through one, singular methodology, rather we need a multiplicity of perspectives and approaches in order to capture the urban phenomenon. The present volume is motivated by the desire to approach the phenomenon of the city of the late Ottoman Empire in the Arab provinces and the Eastern Mediterranean from diverse directions. The significance of urban organization *in* and *of* space, as Yenişehirlioğlu points out in her contribution on the city of Mersin, as well as the architectural production – *Gestalt* and *Gestaltung* – can only be understood by simultaneous reflection in historical context. Urban organization represents a conscious expression of a local conception of state, city and self.

Here architectural sources are important additions to the written sources upon which historiography has depended so much. More than that, they can serve as a decisive corrective to a historical interpretation relying on literary documents alone. As an example, the decoration and pictorial representations in Damascus at the end of the nineteenth century took contemporary Istanbul as its point of reference. Recurrent motives of steamships on the Bosphorus and locomotives flying Ottoman flags are all the more significant as they were located inside private residences in Damascus outside the purview of official narratives, be they Ottoman imperialist or Arab nationalist. A look into the living rooms of the Damascenes tells us a differentiated, complementary story.

The reference to the material culture and the physical expressions of urban centres in the Arab provinces of the late Ottoman Empire constitutes a new research approach. It distinguishes itself not only by choice of topic but also ventures onto new methodological paths. In an interdisciplinary fashion, history of architecture, art history, institutional, social and economic history, urban planning and sociology are delicately interwoven. This approach is carried by the idea that social history can be understood and thoroughly interpreted only when all its forms of expression are studied in interdependent relation to each other. Architecture, urban structures, and material culture are therefore understood as meaningful expressions – as well as carriers of meaning – for political, social and economic change and are used as important sources for the interpretation of these changes. The question the present volume addresses in respect to its source material is how buildings acquire particular meanings, how architectural styles and interior decorations are encoded and decoded.

Material objects are polysemeous. They may have different significance in the realm of the private and the public. They may be decoded in a different way that they were encoded. They may be dialogical, i.e. constructed or put in place with a view to the audience, or they may not have a public message at all. They may mean one thing to the owner and another to the spectator. The spectator may be a targeted addressee or an interpreter in hindsight, such as art- or social historians. One way to overcome the relativism of meanings is to focus merely on 'representational architecture' where buildings are deliberately used to emphasize social standing and political power. But this approach brings with it the tendency to favor particular architectural highlights while neglecting the more mundane and less glamorous sites. Also it ignores the way people themselves interpret and understand the meanings of the built form. As we shall see in the contributions that focus of urban institutions, urban meanings are not constructed through architecture alone. Moreover, Lemke's contribution in this volume shows how places also derive meanings through photographic representations.

To Walter Benjamin, the uniqueness of the city as an art form lies in what he calls 'distracted' perception. People usually perceive facades and interiors of buildings in passing, a marked contrast to the gaze in paintings or literature. Instead of a formal architectural analysis of cities, Benjamin priotitized the transformatory power of 'unconscious processes' and their association with the urban environment. As a concept of analysis, he proposes to explore the "urban aura" in order to establish the underlying fantasies, the wish-processes and the dreams that are locked up in the perception of the city. The concept of the urban aura recognizes that objective meanings of a city's architecture can be located in cultural forms, but also that people interpret these cultural artifacts themselves.[65]

Bodenstein's contribution to this volume in particular explores the multiple and overlapping modes of self-presentation in architecture. Using a number of historical clues, he traces the history of a nineteenth-century villa in Beirut in order to construct a new evidential paradigm for urban research.[66] On the one hand, the analysis of this house demonstrates the inappropriateness of a classificatory approach to architectural style. On the other hand, the architectural hybridity of this particular house is in a way a local manifestation of what Edmund Burke has called – in the context of colonial Algeria – "the first crisis in Orientalism."[67] This crisis was marked by both Europeans adopting 'Oriental' decorative styles and local residents 'Orientalising' themselves – a "willful nostalgia," as Roland Robertson called it in a different context.[68] Bodenstein's approach tunes us into the many layers of interpreting architectural meaning. Are we faced with the representation of the builder's, the owner's or the resident's self-view and *Weltanschauung*? Indeed, are we faced with the representation of a representation? Can we take what we see at face value, or has it already been filtered through the conscious process of self-representation? As a solution to close the gap between what is *visible* in architectural design and what is *legible* Bodenstein proposes to cross-check the architectural material with oral history, cadastral documents, city maps and a comparison of building plans in Beirut and elsewhere in the region. Of necessity, the house requires reading and counter-reading like a literary text or a painting.[69]

Such an approach potentially enables the historian to retrieve the historical subject from archival oblivion. Conventional sources of history (consular reports, Ottoman government correspondence and even court records) are hardly conducive to a 'psychoanalytical treatment' of urban change in the Ottoman Empire. Whilst Mumford's attempt to read the city

---

65 Walter Benjamin, [1968], "The Work of Art in the Age of Mechanical Reproduction," in *Illuminations; Essays and Reflections*, New York 1988, 219-251.

66 For an inspiring theoretical discussion on historical detection, see Carlo Ginzburg, (1986), "Clues: the Roots of an Evidential Paradigm," in his *Clues, Myths and the Historical Method*, Baltimore 1992 (2. Print), 96-125.

67 Edmund Burke, "The First Crisis of Orientalism, 1890-1914," in *Connaissances du Maghreb: sciences sociales et colonialisation*, edited by J.-C. Vatin, Paris 1984, 214.

68 Roland Robertson, "After Nostalgia? Wilful Nostalgia and the Phases of Globalization," in *Theories of Modernity and Postmodernity*, edited by B. Turner, London 1990, 45-61.

69 On this issue, see Chartier, "The Powers and Limits of Representation," in his *On the Edge of the Cliff*, 90-103.

as a text is retained, it is now related to narratives of specific individuals, groups and societies, not to an epoch as a whole. This permits us to recognize the conflicting meanings social groups try to place on the city.

The present volume advocates a return to the archives – in the widest sense of the word. This return is informed by a discursive approach that takes documents not only for what they impart in terms of factual knowledge but one that takes as a focus the grammar in which the texts and images are structured, and the way they themselves are producers (as much as products) of knowledge and representations. To conclude with Michel de Certeau, "the historian [quite literally in this volume] is no longer a person who shapes an empire." Rather "he or she works in the margins… bringing out the differences relative to continuities or to elements from which analysis proceeds."[70] Having set out to glimpse Braudel's "Turkish world" from the 'inside', we now step out of the confines of that world in order to maintain a critical distance at the point of interpretation.

70 Michel de Certeau, "The Historiographical Operation," in his *The Writing of History*, New York 1988, 79.

– I –

Discourse and Practice of Ottomanism

RETHINKING OTTOMAN IMPERIALISM: MODERNITY, VIOLENCE AND THE CULTURAL LOGIC OF OTTOMAN REFORM

USSAMA MAKDISI

In recent years the cause of the Ottomans has undergone a dramatic shift. From being labelled a brooding tyranny incapable of modernization, the Ottoman Empire's historiographical fortunes have changed. Drawing on different methodologies and exploring facets of Ottoman economic, social and cultural history, scholars of the Ottoman Empire have systematically deconstructed the "decline" thesis of the Ottoman Empire.[1] They have replaced a broad, yet static, picture of an empire with a portrait of a vastly complicated empire that sought to modernize, indeed modernized, in the face of uninterrupted European imperialism. Yet in their effort to illuminate the complexities of Ottoman history, Ottomanists have dispensed a little too hastily with a notion of Ottoman imperialism. While several important studies have critically analyzed how Europeans portrayed the Ottomans and how the Ottomans responded and resisted these portrayals, they have only hinted at the implications of these representations for relations of power within the Ottoman Empire.[2] By and large, they have not paid sufficient attention to how changes in Ottoman representation consolidated relations of power that bound imperial subjects, particularly those in the Arab provinces, to Istanbul. Using the case of Ottoman Leba-

---

1 The classic account of the decline thesis of the Ottoman Empire is Bernard Lewis' *The Emergence of Modern Turkey*, Oxford 1961. For an alternative view, see Huri Islamoğlu-Inan, "'Oriental Despotism' in world-system perspective," in *The Ottoman Empire and the World-Economy*, ed. Huri Islamoğlu-Inan, Cambridge, 1987, 1-24. For a more recent evaluation of the Ottomans and the Arab world, see Albert Hourani's *A History of the Arab Peoples,* New York 1991.

2 Zeynep Çelik, *Displaying the Orient: Architecture of Islam at Nineteenth-Century World's Fairs*, Berkeley 1992, Selim Deringil, *The Well-Protected Domains: Ideology and the Legitimation of Power in the Ottoman Empire 1876-1909*, London 1998. Fatma Müge Göçek, *Rise of the Bourgeoisie, Demise of the Empire: Ottoman Westernization and Social Change*, New York 1996, and M. Şükrü Hanioğlu, *The Young Turks in Opposition*, New York 1995.

non, therefore, this essay argues that the nineteenth-century *Tanẓīmāt* reflected the birth of a distinctly modern Ottoman imperialism.

By modern Ottoman imperialism, I mean a set of imperial practices and discourses which were premised on the need to induct forcibly supposedly recalcitrant peripheries into an age of modernity. These practices and discourses defined the late Ottoman Empire's bid to become a modern nation-state. Specifically, Ottoman reformers sought to reshape, improve, and ultimately discipline Arab peripheries of the Ottoman Empire as an integral part of a project of imperial renewal and modernization. Furthermore, Ottoman reformers consistently imagined the Arab provinces as subordinate parts of an Ottoman state despite the development of a language of secular Ottoman nationalism. The Arab peripheries of the empire became a proving ground for Ottoman modernity – physical places that signified both what the modern Ottoman was not, i.e. backwards, primitive and savage and, in addition, the Arab peripheries constituted metaphorical spaces in which Istanbul-centered reformers elaborated a notion what Ottoman modernity was, i.e. rational, scientific and civilized, attributes which were defined against a notion of a premodern periphery.

It is important to note from the outset that this modern Ottoman imperialism was not a throwback to earlier forms of imperial control over the Arab provinces. In other words, the advent of modern Ottoman imperialism was not, as suggested by George Antonius in his classic *The Arab Awakening*, a question of continuing a tradition of a moribund Ottoman "dark" age. Rather, it reflected a far more complicated intersection of modernization with imperial state building that had profound implications for the meaning of modernity in the late Ottoman Empire and its successor states. The primary concern of all Ottoman reformers in the nineteenth century was to maintain the integrity of the empire in the face of European encroachment. Statesmen such as Fuad Pasha urged Ottoman reform because they sought to "catch up" with the European states of Prussia, Russia, England and France. In this sense, modern Ottoman imperialism was a project that sought to break with what was seen by reformers to be a premodern past of the Ottoman Empire and from the hegemony of European power. It was, in other words, a dynamic project that was waged on two fronts simultaneously and dialectically: the domestic and the foreign. It was a project of both reform and violence. More precisely, modern Ottoman imperialism conceived of, justified, and deployed physical and symbolic violence in the name of reform, modernization, and imperial stability.

The Age of Ottoman Modernity

The age of Ottoman modernity was inaugurated in 1839. Maḥmūd II's concerted efforts had begun with the abolition of the Janissaries in 1826 but quickly spread to sartorial and administrative domains and culminated in an era of wholesale modernization known as *Tanẓīmāt*[3]. The centerpiece of the *Tanẓīmāt* reforms was the Gülhane decree issued by Maḥmūd II's successor, Abdülmecid, in 1839 at a time when the Ottoman Empire lay on the brink of total collapse due to Muḥammad ʿAlī's imperial ambitions. Among its provisions was the solemn declaration of the equality of Muslim and non-Muslim subjects before the law. Beginning with the Gülhane decree, imperial reformers abandoned the term *reaya* in favor of *tebaa*.[4] Like the suppression of the Janissaries, the new measures of the *Tanẓīmāt*, which represented a clear break with the past, were couched in a language that suggested a reversion to tradition. However, the Gülhane proclamation, and the 1856 *Hatt-i Hümayun* which followed the Crimean war, formally committed the empire to a course of modernization under effective western tutelage.

The *Tanẓīmāt* opened the empire to what anthropologist Johannes Fabian has described as the evolutionary "stream of Time" – an idea of a "denial of coevalness" that was at the heart of modern European colonialism.[5] Although the discourse of reform in the Ottoman Empire was not itself new, nineteenth-century reform was part of wider culture of modernity.[6] In this culture, the Ottoman Empire sought to culturally define itself as an equal player (especially after the 1856 Treaty of Paris which formally inducted the Ottoman Empire as a member of the European state

---

[3] See Donald Quataert, "Clothing Laws, State, and Society in the Ottoman Empire, 1720-1829," *IJMES,* 29 (1997), 403-425.

[4] This process culminated in the 1869 Ottoman law of nationality, which produced for the first time a juridical definition of the Ottoman citizen without an overt or implied reference to religion. The term *reaya* which literally meant flock was the classical Ottoman appellation for the subjects of the Ottoman government. Although the term included all tribute-paying subjects (including Muslims) it was often used to refer to non-Muslim subjects. The ruling *askeri* class was theoretically entirely Muslim. The term *tebaa* simply means followers, in other words, subjects of a sovereign or state and has no religious connotation.

[5] Johannes Fabian, *Time and the Other: How Anthropology Makes its Object*, New York 1983, 17-26.

[6] Virginia Aksan, "Ottoman Political Writing, 1768-1808," *IJMES,* 25 (1993), 53-69. For an example of pre-*Tanẓīmāt* reform, see Cezzar Ahmed Pasha's *Nizamname-i Mısır* translated by Stanford J. Shaw under the title *Ottoman Egypt in the Eighteenth Century*, Cambridge, Mass. 1962.

system) on a world stage of civilization.[7] It was a world stage dominated, in Ottoman eyes, by mischievous, but modern, European states, and a world stage in which Istanbul was only one of many centers. As part of this project of imperial political and cultural reassertion and redefinition, indeed as part of its own "cultural logic" that placed it on par with other supposedly civilized states, Ottoman modernization generated its discursive opposite, the premodern within the empire, be it in the sands of Arabia or in *cebel-i düruz*.[8] Places like *cebel-i düruz*, or what the Europeans referred to as Mount Lebanon, became locations of the premodern: places of danger and anxiety that threatened to destabilize the course of modernization. Intellectual, architectural and political and social Westernization occurred in Istanbul creating what Göçek has called a "new vision of Ottoman society."[9] Ottoman reformers aspired towards an elusive modernity which they thought was within their grasp if only they could deflect external European hostility which retarded Ottoman advancement while also identifying and eliminating internal premodern problems which invited European interference.

This Ottoman attempt to modernize the empire was both motivated and plagued by a feeling of constant crisis. The first aspect of this crisis manifested itself in the often desperate efforts of reforming officials to outline the exact parameters of modern Ottoman sovereignty in an age of European hegemony: how to reach the nineteenth-century El Dorado – modernity – without becoming a colony of Europe in a century when European empires came to control more than 85% of the surface of the globe. European powers played an increasingly intrusive role in the internal affairs of the empire by emphasizing their duty to protect the non-Muslim minorities from a putative Islamic (and Asiatic) despotism. Ottoman officials, while they were acutely aware of their need to modernize along European lines, decried repeated European interference on behalf of non-Muslim minori-

---

7 It should be added that there was considerable resistance to the reform program even within certain circles in Istanbul. This is a central aspect to Bernard Lewis' classic narrative of positive westernizing reformers opposed by fanatical traditionalists in his *The Emergence of Modern Turkey*. See also Cavid Baysun, ed., *Cevdet Paşa Tezakir*, 3 vols., Ankara 1991, vol. 1, 68, for Cevdet's recollection of the reading of the 1856 Hatt-i Hümayun and the negative reactions it produced not just among what he calls "many of the ehl-i islam" but also the Greek orthodox élites.

8 See Saree Makdisi, *Romantic Imperialism: Universal Empire and the Culture of Modernity*, Cambridge 1998, 181-182 for an analysis of modernization, imperialism and its relationship to time.

9 Göçek, *Rise of the Bourgeoisie, Demise of the Empire,* 119.

ties as sinister attempts to weaken the empire through sectarian means (*mezhebdaşlık vesile*).[10]

In *cebel-i düruz*, because of Eastern Question politics which were centered on the expulsion of the Egyptian troops from Syria following renewed Egyptian-Ottoman hostilities in 1839, and because of episodes of intercommunal violence in the two decades that followed the inauguration of the *Tanẓīmāt*, the crisis of representation expressed itself in dramatic form. For one thing, European intervention was continuous in the region, and European influence was expressed in military terms (through the British defeat of Muḥammad ʿAlī in 1840), in cultural terms (with the introduction of Jesuit and Protestant missionary education and medicine) and in economic terms (with the imposition of the Free Trade Treaties of 1838).[11] For another, local notables and commoners in *cebel-i düruz* and the surrounding region seized the initiative between 1840 and 1860 in interpreting the *Tanẓīmāt*, and did so with the knowledge that European powers played a vital role in their own political, material and cultural future. Some, such as members of the Maronite church establishment, advocated a Maronite-dominated Lebanon in accordance with the *Tanẓīmāt* stipulation to protect non-Muslim subjects; some, such as secular notables from the Maronite Khāzin and Druze Jānbulaṭ families insisted that the *Tanẓīmāt* - because it was premised on an idea of restoring a glorious past – legitimized a full restoration of the old regime social order. And some, such as the Maronite muleteer Tanyūs Shahīn, who led a popular uprising against Khāzin domination in 1859 in the predominantly Maronite district of Kisrawan, understood the *Tanẓīmāt* to mean social as well as religious equality, and therefore, contended that the *Tanẓīmāt* legitimized social revolution. He and his followers demanded what they saw as their right to representation and equality guaranteed to them by the imperial reform edicts because they were Christian subjects.[12]

A second aspect of this crisis lay in the redefinition of the relationship between rulers and subjects in a modernizing empire. The traditional imperial attitude, which had presupposed an inviolable Ottoman domain of obedience, could no longer be maintained. The temporality of traditional

---

10 Başbakanlık Archives, Istanbul (hereafter BBA). IMM 1115. Leff. 8 27 B 1258 [Receb].

11 I have dealt extensively with the relationship between sectarian violence, European colonialism and Ottoman modernization in my book, *The Culture of Sectarianism,* Los Angeles 2000. For more on the economic aspect of European intervention, see Roger Owen, *The Middle East in the World Economy*, London 1981, 153-179.

12 Public Record Office of Northern Ireland. D 1071 H/C/1/1/13.

politics – which had reflected a shared understanding between rulers and ruled of the functioning of politics in a heterogeneous empire, and which had, in fact, regulated an Ottoman accommodation of Druze "heretics" and Christian "infidels" – was effectively broken by the urgency of Ottoman modernization. In their race against destruction by "advanced" Europeans, Ottoman reformers sought to locate and extinguish what they considered to be the premodern within their empire. Politics was no longer simply about bargaining with subjects, as Karen Barkey has described the relationship between the Ottoman state and the *celalis* in the early modern Anatolian provinces of the empire, as much as it was of bargaining and performing with Europeans on the world stage of modernization.

This feeling of crisis was dramatically illustrated by the transformation of the hitherto marginal region of *cebel-i düruz* into a problem of central importance. It was precisely the fact of a rural, neglected and relatively unknown region that caused the Ottomans anxiety, for the questions that confronted them were how to incorporate *cebel-i düruz* into a project of Ottoman modernization, and, more specifically, how to address, mitigate and ultimately resolve *cebel-i düruz*'s premodernity within the context of a modern politics with (and against) Europe? The dispatches and reports of Ottoman officials in the two decades following the *Tanẓīmāt* indicated that they had no clear answer to these questions. For the first time, in fact, Ottoman governors described the region as Mount Lebanon, or "*cebel-i lübnan,*" conforming to European nomenclature. The term *cebel-i düruz* was abandoned. For the first time, really, Mount Lebanon entered Ottoman imperial consciousness in a sustained manner. Ottoman officials began to discuss what they referred to as "*cebel-i lübnan meselesi* (the question of Mount Lebanon)" indicating the location of Mount Lebanon within a constellation of other problems that threatened to thwart imperial modernization. Men like Muṣṭafā Pasha, sent in late 1841 to settle the affairs of Mount Lebanon following sectarian clashes that had earlier erupted in the village of Dayr al-Qamar, epitomized the Ottoman predicament. His mission began by a reassertion of social order.[13] He summoned both Druze and Maronite elites to Beirut and relieved Bashir Qāsim, who had succeeded the famous Bashīr Shihāb in 1840, of his powers; he informed the notables that the return of the Shihāb dynasty was out of the question.[14] Beyond reasserting Ottoman authority in the name of the reforming Sultan,

---

13 *Takvim-i Vekayi*, No.267, 26 Za 1257 [9 January 1842] (Istanbul Universitesi Kütüphanesi/407).

14 Archives du Ministère des Affaires Etrangères de France: Correspondance politique des Consuls, Turquie, Beirut. Vol.3. Bourée to Guizot, 18 January 1842.

Muṣṭafā Pasha symbolically and physically broke with the old regime by finally abolishing the Shihāb dynasty which had ruled since 1697. Yet this rupture was not complete, for although the *Tanẓīmāt* was concerned with building a modern nation, there was very little in the dispatches that indicated how this was to be accomplished.[15] Precisely because the *Tanẓīmāt* lent itself to a variety of interpretations, including a European one that mandated interference, the Ottomans considered the reorganization of local administration imperative to stifling European involvement.[16] The *Tanẓīmāt* placed the Ottomans in a quandary, for while they repeatedly pledged to obey the sultan's will to reform, they viewed the natives as essentially unreformable subjects. Ottoman officials were certain, however, that reform and state violence went hand in hand; public order and security could be guaranteed only by bringing local notables to heel and by removing their "stupid, silly and fickle" followers from the realm of politics.[17] The longer Muṣṭafā Pasha remained in Mount Lebanon, the more insistent he became on the urgent need of the central government to act decisively to restore order. Christian notables seemed on the verge of joining the 1842 Druze rebellion against Ömer Pasha's heavy handed policies. The dispatches of Esad Pasha, the Governor of Ṣaydā, further reflected the weakness of the local Ottoman government – whose troops were unreliable

---

15 In the era of the *Tanẓīmāt*, the central authorities were still hampered by their ignorance of the local populations. With the possible exception of the mission of Selim Bey, a commissioner sent by the Sublime Porte to inquire into the feelings of the *ahali* toward Ömer Pasha's administration (which the European Ambassadors rejected out of hand for being an entirely coercive undertaking), there was no comprehensive knowledge, no ethnography of any kind, no travelers' reports they could rely on to inform them of the "customs and manners" of the rural population.

16 This was evident in the marked persistence of the old regime discourse of social differentiation. If the *Tanẓīmāt* was about equality of communities, the repeated use of the word *zimmi* [*dhimmi*] to describe the Christian inhabitants of Mount Lebanon belittled that. If the *Tanẓīmāt* was concerned with social equality between the "great and the small," the everyday metaphors and practice of the Ottoman masters and their Lebanese subjects blunted its impact. Schools were left in the hands of the clergy or the missionaries. In fact, the only active interest Ottoman officials took in the *ahali* was whether they signed petitions that praised Ottoman rule. The Ottomans referred to these obedient subjects as "loyal people" (*aṣdıqa*). See BBA IMM 1124. Leff.3, 9 B 1258 [16 August 1842]. Inappropriate (*uygunsuzluk*) behavior meant any agitation for the Shihāb; in particular foreign consuls and the Maronite Church were accused of instigating the *ahali* to disavow direct Ottoman rule. Just as European consular reports dismissed as fabrications any petition signed in favor of direct Ottoman rule, the Ottomans also insisted on framing any petition for a restoration of Shihābite rule as the work of conspirators.

17 BBA IMM 1124. Leff.3, 9 B 1258 [16 August 1842].

and unpaid, which had to borrow coal from the English consulate (which, in turn, made it quite clear that it would supply no more), and which had a difficult time in suppressing a Druze revolt against Ömer Pasha, an Ottoman officer of Croatian origin who had been appointed to directly rule Mount Lebanon in 1842. Like Muṣṭafā Pasha, Esad stressed the age-old conflict between barbaric people, they being "in essence two coarse and savage sects ... [who] often need punishment to keep them in order."[18] Ottoman concern reached a climax when Shahīn's calls for Christian social liberation spread to Druze-dominated regions of Mount Lebanon and helped spark sectarian clashes between the Druze and Maronite communities, which in turn led to the infamous war of 1860 in which thousands of Christians were massacred by the Druze in June. In July, to add to Ottoman embarrassment, a riot by Damascene Muslims killed several thousand Christians.[19]

Locating the PreModern

What interests us here are not the details of these sectarian episodes, but how Ottoman reformers took advantage of the restoration of order in Mount Lebanon and Damascus to construct their vision of an Ottoman modernity in contrast to an alleged local premodernity. The foreign minister of the Ottoman Empire, Fuad Pasha – who himself was educated in reformed schools, was fluent in French and had served as an Ottoman ambassador to Russia, and was a statesman who embodied many of the ideals of the *Tanẓīmāt* – went personally to Syria to ensure that *modern* Ottoman law and order was properly imposed. His immediate objective, however, was to stem European influence, for in the aftermath of the massacres the French had sent an army to Syria to "aid" the Ottomans re-establish peace.[20] From the outset of his mission, before he had actually completed any investigations, Fuad Pasha alleged that the violence in Mount Lebanon was a reflection of an "age old" (*kadim ül-cereyan*) tribal struggle, whereas the outburst in Damascus was the work of unthinking and ignorant Mus-

---

18 BBA IMM 1129. Leff.14, 7 B 1258 [14 August 1842].

19 The reasons for the Damascus massacre (as well as the Lebanese war) were complex, but most historians agree that an economic recession among traditional artisanal sectors precipitated by European textile imports played a significant role in fueling Muslim resentment against wealthy Christians who dominated trade with Europe. See Leila Fawaz, *An Occasion for War,* London 1994, for a narrative of the war in Mount Lebanon, the Damascus massacre and the European responses to them.

20 For details on the French expedition see Leila Fawaz, *An Occasion for War*, 110-131.

lims. [21] In report after report, Fuad Pasha contrasted the punishment inflicted by his modern army – whose outfits and organization reflected the new face of the empire – with the supposed tribal savagery of local inhabitants. Tanyūs Shahīn was condemned as a "brigand" and the Kisrawan revolt was suppressed. In Damascus, because of the scale of violence and because of the city's symbolic importance to an Ottoman reconception of their Islamic heritage, scores of "ignorant" Muslims who allegedly took part in the riots were arrested. They were executed after hasty trials because they had "violated" the precepts of the *sharīʿa* and the will of the sultan – both of which Fuad Pasha maintained upheld the equality of Muslim and non-Muslim subjects. He concluded that Ottoman culpability was limited to a neglect of duty at the local level, which resulted in a "stain" on the honor of a modernizing state.[22]

The point here is to understand the implications of Fuad Pasha's convictions rather than their veracity. The descriptions of the conflicts as age-old, in the case of Mount Lebanon, or the work of ignorant rioters, in the case of Damascus, conveniently located sectarianism in a premodern world dominated by fanaticism, ignorance and tribalism. The Ottoman punishment – following supposedly impartial investigations and sentences in accordance with reformed and allegedly unambiguous penal codes and carried out by a *Tanẓīmāt* army in the presence of European representatives – was, by contrast, understood by Fuad Pasha to be modern. Modernity, in other words, was a contest between reforming Ottomans and Europeans. Fuad Pasha was out to prove that the Ottoman Empire was just and tolerant and therefore could be modern. The local setting – be it the city of Damascus or Mount Lebanon – provided the stage upon which two interrelated spectacles could be simultaneously enacted. The first was a modern one which pitted Fuad Pasha and his reforming cohorts against their European rivals. It was a struggle in which a reformed army and officials valiantly tried to snatch the initiative from, and thereby defeat, the hubris of European orientalism, represented by the French army and expressed in the reports of the various European commissioners. This struggle over modernity constituted and defined the second spectacle in which the Ottoman modern crushed the supposed local premodern, that is to say the spectacle of discipline and punishment that went on through 1861. For Fuad Pasha, the local inhabitants themselves were not modern. They did not make or

---

21 BBA. BEO A.MKT.UM. 415/56, 1 M 1277 [20 July 1860]; BBA. BEO A. MKT. UM. 480/28, 11 Z 1277 [20 June 1861] and BBA. IRADE H 9861, 16 Ra 1277 [2 October 1860].

22 See BBA. IRADE MM 851/4. Leff.4, 16 M 1277.

move history as much as they were pawns and objects of a modern historical struggle that pitted, in Fuad Pasha's view, powerful yet scheming Europeans against beleaguered Ottoman reformers.

Another implication was the nature of this modern stage and its impact on the traditional relationship between rulers and ruled in the Ottoman Empire. Although Fuad Pasha deployed the language of the old regime in his reports such as brigandage and the *sharīʿa*, he was acutely aware of the world stage upon which local order had to be restored. "Because the Sublime State never accepts that the slightest harm or aggression should befall any of the classes of imperial subjects who take shelter under its protection," decreed Fuad, "and because the events [that transpired] were contrary to the principle of civilization current in the world and beyond the pale in every manner, the Sublime State, in accordance with its duty to ensure justice, has decided to punish those involved in the events."[23] The ideology of progress allowed Fuad Pasha to deploy the language of brigandage and the *sharīʿa* – thereby tapping into classical Ottoman ruling discourses – to equate the modern Ottoman subject with the tolerant, obedient and quietist subject. Fuad Pasha reminded his soldiers that although they were in Syria "to bring peace and security to this area and to punish the sins of the [Ottoman subjects] because of their cruel acts," they were also there to "show everybody what the worth and value of a soldier is and let all our compatriots (*vatandaşlarımız*) know our Padişah's justice."[24] On the one hand, therefore, the soldiers acted on behalf of their theoretical compatriots in Damascus and Mount Lebanon, who lived (at least in the case of Mount Lebanon) in a 'savage tribal landscape'. The imperial soldiers constituted the vanguard of Ottoman modernity, rationality and nationalism. They were to lead by example, for in addition to being commanded to obey the person of the sultan, the soldiers and their Ottoman compatriots were exhorted to be loyal to an abstract Ottoman nation. They were meant to embody a concept of national allegiance – which like loyalty to the House of Osman of the old regime, flowed up the social order, from periphery to center. Fuad Pasha envisioned an Ottoman modernity which included a modern subjecthood composed of fellow-citizens or *vatandaşlar* who listened, followed and obeyed rather than actively participated in the governance of the empire.

Ottoman modernity introduced a linear progressive understanding of time which created a temporal distance, a gap that separated modern Istan-

---

23 BBA IRADE D 31753. Leff.3, n.d.

24 BBA IRADE MM 851/3. Leff.4, n.d. Also quoted in Baysun, *Cevdet Paşa Tezakir*, vol. 3, 110.

bul from tribal Mount Lebanon within a redefined imperial framework. The closure of this gap became the ostensible goal of Ottoman reform.[25] The inhabitants of Mount Lebanon were not simply savage (for that was a fairly standard Ottoman description of rural mountainous areas even before the *Tanẓīmāt*), but savage in the context of a race of progress against civilized Europe. Fuad Pasha believed that Lebanese savagery and tribalism held back Ottoman reformers in their quest for the holy grail of modernity. In other words, the Ottoman Empire was waging a war of modernization on two fronts. It was desperately trying to close the metaphorical gap between itself and the European states which continued to intervene in the affairs of the empire, while it also imagined an ever widening gap that separated its center from its periphery. The closer the Ottoman reformers edged towards "modern" Europe, the more they drew back aghast at the horror of what they perceived to be their "premodern" subjects. Their own sense of modernity depended not only on their reforms and their emulation of Europe, but also on an increasingly clear representation of their subjects' backwardness and stagnation.

Representing Ottoman Modernity

In the wake of Fuad Pasha's mission, Mount Lebanon and its surrounding regions became the subjects of what Deringil has recently described as the "Ottoman self-portrait," or the official Ottoman representation of their own modern empire. However, Ottoman interest in the region was not simply to "minimize the exotic" as Deringil suggests, but to actually achieve modernity.[26] A reforming Ottoman administration recognized several gradations to modernity. To the Sublime Porte, Europe represented the summit of modernity, a metaphor whose tangible manifestations were advanced technologies and well-organized cities. At the same time, however, Europe also constituted the single most dangerous threat to the survival of the empire. At another level, while Ottoman reformers such as Fuad Pasha and historian and statesman Cevdet Pasha may have considered themselves as individuals to be as modern as their European counterparts, they nevertheless conceived of their task as one to lift the empire as a whole, beginning with Istanbul, to the level of a European modernity. Below Istanbul, there were provincial capitals, such as Beirut after 1888, which became arenas of modernization, and finally there were rural "tribes," for example those

---

25 See Makdisi, *Romantic Imperialism*, 111-115, for a discussion of British modernization in the context of colonial India.

26 Deringil, *The Well-Protected Domains*, 150-151.

of the Caucasus or Mount Lebanon.[27] The official nationalism launched in the wake of the *Tanẓīmāt* was a project of modernization which strove to homogenize different cultures, different regions and, above all, different stages of progress within a coherent culture of an Ottoman modernity and civilization. In this sense, it was a direct parallel to modern British imperialism which sought to incorporate the Highlands of Scotland into a project of British modernization.[28]

Having defined the Lebanese inhabitants as premodern subjects of a *potentially* modern empire, the task before Ottoman rulers was to uplift and incorporate Mount Lebanon into a project of Ottoman modernization.[29] Engin Akarlı's work on the *Mutaṣarrifiyya* (the autonomous special province established by the Ottomans and Europeans in the wake of the 1860 war) of Mount Lebanon has shown how Ottoman statesmen took the lead in reforming local administration; as the Ottoman *salnāmes* (yearbooks) about Mount Lebanon illustrate, Mount Lebanon, its hinterlands and the adjacent coastal cities were studied, mapped, reformed and administered as never before.[30] Beirut, while technically not part of the *Mutaṣarrifiyya* but nevertheless a major influence on it, was redeveloped as a modern Ottoman city.[31] The famous Roman temples of Baalbek, which lay immediately adjacent to Mount Lebanon, were rediscovered by now "civilized" Ottomans. They reclaimed the ruins from a European colonial discourse that had hitherto interpreted them as a metaphor for Ottoman decline, and insisted, to the contrary of European Orientalism, that Baalbek reflected the empire's own rich and dynamic heritage.[32] The entry for Baalbek in the geographical dictionary, *Ḳamus ül-aʿlām* printed in Istanbul in 1888-9, declared it "the most important of the ancient cities famous for

27 Cevdet Pasha, *Tarīkh Jawdat*, trans. ʿAbd al-Qādir al-Dana, Beirut 1890, 329.

28 Makdisi, *Romantic Imperialism*, 98.

29 Ottoman dictionaries which appeared in the late nineteenth century defined Mount Lebanon as a land inhabited by perpetually warring Druzes and Christians. See for example, Ahmed Rifaat, *Lugat-ı Tarihiye ve Coğrafiye*, Istanbul 1881, 3-4: 239-240.

30 Engin Akarlı, *The Long Peace*, Berkeley 1993. See also Ibrahim Bek Aswad's *Dalil Lubnan*, Ba'bda 1906, and Cevdet Pasha's *Tarih-i Cevdet* [tertib cedid], Istanbul, 1884, 249-256.

31 See Jens Hanssen, "'Your Beirut Is on My Desk;' Ottomanizing Beirut under Sultan Abdülhamid II (1876-1909)," in *Projecting Beirut: Episodes in the Construction and Reconstruction of a Modern City*, eds. Peter G. Rowe and Hashim Sarkis, Munich 1998, 41-67.

32 Ussama Makdisi, "The "Rediscovery" of Baalbek: A Metaphor for Empire in the Nineteenth Century," in *Baalbek: Image and Monument, 1898-1998*, eds. Hélène Sader, Thomas Scheffler and Angelika Neuwirth, Beirut 1998, 137-156.

its antiquities," adding that "the ruins of ancient temples and other buildings today attract the attention of visitors and tourists. Both the extraordinary skill [in the construction] of columns and sculptures together with the massive size of the stones used in the buildings provoke the astonishment [of he who views them]."[33]

Ottoman archaeological interest in the pre-Islamic Phoenician and Hellenistic past reflected one more step in the incorporation of the empire into a culture of modernity.

An Imperial Museum (Müze-i Hümayun) had already been founded in 1869, and although the first directors were foreign, in 1881 the French-educated Osman Hamdi Bey was appointed as head of the museum. Under his guidance, various excavations of Phoenician and Hellenistic sites were conducted throughout the Empire; he was instrumental in creating an awareness of the cultural (and hence political) importance of these sites and prompted the Ottoman government to pass a law in 1884 (*Asar-i Atika Nizamnamesi*) which prohibited the export of antiquities from the Empire. The passage of the 1884 law created an exclusive legal and cultural claim for Ottoman antiquities.[34] The Ottoman State directed important finds, among which was the 1887 discovery by Hamdi Bey of the Royal Necropolis of Ṣaydā including the alleged sarcophagus of Alexander, to the recently rebuilt Imperial Museum.[35] Although the museum he directed and the conservation law he oversaw were, in large measure, a reaction to European "pilfering" of (what was now seen as) Ottoman antiquities, Hamdi Bey was nevertheless acutely aware of his debt to European archaeological knowledge and solicited the French philologist and orientalist Ernest Renan's help in deciphering some of the Phoenician inscriptions he found at Ṣaydā. [36]

According to Hamdi Bey the sultan "who has placed himself with a firm will and great solicitude at the head of this *œuvre civilisatrice*, has

---

33 *Ḳamus ül-aʿlām*, 6 vols., Istanbul 1889, vol. 2, 1905.

34 The first law on antiquities promulgated in 1874 had mandated only that antiquities discovered in archaeological digs were to be divided equally between the excavator, the owner of the land on which the excavation was made and the State. See Mustafa Cezar, *Müzeci ve Ressam Osman Hamdi Bey*, Istanbul 1987, 21.

35 See Jens Hanssen, "Imperial Discourses and an Ottoman Excavation in Lebanon," in *Baalbek: Image and Monument 1898-1998*, 165-172, for more information about the excavations of the Royal Necropolis in Ṣaydā.

36 Cezar, *Müzeci ve Ressam Osman Hamdi Bey,* 20. Renan had already traveled to Baalbek and other regions in Syria to study Phoenician inscriptions and ruins in the wake of the French occupation of Syria in 1860. His work is titled *Mission de Phénicie,* 2 vols., Paris 1864.

created, without pause, institutions such as museums, special schools, libraries, etc., appropriate for the regeneration of national art while also introducing modern European sciences into his nation."[37] For Hamdi Bey, places like Baalbek and the necropolis of Ṣaydā reflected national treasures that could be recovered through the science of Europe, namely archaeology and philology. The necropolis was the major display in the imperial museum in Istanbul whose neo-classical facade, as Jens Hanssen has written, suggested an empire able to both reach into the past to set the stage for its own teleological evolution into modernity and at the same time a nation able to translate East for West, and, of course, West for East.[38] The necropolis of Ṣaydā embodied the Ottoman Empire's claim to an ancient pre-Islamic heritage as well as of its own bid for an independent modernity – after all, it had been excavated, transported and displayed as an Ottoman artifact, in an Ottoman museum and for an Ottoman public.

Ottoman modernization reinforced an imperial relationship that explicitly separated a modernizing center from the rest of the empire – through the flow of antiquities from Ṣaydā and Baalbek to the Imperial Museum in Istanbul – at the same time as it increased actual control and authority over the provinces through administrative and urban reform. The irony, of course, is that while Osman Hamdi Bey reacted to and decried European "theft" of Ottoman antiquities, he unilaterally removed local antiquities to Istanbul. On the one hand, the Ottomans wanted to present their modernization by saving and displaying antiquities in a new museum; they wanted to emulate Europe and thereby close the metaphorical gap of progress that separated Ottomans from Europeans. On the other hand, the relocation of antiquities was premised on a distinction between the discerning and cultivated modern center and the ignorant provincial premodern periphery. The Ottomans, in other words, used Baalbek as one of many sites from which to elaborate their own sense of modernity in the face of constant European pressure and in contrast to "the perpetual warfare" of the neighboring Lebanese tribes and the lawlessness of the Arab Bedouins.[39] For example, a plaque erected by Sultan Abdülhamid II to commemorate the visit to Baalbek of the German emperor Kaiser Wilhelm II in 1898 was placed inside the Temple of Bacchus to remind visitors of a civilized Ottoman sovereignty over the ruins. It also intimated in no uncertain terms the de-

---

37 Osman Hamdi Bey and Theodore Reinach, *Une Nécropole Royale a Sidon: Fouilles de Hamdy Bey* (Paris, 1892), 112; see also Hanssen, "Imperial Discourses," 169.

38 Hanssen, "Imperial Discourses," 169. See Çelik, *Displaying the Orient*, 12-13, for a similar point.

39 Rifaat, *Lugat-ı Tarihiye ve Coğrafiye*, 3-4, 240.

sire of the Empire to be treated equally by its "friendly" European allies. Significantly, the plaque was inscribed in Ottoman and German, but not Arabic. The vast majority of the local inhabitants were apparently not deemed worthy enough (or capable, perhaps) of reading or understanding the significance of the imperial visit and its reflection of the elevation of the Ottoman Empire on the world stage.

Hamdi Bey believed that Ottoman modernization could succeed only if it preserved some sense of Ottoman difference from the West. He saw native culture as a timeless patrimony that set the Ottoman Empire apart from the West.[40] He bitterly criticized, for example, some Damascenes for rushing to imitate Western architectural style. This was evidence, according to Hamdi Bey, of a degeneration of taste among "Oriental" peoples.[41] In other words, anticipating what would become a standard, third-world, nationalist claim that modern western science could and should be married to an essential indigenous tradition, Hamdi Bey sought to reconcile Western science and national culture rather than totally emulate the West.[42] Yet in his understanding of native culture of the Ottoman Empire, be it the Islamic architecture of Damascus or the traditional attire of the various peoples of the Ottoman lands which he detailed in his *Les Costumes Populaires de la Turquie en 1873* for the Universal Exposition at Vienna, Hamdi Bey articulated a vision of Ottoman modernity that was hierarchical and imperial. He intimated that it was the task of Ottoman modernizers to save Ottoman heritage not just from the West but also from the Oriental peoples of the Ottoman Empire.[43] He proposed to save the Ottoman subjects of the Arab provinces from themselves – both the supposedly indolent majority in need of uplifting and the active minority who were blindly imitating European style which threatened to destroy any sense of Ottoman uniqueness. Behind Hamdi Bey's romantic discourse of Ottoman difference from the West lay a rhetoric of modernization that necessitated an Ottoman civilizing mission.

In his *Les Costumes Populaires*, Hamdi Bey explicitly outlined where and how tradition fit within a modernized world. He carefully distinguished between what he called clothing and costume. For him, clothing was the

---

40 This point has been made by Çelik, *Displaying the Orient*, 42. The following section on Hamdi Bey is reproduced from an article on "Ottoman Orientalism" forthcoming in the American Historical Review.

41 Hamdi Bey, *Une Nécropole Royale*, 112.

42 See Partha Chatterjee, *The Nation and its Fragments,* Princeton 1993, 6.

43 Osman Hamdi Bey and Marie de Launay, *Les Costumes Populaires de la Turquie en 1873*, Istanbul 1873.

manifestation of the homogenizing and rationalizing impulse of modernization: "Day by day, clothing tends to become more uniform across the world, and to efface not only all distinctions between diverse classes of society, but also those between different nations which seemed otherwise to be permanently separated by natural and moral barriers."[44] Traditional costume, on the other hand, reflected the clearest expression of the innate – and hence for Hamdi Bey authentic – characteristic of a people.[45] Costume, like the archaeological treasures of the Empire, gave the Ottoman state its distinctive cultural and historical code in an otherwise homogenous modernity. For this reason, Hamdi Bey gave an exhaustive account of the myriad costumes, and customs and manners, of the various peoples of the Empire. He began with "Turquie d'Europe" and more specifically Istanbul, which he declared was a link between East and West, and then he proceeded to the Balkan provinces; he next turned to Anatolia, then the Arab provinces, before ending with Africa.[46] Yet in constituting the various popular costumes of the Empire as integral components of Ottoman "tradition" and, therefore, as the authentic underpinnings of any project of modernization, Hamdi Bey paradoxically made it abundantly clear that his ethnographic survey – just like his later archaeological expeditions – both proved and justified an Ottoman mission to civilize quaint, but backwards and often savage, peripheries. For example, Hamdi Bey prefaced his discussion of what he understood to be native dress in Syria, by stating:

> Great historical memories are in abundance in these rich countries, conquered in turn by the Phoenicians, the Hebrews, the Greeks, and the Romans; [these countries] where the Quran and the Bible – two books of peace, fraternity, and tolerance – have long served as a pretext for crusaders coming from all over the Occident and for Arabs who founded Islam to tear each other apart. [This continued] up until the Ottoman conquest contained by force [these] fanatical hatreds, which, on occasion, would reawaken.[47]

Hamdi Bey not only sought to rewrite the history of the Ottoman conquest of the Arab provinces in a profoundly nineteenth-century discourse of tolerance, but he seized on the supposedly timeless costume to underscore other allegedly timeless characteristics of various groups in the Ottoman domains; he sought to adduce what he considered to be the essential char-

---

44 *Ibid.*, 5.

45 *Ibid.*, 6.

46 *Ibid.*, 11-12.

47 *Ibid.*, 258.

acteristics of the native inhabitants of these provinces who were tamed, disciplined and civilized – that is to say, forcibly removed from their endlessly repeated history of putatively endemic and age-old tribal violence - by the Ottoman imperial center. He described "the Muslim of Lebanon" (by which he meant a Sunni) as imbued with "soft and tranquil manners and customs" unlike his "turbulent neighbors," the Druze and Maronites.[48] The Maronites, he declared, were "remarkably intelligent and proud" and were "industrious and rich" but "just like their Druze neighbors, with whom they have never been able to live in harmony, the Maronites have proved difficult to subdue. Only since a few years ago has the joint efforts of the imperial Ottoman government together with its faithful allies succeeded in pacifying [Mount Lebanon]; today the age-old hatreds of the Druzes and Maronites seem to have been finally quelled; obedient subjects, they now live as brothers under the legitimate authority of a Christian Pasha sent by Istanbul to govern Mount Lebanon."[49]

Although Hamdi Bey's main goal was to portray an Ottoman cultural heritage that he feared might be lost, his supposedly objective delineation of the popular costumes of the different groups of the Ottoman Empire – supplemented with innumerable photographs – reinforced once more the notion that Ottoman modernization was not about equality between center and periphery but was a project of imperial benevolence and, above all, power that sought to mitigate an alleged civilizational gap between the modernizers of the imperial center and their subjects in the far-flung peripheries of the Empire. As the Hamidian state continued to battle Western imperialism, and as the Balkan provinces continued to be whittled away in the late nineteenth century, the civilizing Ottoman gaze over a number of different groups and classes (Anatolian, Kurd, Armenian, Serb, Damascene Muslim, Arab, Maronite, Druze, Jew, shaykh, merchant, peasant, and urban elite) was increasingly complicated – indeed redefined – as the desire of the modernizing "Turkish" nation to aid and civilize a backwards "Arab" nation (as well as the Armenians and Kurds). With the rise of the Committee of Union and Progress (CUP) came an increasingly explicit racial articulation of modernization that pitted the Turkish race as the most natural and able leaders of the modern empire.

Race-thinking in the late Ottoman Empire was not, of course, the preserve of the imperial center. However, it is important to note that as Ottoman modernization diminished "traditional" religious differences that had legitimated Ottoman rule in its classical age, it also introduced a discourse

---

48 *Ibid.*, 265.

49 *Ibid.*, 267.

of rational and supposedly scientific race-thinking to justify the domination of the largely Turkish-speaking Ottoman center over the Arabic-speaking peripheries of the empire in its modern age. It is not surprising then that the memoirs of Halide Edib – a woman who was at the forefront of an Ottoman Turkish civilizing mission to educate the women of the Arab provinces during the First World War – reveal a very clear notion of the responsibilities incumbent upon the advanced Turkish nation. Edib claimed that the "Ottoman Turks created an Ottoman citizenship."[50] Such an assertion staked out very precisely and in previously unthinkable racial terms the notion that Turks – as opposed to Arabs, Kurds, or Armenians, and as opposed to the different classes of Turkish-speaking inhabitants that Hamdi Bey recognized in his *Costumes Populaires* – created a modern concept of citizenship to which the other, subordinate, racial and ethnic groups of the empire would have to be gradually and benevolently introduced. "Turkey," she wrote, "must help the Arabs to develop a national spirit and personality, teach them to love their own national culture more than any foreign one [by which she meant the French]."[51] In Edib's view, the Turk was a natural leader whereas the Arab naturally corrupt. Echoing Hamdi Bey's view of the indigenous population of the Arab provinces, and Fuad Pasha's before him, Edib insisted that the Arab was mired in local passions. When she visited Jerusalem, she noted that "there was a hot and unwholesome atmosphere, mixed with religion passion verging on hysteria. The Turk alone had a calm, impartial, and quiet look. He … stood calmly watching, stopping bloody quarrels and preventing bloody riots in the holy places."[52] Such representations underscore the degree to which Ottoman modernization paradoxically elaborated a language of racial discrimination of a Turkish mission to lead and save the other groups of the empire at the same time as it constructed to a discourse of integrative Ottoman nationalism. Ottoman modernization resisted European imperialism but accepted, with a significant twist, its underlying cultural logic: just as modern imperialism can be thought of as the European desire to reshape and discipline non-European places and "peoples without history," so too can Ottoman modernization be thought of as an Ottoman desire to try to reshape and discipline *not-yet* Ottoman places and peoples.

---

50 Halide Edib, *Memoirs of Halidé Edib,* New York 1926, 235.

51 *Ibid.*, 402.

52 *Ibid.*, 426-427.

Conclusion: Future Avenues for Investigation.

Thinking of Ottoman modernization as a project of imperialism which sought to both uplift and discipline the periphery of the empire raises several points that require further investigation. First and foremost was that Ottoman reformers understood the modernity of their empire depended on the reformation of the periphery; at the same time, however, they also viewed the periphery as a foil to modern Ottoman identity. Selim Deringil has used the evocative phrase of an "Ottoman self-portrait" to describe official representations of the timeless Arab subjects of the empire at the Chicago world fair of 1893.[53] Deringil shows how the depiction of Arabs as inferior and backwards was an integral part of an Ottoman effort to counter the Orientalist representation of the barbarous and indolent Turk. Ottoman modernity was torn between a desire to improve and uplift Mount Lebanon, Syria, and Arabia in order to counter, and ultimately negate, a European discourse of the fanatical Turk, *and* an underlying refusal to ever acknowledge the equality and similitude of these regions and their inhabitants to Istanbul and its inhabitants. Arab subjects and provinces, as indicated earlier, constituted a proving ground of Ottoman modernization. This is not to deny that Sultan Abdülhamid paid more attention to the Arab provinces as part and parcel of his attempt to consolidate imperial control, nor that certain Arab subjects played an important and increasingly visible part in imperial politics.[54] It is only to bear in mind that the process of Ottomanization of the Arab provinces went hand in hand with a process of redefinition of imperial power through a discourse of modernization that was ultimately articulated in architectural, administrative, and sartorial terms but also in ambivalent racial terms.

The second major point is the relationship between reform and violence. Ottoman modernization was inseparable from the language of preservation of empire – in other words, it was marked by a sense of crisis that culminated in the First World War. Underlying the physical reformation of cities – from the architectural reorganization of Beirut to the introduction of municipalities – was a project of imperial preservation as well as national salvation. Anything that stood in the way of these twin goals was eliminated. Modernization, put differently, had an enormous cost. From the abolition of the Janissaries in 1826 through the massacre of Armenians,

---

53 Deringil, *The Well-Protected Domains*, 158.

54 Stanford J. Shaw and Ezel Kural Shaw, *History of the Ottoman Empire and Modern Turkey. Volume II: Reform, Revolution, and Republic: The Rise of Modern Turkey, 1808-1975*, Cambridge 1977, 259-260.

and suppression of Arab nationalists in Syria in WW1, an intimate and ever more lethal and efficient relationship between modernization and putative national security developed. Is it not time that we, as scholars of the Ottoman Empire, should take seriously *all* aspects of modernization rather than reproduce the conceit of the Ottoman reformers themselves – that all that they did was for the benefit of the local populations?

Cemal Pasha, for example, may not have been the ghoulish figure that Arab nationalists have made him out to be. Hasan Kayalı's recent work on *Arabs and Young Turks* certainly points in this direction, for it indicates that Cemal Pasha was genuinely interested in reform and urban renewal in Syria. But what Kayalı dismisses far too easily are the implications of representation for imperial modernization.[55] Cemal Pasha's memoirs are suffused with a language of race-based distinctions. This language informed his attitude towards supposedly backward Arabs, whom he first tried to uplift, and then – during the First World War – subjected to a reign of terror. It is an indisputable fact that Ottoman reformers relentlessly battled against Orientalism and imperialism. But in this battle did they not elaborate a language and attitude towards their Arab (and non-Arab) subjects that was analogous to Western Orientalism and imperialism? This is precisely the question that has not been sufficiently theorized.

---

55 Hasan Kayalı, *Arabs and Young Turks*, Berkeley 1997, 199-200 for a discussion of Cemal Pasha from an Ottoman perspective.

PRACTICES OF INTEGRATION – CENTER-PERIPHERY RELATIONS IN THE OTTOMAN EMPIRE[1]

JENS HANSSEN

Until recently, the assessment of the *Tanẓīmāt-i Ḥayriye* ("beneficent regulations") or reform era from 1839-1878 has tended to fall into two dominant heuristic categories. There were those scholars who followed the enthusiastic line of contemporary politicians and observers. They saw in the men of the *Tanẓīmāt* around the foreign minister Reşit Pasha enlightened visionaries imbued with the qualities of European democracy and representative government which culminated in the establishment of the Ottoman parliament and the promulgation of a constitution in 1876.[2] The reformers' subsequent failure is attributed to the autocratic rule of Abdülhamid II.[3] The second school has been more skeptical from the outset. It holds that any reform was either imposed by the Western powers or what British diplomatic circles referred to as 'paper organization' or a 'dead letter' in the first place, i.e. an Ottoman attempt to evade European military pressure by pretending to be reform-minded when in fact the Ottoman politicians were never really interested in 'true' democracy, equality and liberty. This view was vindicated by Abülhamid II's authoritarian policies which were seen as nothing else but the real face of Ottoman politics. Both approaches echo the words of one of the earliest (French) commentators who states that the *Tanẓīmāt* decrees were a "veritable bilateral contract" between the European powers, in particular Britain and France, and the Ottoman government and that "everything that was successful about the Tanẓīmāt was done in collaboration with foreigners."[4]

---

1 I would like to thank Isa Blumi, Ussama Makdisi, Robert McCaw and Eugene Rogan for their valuable and constructive criticism on previous drafts.

2 See for example Şerif Mardin, *The Genesis of Young Ottoman Thought, a Study in the Modernization of Turkish Political Ideas*, Princeton 1962, 10-80.

3 See for example, Bernard Lewis, *The Emergence of Modern Turkey*, Oxford 1961, 169-170.

4 E. Engelhardt, *La Turquie et le Tanzimat, ou histoire des réformes dans l'Empire ottoman depuis 1826 jusqu'à nos jours*, vol. 1, Paris 1882-1884, 260.

Initially, this essay represents a rereading of the very 'classics' of Ottoman historiography that constitute Ottoman imperial history.[5] I argue that, disposed of their progressist meta-narratives, these 'classics' have still a lot to offer. Despite the validity of recent criticism, dismissing their work outright is hypocritical (given that we all depend on their groundwork) and inconsistent (because it amounts to a weak subterfuge not to read them). These studies can hold a stock of information which may be marginal within their own progressist presentation, but can be refocused, enlarged and reformulated into a new analytical framework with the help of new critical historians of the Arab provincial periphery (like, *inter alia*, Doumani, Thompson, Makdisi and Hakim). Piecing together historical clues for a narrative that contradicts their original 'emplotments' is, in a sense, an exercise in 'reading history against the grain' of Ottomanist 'classics'.

Any enterprise to situate the Arab East in the framework of Ottoman imperialism must inevitably come into contact with Stanford Shaw's systematic work on Ottoman state archives. Shaw's two-volume account of the *History of Ottoman Empire and Modern Turkey* and the innumerable articles that preceded it, have been the most ambitious and well-researched Ottoman institutional history. Although he must be credited with having provided an authoritative alternative to previous studies that relied solely on European sources, his own accounts were necessarily shaped by the limits and categories of the Ottoman state documents he used. Thus his greatest achievement – the reconstruction of the politics in Ottoman government institutions – is at the same time his greatest limitation. Shaw's (like Lewis') obsession with tracing "the foundations [that] had been laid…for the Republic of Turkey" has had the historiographical effect of having invested the Ottoman past with a historical purpose of national becoming.[6] This, he has masterfully achieved by reassembling the empire's textual remainders into a narrative of Ottoman state formation from within the confines of that state's own archives.

The two main arguments in what follows are, first, that the processes and practices of integration within the Ottoman Empire in the nineteenth century also brought about new regional and imperial dimensions of local political participation. It is pertinent to develop this argument a step further, against the somewhat conventional game-theory view of zero-sum relations between imperial integration and local self-government. In fact, it

5 In particular, the pioneering works of Bernard Lewis, Niyazi Berkes, Standford Shaw, Şerif Mardin, Halil Inalcık, Roderic Davison and Robert Devereux.

6 Stanford and Ezel Shaw, *History of the Ottoman Empire and Modern Turkey*, Vol. 2, Cambridge 1977, viii (Preface).

will be argued that, for better or worse, the processes of 'Ottomanization' and 'localization' took place virtually simultaneously rather than the one at the expense of the other. Second, it will be argued that in the search for a solution to the crises of provincial rule in the first part of the nineteenth century, the Ottoman state recurred neither to 'time-honoured' principles nor to outright adoptions of 'western' models of governance. The imperial government looked instead at what had happened and indeed changed in the Arab provinces in the absence of direct Ottoman rule during the Egyptian occupation of Syria and during the early phases of Ottoman centralization in order to find blue-prints for the adoption of future reforms at the center in Istanbul. Within this process of integration, the determining forces of change were imperial inspection tours, local petitions, local councils and model provinces.

The following part will be a rather cursory tour through the two centuries that preceded the age of the *Tanẓīmāt*. In a sense this prehistory offers a '*longue durée*' backdrop against which claims of nineteenth-century continuities and changes can be better substantiated. On the one hand, the notion that change (as state modernization) was abrupt, all-embracing and came from outside forces in Europe needs to be reviewed. On the other hand, given the near total eclipse of state authority at the center of power in Istanbul by the beginning of the nineteenth century, subsequent developments during the *Tanẓīmāt* were neither moments of decline in Ottoman history nor marked by *déjà vu* banality. However, the newness of the relations between imperial center and provincial periphery during the *Tanẓīmāt* lies not so much in the long process that substituted new for old institutions.[7] Where such substitution occurred, it did so because the dia-

---

[7] The term 'periphery' has strong world-economic connotations. Here, however, it is not used in relation to a European economic and military core whose expansion since the sixteenth century shaped a dependent periphery in a capitalist system. Rather, the terms "centre" and "periphery" are used to denote political, social and cultural relations *within* the realms of the Ottoman Empire. For clarity, I will add two adjectives and speak of "imperial centre" and "provincial periphery". As we shall see, these relations are determined by geography as much as by identity politics and social hierarchy. As such, centre and periphery are necessarily simplifications of complex and multipolar relations. As an ultimately imprecise working hypothesis, I consider politicians and officials of the imperial government as representing the interests of the imperial centre. Provincial governors and special envoys like Fuad or Midhat Pasha and Selim Bey, for example, represent instances of "the centre in the periphery" regardless of their 'conservative' or 'liberal' inclinations. Provincial notables who have entered into government positions in Istanbul, like the provincial deputies in parliament or the Malhames and ʿIzzat Pasha represent instances of "the periphery in the centre" specifically in relation to their place of origin.

lectic communication between capital and province suggested it. From here this essay's own suggestion is to refocus the analysis and to prioritize the spatial dimension of the *Tanẓīmāt* over the conventional temporal dimension.[8] As such it is an attempt to cut the cord of temporally arranged, evolutionary causality of the *Tanẓīmāt* era and offer as an alternative geographically, politically, socially and culturally determined reference to an imperial center and a provincial periphery. This is not to say the Ottoman past has become insignificant to nineteenth-century transformations. Within the framework of this spatial conception, time, it will be argued, served as a powerful referent for reforms (or as a repertoire for what Blumi calls "strategic utilitization") rather than merely containing those reforms' causal origins.[9]

Center-Periphery Relations prior to the Tanẓīmāt

Throughout the Ottoman centuries political challenges from the provincial periphery were marked neither by outright rejection of the new Ottoman rulers nor by fixed religious, ethnic, or linguistic antagonism. On the contrary, the Ottoman centuries in the Syrian land revealed recurring patterns of interaction and assimilation between the local and the imperial elements. On a socio-cultural level, patterns of integration and assimilation, of 'Ottomanization' and 'Localization', unfolded in reciprocal directions. This dual process, as I see it, took place not so much in chronologically distinct "waves" as implied by Halil Inalcık;[10] rather, Ottomanization and localization coincided and mutually complemented each other in "confluence and continuum" to borrow from Hannerz.[11] In other words, localization did not occur outside the Ottoman context but depended on political and infra structural centralization (against which resistance began to form at the beginning of the twentieth century). Therefore, this essay suggests that only when the Ottoman state embarked on its centralizing reforms in the nineteenth century, did a sense of locality (urban, confessional, political, cultural, etc.) crystallize.

---

8 See Isa Blumi's contribution to this volume on these dimensions of analysis.

9 For a succinct discussion of the 'fallacy of origins' in 'History', see Roger Chartier, "The Chimera of the Origin", in his *On the Edge of the Cliff; History, Language and Practices*, Baltimore 1997, 51-71.

10 Halil Inalcık, "Centralization and Decentralization in Ottoman Administration," in *Studies in Eigtheenth Century Islamic History*, edited by Thomas Naff and Roger Owen, London 1977, 27-52.

11 Ulf Hannerz, *Transnational Connections,* London 1996, 67.

By the end of the sixteenth century, the Ottoman government found it increasingly difficult to finance the large standing Ottoman armies. As a solution, the central government decided to modify the system of land administration. It introduced the principle of tax-farming, or *iltizām*, according to which plots of land were auctioned. The bargain struck between government and tax farmer signified an important shift in the center-provincial relationship inside the empire, effectively marking the beginning of the process known as decentralization. Where and when land lease passed from the imperial sipahis and the janissaries into the hands of local, landed potentates, the Ottoman military administrators gradually lost their economic power bases. Conversely, provincial notables could localize their socio-economic status and were beginning to share a stake in the Ottoman state. This process was marked by two significant changes in the center-periphery relations: First, the replacement of sultanic representatives, or *kul*s, by local notables to establish quasi-hereditary '*ayanliks*', and second the rise of new urban – especially coastal – centers into a system of economic rivalry. The rise and fall of Acre around the turn of the eighteenth century as outlined in Thomas Philipp's contribution to this volume is a case in point for the wider phenomenon of the emergence of local 'power houses' in the Fertile Crescent based on their direct access to trade with Europe.

However, the presentation requires qualification in so far as the age of decentralization was viewed as constituting a measure of "externalization of the Ottoman state's socio-organizational capacity"[12] in commerce, land and agriculture that weakened the formal Ottoman economic system of fiscal redistribution. As Salzmann argued recently, statist and functionalist perspectives tend to assume that the degree of centralization of administrative and coercive capacity is a measure of progress in state development, while fiscal practices that auctioned off economic assets to the gentry, entrepreneurs or merchants are seen as a detour to Smithian principles of economic development.[13] Rather, lifetime tax-farms and commercial estates "created diffused but interrelated loci of state power [through an] extensive fiscal network that sustained old-order power, knitting center and periphery together over the eighteenth century, and laying the social foundation for the centralizing policies initiated from 1812 onwards."[14] In

---

12 Ariel Salzmann, "An Ancient Régime Revisited: 'Privatization' and Political Economy in the Eighteenth Century Ottoman Empire," *Politics and Society* 21 (1993), 393ff.

13 See Robert Brenner, "The Origins of Capitalist Development: A Critique of Neo-Smithian Marxism," *NLR* 104 (1977), 25-91.

14 Salzmann, "An Ancient Régime Revisited," 395.

this scenario, the Ottoman government did formally sell off economic assets to imperial and local notables, but at the same, state revenue increased and so did the stake that local notables held in the well-being of the state.

A Lifeline for Istanbul: the Province Rescues the House of Osman

By the beginning of the nineteenth century, political events in the capital Istanbul had more immediate seismographic effects on the provinces than ever before. At the same time the provinces became ever more involved in the dramatic changes at the center of imperial power in the capital. Sultan Selim III's rule (1789-1807) was marked by central bureaucrats' efforts to (re-) align political power to the imperial government. However, before their attention could be turned towards the semi-autonomous provinces, the struggle concentrated on Istanbul itself. Throughout the eighteenth century the Ottoman capital had been receiving growing numbers of immigrants driven from the Anatolian countryside by the economic hardship inflicted by an encroaching world-economy, and by refugees driven from war zones in Ottoman Europe. Food shortages and dissatisfaction in the barracks and religious schools frequently led to urban riots which occasionally even cost sultans their lives. By the turn of the eighteenth century the city was in a state of simmering civil war. Projects of social reforms introducing European methods and technology were aimed to reassert the state's control over the city. A population census was attempted to restrict the influx of unaccountable migrants. Coffeehouses and taverns were closed as potential abodes of sedition, and a rigid dress code was issued attempting to make social and ethnic difference legible and hence controllable. In the protracted battle over their enforcement, city quarters were looted and burnt, wealthy Jews and Christians attacked on the streets, the sultan's palace invaded by an angry mob of janissaries and a group of reformers killed.

This intense internal crisis finally abated with the accession of Maḥmūd II, the penultimate remaining Ottoman heir to the throne, in 1808. His term of office came at the most precarious moment in the history of the Ottoman Empire. Not since Istanbul was captured in 1453 had "war been waged on such a scale in the streets of the city" and never before had Ottoman state authority been challenged so fundamentally by its urban population.[15] It is significant that in such a moment of siege and threat of dynastic obliteration, the sultan received vital support from provincial notables under Alemdār Muṣṭafā Pasha who marched on Istanbul from

---

15 Andrew Wheatcroft, *The Ottomans; Dissolving Images*, London 1993, 120.

southern Bulgaristan in support of the sultan and the Ottoman dynasty[16]. While, as Abu el-Haj argues, "the rapprochement between the sultan and the ruling elite was uneven and never without ambivalence…the impression remains that some groups among the provincial notables and a sector of the centrally based power-holding elite were willing to cooperate for the purpose of strengthening the Ottoman dynasty."[17]

The new center-province reform coalition was codified in the short-lived, so-called Deed of Alliance (*Sened-i Ittifak*) of October 7, 1808. It followed extensive meetings attended by provincial notables from Anatolia and Rumelia and was supported *in absentia* by Arab notables unable to travel the distance in enough time. The draft expressed loyalty to the sultan, mutual respect and cooperation in the administration and taxation of the empire and commitment to recruiting Ottoman conscripts. The notables, in effect, agreed to Maḥmūd II's renewed state-centralization on the condition that the Ottoman government endorse their brokering role in local and regional matters.[18]

The Eastern Question: The Internationalization of Ottoman Center-Periphery Relations

The efforts at provincial realignment came at the time of the 'Eastern Question', which war and diplomacy tried to 'solve'. From our perspective the Eastern Question was in a way a raising of the stakes, an 'internationalization' of the center-periphery 'tug-of-war' between Istanbul and the provinces. European rivalries first swept into the European provinces of the empire in the Balkans, Egypt and some decades later into the Arab provinces. These developments engaged the Ottoman state in a series of defensive wars in which it was faced not only with the armies of other European empires but also with provincial breakaway movements. Separatist movements managed to involve European states by successfully playing religious or nationalist emancipatory themes to advance their causes. The internationalization did mark a significant rupture in the conduct of center-province relations. In the breakaway provinces – like Serbia or Greece – as well as the provinces remaining under Ottoman rule, like Mount Lebanon – race, ethnicity and sectarian identification became essentialist, political vocabularies of difference that fed international claims

16 See Christoph Newman's contribution to this volume.

17 Rifaat Abou-El-Haj, *Formation of the Modern State*, Albany 1991, 68.

18 Halil Inalcık, "Sened-i Ittifak ve Gülhane Hatt-i Hümayunu II," *Beleten* 28 (1964), 603-622.

for 'national' emancipation. Yet, despite tense center-periphery relations between Istanbul and the Arab provinces during the nineteenth century, these relations were never entirely severed by either party. By 1840, the Ottoman Empire was enjoying the support of most European powers, as it established itself as a vital link in the balance of power. Itself militarily vulnerable, the geopolitical constellation gave it power to manœuver in its provinces.

Imperial Crisis Management looks for Inspiration in the Provinces: Inspection Tours, Petitions, Rule by Council, Model Provinces

From the sublime Topkapi premises on the Golden Horn, the world looked grim in 1839. In 1830 Serbia had gained autonomy and was pressing for territorial expansion at Ottoman expense; the Treaty of Edirne in 1829 rewarded the Greek rebellion with independence and Russia gained footholds on the Danube and in the north-eastern Anatolian provinces stationing troops dangerously close to the capital. To top the disastrous performances of the new Ottoman army, Egypt's own new model army had not only invaded and occupied one of the empire's most precious provinces, Syria (1831-1840), but in 1832 had advanced to within a few days' march of Istanbul itself.

Faced with such paramount crises in the provinces, the central government resorted to four strategies in order to reorganize fundamentally the structure of Ottoman provincial rule:

1. dispatching fact finding and inspection missions to the troubled provinces;
2. encouraging local petitions and delegations to Istanbul;
3. setting up local councils to channel the center-periphery relations into *in situ* institutions;
4. setting up model provinces which were then applied as blueprints to other provinces.

The production of imperial knowledge about the provinces involved classifications according to territorial and communal categories that emerged out of the practices of integration. Inspection tours and local petitions formed the stock of experience and information upon which a major part of the official knowledge about provincial society in Istanbul depended. The inspectors' provincial reports effectively provided authorized knowledge about Ottoman provincial societies, on the basis of which model provinces were created in order to test the efficacy of its application. To paraphrase

Richard Smith, "to 'know' was to know what was good for [a provincial society]... Here, one should not assume that the reports were not merely a natural product of administration, without a beginning or a dynamic of its own."[19] It is in this sense that the "beneficial regulations" of the Ottoman reform era should be understood as an epistemological leap through acts of abstraction from provincial situations to imperial policy.

As in the case of British imperialism in India discussed by Richard Smith, the Ottoman government was trying to adjust its prospective central rule over the provinces to what was perceived as constituting the needs and interests of their inhabitants and its own officials. Whereas British rule was marked by the extra geographical, cultural and administrative distance between ruler and ruled, by contrast, the Ottoman system of provincial rule, as argued above, had a long and diverse tradition of interaction at all levels of society between the imperial center and the provincial peripheries.

Local petitions were, in a reversal of perspective, a kind of bargaining chip in this "ambivalent" – to use Homi Bhabha's catchphrase[20] – yet ultimately unequal center-periphery power relation. The reports engineered provincial development on the basis of textualized facts on paper whose "categories used by state agents [we]re not merely means to make their environment legible; they [we]re an authoritative tune to which most of the population must dance."[21] The authors of the local petitions provided the confessionalized script of self-imagination and self-representation of the respective communities. Rather than reflecting inherent, primordial socio-religious structures and sentiments of the undersigned, the authors of the petitions themselves opportunistically produced (and invented) the trope of fixed, natural entities as a culturalist instrument to stake out favorable claims for the political future of their locality.[22]

Within Ottoman center-periphery relations, imperial inspection and local self-representation merge Foucault's technologies of modern governmentality and epistemological power on the one hand,[23] and the processes

---

19 Richard Smith, "Rule-by-Records and Rule-by-Reports: Complementary Aspects of the British Imperial Rule of Law," *Contributions to Indian Sociology* 19 (1985), 154.

20 See Robert Young, "The Ambivalence of Homi Bhabha," in his *White Mythologies; Writing History and the West*, London 1993, 141-156.

21 James Scott, *Seeing like a State; How certain Schemes to Improve the Human Condition Have Failed*, New Haven 1998, 83.

22 Arjun Appadurai, "Life after Primordialism," in his *Modernity at Large*, Minneapolis 1996, 139-157.

23 G. Burchell, C. Gordon, P. Miller, *The Foucault Effect; Studies in Governmentality*, Chicago 1991, especially chapter 4.

of adaptation, negotiation, experimentation and contestation by those people subject to these imperial practices on the other.[24] It is not that community or confession as principles of social organization had been irrelevant prior to the *Tanẓīmāt*, nor did they replace other forms of identities during and after the age of reform. In this sense, Hakim's point is taken that the new Ottoman order in Mount Lebanon under the Şekib Efendi Réglement of 1845 "was important because it introduced for the first time the communal factor at the institutional and political [and one might add: the territorial] levels."[25]

Inspection Tours

The foundations of Ottoman authority in the entire empire were deeply shaken by the Egyptian occupation of Syria, Palestine and Mount Lebanon and only the diplomatic logic of the concert of Europe's balance of power saved the empire from collapsing. Meḥmed ʿAlī was ousted from Syria following a joint European naval landing near Beirut. Thus, the fragile integrity of the Ottoman Empire was reestablished and the *status quo ante* in Syria nominally restored. The resolution of the Syrian crisis also fell amidst a shift of imperial power at the center of empire – away from the sultan to what came to be known as the "men of the *Tanẓīmāt*," a corps of Ottoman bureaucrats, several of whom had spent time in European capitals on training missions at Maḥmūd II's behest. While these new European-trained Ottoman bureaucrats had a fair knowledge of the politicians in Paris and London, few of them had ever been to Arabistan – as the Arab provinces were collectively referred to in Istanbul.

Under these circumstances, the Ottoman government required inspectors who would go into the provinces, talk to the inhabitants, record peculiarities and return with suggestions as to how best to administer the provinces. Shortly after the *Hatt-i Şerif* of 1839, imperial officials were sent out to the provinces to form an idea about the state of affairs in the provinces. These "commissions of improvement" investigated the administration of taxes, the operation of the local councils and their relationship with the

---

24 See especially the works of E. P. Thompson, *Customs in Common, Studies in Traditional Popular Culture*, London, 1995, James Scott , *Weapons of the Weak: Everyday practices of Peasant Resistance*, New Haven, 1985 and the subaltern historiography in India.

25 Carol Hakim-Dowek, *The Origins of the Lebanese National Idea, 1840-1914*, Oxford: D.Phil. Thesis 1997, 83. This judgment concurs with Smith's view of 'caste' and a classificatory category in British India that "in this sense, the British did invent 'caste' by institutionalizing it. Smith, Richard S., "Rule by-record," 171.

governors, they drew maps, attempted cadastral surveys, assessed roads and the potential for public works. As such their strategies of spatial representation combined to produce a new quality of transformation that was based on establishing an order of geographical homogeneity rather than temporal linearity.

Upon return to Istanbul, these inspectors were met by ministers and legislative councils. Following their discussions, the Ottoman government "decided to direct the development of public works more closely to the provincial recommendations," to concentrate on training bureaucrats and to establish model provinces.[26] One such inspection report on the situation in Mount Lebanon was prepared for the Porte by Selim Bey[27] who toured Mount Lebanon from April to August 1842 in the wake of what is widely considered the starting point of Maronite-Druze clashes for the subsequent two decades.[28]

Selim Bey's report was the basis of diplomatic negotiations between the Great Powers and the Ottoman government in Istanbul.[29] In the event, Selim Bey's recommendations for direct Ottoman rule, propped up by what the Europeans considered illegitimate local petitions, were rejected by France whose agenda involved the restoration of the old Shihābī regime (and whose 'men on the spot' had supplied information contrary to that provided by Selim Bey). It is not surprising that the Ottoman government should aspire to direct rule given that unity, centralization and state-led modernization were the main tenets of the Ottoman reforms. What was new in the context of the center-periphery relations within the reforming Empire and what contrasted with the *Sened-i Ittifak* of 1808, was that the

---

26 Stanford Shaw, "The Origins of Representative Government in the Ottoman Empire: The Provincial Representative Councils, 1839-1876," in *Near Eastern Round Table, 1967-68*, edited by R. Winder, New York 1969, 84-85.

27 Born into a family of high-level Ottoman officials, he was an experienced inspector. However, according to Baron de Testa, he professedly had little knowledge about Mount Lebanon before his departure. Caesar Farah, *The Politics of Interventionism in Ottoman Lebanon*, London 2000, 181, fn. 96.

28 The multilateral negotiations over the future administration of Mount Lebanon leading up to the 1842 agreement had themselves depended in part on inspection tours commissioned by the sultan of foreign agents such as Wood and Jochmus. Farah, *The Politics of Interventionism*, 53, fns. 7, 9, 10.

29 "Protocole de la Conférence qui a eu lieu dans la Maison de Campagne du Reis Efendi, 15. Septembre, 1842," in Adel Ismail, *documents diplomatiques et consulaires relatifs à l'histoire du Liban*, Vol. 7, Beirut 1976, 200-214.

government should insist that Selim Bey's report reflect "but the free voice of the populations," the recording of which had his original mandate.[30] Selim Bey's mission set a precedent for a number of high ranking investigative missions into the violence in Mount Lebanon by Ottoman politicians such as Kapudan Halil, brother-in-law of the sultan, the General Meḥmed Emin, Ata Bey, Şekib Efendi and Fuad Pasha, the last two both Ottoman foreign ministers during their respective inspection tours between 1845-6 and 1860-61. In sum, during the *Tanẓīmāt*, Ottoman statesmen began to discover the backyards of 'their' empire.[31] And they did so invariably in times of crisis.

Elsewhere in the empire the application of the *Tanẓīmāt* in the provinces had similar repercussions on the social fabric and center-periphery relations. As Inalcık put it, "far from remaining a dead letter, the Gülhane Hatti led to unrest and large scale movements in many parts of the empire."[32] But our point here is a subtler one than the latent narrative of "local reaction to modernization attempts." For neither 'modernization' *per se*, nor the provincial inspections were neutral, or self-evident, endeavors. Thus on the one level the inspector of a given province might have been anything between a participant observer – akin to an early social anthropologist – who patiently sat in council sessions amongst the 'native chieftains' and meticulously recorded his findings, and a development agent who assessed a province's feasibility for modernization in general and public works projects in particular. From here to the discursive practices of Ottoman imperialism as discussed in other contributions to this volume it is but a minor leap.

The practices of reporting and recording ushered in new dimensions of planning based on imperial application and provincial response. These dimensions were to determine notions of effective provincial government beyond the appearance of a standardized and uniform provincial law in 1864. It is significant that rather than evoking the formulaic return to the great days of Sultan Suleymān the Lawgiver common since Koçu Bey's

---

30 Adel Ismail, *Histoire du Liban, redressement et déclin du féodalisme libanais (1840-1861)*, Beirut 1958, 184.

31 The number of high-level bureaucrats who earned their spurs in the troubled provinces and moved on to ministerial posts in Istanbul was ever increasing since the mid-nine teenth century. Of the first generation, Necip, Kibrisli and Izzet Pasha, reluctant reformers in their respective Syrian provinces went on to become grand vezirs. Likewise, Mustafa Nuri, Said and Kamil Pashas had been ministers of War before their provincial assignments to Syria and Mount Lebanon. This trend continued well into the Hamidian period and beyond. See also the contribution of Herzog to this volume.

32 Halil Inalcık, "Application of the Tanzimat and its Social Effects," *AO* 5 (1973), 98.

trope of imperial or Ottoman decline in the late sixteenth century, imperial planning became forward-looking, future-oriented and shrouded in the vocabulary of just and equitable provincial rule. Rather, with the Ottoman reconquest of the Syrian provinces there developed a self-referential discourse within the dialectic process of reform whose referents were the provincial fields of application themselves. The compression of Ottoman political space not only offered new modes of social control, but also new ways for the provincial periphery to take the imperial government up on its *Tanẓīmāt* discourse of modernization. Provincial élites and commoners alike had become familiar with the modern tunes of legitimacy and accountability of Ottoman rule. In fact, as we shall see, the local vocabularies of self-representation were a powerful antiphonal variation to that tune.

Petitions

The populations and societies Ottoman inspectors were supposed to comprehend and classify prior to the implementation of the centralizing reforms were hardly the uninformed, oblivious entities once assumed. Various local élites, religious establishments, landowners and commoners naturally had vested interests in determining their localities' future. They were quick to understand that the best way to push their cases was by popular support manifested in petitions.[33] The topics of petitions traditionally varied from complaints about too high taxation, requests for debt relief after droughts or the perceived injustice of a *qāḍī*. What was new in the *Tanẓīmāt* era was the political quality: campaigns for new administrative boundaries or public construction (a port or seray), for elevation of a city to a provincial capital (as in Beirut) or for improved modes of local representation.[34] At the same time, provincial notables were encouraged by frequent formal and informal invitations to Istanbul to present their demands.[35] Imperial cere-

33 Petitions, or *arẓuhalat* were "a time-honored tradition in Islam". See Ehud Toledano, *State and Society in mid-nineteenth century Egypt*, Cambridge 1990, 213. In the Ottoman provinces, petitions were a powerful instrument for local *ayan* who used them to express "their opinions on the appointment [and tenure] of urban public officials and of religious functionaries, including the kadi...causing their dismissal." "Examples of petitions by ayan attempting to influence the decisions of the government throughout the seventeenth century abound in the kadi records." In the eighteenth century "such petitioning activities took a more organized form". Inalcık, "Centralization and Decentralization," 44 and fn. 63.

34 Jens Hanssen, *The Effect of Ottoman Rule on Fin de Siècle Beirut*, Oxford, Ph.D. thesis 2001.

35 Shaw, "The Origins of Representative Government," 136.

monies and processions, as well as the bestowal of imperial medals, were favored techniques of displaying imperial grandeur.[36] In return the government could be sure the notables would recount metropolitan tales at home.

Once the petitions reached the Porte, they were processed by specially formed commissions inside new departments tending to provincial affairs. From the 1860s onwards, the new state *niẓamiye* courts dedicated one out of three sections to servicing petitions. When the Ottoman constitution was promulgated, article 52 stipulated the right of petition, while the parliament had a special petitions committee.[37] In sum, these institutional provisions enhanced the Ottoman state's knowledge of the provinces and provided it with an authoritative mnemonic repository on which to base provincial rule. Once processed and classified into drawers of imperial departments, the petitions and letters of complaints counted as social facts and valid representations of provincial realities. However, the social facts and representations of provincial realities they project had already been pre-molded at the point of gathering. More often than not they emerged out of particular power struggles whose local origins were lost to the departments in the capital or were deliberately obscured, pre-processed or translated into macroscopical imperial categories by the petitioners.

To elucidate the 'micro-politics' of petitions, let us leave Istanbul's government offices and return to Mount Lebanon again. According to the recent studies by Caesar Farah and Carol Hakim, the 1840s were ripe with political statements and claims to social belonging enshrined in petitions. There raged, according to both authors, a veritable "battle of petitions" often with contradictory messages, apparently signed by the same people, calling for anything from the reestablishment of Ottoman central rule to the annexation of Mount Lebanon to France.[38] The messages conveyed were determined by who the addressee was. Bent on gaining the international recognition they felt they deserved, respective clergy and notables reified conceptions of primordial enmity, to produce the new 'culture of sectarianism' in Mount Lebanon. In his study on nineteenth-century Lebanon, Ussama Makdisi demonstrates how the sectarian nature of the conflict was projected back in history (or, more precisely, taken out of history's progressivist flow and reduced to forces of nature), when, in fact, the vio-

---

36 Selim Deringil, "Invention of Tradition as Public Image in the late Ottoman Empire, 1808-1908," *CSSH* 35:1 (1993), 3-29.

37 Robert Devereux, *The First Ottoman Constitutional Period; a Study of the Midhat Constitution and Parliament*, Baltimore 1963, 175-6.

38 Hakim, *The Origins of the Lebanese National Idea,* 80.

lence that occurred was historically produced by a confluence of factors particular to the nineteenth century.[39]
The imperial parties read the signs of violence in accordance with their political agendas: For France the protection of the Christians by way of establishing a Christian entity within the Ottoman Empire and for the Ottoman government pacification through direct rule. Ottoman inspectors were prime movers in this battle. For while roaming the mountain, they were rallying for pro-Ottoman voices, or rather signatures on petitions, to strengthen the Ottoman case against the foreign consuls and special envoys.[40]

In the event, these petitions created a maze of local self-representations in which the French political establishment – itself embroiled in contradictory colonial visions concerning Mount Lebanon – and the Ottoman governments took the claims of the petitions at face value as the texts were formulated in a way that anticipated imperialists' criteria. They reaffirmed notions of primordial identities and passions whose violent potential could only be quelled through the petitioners' political recognition. In a way, there existed an uncanny, tacit alliance of purpose between the imperial powers, including the Ottoman, and the local élites under the banner of stability and order with a purpose of suppressing 'the disruptive aspirations of the commoners'. The alleged ignorance of their accustomed place in society was universally blamed for the communal violence. The notables and clergy derived legitimacy precisely from their claims to speak for these 'ignorant' commoners.

What is pertinent in these "mirror games"[41] is that they corroborate for Mount Lebanon what E. Thompson and B. Doumani have established for Damascus and Palestine respectively. Namely that local societies are using the very institutions and mechanisms of the *Tanẓīmāt* to push for their own – often recently invented – agendas and identities. These local agendas only emerged as a consequence of the new center-periphery relations during the *Tanẓīmāt*. As the Ottoman state changed its legitimacy structures there emerged room for certain local inhabitants to 'fill gaps' created by the readjustment.

---

39 Ussama Makdisi, *The Culture of Sectarianism; Community, History and Violence in Nineteenth Century Ottoman Lebanon*, Los Angeles, 2000.

40 See Farah, "The investigative Commision of Selim Beg," in his *The Politics of Interventionism*, 183-208.

41 Hakim, *The Origins of the Lebanese National Idea*, 72.

Rule by Council

From the dynamics that evolved around inspection tours and petitions, there emerged a recurring pattern in the application of central reforms that enables us to go beyond normative, functionalist and institutional frameworks of analysis. This is not to say that the central institutions that developed in the early *Tanẓīmāt* period did not shape the center-periphery relationship between Istanbul and the provinces. On the contrary, from the point of view of the center, as Shaw puts it, "representative government entered the Ottoman system in the nineteenth century as part of the integration process by which the central government effectively extended its power into the provinces."[42] Viewed from the provinces, however, the representative councils were vital arenas that channeled the evolving bargaining process both in Istanbul and in the provinces.

Immediately following the promulgation of the Gülhane *Hatt-i Şerif* in 1839, an imperial *firmān* was issued which determined the organization and structure of the new councils. Provincial notables were summoned to Istanbul to attend the Assembly of Provincial Notables and to consult the government on situations and opinions in the provinces.[43] Quite apart from the obvious concern for the centralization of knowledge, the gathering of provincial notables in Istanbul also both aligned leading political figures of the provinces and tied the economic élites to the survival and prosperity of the new and contested reforms. The 'councilization of politics' created an institutional buffer between imperial center and provincial periphery. Unpopular measures, such as fiscal or penal matters, were carried by the local councils, thus effectively implicating local members in imperial rule. In terms of the politics of petitions, the councils also provided local channels of criticism that would be leveled against the Ottoman governor with an institutionalized legitimacy on a more routine, day-to-day basis.

Two recent studies have greatly changed our view and enhanced our understanding of the role of the local administrative councils in the provinces. Discussing the first Damascus Administrative Council of the new order in 1844-45, Thompson claims the council "represented an opportunity for reform from below." Unlike earlier councils which had often been "an *ad hoc* body controlled by the provincial governor, the council had become a pillar of Ottoman provincial rule intended to balance the power of the governor". As such it had "more autonomy, and broader powers

---

42 Shaw, "The Origins of Representative Government in the Ottoman Empire," 56.

43 Lütfi, Ahmet, *Tarih-i Lütfi*, edited by Abrurrahman Sherif, Istanbul, 1873-1910, Vol. 8, 9.

than any of its predecessors."[44] The twelve members had to deal with everyday welfare requested in petitions arising from natural disaster, with complaints about hardship brought about by market forces and related requests for tax and debt relief. Largely concerned with specific and practical matters, the council functioned as a kind of political and economic regulator.

Doumani's study on Ottoman Nablus confirms the provincial council's role in defending the merchants and the town's interests *vis à vis* an encroaching world-economy, an encroaching revenue-seeking Ottoman state and, later, an encroaching body of Beiruti merchants and moneylenders. Doumani dissects a crucial point regarding the interpretative strategies of the council *vis à vis* the central authorities:

> The argument of 'tradition' was often used as a weapon against those innovations that the council members deemed not to be in their favor (they did not complain about innovations they approved of, even those that did in fact challenge established practices). Indeed, the council consciously arrogated to itself a monopoly in the meaning of tradition – hence the position of interpreter of local realities – in order to strengthen its hand in dealings with the central authorities.[45]

Such strategies reiterate the argument made earlier in this study that the *Tanẓīmāt* represented a break with the past. Here, the element of strategic choice, in referring to tradition, is in itself an aspect of self-referentiality, one that enhanced the powers of the provincial social actors with regard to the state structure into which they were incorporated.

In both cases, in Damascus as in Nablus, the administrative council became the forum of a new composite urban elite which included first many *multazims*, and then merchants, moneylenders, manufacturers and small industrialists. "These notables used the council to bargain with the Ottoman government over the boundaries of political authority."[46]

Model Provinces

Again shortly after the *Hatt-i Şerif* of 1839, representatives of the provincial councils were invited to Istanbul to report on the needs and desires of

---

44 Elizabeth Thompson, "Ottoman Political Reform in the Provinces: the Damascus Advisory Council in 1844-1845," *IJMES* 25 (1993), 457f.

45 Beshara Doumani, *Rediscovering Palestine, Merchants and Peasants in Jabal Nablus*, Los Angeles 1996, 148.

46 Doumani, *Rediscovering Palestine*, 241.

their provinces.[47] Following these recommendations the Porte decided in late 1845 to designate certain provinces as models to overcome the burdensome task of reform. Here the best qualified administrators were concentrated to adopt what the provincial notables had reported to the imperial center and what the imperial commissions discovered in the provinces. The first provinces to benefit from such special attention were the *sancaḳs* of Izmit, Gallipoli and slightly later Izmir, Salonica, Varna, Trabzon and Samsun, notably all maritime provinces. In these model provinces the members of the councils were subjected to tighter central control by way of keeping biographical files on each representative stored in Istanbul in what was to become the *sicill-i ahval* imperial archive under Abdülhamid II.

After the success of these pilot projects the reforms were extended to the provinces of Edirne, Bursa and Sidon where the experiences in the first new provinces were adapted to fit the local conditions of the latter. With the breakout of new social and sectarian conflicts in the Ottoman provinces in the 1850s, culminating in the civil wars of Damascus and Mount Lebanon in 1860, new efforts to revise provincial administration were undertaken. Whereas the emphasis in the first set of models was placed on devolving central power and engaging local notables, the second set of provincial reforms in the late 1850s and early 1860s was designed to strengthen the authority of the provincial governors both *vis à vis* the central government and the local councils. Charged with an emergency mission to resolve the atrocities committed against the Christians, the foreign minister Fuad Pasha successfully abated the imminent European military intervention in Mount Lebanon. Basing his judgment and verdicts as much on the extensive trials as on the body of previous reports available in government archives, Fuad Pasha's new order in Mount Lebanon was to be adopted in other provinces and ultimately served as one of the provincial blueprints for the provincial law of the entire empire in 1864.

Midhat Pasha was another prominent Ottoman reformer whose very political clout in the imperial capital was closely connected to his achievements and his support in the provinces. His successful experiments in social pacification and public works as governor in the Balkans were to shape his later policies as grand vezier in Istanbul. The province of the Danube was a particularly formative testing ground both for Midhat and for the empire, as he was able to deal with subduing Bulgarian nationalists,

---

47 Shaw, "The Origins of Representative Government," 84-85.

resettling refugees while improving the infrastructure, establishing schools and constructing public buildings.[48]

The new, highly structured system of provincial government acutely affected the local populations who vented complaints against certain measures of state encroachment. Their complaints were taken seriously by the government and a new batch of prominent inspectors was sent out. "Far from the simplistic, vague, and general reports of most European observers of the *Tanẓīmāt* at this time, Ahmed Cevdet provided 'all those who could see' with highly detailed – and apparently quite accurate – reports about Ottoman provincial administration."[49]

Particularly when inspection reports were beginning to be published in Istanbul's press during the 1860s a specific knowledge of the savage and ignorant provincials ('ignorant', because they were unable and unwilling to follow Ottoman leaps into modernity) was disseminated amongst the 'cultured circles' of the capital.[50] Indeed, in the prose of Stanford Shaw's imperial history, "the reports of these inspectors were made available to officials at the Porte, but in addition, most of them also were printed in the official newspaper *Takvim-i Vekaii* so that the Ottoman public and foreigners alike could see what the problems were and what was being done to correct them."[51]

The complex involvement of metropolitan culture in creating 'colonial others' in the Arab provinces is dealt with in other essays in this volume.[52] Yet, there were also foundational ways in which the provinces influenced central state structures prior to the canonization of central institutions and laws in the 1860's and 70's. The *Tanẓīmāt* did not just affect existing state structures. With time – and through practice and implementation – the changes they brought about became state structures themselves.

---

48 Roderic Davison, *Reform in the Ottoman Empire, 1856-1876*, Princeton 1963, 151-157.

49 Shaw, "The Origins of Representative Government," 93-96.

50 See Herzog and Makdisi in this volume.

51 Shaw, "The Origins of Representative Government," 95. See also Davison, *Reform in the Ottoman Empire*, 105-108, 142: "A number of influences which converged in the early 1860's help to explain the climate in which the new [provincial] law was born … One such influence was the series of provincial tours of inspection by Kibrisli Mehmed and by groups of imperial commissioners from 1860 on. Four inspectors had gone out in 1863 with instructions to check on local officials, effect economies, inspect police and prisons and vaqif administration, advise on measures to improve communications and agriculture, and reform the conduct of the local councils and village notables."

52 See, for example, Thomas Kühn's or Christoph Herzog's contributions.

Through the model provinces the *Tanẓīmāt* created its own system of administrative and territorial references. Local petitions and imperial inspection tours combined to produce the vision of an ideally bounded and administered province.[53] Mount Lebanon after the *Règlement Organique* of 1861 came to be represented as one such ideal province. Indeed the self-referential nature of the evolving reforms represented one of the most important carriers of rupture both in the eyes of those who practiced and opposed the reforms, and those who were to engage in the nationalist visions for Lebanon in the early twentieth century.

The creation of a coastal province of Beirut – as distinct from Mount Lebanon – was repeatedly raised as the subject of Beiruti petitions to Istanbul between the reorganization of provincial boundaries in 1864 and the eventual granting of the status in 1888. These petitions aimed at upgrading their city's politico-administrative position within the evolving parameters of the *Tanẓīmāt* by requesting Beirut be made provincial capital. In 1865, a first petition reached the Sublime Porte calling for the establishment of an Ottoman provincial capital in Beirut.[54] Written, probably, by the Greek-Catholic Patriarch, Gregorius and signed by 200 notables, the petition first thanked the Sublime Porte for the recent construction work in Beirut, " as a reinvestment for the tax collections in Beirut."[55] To nip criticism from Damascus in the bud the petition went on to assure that, Beirut

> is not envious of Damascus or other inland cities, since commerce the annual pilgrimage and the surrounding agriculture of Damascus had made it a successful but a different city. Damascus does not need the status of a capital, as the most important factors are its hinterland and the headquarters of the imperial army. By contrast, our city has only flourished at the time it became a seat of government for the province of Saida. Beirut's progress is dependent on attracting more people to the city. At the moment, imperial coffers do not provide for that. It is a pity after Beirut has progressed so much in the architectural domain.[56]

The wording of the petition suggests a high degree of internalization of the workings of the *Tanẓīmāt* to appropriate the rules provided by the

---

53 Engin Akali, *The Long Peace*, London 1993.

54 According to French consular reports, some circles in Beirut were contemplating moving the provincial capital of the province of Syria from Damascus to Beirut altogether. Adel Ismail, *Documents Diplomatiques et Consulaires*, vol. 11, (Beirut, 1979), 162-163.

55 BBA, Istanbul, *Dahiliye Iradeleri* 37280, April 29, 1865.

56 *Ibid.*

Ottoman reforms. Moreover, the way the Beirutis presented their argument reveals the self-conscious interaction between the petitioners and the geography within which they thought. To create a new model province around Beirut – the argument ran – was in the Ottoman government's own interest as it contributed to Beirut's *and* Istanbul's flourishing.

The political struggle for the capitalisation of Beirut was finally won in 1888, when despite the ongoing protests of the Ottoman administrators and the notables in Damascus, Sultan Abdülhamid II finally issued the long awaited *irade* to make Beirut the capital of its own province, effectively severing it from Damascus. As of 1888, provincial offices settled in Beirut and bureaucratic ranks swelled with local Beirutis to hundreds of posts administering rival towns like Tripoli, Lattakia in the north and Haifa, Saida and Acre in the south. The memoirs of Bishāra al-Khūrī – ex-president of the Republic of Lebanon – who was born in Beirut two years after the creation of the province of Beirut captured this tendency aptly:

> Ever since I opened my eyes onto this world I found myself in an ocean of bureaucrats... Office in those days was everything. It was the object of ambition and the source of all influence and prestige. They engage in internecine fighting to attain them... they break down for their victory, it was the reason for feuds, the determining factor to exhaust their economic resources.[57]

The conception that first the central state structures were reformed while the provinces remained unaffected until 1864, requires modification at least to the extent of conceding that the practical administrative experiences in the model provinces – the negotiating processes in councils and petitions – were central to operating the reforms at the center. To be sure, Istanbul remained the political center from where power emanated ever more pervasively given the new systems of instant communication and transportation that were introduced to the Ottoman Empire from the middle of the nineteenth century onwards.[58] Yet – and this proved to be one of the main characteristics of the *Tanẓīmāt* – the provincial periphery main-

---

57 Bishāra al-Khūrī, *al-Haqā'iq al-Lubnāniyya*, Vol. 1, Beirut 1960, 30.

58 Roderic Davison, "The Advent of the Electric Telegraph in the Ottoman Empire," in his *Studies on Turkish History*, Princeton 1994, 133-165. See also, more recently, Eugene Rogan, "Instant Communication: The Impact of the Telegraph in Ottoman Syria," in *The Syrian Land; Processes of Integration and Fragmentation*, edited by Thomas Philipp and Birgit Schaebler, Stuttgart 1999, 113-128.

tained and created channels through which it could influence and determine the political power in Istanbul. The rise to power of Midhat Pasha who was to have successful stints as governor in Baghdad (1869-71) and Damascus (1878-80) was based on the strong support not only of European diplomats but also on the support rendered by the provincial notables with access to power in Istanbul.

The Changing Nature of Relations Between Capital and Province under Abdülhamid II

Before the tide was to turn against reformers like Midhat Pasha under the new autocratic sultan Abdülhamid II (1876-1909), the system of provincial administration that he had helped shape had become standardized law in 1864 and applied uniformly across the empire in 1867. The brief episode of the Ottoman parliament between 1876-78 saw the manifestation of a principle that Midhat Pasha's British contemporary Benjamin Disraeli had uncharacteristically toyed with briefly in London, and, indeed, once publicly advocated for the British empire: an imperial parliament uniting the local ruling élites of the entire British empire.[59] – It would have been unthinkable to allow Indian notables a seat in Westminster.

The Ottoman Parliament was in many ways the culmination of the *Tanẓīmāt* process of incorporating the provincial periphery. When deputies arrived for the first parliamentary session in Istanbul they attracted huge crowds of spectators and euphoric journalists on the docks of the harbors. To the Ottoman government, the spectacle of exotic deputies arriving from all corners of the empire was welcomed as an expedient ceremony that symbolized to the population in the capital its imperial might. However, inside the Parliamentary sessions, these provincial notables were quick to set their own agendas. As the British ambassador pointed out, "if such deputies were mere nominees of the Porte, they showed [remarkable] independence and intelligence."[60]

The Ottoman Parliament had more far-reaching direct effects on Istanbul than in the provinces where the elections drew little public participation. Indeed, Istanbul witnessed its own first provincial elections for the very purpose of nominating five deputies to Parliament in January 1877. The Ottoman capital had not been organized as a province, but had been

---

59 Victor Kiernan, *Imperialism and its Contradictions*, edited by Harvey J. Kaye, New York, London 1995, 174.

60 Devereux, *The First Ottoman Constitutional Period,* 148.

directly under the jurisdiction of the Minister of Police.[61] During the two months of the second session, the population of Istanbul witnessed the "amazing spectacle of seeing ministers consent to appear before the Chamber to undergo the most vigorous cross-examination concerning their action." The *Times* continued, "there are signs of party organization... Curiously enough, those who have rendered themselves most conspicuous are men of the provinces and not the capital... and yet [sic] they display an amount of political insight which could scarcely have been expected of them."[62] The extent of provincial self-confidence is captured in the almost arrogant exclamation in a Parliament session of the deputy of Tripoli, Syria, Niqūla Nawfal:

> We are from the provinces, we have been voting since the beginning of the Tanzimat, Istanbul, however, has encountered elections only this year.[63]

Under Abdülhamid II's reign the nature of center-periphery relations clearly changed. His decision to dissolve parliament can be seen as a reaction of the central forces around the new sultan against the growing power of the provincial peripheries. In particular the deputies of Jerusalem (Khālidi), Aleppo (Jābiri), Beirut (Bayhum) and Tripoli (Nawfal) came to be considered the oppositional forces in parliament.[64] After abrogating Parliament, Abdülhamid ceremonially 'upgraded' the Arab provinces whose notables he began to integrate into his personalized system of rule by placing them at the head of the list of imperial ceremonies.[65] Not least, the city of Beirut benefited from the uncanny attention of the sultan when the Beiruti petitioners finally struck a cord with the Ottoman government to be granted the administrative status as provincial capital they had struggled for since 1865. Beirut's new 'rule by council' favored the city as now the members of the provincial council not only met for (irregular) sessions

---

61 *Ibid,* 133.

62 *The Times*, Jan. 15, 1878. Quoted in Devereux, *The First Ottoman Constitutional Period*, 150.

63 Tarik Hakki Us, *Meclis-i Mebusan Zabit Ceridesi*, 17. April 1877 session, 84-85, taken from İlber Ortayli, "From the Ottoman Experiment in Local Government to the First Constitutional Period of 1876-77," *Studies on Ottoman Transformation*, Istanbul 1994, 115.

64 Abdu-l Latif Tibawi, "Greater Syria, 1876-1890: Divided Loyalties – Ottoman, Muslim or Arab?," *Islamic Quarterly* 11 (1967), 9, 10.

65 Kemal Karpat, "The Transformation of the Ottoman State, 1789-1908" *IJMES* 3 (1972), 271. On Abdülhamid II's concern for public image, see Selim Deringil, "Invention of Tradition as Public Image."

in Beirut, but the council was quickly dominated by residents of Beirut.[66] As a consequence, the council's planning of provincial and regional infrastructural projects strongly favored the city of Beirut in terms of connecting the city to its hinterland. Moreover, provincial tax revenues were now reallocated by the Beirut-dominated provincial council, a fact that contributed to the city's Ottoman building frenzy in the 1890s.[67] Ultimately the 'capitalization' of Beirut paid dividends as hitherto hesitant international investment capital flooded into Beirut to finance the new port constructions (completed in 1893), the Beirut-Damascus railway (completed in 1895) and the tramway (completed in 1909).[68]

Abdülhamid's policy towards the Arab provinces through state education and the cultivation of direct ties with select provincial notables has recently been examined.[69] New human networks between the Arab provinces and the Yıldız Seray were drawn.[70] Many local notables from the Arab provinces found, or were forced to seek, new ways of preserving or recovering their power and prestige by forging links with the central administration and, as a consequence, readily seized opportunities of imperial or sultanic patronage.[71]

Within the rapidly unfolding network, ʿIzzat Pasha al-ʿĀbid from Damascus, al-Sayyid Abū 'l-Hudāʾ from Aleppo[72] and the Maronite brothers

---

66 The six yearbooks (salnames) for the province of Beirut between 1888 and 1908 reveal an overwhelming majority of Beiruti concessionaires, merchants and dignitaries on the provincial council where before there had been mainly Damascenes. The permanent council positions of *muftī* and *naqīb al-ashrāf* were *ʿulamā'* from Beirut. The following families dominated the provincial councils under Abdülhamid: Sulḥ (recent resident in Beirut with constituency in Sidon), Bayhūm, Sursuq, Ghandūr, Tuwaynī, Faraʿūn, Trad, Hānī, Ṣabbāgh, Mutrān, Qabbānī, al-Dana, Baydūn, Dimashqiyya.

67 Hanssen, "'Your Beirut is on my desk': Ottomanizing Beirut."

68 On the political and financial 'capitalization' of Beirut, see Jens Hanssen, *The Effect of Ottoman Rule on* fin de siècle *Beirut*.

69 Eugene Rogan, "Aşiret mektebi: Abdülhamid II's School for Tribes (1892-1907)," *IJMES* 28 (1996), 83-107; Engin Akarli, "Abdülhamid II's Attempt to Integrate Arabs into the Ottoman System," in *Palestine in the Late Ottoman Period*, edited by David Kushner, Leiden, 1986, 74-89. See also Tufan Buzpinar, *Abdülhamid II, Islam and the Arabs: the Cases of Syria and the Hijaz (1878-1882)*, Manchester, Ph.D. thesis 1991.

70 For two interesting methodological elaborations of political networks in the late Ottoman Empire, see Andreas Tunger-Zanetti, *La Communication entre Tunis et Istanbul, 1860-1913: Province et Métropole*, Paris 1996; and Corinne Blake, *Training Arab-Ottoman Bureaucrats: Syrian Graduates of the Mülkiyye Mektebi, 1890-1920*, Princeton, Ph.D. thesis 1991.

71 Hasan Kayalı, *Arabs and Young Turks; Ottomanism, Arabism and Islamism in the Ottoman Empire, 1908-1918*, Los Angeles 1997, 19.

72 See Gonnella's contribution in this volume.

Najīb and Salīm Malḥama from Beirut managed to attain prestigious posts as ministers and personal confidants of the sultan. These notables were able to amass vast fortunes through the pivotal positions held in the fields of *waqf* administration, public works and concessions. As such, unlike their elected predecessors, their personalized access to power was not representative of a political constituency back home but obeyed the rules of cronyism. Moreover it had become popular lore that Arab Christians featured prominently in the sultan's espionage circles, with Najīb Malḥama as a director of the secret service, the so-called *jurnalci*s, of the empire. The involvement of "Hamid's Arabs" as they were called on the streets in Istanbul, in newspaper cartoons of the post-Hamidian period and in diplomatic circles alike, was a main tenet of the Young Turk opposition, which also contained large numbers of Arab intellectuals.[73]

So much had Abdülhamid II's rule become associated with his Arab political clientele that the Young Turk Revolution also constituted to a significant extent a revolt against the Arab provinces' assumed control over the empire's centre of power. On the morning of the Young Turk revolution, according to a Francophone, Greek Young Turk, a popular song to the tune of the cadet-Roussel on the streets of Istanbul revealed the wicked power 'Hamid's Arabs' were perceived to have wielded over the affairs of the empire:

Ceux qu'on ne doit pas oublier,
Que sans pitié il faut chatier,
Ce sont les *Mélhamés*, mes braves,
Qui au pays mir'nt des entraves,
Allons, les nouveau-nés,
Crions à: bas les *Mélhamés*!

Tous ces crapauds de Mélhamés,
Seront de suite consués,
Et tout leurs faits d'espionage,
Leur seront crachés au visage,
Car ils sont tous des Malfamés!

Que vous dirais-j' d'*Izzet* Pasha,
Qui va danser une polka,
Il ira purger à Damas,
Les quelques millions du Hédjaz.

73 Šukri Hanioglu, *The Young Turks in Opposition*, Oxford 1995.

Cert's, oui, *Izzet* Pasha,
Tous ces millions il les crach'ra.[74]

Summaries

The practices of integration that evolved during the stormy mid-decades of the nineteenth century represented multiple processes of negotiation between imperial and local interest groups and their representations. Focussing specifically on certain imperial strategies of crisis management in the Arab provinces, such as imperial inspection tours, local petitions and councils, and model provinces, there emerged distinct and subtle modes of contestation, appropriation and co-optation in the provincial peripheries that determined the application of *Tanẓīmāt* reforms. Moreover, what have consistently been considered impositions of state power, malicious or benevolent, under closer scrutiny turned out to be attributable to socio-political processes and agencies in the provincial peripheries that were then adopted in Istanbul as imperial legislation.

In order to highlight this perspective, we have consciously resorted to a geographical and spatial emphasis of analysis at the expense of the conventional temporal bias. Nevertheless, conceptions of time – such as the tropes of tradition or modernity – shaped the strategic constructions of local and imperial identity politics through which the diverse interpretations of the *Tanẓīmāt* were articulated.

Under Abdülhamid II, the processes of integration became more entrenched. During his rule the notables of the city of Beirut were able to perpetuate their political economic position in the city. They were able to expand their radius of action geographically over the new province under their jurisdiction through the channels of center-periphery relations – the petitions, the struggle for the ideal province and the rule by council.

While acknowledging the unequal means of coercive imperial authority, we have nevertheless traced instances where the provincial periphery has managed to appropriate the new rules of the *Tanẓīmāt* to advance local interests. The struggle for the province of Beirut, or ʿIzzat Pasha and the Malḥamas who subverted their imperial authority as Hamidian bureaucrats to the extent that they became equated in Istanbul with the Hamidian regime are examples of a new departure of practices of integration. Taken together, the instances examined in this essay outline the cultural geography of modern Ottoman imperialism.

---

74 H. Diamantopulo, *Le Réveil de la Turquie*, Alexandria 1908, 109. This source has kindly been availed to the author by Youssef Mouawad.

– II –

The Empire and the European in Arab Provincial Capitals

ACRE, THE FIRST INSTANCE OF CHANGING TIMES

THOMAS PHILIPP

Most contributions in this volume relate firmly – as indeed the title of the book suggests – to the last epoch of Ottoman rule, that is to say the period stretching from the *Tanẓīmāt* to the Young Turks. By far the most articles deal with the geographic region of Syria. Only a few stray beyond these geographical or the temporal limits, with the present article falling into the latter category.

The epoch dealt with is a time of reintegration of the empire, of the strengthening of the center, and of its power bearing upon the provinces. But it was also a time in which the empire was opened to new influences from outside. The reintegration of the empire was attempted in many different ways: Government administration was reorganized on the imperial as well as the local level, establishing in the provincial centers councils which gave certain local elements a voice in the management of local affairs but also enticed those elements to work closer with the central government. For the same purpose legislation and the law was reconstructed. Legislation supported by the central administrative authorities penetrated and shaped to a heretofore unknown intensity local society, with a host of laws covering aspects of life which had previously never been regulated by the central government. Some of the most visible ones were building regulations but also laws concerning health and education took a prominent place. Finally, technological developments drew all parts of the empire together. Ships, railways, roads, and telegraph brought Istanbul closer to the provinces then ever before.

All administrative and legislative integration had its source and its focus in Istanbul. The technological innovations that brought about a greater integration within the empire also drew its different regions much closer to Europe. With the establishment of regular steamship service, the construction of railway connections and the promotion of European financial institutions industrialized Europe could relentlessly and efficiently pursue its permanent quest for cheaper raw materials and new markets. This had, possibly, an even greater impact on the economic fiber and structure of local society than all the administrative and legislative measures emanating from Istanbul.

The result was a society in transition with two points of reference: Europe and Istanbul. The added twist was that much of what came from Istanbul in this period also had its origins in Europe but reached the provinces filtered through the intermediacy of agendas, ideas, and self declared aims of the ruling élites in Istanbul. We have to do, as Makdisi has formulated so aptly in his contribution to this volume, with a "dynamic project that was worked on two fronts simultaneously and dialectically: the domestic and the foreign." The Ottoman élites wanted to catch up with Europe and at the same time "reform" the provinces.

In the Arab provinces much of the new technology consisted of direct imports from Europe: streetcars and railways – but also iron girders and roof tiles. Architecture and urban design as well as the decorative element had to do as much with Ottoman as with European ideas of representation and functionality. It is remarkable that in the interior of private residences, decor and pictorial representation clearly took contemporary Istanbul as its point of reference: steam ships on the Bosporus, trains going to Istanbul.[1] We do find the occasional pictorial reference to the world beyond the Ottoman Empire. But what is noticeably absent is any decorative or pictorial citation or symbolism pointing toward an Arab frame of reference. This is so remarkable because, at least in the later part of this period, Arab identity already becomes a central theme in the literary and historiographic debate.

The issue of two frames of reference, the European economic impact and the political orientation towards Istanbul, was, however, not new to the region. Since the middle of the eighteenth century, the very beginning of the modern period in the region, the tension and the creativity of such duality can be observed. This duality is perhaps the very characteristic of the new epoch. In the following discussion I would like to take a look at the city of Acre, which actually flourished precisely due to this dual frame of reference. In the period preceding the age of Ottoman reforms, Acre became the third largest and politically, for a while, the most important city in Syria. Though the similarities to the later period are striking, so are the differences, and the fate of the society and the city of Acre took a very different course to that of the later provincial centers.

The importance of Acre's history during this time lies in its role as precursor. It signifies the beginnings of a truly new epoch in the Eastern Mediterranean, distinguishing itself profoundly and in many aspects from

---

1 See Stefan Weber's contribution to this volume.

preceding periods. For lack of better terms, we can call it the beginnings of the modern period in what became later known as the Middle East.

It is here, and not in Egypt, that the first momentous changes happen. An argument has been made for the development of an indigenous capitalism in Egypt or at least the roots of such capitalism; enlightenment has been detected in the eighteenth century Cairo. Most recently the argument has been simplified to the claim that a similar amount of change and upheaval occurred in seventeenth and eighteenth century Egypt as in Europe; hence, it is concluded, the former must also have been in the throws of modernization.[2] These are patriotic but spurious arguments, based often on the observation of increased exports from Egypt to Europe during a short period. A period which coincides more or less with the rule of ʿAlī Bey al-Kabīr and only proves that for a short moment he was able to reestablish – with rather conventional means, I may add – law and order, i.e. security of trade in the land, but neither new products nor new methods of production were involved.

Acre and its realm was the first region of the Eastern Mediterranean to be linked to the European world market through a commodity whose consumption and price in Europe increased relentlessly through almost all of the eighteenth century: *cotton*. Closer integration into the European world system initiated profound change and dislocation for the economy, society and politics of the region.

To begin with: there was no "Acre and its realm" before the cotton boom. Acre existed only as a small fishing village and did not have any kind of economic or political "realm." Administratively, the region was somewhat casually divided between the governor of Sidon and the governor of Damascus with tribal and ethnic groupings such as in Jabal ʿĀmil and the Druze region forming fairly autonomous societies. The estabishment of Acre as a port city and its integration with the hinterland, first and foremost the Galilee, from the Bridge of Jacob's Daughters to the prime cotton growing coastal region, were the political achievement of Ẓāhir al-ʿUmar (r. 1740-1775). He was quick to realize that political control over the region gave him economic control over increased cotton production and over the export trade to Europe. The political realm that grew under his rule and that of his successors – unique in the history of the region – always included the Galilee and stretched ever more over the coastal region. This movement had a twofold aim: the extension and securing of cotton cultivation, and the banning of cotton exports from the Syrian coast from any port but Acre.

---

2 See the works of Peter Gran, *Islamic Roots of Capitalism*, Austin 1979; Reiner Schulze, "Das islamische achtzehnte Jahrhundert. Versuch einer historiographischen Kritik," *WI* (1990), 140-159; Nelly Hanna, *Making Big Money in 1600*, Cairo 1998.

The Politics of Monopolies

Ẓāhir al-ʿUmar made use of an economic instrument well known in Islamic history but only sporadically applied heretofore: monopoly control over certain goods and produce, their pricing and their trade. He used his political and military strength to exercise monopolistic control over the economy of cotton and in return his control over the profits from cotton exports strengthened his military and political position. In an informal sense one could speak of him as the only large landowner of the region and the only trader of cotton – a merchandise much in demand at this time in Europe. His successors refined the system, making it more comprehensive, including ever more economic aspects, and making it more efficient, with more of the profits going to their own coffers, and ensuring that no competitors join the fray. In addition grain was also occasionally sold on the European markets. The needs of European markets became of fateful importance for Acre and its realm; best illustrated by the measures taken by Sulaymān Pasha upon the news that the Continental Blockade had come to an end. Anticipating that the bottom would drop out of grain prices he sent troops to the villages forcing the farmers to plow under the grain crop and to work day and night to plant cotton, just barely catching the end of its season.[3] Muḥammad ʿAlī applied similar monopolistic policies in Egypt concerning grain during the Continental Blockade and would later extend them successfully to cotton.

In many ways Acre's boom in the eighteenth century foreshadowed features that would become typical for the Syrian region in the nineteenth century. The supply of raw materials, cotton, grain, silk, tobacco, etc. to the expanding industrial economies of Europe could be highly profitable. However the recipients of this wealth seem to vary: in the case of Acre it was the ruler and a few top administrators, in other Syrian cities it was the new mercantile classes. One thing seems certain: the new wealth did not have a trickle down effect, never reaching the peasants.

The commercial integration into the European economy was so powerful that it created new trade links, caused cities to grow where there had been none while decreasing the size of others. New infrastructures came into existence and the administrative organization of the region was reshuffled. Beginning with the rise of Acre we can observe a profound and permanent shift of gravity of economic and commercial activities from the Syrian interior to the coast. This shift of gravity, however, also ended at

---

3 Archives Nationales, Affaires Etrangères, Correspondence Consulaire, Acre II, Nov. 18, 1814 and May 14, 1817.

the coast, that is to say, in the nineteenth century just as in the eighteenth century overseas trade and overseas transport was firmly in the hands of Europeans – including to a large degree the trade between the local coastal harbors. At no time did local merchants or governments establish their own commercial representation in Europe or control over the transport business.

There were also significant differences between Acre in the eighteenth century and the Syrian cities a century later. The rulers of Acre were strong enough to keep foreign merchants out of the intermediary business and, indeed, out of the country. In fact Ẓāhir al-ʿUmar threw the French merchants out of the Galilee and reduced them to residing in Acre – making himself the sole middleman between cotton producer and the French merchants. Half a century later al-Jazzār expelled the French resident merchants from Acre without political consequences – albeit to his economic disadvantage. The French state could not project its political and military power to distant Palestine to enforce the privileges of her merchants there. A certain measure of equilibrium can be observed during the eighteenth century. True, the local cotton production depended on French merchants for its purchase and transport to Marseille. But these merchants depended on the local rulers for the production and the supply of cotton. In the climate of ever-rising prices both parties could participate in the profits of this arrangement.

This balance of interests and power began to disintegrate when toward the end of the century French merchants found other sources supplying cotton, and was finally destroyed with the French invasion of Egypt, Bonaparte's siege of Acre and the British navy's efforts to relieve Acre. With these steps the Europeans had made it abundantly clear that they had the capability to project superior military strength in the eastern Mediterranean. The first subtle changes can already be observed in Acre. When in 1806, after a 15 years absence, a consul was appointed again to Acre as representative of the French empire, he proceeded to tell Sulaymān Pasha what he should do in agriculture such as what new crops he should try to cultivate. He concluded with the observation that, if it was not for the intrigues of a certain Catafago, Acre could become a profitable "*colonie*" of France.[4] Surprisingly this comes at a time when French trade with Acre was non-existent and the French government had hardly any energy to spare to interfere in the region directly. But the consciousness had changed and the presence of Europe began to acquire a new quality. By 1840 only a short bombardment of Acre was needed to force the Egyptians to withdraw

4 AN AE, CC Seyde 1792-1815, Oct. 10, 1810, Nov. 12, 1812.

their troops from Syria, and, for the Ottomans, the London treaty of 1838 was sufficient to open up all its regions to direct British trade. French troops in Lebanon in 1861 were rather of symbolic strength, but the political force of Europe behind them was well understood. The tone had changed, the European presence became much more direct in its political interference and its implied military potential. It became more tangible in the economy through European merchants but also entrepreneurs of all sorts and administrators all traveling, settling and dealing freely in the Syrian region. By the second half of the nineteenth century European imperialism had truly gained full strength in the region.

Among urban and social historians the link between the economic and political conditions of a society and the layout of a city and its architecture and style is a well accepted fact. The challenge is to uncover these relationships and interpret them. A number of contributions in this volume deal specifically with this issue. In the late Ottoman period buildings were constructed for new functions: railway stations, townhalls, hotels etc. On the one hand a new political sense of public space and representation led to the construction of boulevards, squares and monuments. On the other hand the design of private residences changed from being turned strictly inward on an interior court to façades with galleries and windows facing the street, reflecting a new perception of the relation between private and public space. To these examples one would also have to add new technological innovations and requirements as well as the question of decorative elements in architecture and city planning. Here again, a lot was introduced from Istanbul whilst a certain amount came directly from Europe.

Can we observe any of these changes a century earlier in Acre? The question is particularly pertinent because, in contrast to most other cities, Acre was newly constructed in the eighteenth century, rebuilt on the rubble of a crusader town. A look at the map of the city (fig. 1) – and also travel descriptions – tell us that the streets were as narrow and crooked as in other towns of the region. Some thoroughfares existed, providing access to the typical cluster of blind alleys which formed small neighborhoods. The houses seem to distinguish themselves by a certain narrowness and probably by the frequency of two storied houses, containing an independent apartment on each floor.

Noticeable is the number of large *khāns* (see map Nos. 24 and 27) located close to the quay. They served as warehouses for cotton and as the residences of foreign merchants. In contrast to the layout in other cities they were not connected to the *sūq* (no. 1). The latter served only as a market for local needs, while the *khān*s, as their location close to the water reveals, were used solely for the export trade. The architecture of the *khāns*

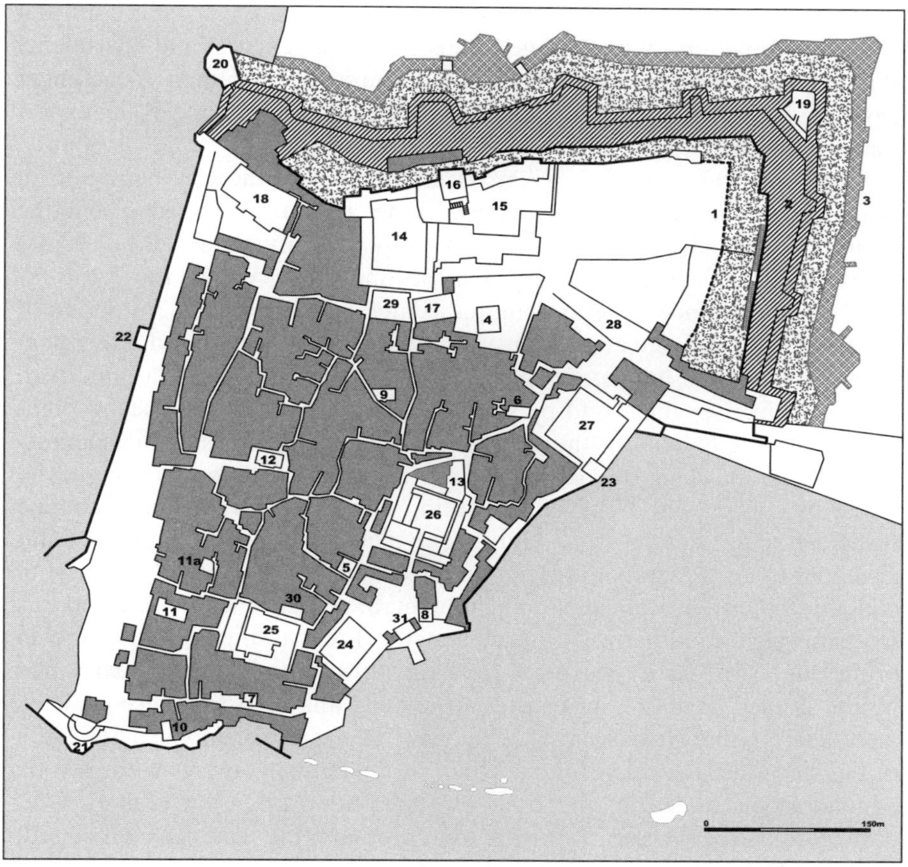

Acre

1 Inner Wall (Ẓāhir al-ʿUmar)
2 Outer Wall (Aḥmad Pasha al-Jazzār)
3 Earth Works (ʿAbdallāh Pasha)

4 al-Jazzār's Mosque
5 al-Muʿallaq Mosque
6 al-Raml Mosque
7 Shaykh Ghānim Shrine
8 Sinān Pasha Mosque
9 al-Zaytūn Mosque

10 St. John's Church
11 St. Andrew's Church
11a Our Lady Church
12 St. George's Church
13 Latin Convent

14 Barracks
15 Arsenal
16 Citadel (Burj al-Khazna)
17 Old Serail (Bustā)
18 Residence of ʿAlī Pasha Katkhusā

19 Burj al-Kumandār
20 Burj Kurayyim
21 Burj al-Sancak
22 Burj al-Ḥadīd
23 Burj al-Sulṭān

24 Khān al-ʿUmdān
25 Khān al-Shūna
26 Khān al-Faranj
27 Khān al-Shawarda
28 al-Sūq al-Abyaḍ

29 Ḥammām al-Bāshā
30 Ḥammām
31 Customs House

Fig. 1: Acre ca. 1820.

did not display any unknown or uncommon features. They were built in a well-known pattern, with storage rooms on the lower floor and apartments for merchants on the upper. But their prominence and their detachment from the local market clearly indicated the central importance of the export trade to Europe.

The only – but by far the largest – structure in the city betraying in shape and layout its European origin was the city wall. Nowhere else in the region do we find this sort of fortification. In fact city walls had fallen into disuse by 1800 and cities had grown beyond them. Where they still existed, as for instance in Jerusalem, they dated from a pre-modern period of warfare. The elaborate and expensive, one may add, design of the fortifications of Acre was unique: it consisted of a rampart, a moat, a wide wall with a projecting glacis and bulwarks. It was designed to withstand bombardment by any state-of-the-art artillery by land. The famous unsuccessful two months siege of Acre by French troops under Bonaparte comes to mind, of course. The irony is that during the siege of 1799 this elaborate fortification did not yet exist. Only a one meter thick wall – built by Ẓāhir al-ʿUmar to keep marauding Bedouin out – blocked Bonaparte's attempt to conquer the city. It was not so much the heroic defense which effected this outcome as the embarrassing fact that the French ships which were to bring Bonaparte's heavy artillery from Egypt to Haifa had been intercepted by the British. Rather than tearing apart the walls of Acre, these cannons were used by the British navy to bombard Bonaparte's troops. The lesson of the siege and the role of the artillery of the British navy was not lost on Aḥmad Pasha al-Jazzār, the ruler of Acre. Soon after the French withdrawal he began a vigorous fortification program, the results of which still can be seen. Most likely al-Jazzār had seen similar fortifications as a youth in his homeland Bosnia. He is also said to have had some engineering and architectural skills, though it is not evident how or where he obtained them. Already in 1772, when he had taken control of Beirut, he displayed his engineering skills. Expecting a siege by the Druze, from whom he had taken the town, and a bombardment from the sea by the Russian fleet, al-Jazzār personally supervised the reconstruction of the city walls with soft sandstone and a wide glacis so that most cannon balls inflicted their destructive power on the walls of the fortifications without causing much damage.[5] A few years later he initiated the construction of the great mosque of Acre and is said to have drawn the plans for it himself.

---

5 Ḥaydar Aḥmad Shihāb, *Tārīkh al-Jazzār*, Beirut 1955, 51-53. Mikhā'il Mishāqa, *Murder, Mayhem, Pillage and Plunder,* Albany 1988, 14-15.

The construction of the new fortifications around Acre drew not only al-Jazzār's attention and energy. His successors, Sulaymān Pasha and ʿAbdallāh Pasha, also considered it a project of prime importance, mobilizing forced labor from the villages and "volunteers" among the townsmen. In the subsequent years the new fortifications were twice put to the test. In 1821 a combined force mobilized by the governors of Aleppo and Damascus tried, under order of the Ottoman government, to dislodge ʿAbdallāh Pasha from Acre in a siege that lasted nine months. The army was ill equipped and possessed no noteworthy artillery. It is probable even that the old walls of Acre, built by Ẓāhir al-ʿUmar, would have easily withstood this siege. In the end, the Ottoman army was called back and ʿAbdallāh Pasha was reconfirmed as governor. The second attack came in 1831 when Egyptian troops under Ibrāhīm Pasha besieged the city. Even the considerable Egyptian artillery needed six months to bombard it into a heap of rubble, with that act ending Acre's moment in modern history.[6]

These fortifications, the largest structure in Acre, were constructed according to European designs, with European war technology in mind, and most likely with the help of some European engineers. These fortifications dominated in many ways the life, economy, and design of the city. Ironically, they were built after the historically most decisive siege had already taken place and were of not much military use later on.

Being Ottoman in Acre

The flourishing of Acre coincided with the nadir of power of the central government in Istanbul. The Ottomans were involved in a series of wars with Russia, Austria, and even Acre's trading partner, France. More than once the empire was threatened with complete disintegration.[7] The government in Istanbul more often than not had to accept developments in the provinces without being able to interfere. It was a period in which a number of centrifugal forces made their appearance, aiming for autonomy in the provinces: The Mamluks of Egypt, especially under ʿAlī Bey al-Kabīr, consistently diminished the authority of the central government; the dynasty of the ʿAẓm Pashas in Damascus followed a similar trajectory; and the split of the Uniate church from the Greek Orthodox church in 1724

---

6 In spite of the role the British navy played during the French siege, neither al-Jazzār nor his successors gave any thought to attack from the sea and the defenses on that side were woefully neglected. The British naval bombardment of Acre in 1840 encountered no resistance.

7 See Hanssen's contribution in this volume.

reflected weakness at the center as the Greek Orthodox Patriarch in Istanbul could no longer establish his authority over all his Arabic speaking flock in Syria; the Druze had always been fairly autonomous; in addition a new economic and political center rose on the Syrian coast. Not only Acre as a port city, but its hinterland and long stretches of the coast line were brought together into a new political realm, carved out between the official provinces of Sidon, Tripoli, and Damascus. The rulers of Acre were fairly free to do as they pleased. They would fight with their neighbors, take over more territory, sell cotton without paying taxes and export foodstuff in spite of the explicit Ottoman prohibition from doing so. So great was the autonomy of the rulers from the imperial government that occasionally the Ottoman Empire would declare them rebels, e.g. Ẓāhir al-ʿUmar and Aḥmad Pasha al-Jazzār, only to make up with them later and reappoint them in their positions.

But were these movements toward provincial autonomy or indeed local rebellions clamoring for independence? I would argue that the centrifugal tendencies were more the result of an opportunity, born out of the weakness at the center, than a programmatic demand for local autonomy. Certainly such movements should not be mistaken for proto-nationalist movements, which they were not. In fact, the military and political weakness of Istanbul which allowed local power centers to mushroom was not accompanied by any weakening of the Ottoman-Muslim world view which considered the Ottomans the legitimate rulers of the realm and obedience to them the only legitimate political behavior. What this obedience consisted of had to be negotiated anew every time, but there was no doubt that loyalty was due to the sultan. Every time Ahmad Pasha al-Jazzār was dismissed from the governorship of Damascus he would obediently return to Acre. He, just like the al-ʿAẓms, his great adversaries, spent a lot of energy and money in Istanbul to ensure their regular reappointment in their positions. The factional and unruly Druze sought, in turn, for their chosen *amir* official appointment from the governor of Sidon. The only imaginable form of legitimate government was a delegation of power from the sultan downwards. In contrast to the end of the nineteenth century, we cannot observe any cracks in this overall worldview or any competing sources for the legitimization of power such as nationalism was to become. The eastern Arab provinces were far away from the Balkan and the Black Sea fronts, and far away from the crises, which shook the empire. Perhaps because of this the disappearance of the Ottoman order, already discussed in the European capitals, seemed unimaginable. The strength of this worldview is demonstrated by the validity it had in the provinces precisely at a time of enormous weakness of the empire. But if the local autonomy was basically the result of central weakness this also meant that no political changes, no institutional developments, no ideological transformations were up for discussion. The local potentates ruled *en detail* more or less as the sultan ruled *en gros*.

The Friday mosque of Acre gave architectural expression to this political context. Aḥmad Pasha al-Jazzār began its construction in 1778, three years after being appointed governor of Sidon. It is probably the most graceful piece of Ottoman architecture in all of Palestine. It manifested – and this is important – an entirely Ottoman piece of architecture. Its beauty and size clearly were not aimed so much at serving the faithful as impressing the subject. It demonstrated the power of al-Jazzār and legitimated it at the same time. To enable the believer to lead a pious life was still the basic justification for political power.

So all-pervasive and generally accepted was the Ottoman – Muslim political order that it was also fully accepted by its non-Muslim subjects. The fact that the population of Acre was for a long time Christian in majority, and the fact that the whole administrative apparatus of the government was managed by local Christians and the financial administration controlled by a Jew, did not challenge this order in any way. All the non-Muslims, with the possible exception of some Greek Catholics, considered themselves loyal subjects of the sultan and considered Istanbul the center of the political order they lived in.

Absorbing Europe in Acre

Lest a too one-sided impression arise, it should be added here that Europe did have also an impact on the politics of Acre, though not as a model for, or source of, new political concepts. If any, the reverse was the case: Acre, and its ruler Aḥmad Pasha al-Jazzār in particular, served in the political debate of pre-Revolutionary France and later as the perfect example of "*tyrannie et despotism*" and their evil consequences.[8] Neither was the European political impact felt through direct military interference. Neither the French expedition to Egypt nor a short-lived appearance by the Russian fleet in 1772 had a profound effect on Acre's regional power. Rather the impact was an indirect one largely linked to economic developments. The weakness of the center of the empire described above could be so dramatically exploited by local potentates in Acre only because the export of cash crops provided them with the means to realize their political ambitions.

---

8 Thomas Philipp, *Acre, the Rise and Fall of a Palestinian City 1730-1831, New York 2001, 48 ff.*

Since all the revenues went to the ruler thanks to Acre's system – of trade monopolies, the dramatic shift from subsistence agriculture to cash crop exports seemed to support and enhance, in the first instance, traditional and localized patterns of politics. Naturally, a dependency on these revenues developed, and once the European markets for the cash crops of Acre and its realm disappeared, the local rulers could not maintain their power any longer.

But over the period discussed here, from about 1750 to 1830, changes did occur in spite of an apparent continuity in the political patterns of power and worldview. Eventually the shift in the balance of power in the Eastern Mediterranean made itself felt, and toward the end of the period we can observe a curious cultural opening toward Europe with a simultaneous deterioration of relations between Muslims and non-Muslims of the realm.

Under the rule of Ẓāhir al-ʿUmar French merchants had been driven out of the hinterland of Acre and were forced to reside only in the Khān al-Ifranj in Acre. Ẓāhir al-ʿUmar introduced a strict segregation between French and local residents, prohibiting any direct contact between the two elements. This he did, however, not because of any perceived cultural or religious threat but strictly for economic reasons. He hoped in this way to interdict any direct dealings in cotton between local producers and French merchants, thereby circumventing his monopoly on all buying and selling of cotton. After al-Jazzār had expelled the French from Acre altogether in 1792, only the occasional European resident was to be found in Acre while European travelers passed through Acre more regularly.

European influence had been indirect and not apparent in aspects of local life style. During Ẓāhir al-ʿUmar's rule all women "even the catholic and European women" had to be veiled in public.[9] As late as 1797 al-Jazzār could tell the vice consul to order the wife of one French merchant to cease wearing dresses " à la Constantinopolitaine" because this was the exclusive privilege of al-Jazzār's harem.[10] In 1806 "Turcs," i.e. local Muslims, assaulted people wearing European dress. The French exacted a promise from Sulaymān Pasha that they could wear the *cocarde* with his protection.[11] Twenty years later ʿAbdallāh Pasha, religious minded as he was, took pleasure imitating the Europeans: "He sits only on chairs, drinks nothing but wine and Champaign and uses a European saddle and stir-

---

9 G. Mariti, *Voyage dans l'Isle de Chypre, la Syrie et la Palestine,* 2 vols., Paris 1791, II, 95.

10 AN AE, CC Acre, 19 Floreal, ans 5 (April 25, 1797).

11 AN AE, CC Seyde XXVI, March 26, 1806.

rups."[12] His nephew was *mutasallim* in Sidon and dressed totally in European style – only his mustache was oriental.[13] Catafago gave dinners *à la Franca*, at which ʿAbdallāh would get very drunk. Reportedly, Madame Catafago dressed "half European" and spoke French very well.[14] Another, more frivolous example is the popularity of cuckoo clocks which came to be highly appreciated presents from European travelers.

The European presence found also expression in the internal political structure. Ibrāhīm al-Ṣabbāgh (d. 1776) and Ḥaym Farḥī (d. 1820) had been local *dhimmīs* whose own power was entirely derived from the protection their masters granted them. The prominence of *dhimmīs* in high positions was, of course, long established policy of Muslim rulers. Catafago played in some ways a comparable role under ʿAbdallāh Pasha. It was never quite clear, though, whether he was a *dhimmī* or an Italian. He tried to buttress his position in Acre by becoming vice consul of as many European nations as possible.

Just as profound was another change which suggested a changing world view: Ẓāhir al-ʿUmar had relied totally on local physicians, trained in traditional concepts, such as the physicians Sīwān and later Ibrāhīm al-Ṣabbāgh. For the latter, in fact, his medical skills were instrumental for his career as the most powerful and intimate consultant to al-ʿUmar. The chief physician of Sulaymān Pasha was an Italian from Naples, one Francesco. He had no political influence whatsoever but quickly sent off the traditional physicians still at the court of Sulaymān.[15] ʿAbdallāh Pasha also had an Italian physician, Bosio from Piedmont; though he maintained a profound distrust of him and always made the physician swallow the same medicine he prescribed for the pasha.[16]

These first inklings of a cultural reorientation towards Europe, superficial as they might have been and limited more to "life style" than anything more substantial, were accompanied at the same time by a clear deterioration of intercommunal relations. Ominous forebodings of developments which would lead to major crises by mid-century and whose outcome were to determine much of the policy of Europeans and the Ottoman government in the last phase of Ottoman rule. Two issues were the precursors of later developments.

---

12 M. Michaud, *Correspondance d'Orient 1830-1831,* 6 vols., Paris 1833,V, 85.

13 *Ibid.*, VI, 212, 305.

14 *Ibid.,* VI, 268.

15 I. al-ʿAwra, *Tārīkh wilāyat Sulaymān Pasha al-ʿĀdil*, Sidon 1936, 334.

16 Michaud, *Correspondance*, VI, 276.

In the 1810's local notables in Acre began to push their political interests after Ẓāhir al-ʿUmar and Aḥmad Pasha al-Jazzār had ruthlessly repressed any local participation in the politics of the realm. The beginning of this development lay probably in the circumstance that ʿAlī Pasha, the father of the last ruler of Acre, ʿAbdallāh Pasha, liked to establish himself as patron of the local *ʿulamā'*. Shaykh Muḥammad Efendī Abū 'l-Hudā, *muftī* and *qāḍī* of Acre during Sulaymān Pasha's and ʿAbdallāh Pasha's regimes, belonged to this circle. The Abū 'l-Hudā were a Palestinian family of learned men who over several generations held different religious positions in Jerusalem, Nablus, Ramla and other towns.[17] Another *ʿālim* belonging to this circle was ʿAbd al-Ḥalīm al-ʿAḍwī from the lower Galilee. He became the tutor of young ʿAbdallāh.[18] A further member of this circle – though not an *ʿālim* but a local notable – was Masʿūd al-Māḍī. He was of peasant origins and belonged to a family of village shayks in Ṭanṭūra, south of Haifa. These three were the nucleus of a group that supported and was protected by ʿAlī Pasha and later would wield decisive influence on his son ʿAbdallāh. It was they who succeeded, through ʿAbdallāh, in having the powerful Ḥaym Farḥī liquidated.

From within this circle, a patron-client network, a political discourse emanated with distinct religious overtones. During the devastating plague of 1812/13, which the Christians in Acre survived so well thanks to their quarantine measures, ʿAbd al-Ḥalīm al-ʿAḍwī, together with the superintendent of the al-Jazzār mosque, instituted anti-Christian measures. This religious discourse was to have its effect on ʿAbdallāh. Since his childhood ʿAbdallāh Pasha received regular religious instruction, the first ruler of Acre to do so. Later he was not only to heed the counsel of these *ʿulamā'* but in 1819 ʿAbdallāh "gave up coffee and joined a community of dervishes."[19] He had regular sessions with Sufi dervishes, going through ritual exercises, dancing, and reciting the name of God.[20] Being an impressionable and somewhat unstable young man, exposed for years to religious learning, ʿAbdallāh must have appreciated the argument of religious impropriety for a Jew to lord over Muslims. Interestingly, in the short period between his official appointment as governor of Sidon and the assassination of Ḥaym Farḥī, ʿAbdallāh (Jan.-Aug. 1820) reintroduced the traditional – but in Acre never applied – laws of special dress codes for the

---

17 ʿĀdil Manāʿ, *Aʿlām Falastīn*, Jerusalem 1986, 39.

18 *Ibid.*, 274.

19 AN AE, CC Acre, IV, "Mémoire par Ruffin en 1821."

20 AN AE, CC Acre, IV, "Relation des événements éprouvés par le consulat de France à Saint Jean d'Acre en 1821."

dhimmīs. It was clearly a strategy to undermine the position of Ḥaym Farḥī and most of the government administrators, who were Christians. Probably all this was inspired by the clique of *ʿulamāʾ* surrounding ʿAbdallāh Pasha. The Christian *dhimmis,* too, understood the whole affair as a heightening of intersectarian tensions and some of them began to leave Acre.[21] The religious discourse was first used by some local elements of Muslim Arabs trying to articulate and assert their own political interests. This group of *ʿulamāʾ* and notables appeared, however, too late and remained too weak to influence the fate of Acre and its realm in any decisive way. Soon international forces were to sweep away altogether the political relevance of Acre.

There may have existed a correlation between the new religious-mindedness of the Muslims of Acre, economic decline, and the greater visibility of the European presence. Abdel Nour observes a "*regroupement confessionel*" and a "*crystallisation religieux*" in all the cities of Syria during the nineteenth century. He implicitly addresses the deterioration of intercommunal relations; he points out this trend in various cities, but does not provide a common explanation.[22] In the first decades of the nineteenth century the reasons for such trends seemed to differ greatly. Barely a few years before such confessional tendencies appeared in Acre, Kanj Yūsuf Pasha had established stringent rules for Christians and Jews in Damascus.[23] In his case it was an attempt to legitimize his own position in view of his failure to defeat the Wahhābī forces.[24] In Acre anti-*dhimmī* politics were intensified in 1821. After Greek nationalists had started their uprising in the Morea in March, the sultan sent orders to all provinces to fortify the coastal towns and to disarm the Christians. ʿAbdallāh Pasha not only obeyed this order but also evicted most Christians from Acre.[25] Christians were also paid to convert to Islam and young boys were trained to become Mamluks.[26] These measures were not applied very vigorously, but the mood had changed. Where once the Christians had constituted at least half

---

21 Mishāqa, *Murder, Mayhem,* 107-08.

22 A. Abdel Nour, *Introduction à l'histoire urbaine de la Syrie ottomane (XVIe – XVIIIe siècle)*, Beirut 1982, 170-180.

23 His closest advisers, however, remained throughout the Greek Catholic Baḥrī brothers; see T. Philipp, *The Syrians in Egypt 1725-1975*, Stuttgart 1985, 65.

24 Mīkhāʾīl al-Dimishqī, *Tārīkh ḥawādith al-Shām waʾl-Lubnān*, Damascus 1983, 113-114.

25 Ḥaydar Aḥmad Shihāb, *Lubnān fī ʿahd al-umarāʾ al-Shihābīīn*, ed. by A. Rustum and F. Bustānī, 3 vols, Beirut 1984, vol. III, 668.

26 AN AE CC Acre, IV, Bulletin March-April 1821.

the population, if not the majority, by 1829 they constituted perhaps only one fifth.[27]

What ties the situation in Damascus with that of Acre is not the visibility of the European impact, nor necessarily the general weakness of the Ottoman Empire. The weakness of the center was well known and had given space to different expressions of localism and the assertion of peripheral vis-à-vis central power. The case of Wahhābī and Greek assaults on the empire had a different connotation: neither the puritanism of the former nor the nationalism of the latter accepted the (religious) legitimization of the Ottoman ruler as a given. The first response to this challenge was almost reflexive: reasserting publicly the Islamic order by strict application of the *sharīʿa*. As it turned out it was only the beginning of a long process within which the Ottoman Empire to redefine, nay, reinvent itself, trying to give new content to its legitimacy, to give new meaning to the relations between center and periphery, as well as between ruler and subject, and to interpret its relation to Europe anew.

27 Jews never had a strong numerical presence in Acre.

FOREIGN PRESENCE AND PERCEPTION OF OTTOMAN RULE IN BEIRUT

LEILA FAWAZ

The long struggle for power between European consuls and Ottoman officials in the Ottoman Empire in the nineteenth century played itself out in Beirut where the city's status gave both sides ample opportunity to compete in influencing the course of events. Struggles for power were common in all the ports of the eastern Mediterranean in the age of European economic penetration, but in the case of Beirut, the struggle was political as much as it was economic and cultural. Beirut was a center of both trade and government, the seat of Ottoman power on the Syrian coast and therefore the place where the foreign consulates were located. After 1888, it was also the center of an Ottoman province, or *vilayet*; in the 1840s and 1850s it had to contend with a state of chronic unrest in neighboring Mount Lebanon, and, after 1860, had to deal with the aftermath of the most bloody civil war in the history of Ottoman Syria.

In the first half of the nineteenth century, the foreign presence and particularly the growing role of entrepreneurs in the economy and society had already made it impossible for the Ottomans to take control of the city without European interference. The duality of European and Ottoman influence in Beirut insured a certain political and social openness that remained characteristic of the city in modern times. In some ways, the struggles for influence between European and Ottoman officials, the rivalries over cultural and economic control, and the proliferation of schools, newspapers, and social functions that these generated, contributed to the establishment of the liberal tradition in Beirut that prevailed for most of the twentieth century, long after the Ottoman Empire had waned and the Europeans had withdrawn from the region.

This paper will concentrate on the duality of the Ottoman and European presence in Beirut between 1840 and 1860, as it set the tone for the rest of the century. The crisis of 1860 and the increasing economic prominence of Beirut in the second half of the century gave Europeans the leverage needed to control the affairs of Beirut and the coast. The Ottomans had returned to Syria in 1840 after having seized it from their vassal Muḥammad ʿAlī Pasha of Egypt, who had appropriated it in the 1830s, and set about imposing the *Tanẓīmāt* and its concomitant policies of direct control. But by then, the European consuls-general were already a force to be reckoned with especially in Beirut, which Muḥammad ʿAlī had made – and the Ottomans kept as – the seat of the regional administration. The British in particular had wanted to see the end of Muḥammad ʿAlī Pasha's rule in Syria, and they helped arm the local Christian population in the late 1830s to help the Ottomans defeat him.[1] This involvement and, after 1840, the dominant influence of the British in Istanbul supported the pretensions of British representatives in Beirut.

After the British and Ottoman troops entered Beirut in 1840, Major General Sir Charles Smith, who commanded the land troops, commented to Ponsonby, the British ambassador in Istanbul, that "when the last Egyptian soldier shall quit the Country, then will commence the *real* difficulties of the Turks – for the elements of good government are not discernable amongst them," adding (perhaps charitably) that the task "will be difficult in the hands, even, of the most able and practiced of the Political Economists."[2] Because the Ottomans were vulnerable and dependent on British military force to reconquer Syria, the British were in a position to make their decisions for them.

The struggles for influence between the French and the British that were characteristic of the century were particularly evident during the crisis of 1840, as the two Great Powers took opposite sides in the conflict between Muḥammad ʿAlī Pasha and the Ottoman government. Richard Wood, a British agent in Syria, concerned that French warships along the Syrian coast might carry dispatches from Muḥammad ʿAlī Pasha in Egypt to his son Ibrāhīm Pasha in Syria, ordered the establishment of a quarantine along the entire Syrian coast, ostensibly for health reasons but in fact to check the boats for any correspondence they might be bringing the Egyptians. All vessels had to stop in Beirut so that their passengers could be checked out. He felt that it was his "imperative duty" to institute this control, though he added that he had enforced the measures "after procuring the assent of Their Excellencies Izzet Pasha and Sir Robert Stopford,"

---

1 Great Britain, Public Record Office, Foreign Office Archives, London, (henceforth referred to as F.O. followed by series and volume numbers) F.O. 195/127, No. 9, Moore-Ponsonby, Beirut, 4 June 1838, mentions that arms sent on the 30th of May had been distributed among the Christians and that further supplies were coming from Sidon.

2 F.O. 195/171, C.F. Smith-Ponsonby, No. 12, 24 November 1840.

though clearly, he did not ask for Ottoman permission before taking that step.[3] When the Ottomans tried to enforce the new sanitary laws the French did not take it quietly. In October 1840, when the captain of a French warship sailing from Alexandria to Beirut was brought in for inspection, the French consul, accompanied by officers of his consulate and several French merchants, "took it upon himself to repair to the landing place, in full dress," and ignoring the remonstrances of the quarantine director, he set the commander free. The result, commented Wood, was that the letters from Egypt to Ibrāhīm Pasha reached him through a French agent in Damascus.[4] Wood also asked his ambassador to exert pressure on the Sublime Porte to pay their officers in Syria the back pay owed them as they had suffered greatly from the bombardment of the coastal towns.[5] This habit of commanding the Ottomans in times of conflict proved difficult to give up in times of peace.

Even after the defeat of the Egyptians in Syria and the restoration of Ottoman rule, the British and the French continued their political and economic rivalry in the region, especially as political tensions escalated in Mount Lebanon with the end of the Shihab emirate and throughout the Double Qaymaqamate in the 1840s and 1850s. Each side monitored the other: the British suspected that the French were undermining the Ottomans by supporting the Shihābs, arming local rebels, and establishing alliances among the local population. British agents, following the movement of ships along the coast, suspected that the French were smuggling ammunition into Syria. On May 4, 1842, Moore, the British consul-general in Beirut, wrote that a French battleship had stopped at Beirut for three days with the "ostensible object" of bringing stores to the French ships on the coast. He followed closely the comings and goings of the men on the ship. One night in particular, seven or eight boats left the ship for Ras Beirut, then "a promontory about a mile south of town." Moore reported to Stratford-Canning, by then British ambassador in Istanbul, that the French officers had rented a small house there "for amusement," and that evening a party was given there, possibly "intended to divert attention" from the departing boats. Moore became even more suspicious when the French consul explained, without being asked, that the warship had brought supplies for other ships. Moore also reported that a shaykh from Kisrawān met

3 F.O.195/171, No. 18, Wood-Ponsonby, 28 November 1840.

4 F.O. 195/171, No. 28, Wood-Ponsonby, 21 December 1840, and the enclosed report from the quarantine board to H.E. Izzat Pasha on the violation of the sanitary laws by the French consul.

5 *Ibid.*

frequently with the French officers in their house and once went on board the warship, speculating that the French might see tensions in Mount Lebanon as an opportunity to regain their influence, especially by smuggling in arms.[6]

In October 1842, Moore was told by the Foreign Office that he could stop sending political dispatches since a consul-general – Colonel Rose, who had been secretary to the ambassador at the Sublime Porte since 1851 – had been sent to Beirut for that purpose. So long as Rose was in residence in Beirut or nearby, Moore should confine himself to "strictly consular" matters.[7]

Even in the 1830s when there were few Europeans in Beirut[8], European consuls-general had assumed that they had a perfect right to be involved in local affairs to a degree out of all proportion to their number. Their interference took many forms, some philanthropic and educational. When an earthquake hit Syria, including Palestine, in December 1836 and the first week of January, British consuls provided modest funds for the immediate relief of the survivors.[9] Throughout the century, epidemics – or the fear of them – brought out the best of European philanthropy.

During the Double Qaymaqamate period (1843-61), British agents in Beirut refused requests by petitioners from Mount Lebanon to intercede in the affairs of the Mountain, telling them to refer their problems to the Ottoman authorities, but French agents could not be counted on to do the same. The French were establishing ties with the Christian communities of Mount Lebanon, particularly the Maronites.[10]

Despite their rivalries over politics, resources, and influence, the French and the British in *Bilād al-Shām* shared similar opinions of the Ottomans. The British policy of supporting the Ottoman Empire did not prevent them from belittling Ottoman local officials as enthusiastically as French agents in Syria did. Corruption was a common European complaint. The *majlises* of Beirut and Ṣaydā "are known to be corrupt," commented Rose to Stratford-Canning in 1844[11] – perhaps with some truth –

---

6 F.O. 195/195, No. 13, Moore-Statford Canning, 25 May 1842.

7 F.O. 195/221, No. 3, Aberdeen-Moore, 4 October 1842. For Rose's assignment to Istanbul, see F.O. 195/351, Rose-Palmerston, 15 March 1851.

8 F.O. 195/127, Moore-Ponsonby, Beirut, No. 1, 9 January 1837.

9 *Ibid.*

10 Excellent information on French-Maronite relations in the eighteenth and nineteenth century can be found in the works of Dominique Chevallier, Boutros Labaki, John Spagnolo, Kamal Salibi, Toufic Touma, and Richard van Leeuwen, among others.

11 F.O. 195/234, No. 19, Rose-Stratford-Canning, 2 April 1844.

as in 1850 all government officials took a public oath never to accept bribes or gifts or to show partiality in the performance of their duties.[12] In 1850, he commented that his suspicions, "founded on long local observation of Turkish bad faith towards British engagements to Syrians," led him to expect that the Ottoman government would not admit the validity of Christian evidence against Muslims (and Druzes) in the tribunals of Mount Lebanon.[13] The British consul in Jerusalem, William Young, complained to Rose about Ḥaydar Pasha, the local governor, in 1855, but he added that it was not entirely the pasha's fault since the instructions of his superior in Beirut "could not have been of a proper character."[14] The abuse of local groups by Ottomans, such as the "great and wanton cruelties practiced by Turkish Troops at Gazir" in the Kisrawān not only on the townfolk but also on the priesthood, was pointed out over and over again.[15] In 1846 Rose complained that a new governor, "Kiamil" Pasha, had not carried out sentences against six convicted murderers.[16] The French complained about the lack of statistics needed for their trade and navigation; the few that were available were unreliable, gathered as they were from the customs office, a private enterprise and therefore reluctant to open its records to the public. It provided information that inspired only "mediocre confidence" with its approximations of the commercial traffic in Beirut and other ports.[17] Entrepreneurs were frustrated by the absence of exact statistics on the value or quantity of merchandise and customs operations, aware that it was in the interest of customs officials and of cultivators to keep the records of imports and exports secret and make the compilation of accurate figures impossible. As trade picked up in Beirut in the middle decades of the nineteenth century, complaints from European consular agents and the commercial interests they represented continued to grow.

---

12 F.O. 195/351, Moore-Palmerston, No. 12, 28 February 1850. Those who took the oath included the governor, the defterdar, the president and the members of the *majlis*, the *qāḍi*, and the *muftī*. The oath, clearly part of the *Tanẓīmāt* reform efforts, was to be administered regularly to all functionaries both Christian and Muslim on taking office.

13 F.O. 195/351, Rose-Palmerston, Bikfaya, Mount Lebanon, No. 44, 17 September 1850.

14 F.O. 195/234, Consul Young-Rose, Jerusalem, 21 April 1844, enclosed in ibid., Rose-Aberdeen, No. 20, 10 May 1844.

15 F.O. 195/251, Rose-Stratford-Canning, No. 94, 1 November 1845.

16 F.O. 195/260, Rose-Stratford-Canning, No. 28, 4 July 1846.

17 A.E., CCC/7, Lesseps-Walewski, No. 30, 17 August 1856 (henceforth referred to as A.E./CCC, B/7), Lesparda-Lhys, No. 78, 7 February 1854.

Even when Europeans refrained from voicing their opinions, their descriptions managed to convey the impression that the Ottomans were not in control. In 1856, the price of meat was unstable; every butcher imposed a price at will and the local authorities were unable to regulate that price or to impose conditions on the sellers as they had done through the *majlis* at other times.[18] Sometimes it seemed that, on the contrary, the government controlled too much. In 1856, in an effort to check usury and corruption, the government issued a memorandum to regulate interest rates and the sale of grains between foreigners and Ottomans. The consuls protested that the new measure meant that all contracts between foreign and local traders would have to be cleared by local authorities, thus creating a new obstacle to trade. Yet another layer of official supervision of contracts would be hard on merchants, even when authorities were competent, and even harder in remote areas where there were no government officials at all. Instead of tightening control over contracts between foreign and local tradesmen and adding layers to transactions between them, the government should make it easier for them to deal directly with each other.[19]

Every matter was seen as a struggle between Ottoman and European authorities. In 1845, the Sublime Porte circulated a regulation that subjects of "Allied Powers" who entered Ottoman territory with passports from their respective countries would have also to have "a Teskere or Permission to pass" before they would be allowed to enter the empire. This regulation was not enforced, however, since it ran counter to the customs followed in the country, "plus," as Rose added, "there is no order or public security in any part of Syria, and no Establishment of Offices for Passports, as in those Countries where they are required." He expected the new regulations to lead to an abuse of power from "the more than semi-barbarous Sheiks and Authorities in the South of Syria," who would demand to see whether English travelers were provided with the right papers.[20] Rose "acceded temporarily" to the demand of the Ottoman authorities, as had the French and Prussian consuls, but he continued to find the system of *teskeres* "objectionable." If his embassy were willing to admit the principle of *teskeres*, it would do so only if it were made "indispensable" that a *teskere* "always be given at the demand of the Consul" and that "an inspection of the Teskere should not be demanded by any Authority where there is not a Consul, or at any rate that the Authority demanding

18 A.E., CCC/7, Lesseps-Walewski, No. 26, 16 February 1856.

19 A.E., CCC/7, Lesseps-Walewski, No. 23, 5 January 1856.

20 F.O. 195/250, Rose-Stratford-Canning, No. 17, 7 March 1845 and enclosure, "Translation of a letter from Assaad Pasha to Colonel Rose," dated 11 Safar 1261."

must be a Commissioned Officer," and that authorities in the frontier towns specify where the necessary papers could be obtained.[21]

Europeans did not respect the local institutions either. They believed that "a people so intelligent as the Syrians"[22] would be quick to understand the superiority of European commercial law, "the result of ages of civilization and experience," on which the new *Tanẓīmāt*-based commercial laws were based, over Islamic law which was "the offspring of a dark age adopted by a people wholly unacquainted with Foreign Commerce."[23]

British agents in Syria found themselves at odds with local Ottoman authorities on all sort of issues. Together with other consuls, they complained in 1851 that the authorities expected guards working in the consulates to be eligible for conscription, which violated the Capitulation stipulating that all persons working for the consular service should be exempt from military service.[24] They brought up the question of "character" every time the Ottomans disagreed with them, instead of admitting that each party might have different interests or priorities. Many of the middle-level European agents stationed overseas would have agreed with Moore's comment that Ottoman authority in Syria depended less upon military force than upon "the character and capacity" of the government functionaries who administered the province, "supported as they are by the moral influence of the Agents of the Sultan's Allies."[25]

British consuls also criticized the Ottomans at every opportunity. One such occasion was the case of the governor of Ṣaydā, residing in the mid-1850s at Beirut, who displeased the British by not showing them proper deference. They recommended that he be moved to Aleppo, whose pasha was about to vacate his post, ostensibly because someone else would get along better with his counterpart in Damascus than he did. Dignitaries including the governor in Beirut, the *qāḍī*, the *muftī*, and other officials called the chancellor at the British consulate[26] to a meeting and asked him to suggest to the consul-general in confidence that the pasha replace the

---

21 F.O. 195/250, Rose-Stratford-Canning, No. 25, 31 March 1845.

22 F.O. 195/351, Moore-Palmerston, No. 30, 30 May 1850.

23 *Ibid.*

24 F.O. 1950351, Rose-Stratford-Canning, 28 February 1851.

25 F.O. 195/479, Moore-Redcliffe, No. 29, 4 June 1855.

26 In the 1840s, members of two local families worked at the British consulate. The first was a man from the Mussali family who worked as "scribe or secretary" for Moore. The second, Noeme (Naʿma?) Tabet, was Moore's "pro cancellier" whom he lent to Rose "to write his dispatches" (F.O. 195/250, Rose-Aberdeen, No. 13, 13 February 1845).

departing pasha. "The Pashalick of Damascus is so intimately connected with that of Saida that unless the Walis in the two provinces are sincerely attached to each other and understand each other exchanging constantly between them those relations of confidence and cordiality, the Public Service cannot but suffer."[27] Moore, however, revealed the real reason for removing Wamik Pasha when he complained openly two months later about "how great must be the degree of subserviency of Turkish officials towards French Agents," for a functionary of the rank, ability, and experience of Wamik Pasha, "at the mere wish of a French consul" slighted a British representative in a matter "of precedence."[28]

French officials, on the other hand, seemed quite able to get their way with Wamik Pasha, sometimes at the costs of local or Ottoman self-interest. In February 1854, G. de Lesparada, the French consul-general, wrote that partly because of a drought, the pasha had prohibited the export of wheat. The measure seems quite sensible, but it went against French and English requirements for wheat export, so the consul interfered "quite actively," demanding that the pasha refer the matter to an ad hoc committee whose decision, wrote the consul, "would satisfy the just complaints of our commerce." The consul then reported that several French and local ships were in the process of loading grain destined for Marseilles.[29]

Ottoman officials fired back with complaints of their own. In 1850, Mehmet Emin Pasha, governor of Beirut, lodged a complaint against Colonel Rose for unfairly accusing him of plotting against the government in Lebanon.[30] After each sectarian clash in the 1840s and 1850s and especially after 1860, Ottoman officials complained repeatedly about Europeans' stirring up local tensions and interfering in relations between the government and its subjects.

Occasionally Europeans had a good word to say about government employees in Syria, usually when they found them receptive to their rec-

---

27 F.O. 195/479, Tabet (signed)-Moore, 7 December 1855, enclosed in Moore-Redcliffe, No. 64, 8 December 1855.

28 F.O. 195/519, Moore-Redcliffe, No. 6, 14 February 1856.

29 France, Archives du Ministère des Affaires Etrangères, Paris, correspondance consulaire et commerciale, Beyrouth, volume 7 (1854-63). (henceforth referred to as A.E./CCC, B/7), Lesparda-Lhys, No. 78, 7 February 1854.

30 F.O. 195/351, "Translation of a Protest from Emin Effendi against Colonel Rose," enclosed in Rose's dispatch No. 59 [to Statford-Canning], 26 November 1850. On the accusations against the pasha, see ibid., Moore-Stratford-Canning, 29 November 1850 and Rose-Stratford-Canning, No. 63, 7 December 1850 and enclosure, "Translation of a Secret Letter from H.E. the Christian Kaimakam to his Banker and Agent in Beirut to be shewn to Colonel Rose."

ommendations. On one such occasion, Rose praised the chief customs-house officer in Beirut for following his recommendation not to open antiquities sent from Baghdad to England via Beirut, and commented that this was "one of the many proofs of the esteem in which the word of a British Agent stands in this Country."[31] When a projected railway between the Mediterranean and the Persian Gulf was discussed in the 1850s, R. A. Chesney, a British major general wrote to the British ambassador in Istanbul from Aleppo that "the local government has been very active and useful." He also reported that the project was very well received in Aleppo by everyone except "the Arabs" (by which he meant the bedouins) who threatened war under the "reasonable impression that the projected railway would put an end to their state of independence.[32] French agents also do not dwell on any negative points about Ottomans when their entrepreneurs were given the concessions they were after. Such was the case with Baron Edmond de Perthuis, a former French marine officer who resided in Beirut in the 1850s where he became a prominent entrepreneur: he introduced cochineal to the cultivation of mulberries in Syria. In 1857 he was given the right to build a road between Beirut and Damascus and, if he chose, between Tripoli and Hama and between Acre and the Hawran as well.[33] E. de Lesseps, the French consul-general in Beirut in the 1850s, described these projects and mentioned that very recently talks had also taken place about the possibility of constructing a new harbor in Beirut. He remarked that Emin Pasha was "a man very rich in ideas" ("*homme très fécond en projets*") who had once before put that project in the forefront of the public works he wanted to see happen in Syria and had even asked Perthuis to do some preliminary work for it. But "like most of his [Emin's] ideas, the matter was not pursued." Lesseps commented that the project was again being considered, and this time it had a chance of succeeding because an English company – as opposed, presumably, to a purely Ottoman one – would be in charge of making it happen and covering its expenses.[34]

The views of consuls were shared by their co-nationals. Consular reports refer to the slender protection foreign merchants were given by the

---

31 F.O. 195/351, Rose-Palmerston, No. 56, 9 December 1850, enclosed in Rose-Stratford-Canning, No. 2, 8 January 1851.

32 F.O. 195/460, Chesney-Stratford-Canning, Aleppo, 15 October 1856.

33 A.E./CCC, B/7, Lesseps-Walewski, No. 43, B, (no day) September 1857.

34 In the end, although the project of a new harbor was discussed in the 1850s, it was not built until the 1890s, by a French company which had reconstituted itself in 1888 under an Ottoman umbrella, though keeping Paris as its base. In 1926, the company became French again and in 1960 it became Lebanese (Leila Fawaz, *Merchants and Migrants in Nineteenth-Century Beirut*, Cambridge, Mass. 1983, pp. 71-72).

local government, especially in the interior of Syria, which prevented them from extending their operations.[35] They also mention the refusal of local authorities to reorganize the commercial court in Beirut and its impact on settling litigation.[36] As late as 1862, the commercial court at Beirut had not been constituted as required by regulations in force in the capital.[37]

The European agents and the Lebanese and Syrians with whom they worked shared a low opinion of the Ottomans. Who influenced whom is a matter of speculation, but it makes sense to think that those among the local population who were close to Europeans influenced them as much as they were influenced by them. After all, they were not passive recipients of Western opinions; they were agents who must have helped shape those opinions. European biases about the Ottomans were passed on to local clients and partners and local prejudices about Ottomans were passed on to the Europeans. After the civil war in 1860 the French troops who landed in Lebanon assumed that the Christians were the victims and then worked hard to provide them with resources that they took from Druzes and other non-Christian people. This must have been true earlier as well. In the middle decades of the nineteenth century local entrepreneurs, most of whom were Christians, worked closely with European traders and others in developing Beirut. In 1854, for example, leading Beiruti merchants and representatives of French commercial houses in the city met to discuss current and new trade taxes and, in the process, all the inconveniences that resulted from leaving the silk trade – Syria's and their principal source of revenue – to the "arbitrary" assessments of customs officials.[38]

Popular opinion of the Ottomans in Syria was low, at least according to European sources. In 1856, the Ottoman government asked its governors to enroll men in the army. Moore commented that there was little chance of any considerable number of men responding, as there was a great disinclination on the part of the Syrians to enter the service after the treatment they had received at the hands of the Ottomans in 1853-54 (probably a reference to the Crimean War when, according to him, their commander

---

35 F.O. 195/647, 1858-60.

36 *Ibid.*

37 According to a letter signed Etienne Pisanisent and sent to Bulwer (No. 19, Pera, 1 February 1862), as a result of representations made by the British ambassador to the Porte, instructions had been sent to the *mushir* of Sidon to establish a commercial court.

38 A.E./CCC, B/7, Lesseps-Lhys, 7 November 1854 and enclosures.

failed to provide them with any means of subsistence).[39] In times of crisis, the government was blamed. Local accounts of the 1860 crisis were written mostly after the fact and mostly by Christians who were very critical of the role of the Ottoman irregular troops, the local government, and even the Sublime Porte.[40] As peace was reestablished in the area in the later part of the nineteenth century, local notables worked closely with the Ottomans and were careful to stay on good terms with the local authorities, but in the troubled middle decades of the century, it was easy to include the Ottomans among those to blame for the years of turmoil.

As Europeans became more involved in local affairs in the 1840s and 1850s, they made their own enemies as well and invariably they overreacted, although the balance of forces had clearly shifted in their favor. In Ṣaydā, for example, a shaykh, according to a French source, had stirred up the Ottomans to kill Christians entering the French khan in the heart of the city where Europeans resided. He hit a French agent who told him to leave. The consul-general in Beirut lost no time recommending that a ship of the Ottoman imperial navy be sent to the Syrian coast and forty cavalrymen be sent to Ṣaydā, their leader was expected to replace the *qā'im maqām* (it is not specified who) and to send the shaykh and any other guilty parties to Beirut. Presumably, the French took these decisions in consultation with Ottoman authorities, but that is not mentioned in the correspondence; what is mentioned is that the governor wrote a letter of apology to Durighello, French consul in Ṣaydā.[41]

In Tripoli, another incident pitted French agents against local Muslims and, once again, the French overreacted to what might be considered a minor slight. This time a Muslim child hit the horse of the dragoman of Blanche, the French vice-consul in Tripoli, with a piece of metal that wounded the horse. When the dragoman scolded the child, his parents sent for the "Turks of the quarter" to come to the office of the Messageries Maritimes, the main French steamship line on the Mediterranean, where they insulted Blanche. The authorities made no arrests, which provoked

---

39 F.O. 195/519, Moore-Redcliffe, No. 10, 28 February 1856. For aspects of Ottoman rule which the local population appreciated, consult in this volume the findings of Stefan Weber, who concentrates on the late 19th century in Damascus.

40 Leila Fawaz, *An Occasion for War: Civil Conflict in Syria and Lebanon in 1860*, Berkeley 1984; Engin Akarli, *The Long Peace: Ottoman Lebanon 1861-1920*, London 1993; Caesar E. Farah, T*he Politics of Intervention in Ottoman Lebanon 1830-1861*, Oxford 2000. See also Ussama Makdisi, *The Culture of Sectarianism,* Los Angeles 2000.

41 A.E./CCC, B/7, Lesseps-Lhuys, No. 6, 31 May 1854; ibid., Lesseps-Lhuys, No. 7, 17 June 1854.

Blanche into asking the consul-general to jail the father of the child and his "seditious" companions. He also demanded that the notable whom Blanche regarded as most hostile to him in the local *majlis* hear the case and condemn the dragoman and that the governor severely reprimand the *qā'im maqām*, apologize to the French agent and the French marine for the incident, and remove the man in charge of the docks who had encouraged the gathering of "fanatics." The French got their way on all counts.[42]

Occasionally, as during the Muḥammad ʿAlī Pasha's takeover of Syria in the 1830s and after the civil war of 1860, the Ottomans had the upper hand, thanks to European rivalries that secured British support for the Ottomans to maintain the status of Lebanon and Syria, or because of an exceptional leader such as the vizier Fuad Pasha who governed Syria after the 1860 civil war. However, throughout the century, Europeans were a force to reckon with in *Bilād al-Shām*, particularly on the coast where European commercial interests were at their most concentrated. The tugs-of-war between the men in charge in Beirut in the 1840s and 1850s resulted in decades of political and commercial interference that ended in direct colonial rule when the Ottoman Empire came to an end.

42 A.E./CCC, B/7, Lesseps-Lhuys, No. 8, 6 July 1854.

HOUSING THE FOREIGN

A European's Exotic Home in Late Nineteenth-Century Beirut

RALPH BODENSTEIN

When searching for sources for the study of global and local change in urban societies in the late Ottoman Empire, the study of domestic architecture can provide enlightening insights into the evolving quality of the practices of daily life, tastes and life styles of the local population. The starting point and focus of this paper, however, is not a grand hypothesis or a general theory about the kind of change that would be verified with the help of evidence from material sources. Instead we will primarily deal with some aspects of the individual history and architecture of a single late nineteenth-century mansion in Beirut as a case study, which – when related to its context – will soon confront us with some more general problems and questions concerning the architectural and social history of late Ottoman Beirut.[1]

The background of this paper is the attempt to reconstruct the history of Qaṣr Heneiné (Qaṣr Ḥunayna), a stately mansion in the quarter of Zokak al-Blat (Zuqāq al-Balāṭ).[2] This quarter is one of the early extensions of Beirut *extra muros*, developing from the middle of the nineteenth century

---

1 This paper is based on the research, which I have done in Beirut in 1998 and 1999 for my M.A. thesis in Oriental Studies at the University of Bonn, Germany. The thesis – titled "Qaṣr Heneiné – Memories and History of a Late Ottoman Mansion in Beirut" – was supervised by Prof. Stefan Wild and Prof. Dorothée Sack. During my research in Beirut, I was associated researcher at the German Orient Institute in Zokak el-Blat. I am therefore very grateful for the support I enjoyed by the Orient Institute and its then director, Prof. Angelika Neuwirth. I also would like to explicitly thank: Jens Hanssen, Anne Mollenhauer, Stefan Weber, and Carlos Heneiné – they know best why. My research could not have been finished without the generous sponsoring by GROME MESMA (Jdeidet el-Metn), LITHOG-RAFFI (Beirut), and Mr. Fouad N. Issa (el-Rabieh).

2 Names of places and streets in Beirut are given according to the locally established and most widely used transliterations as found on maps, on streets signs, and in newspapers. They also correspond to a semi-official street list, the *Fihriz shawāriʿ madinat Bayrūt*, publ. by Alfred Dibs (Mudīr ʿĀmm al-Ṣināʿa), Beirut 1978.

onwards mostly as a residential quarter for the old and new Beiruti bourgeoisie who moved out of their old houses *intra muros* and built new and representational villa residences in the orchards and garden lands on the hills overlooking the old town and the sea. Until the 1830s, Beirut had only been a minor harbour city of the Levant, ranking behind Tripoli, Sidon and Acre. During the Egyptian occupation in 1832-1841, Ibrahim Pasha made Beirut an administrative centre. After regaining control of the Syrian provinces, the Ottomans made Beirut the capital, first, of the *vilayet* of Sidon in 1842 and, then, of the newly created *vilayet* of Beirut in 1888.[3] This growing political importance was accompanied by the development of Beirut's harbor into the major import-export trading centre for Mount Lebanon and the Syrian hinterland, which also gave rise to a new urban commercial bourgeoisie. The population of the city rose from around 10,000 inhabitants in 1840 to around 120,000 in 1900, leading to the mushrooming development of new residential quarters *extra muros*. Numerous foreign consulates, missionary and educational institutions were established; the intensified trade and the increasing political presence of European powers – particularly in the wake of the 1860 civil clashes in Mount Lebanon and Damascus – made Beirut an interface between the European countries and the United States on the one hand and the Syrian provinces of the Ottoman Empire on the other hand.

The quality and extent of the cultural, social, and architectural transformations in Beirut, which were triggered by the import and adoption of goods and ideas, constitute the underlying problem of this paper. Nada Sehnaoui once labelled this transformation the "westernisation of daily life",[4] which – according to Sehnaoui – also found its expression on the architectural level. In contrast to the introverted character of the traditional urban house, the new suburban houses of the wealthy Beiruti aristocracy and merchant bourgeoisie – starting at some point in the middle of the nineteenth century – had a much more extroverted character, with numerous large windows, balconies, and galleries looking onto the surrounding gardens and neighbouring streets. In addition, they were often decorated with marble, stone and stucco elements in historicist styles of a European kind. Their plans were different from the traditional urban courtyard houses as well; they show a central-hall plan with rooms lined up along

---

3 Jens Hanssen, *The Effect of Ottoman Rule on* Fin de Siècle *Beirut*, Oxford, Ph.D. thesis 2001.

4 Nada Sehnaoui, *L'occidentalisation de la vie quotidienne à Beyrouth, 1860-1914*, M.A. thesis, Paris X 1981.

both sides of a large main hall going all through the building.[5] If it is true that this change clearly reflects a shift in the taste and in the life style of the urban bourgeoisie, their preference for ostentatious luxury and their wish to see and to be seen, we may nevertheless ask, if this shift can correctly and sufficiently be described as a process of westernisation, and in how far these houses allowed for an *a priori* "western" way of life. Naturally we will not be able to answer this question in an exhaustive manner within the frame of this paper. A closer look at Qaṣr Heneiné however will shed a new light on this question.

Narratives of Origin

Qaṣr Heneiné (Fig. 1 and 2) is located on the corner of rue Hussein Beyhum (Sh. Ḥusayn Bayhum), rue Abdel-Kader (Sh. ʿAbd al-Qādir), and avenue Fouad Chéhab (Jādat Fu'ād Shihāb), hence on the western limits of present Zokak al-Blat, a location which – at least until the cadastral reorganisation in the French Mandate period – was perceived to belong to the quarter of al-Kantari (al-Qanṭārī).[6] The avenue Fouad Chéhab – as part of the ring road – was only cut through the existing urban tissue by the late 1960s, early 1970s, replacing a small secondary road, which earlier had constituted the northern limit of the plot.

Before dealing with the house's early history, I shall briefly outline some parts of its later history, as this is important for the sources I had at my disposal for the reconstruction of its earlier history. From around 1903 to 1914, the house served as residence for a certain Dr. Justin Calmette, who was a professor at the Faculté Française de Médecine in Beirut. A photo-postcard showing the interior of the great hall of Qaṣr Heneiné (Fig. 3) is probably the only remaining document for this period.[7] From 1914 to 1936, the mansion served as premises for the U.S. Consulate General in Syria, with a short interruption between 1917 and 1919, when it was temporarily taken over by the Dutch Consulate General. For this period, especially, the regular inspection reports of the U.S. Consulate proved a rich

5 Compare the contribution of Anne Mollenhauer to this publication.

6 This is recognisable on maps dating from the beginning of the 20th century, e.g. the Ottoman *Beyrūt Planı* (reproduced in: May Davie: *Beyrouth et ses faubourgs (1840-1940). Une intégration inachevée*, vol. 15 of *Les Cahiers du CERMOC*; 15, Beirut 1996, 150.

7 I have to thank the chief-librarian of the Orient Institute, Wolf-Dieter Lemke, for providing me with a copy of this postcard. A reproduction of the postcard can also be found in Fouad Debbas, *Beirut. Our Memory. An Illustrated Tour in the Old City from 1880 to 1930*, Beirut 1986, 126-27.

source. Only after the U.S. Consulate had moved out, the house became the residence of its owners, Dr. Joseph Heneiné and his wife Marie Mezher (Muzhir). Members of the older generation of the Heneiné and Mezher families were very helpful in relating to me what they remembered of the house's history; their accounts served as the starting point for further research. But for the periods before their lifetime and before the house became the residence of the family – i.e. the time before the 1930s – their accounts are extremely flimsy, full of gaps, and even contradictions. Their information had to be cross-checked and complemented by sometimes very scattered pieces of information from different written and photographic sources, and – last but not least – the architecture of the house.

As it is the case with many houses in Beirut, the date of construction is unknown to the living members of the owner family. Two informants even date it back to the beginning of the nineteenth century – a claim which can easily be rejected in view of the basic constructional features of the building: with its two residential storeys on a partly vaulted ground-floor and the red-tiled hip-roof, the house is clearly a structure of the second half of the nineteenth century or the beginning of the 20th century. Add to this the use of iron beams for the ceilings, the window glazing, the wooden lamella shutters of the windows, and their stone lintels with a classical S-profile: all features which clearly point to a date of construction in the late nineteenth or early twentieth century.

In order to narrow down the possible date of construction, I had to refer to two other sources: the 1876 "Löytved" map of Beirut shows an empty plot where the house should have been. On a photograph with a panoramic view of Beirut taken from the clocktower of the Syrian Protestant College (the later AUB) around the mid-1890s we can already spot the house. Thus Qaṣr Heneiné must have been built between the mid-1870s and the mid-1890s.[8]

So far the date of construction could not be specified more exactly on the basis of available sources. Information about the builder and the first occupant is contradictory: One account has it that the house was built by a member of the Mezher family. The Mezhers (as the Heneinés who are related to them) were a wealthy Maronite family who owned lands and houses in the neighbourhood; hence it appears quite plausible that they

---

8 See *Plan de Beyrouth dédié à S.M.I. le Sultan Abdul Hamid II*, Julius Löytved 1876, scale 1:12,200. The plan is reproduced in May Davie: *Beyrouth et ses faubourgs*, 148. The panorama photo is published in Debbas, *Beirut. Our Memory*, 130-131. This photo is not dated; but from a comparison with other dated photos and from the buildings of the Syrian Protestant College, which are shown (or not existing) on the photo, we can conclude that it must have been taken between 1894 and 1897.

Fig. 1: Qasr Heneiné, View from North.

Fig. 2: Qasr Heneiné, Western Front.

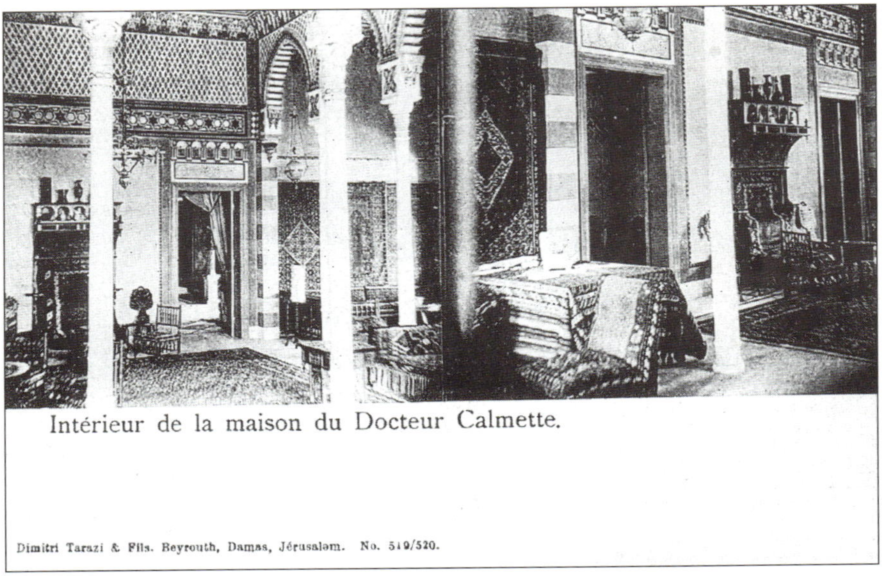

Fig. 3: Postcard Showing the Interior of the Great Hall of Qasr Heneiné; Published ca. 1903-1905 (Courtesy of W.-D. Lemke).

Fig. 4: Qasr Ibrahim Sursock, View of Central Hall.

Fig. 5: Qasr Heneiné, Arcades and Ceiling of the Great Hall.

Fig. 6: Alhambra, Granada, Arcades of the Myrtle Court.

Fig. 7: Qasr Heneiné, View into the Northern Aisle of the Great Hall, Late 1960's (Courtesy of Carlos Heneiné).

Fig. 8: Wall in a Courtyard House in Damascus (D.O.C- ca. 1800).

Fig. 9: Qasr Heneiné, Side Wall
of the Northern Aisle
of the Great Hall.

Fig. 10: Qasr Heneiné, Great Hall,
Late 1950's (Courtesy
of Carlos Heneiné).

have built this house as well. According to this account, the Mezhers rented it out to a Russian count in the nineteenth century. This Russian reportedly altered the interior by adding the extraordinary interior decoration to the first floor. (We will deal with this interior below.) When the Russian count died or left, the Mezhers took their property back. But there is another version, which is more common among the family members and which has it that the house was originally built and lived in by a Russian count, and only after his death or his departure the Mezhers took over the estate.

Both versions harmonise in ascribing an important role to the Russian count in the house's history. Nevertheless, nothing is known concerning the identity of this Russian count, his activities in Beirut and whether he left Beirut or died there. From the information that he built the house for himself – or furnished the interior – we may conclude that he should have been rather wealthy and that he lived for a sufficiently long time in Beirut. Possibly he even came to Beirut to stay. We might expect such an unusual personality to figure in the historiographic literature dealing with the Russian community and the role of Russians in Beirut and the Levant during the later nineteenth century. This, however, is not the case: The literature which I surveyed did not mention a person who would meet the demands of chronology and circumstances,[9] Russian biographical dictionaries and almanacs of the Russian nobility could not be used because the Russian count's name is unknown to us. Relevant archival sources were not at my disposal. However we know that – from the 1880s onwards – there was an increasing presence of Russians in Beirut and Mount Lebanon in connection with their missionary and educational activities.

Taking into account that foreigners in late nineteenth century Beirut[10] usually rented houses or sub-units of houses for their residence – this at

---

9 M. Daher, *Bayrūt wa-Jabal Lubnān ʿalā mashārif al-qarn al-ʿishrīn. Dirāsa fī l-tārīkh al-ijtimāʿī min khilāl mudhakkirāt al-ʿālim al-rūsī A. Krīmskī (A. Kremsky) – rasāʾil min Lubnān 1896-1898*, Beirut 1985. Marlene P. Hiller, *Krisenregion Nahost. Russische Orientpolitik im Zeitalter des Imperialismus 1900-1914*, (Europäische Hochschulschriften, R.3, Bd. 267), Frankfurt a.M. & Bern 1985. Derek Hopwood, *The Russian Presence in Syria and Palestine 1843-1914. Church and Politics in the Near East*, Oxford 1969. Hans-Jürgen Kornrumpf & Jutta Kornrumpf, *Fremde im osmanischen Reich 1826-1912/13. Bio-bibliographisches Register*, Stutensee 1998 (private print by Kornrumpf). Jamīla Kūstā Kūstī, *Madrasat Zahrat al-Iḥsān. Khaṣāʾiṣ al-nashʾa wa-l-taṭawwur min khilāl »ʿaqd al-jumān« (1881-1928)*, Beirut 1996.

10 We should note that the number of foreigners in Beirut was very limited: Until the French Mandate Period, they only constituted 1-3% of the population. See Leila Fawaz, *Merchants and Migrants in Nineteenth-Century Beirut*, Cambridge (Mass.) 1983, 52.

least is the picture we get from many travel accounts and contemporary testimonies – we might be tempted to reject the claim that Qaṣr Heneiné was *built* by this Russian count, and either favour the version according to which the Russian rented the house, or even go further and dismiss the "Russian count" as a mere invention which was introduced into the recollections, maybe to give the house's history more colour and prestige.

Two sources however counter this conclusion:

a) The architecture of Qaṣr Heneiné: there are no signs or traces, which would indicate that the interior was altered. On the contrary the interior design constitutes an integral part of the structure and must be original. So if the Russian nobleman played a role in the building activities, he cannot only have provided the interior furnishing, but should have built the house as a whole.

b) The inspection reports of the U.S. Consulate General do in fact mention a Russian nobleman: the inspection report for the year 1922 (which is the first to deal with Qaṣr Heneiné as premises of the consulate) says that the house "was originally designed and occupied by an exiled Russian prince", and the 1931 report states: "The house was built for a private residence by a Russian count."[11]

Consequently the Russian nobleman was not an invention, and he must indeed have built the house for himself. By the time these reports were written, there should still have been enough people alive who knew the Russian nobleman – who must have died (or left Beirut) at the turn of the century. Yet, the fact that the nobleman is mentioned as "exiled prince" in 1922 and referred to as "count" in 1931, clearly shows that already around 20-30 years after the Russian's death or departure the message-transforming processes of oral history had affected this information. The U.S. staff personal who provided the information for the report obviously faced a similar problem with the (oral) history of the house then as we do now.

Since oral history and available written documents cannot provide any further information on the 'genesis' of Qaṣr Heneiné, we shall now turn to the architecture of the house as an historical source, which – in this case – has remained mostly unchanged.[12]

---

11 U.S. National Archives, Maryland, Beirut Inspection Reports 1922 and 1931, (MLR 865; I-15; Entry 865; 250/48/12/1, Box 17).

12 The minor changes which were effected on the building during the roughly 110 years of its history could mostly be identified with the help of a detailed architectural analysis, some historical photographs, building plans from the U.S. inspection reports (dating from 1922), and oral testimony. Our following analysis is therefore made on the grounds of the reconstructed original plan of the building (Plan 1 and 2). As far as the

Searching for an Evidentiary Paradigm

Houses are people. A house reflects the personality, the life style, the taste, the social standing, and the cultural background of its builder.[13] At the same time its architectural style, the technical solutions and the building material are a product of the time and place of its construction. Bearing this in mind we have to ask: What does Qaṣr Heneiné have in common with other mansions in *fin-de-siècle* Beirut, and what are the peculiarities of Qaṣr Heneiné which would allow us to draw conclusions on the builder's life style, taste and cultural background and – by means of contrast – on the taste and domestic culture of the local bourgeoisie?

As we already pointed out, the house does in fact share important features with other local contemporary structures, as far as building material and some constructional and design features are concerned. These are – to name only a few – a red-tiled hip roof,[14] the two residential floors on a partly vaulted ground floor, the compact cubic shape of the house, the fact that all walls are structural walls, the extreme storey height (around 6 metres), the rectangular windows with glazing[15] and wooden lamella shutters, the use of iron girders, the vaulted kitchen, the paving of the floors with marble or terracotta tiles, and the fact that the interior walls are not covered with wall-paper, but instead with a – sometimes decorative – painting.

Many building materials which were used for the construction of the mansions and houses of wealthier families in Beirut during the second half of the nineteenth century – i.e. roof tiles, marble, iron girders, glass – were imported from Europe. That they were used at most of these houses shows

---

interior decoration is concerned, we should note that the coloured stucco decoration of the great hall is – apart from some recent war damages – mainly preserved today as it was at the turn of the century. The painted wall decoration of the other rooms is mostly lost or covered by later painting.

13 Susie West, "Social Space and the English Country House," in *The Familiar Past? Archaeologies of Later Historical Britain*, eds. Sarah Tarlow & Susie West, London & New York 1999, 103-122, here 105.

14 Red tiled roofs are first documented for Beirut in 1860 and became common during the last decades of the nineteenth century. The tiles were not locally produced, but imported from Europe, mainly Marseilles. Only in 1897 a factory for roof tiles was set up near Beirut. See Sehnaoui, *L'occidentalisation*, 87-88.

15 Glass windows were unknown in Beirut until the 1840s and were then introduced as luxury in the houses of the rich families. See Sehnaoui, *L'occidentalisation*, 89. From my observations it appears that they only became more widely used also by less wealthy families around the end of the nineteenth century. More research has to be conducted on this topic.

that the local masterbuilders[16] and building craftsmen had successfully adopted their use. As Qaṣr Heneiné shares essential constructional features with the bulk of contemporary Beiruti houses we may conclude that it must have been built by local craftsmen, probably under the direction of a local masterbuilder.

By sharing the essential constructional features with other Beiruti houses of its time, Qaṣr Heneiné also shares their 'built-in' disadvantages. These are, for instance, the humidity of the walls during the rainy winter months, which is caused by the porosity of the Beiruti sandstone,[17] or the deficient sanitary facilities: The toilets (*à la turque*) were generally inside the kitchen (as in Qaṣr Heneiné) or ventilated towards to the kitchen, causing annoying smells and even hygienic problems.[18]

I had to point to these details because we cannot avoid the question why the alleged European – or more exactly Russian – "designer" of the house did not avoid these surely annoying deficiencies resulting from the local building techniques which might not have disturbed the locals as much as a foreigner. Why did he not equip his house with more elaborate sanitary and heating facilities (like ovens or fireplaces), which would generally be found in central and eastern European bourgeois houses and would have been useful for a house in Beirut as well? Now, if the builder of Qaṣr Heneiné was a Russian nobleman, he did either not care for these deficiencies, or – more likely – he simply had no other choice than to accept them as part of the usual set of technical features offered by the local craftsmen. The question behind this is: How far could a builder influence at all the design of the house that he wanted to have built by local masterbuilders and craftsmen? We will see in the following that he obviously

---

16 Until 1913 there was no professional engineering education in Beirut (see Robert Saliba, *Beirut 1920-1940. Domestic Architecture Between Tradition and Modernity*, Beirut 1998, 23). Most of the houses in Beirut until then where built by local masterbuilders who had learnt their craft by practical apprenticeship with experienced older masterbuilders. This explains why even with the introduction of new building materials, traditional ways of building were basically preserved but further elaborated.

17 Witness the complaints made by the Russian orientalist Kremski (Daher, *Bayrūt wa-Jabal Lubnān*, 111), and the remarks on the Beiruti building stone made by the British missionary Thomson (W.M. Thomson, *The Land and the Book; or, Biblical Illustrations Drawn from the Manners and Customs, the Scenes and Scenery of the Holy Land*, London, Edinburgh and New York 1874, 33).

18 The French physician Dr. B. Boyer pointed to this hygiene problem in his report on the typhoid epidemic which took place in Beirut in 1895: "Les latrines à la turque s'ouvrent largement...par leur orifice de chute, à la côté de la cuisine où elles déversent des torrents de gaz ammoniacaux et fétides." (Cf. Dr. Benoît Boyer, *La fièvre typhoide à Beyrouth (Syrie). Extrait du Lyon Médical*, Lyon 1897, 11.)

could influence the design in an essential manner, but we can already say that this did not include the basic construction techniques – which were determined by what the local craftsmen were trained to do – and the basic building materials – which were determined by what was locally available.

Despite these shared local characteristics, the outer appearance of Qaṣr Heneiné is unusual. One of the very characteristic design features of the main façade of Beiruti houses, the superposed pointed triple arches, is not found here. Instead there is a long open gallery on the western main façade, and superposed galleries on the eastern garden façade (these eastern galleries were originally open as well, but were then enclosed with glass some time in the early 20th century). We do find a pointed triple arch above the main entrance on the western façade, but only on the first floor. With its huge dimensions, massive piers, and the geometric woodwork of its glazing, it is rather austere or even coarse when compared to the more elegant triple arches with marble columns and elaborate wooden traceries which we would find at the houses of wealthier Beiruti families. The overall austerity of the exterior of Qaṣr Heneiné is especially irritating if we take into account that the house is one of the biggest (surviving) mansions in Zokak al-Blat. Mansions of Qaṣr Heneiné's size generally display the wealth of their builders in a more ostentatious and opulent manner by an extensive use of imported materials like cast iron balusters, marble brackets and columns, porch and window framings etc.[19] Judging from the size and the interior decoration of Qaṣr Heneiné, the builder must indeed have been wealthy. But from the unobtrusive exterior of Qaṣr Heneiné we may conclude that its builder obviously had a taste that was quite different from the taste of the wealthy local families.

But the differences between Qaṣr Heneiné and its Beiruti contemporaries turn out to be much more fundamental when we take a look at the interior spatial organisation (Fig. A). We should recall that the new (we should say: modern) mansions of the Beiruti bourgeoisie generally and characteristically show a plan with a central hall structuring the building and giving access to the adjoining rooms on both sides. The central hall serves as main living room for the family and often is the most representatively decorated room of the house. Depending on the wealth of the builder and the availability of space, the access to the first floor is provided by a representative exterior two-flight stair in the garden and/or in front of the main façade, which leads directly into the entrance part of the central hall.[20]

---

19 See also Saliba, *Beirut 1920-1940*, 46.

20 Compare the plans of Qaṣr al-Khūrī and Qaṣr Mukhayyish in Anne Mollenhauer's contribution.

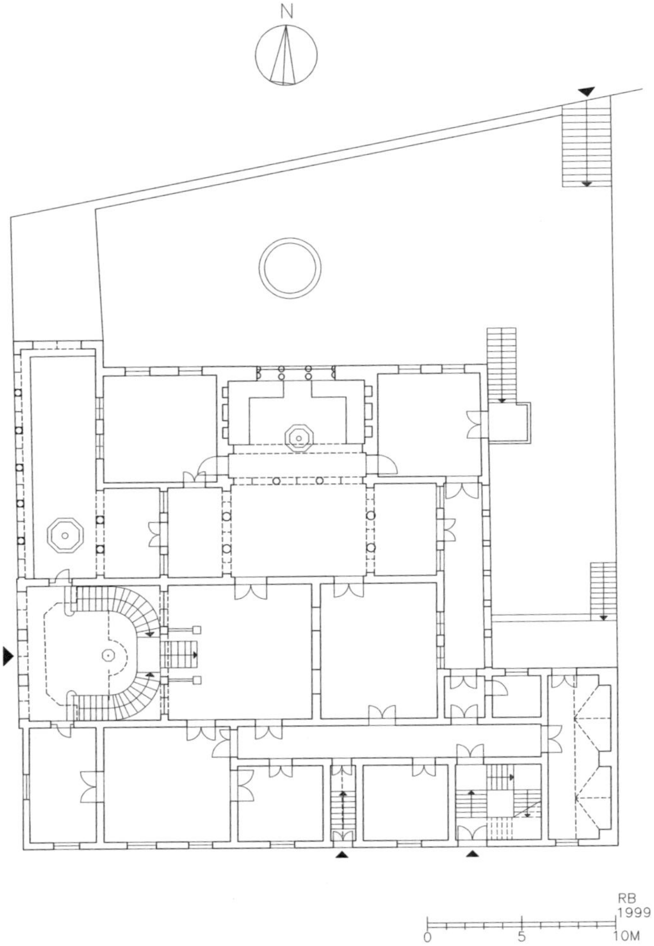

Fig. A: Qasr Heneiné, Plan of the First Floor, Reconstructed Original State (End 19th Century).

This characteristic organisation of space clearly reflects a similar life style of the emerging Beiruti bourgeoisie – be it Christian or Muslim.[21] What is more, the central-hall plan appears to have constituted such an essential condition for the life style of the new Beiruti commercial bourgeoisie that even houses in Mersin, built by Beiruti merchants during the late nineteenth century, show this plan in different variations.[22] Variations of the

21 Saliba, *Beirut 1920-1940*, 35.

22 See Yenişehirlioğlu's contribution to this volume.

central-hall house can also be found in other parts of the Ottoman Empire in the late nineteenth century. This expression of a new domestic culture can therefore not be limited to the Beiruti bourgeoisie or to the new quarters of cities on the Syrian coast, but should be considered as a phenomenon in the larger context of the Ottoman Empire in the second half of the nineteenth century.[23]

The spatial organization of Qaṣr Heneiné, however, is alien to this context in many regards. The first outstanding feature is the entrance area. Through the main gate giving immediately onto the street on the western side of the house, we enter a large hall at street level with a height of two storeys. A curved two-flight staircase – resembling those stairs we would normally find outside a wealthier house in Beirut – is *inside* this entrance hall and leads up to the first floor level into a second entrance hall. The spatial quality of the lower entrance hall is very peculiar: It is already secluded from the street, protected from the summer heat and winter rains, the dust and the noise, embracing the visitor with its cool, calm and spacious atmosphere which is very much enhanced by the marble fountain in the centre of the hall (the fountain is missing today). In a way, this entrance hall is a substitute for a representative garden entrance, which – because of the small lot and the interior organisation of the house – was not feasible in Qaṣr Heneiné. It could also be argued that this staircase was inside because of stipulations of the new Ottoman building laws issued in 1880/1881 which forbade any disturbing protrusions into the road or across the building line of newly built buildings.[24] However, no comparable examples can be found in Beirut today (maybe because they did not survive). The entrance hall of Qaṣr Heneiné is an exception to the domestic architecture in late nineteenth-century Beirut.

The same is true for the upper part of the entrance area: This second entrance hall serves as a kind of *vestibule*; it is mainly a through space, which gives access to the adjoining areas of the first floor. The vestibule therefore provides a higher degree of privacy than the spatial organisation of a central hall would allow. In a central hall house a visitor would already enter the first part of the central hall and consequently almost enter

---

23 Take for instance the traditional *sofa* houses in Anatolia (see Önder Küçükerman, *Das alttürkische Wohnhaus*, Istanbul 1992, 47-60), the *sofa* houses in later nineteenth-century Damascus and Aleppo, or the central-hall houses in Sanaa, Yemen, or in Bulgaria (I owe this information to Stefan Weber, Anne Mollenhauer and Prof. Dorothée Sack).

24 For the Arabic translation of these laws see Amīn ʿAbd al-Nūr, *Tarjama wa-sharḥ qānūn al-abniyya wa-qirār al-istimlāk*, Beirut 1896. The protrusions are dealt with in chapter 4, §§ 26-32.

the main living area. In contrast to the sumptuously decorated entrance part of a central hall, the entrance hall and the vestibule of Qaṣr Heneiné are of a rather simple design which is everything but ostentatious. Once again the builder of Qaṣr Heneiné proves to be keen on *not* displaying his wealth in such an ostentative manner as rich Beirutis generally did. What is more, this quality of the vestibule is in a striking harmony with the concept of a vestibule in the modern domestic architecture of the upper classes in France and other parts of Europe at the end of the nineteenth century, where – against the earlier pomp of the entrance areas – a strong trend towards simpler entrance areas and richer decoration of the interior rooms can be observed.[25] We can hence see from the way privacy is created and from the decoration, that the entrance area of Qaṣr Heneiné is very different from the new domestic architecture in Beirut. Instead it resembles modern domestic architecture of the European bourgeoisie.

The areas, which were accessible from the vestibule, can be defined as four distinct areas: The first is the larger decorated room with two adjoining smaller rooms in the south-western corner of the house.[26] The second area is the interior corridor leading eastward to the secondary entrances, the staircase between first and second floor, and the service area with the kitchen. The third is a large decorated room located on the axis of the entrance hall and the vestibule. It is accessible from the vestibule, from the great hall and from the corridor. For reasons of its location close to the kitchen and its accessibility from other rooms, this room can be identified as the dining room – as, in fact, it was used in the days of Dr. Calmette and later the Heneinés. The fourth area is the lavishly decorated great hall with its two adjoining rooms on the northern side of the house. With regards to

---

25 See Monique Eleb-Vidal & Anne Debarre-Blanchard, *Architectures de la vie privée. Maisons et mentalités, XVIIe-XIXe siècles*, Brussels 1989, 268. The *Nouveau Larousse Illustré* from 1905 describes the vestibule as follows: "*Un vestibule ne comporte, en aucun cas ni meubles, ni glaces, ni tableaux, ni riches ornements, il est décoré avec des pilastres, des colonnes simples, quelquefois, mais rarement des statues*." (cf. Eleb-Vidal & Debarre-Blanchard, *Architectures*, 298). This description corresponds exactly to the vestibule of Qaṣr Heneiné. For vestibules and their function in German domestic architecture of the late nineteenth century (which remind one very much of the entrance and vestibule in Qaṣr Heneiné) see also Wolfgang Brönner, *Die bürgerliche Villa in Deutschland, 1830-1890*, (Beiträge zu den Bau- und Kunstdenkmälern im Rheinland; 29), Düsseldorf 1987, 58-59.

26 The decoration of this large room and the other large rooms of the first floor (except the great hall) originally consisted of painted coloured patterns on the wooden girder casings of the ceilings (which are all combined iron-wood constructions without stucco) and of similar coloured frieze patterns on the walls. The wall decoration has mostly disappeared today, only the ceiling decoration is preserved.

its function, location and decoration, the great hall could be called a *grand salon* – if we want to apply the corresponding vocabulary for European domestic architecture. Together with the two adjoining rooms in the north-western and north-eastern corner – one of which is reported to have been the *petit salon* at least during the period when the Heneinés lived in the house – these rooms constitute the main reception and living area of Qaṣr Heneiné. They contain rich decoration – especially in the great hall; they are located towards the calmer and cooler garden side of the house, and they have the advantage of direct access to the galleries on the western and eastern side of the house. The grouping of these rooms again shows a close resemblance to the grouping of the different *salons* in European bourgeois mansions of the late nineteenth century.[27]

Without going into further detail, we shall only stress a few important aspects of the plan:

1. The high complexity of the plan: a specifically designed entrance area gives access to different complexes of rooms with different functions. This subdivision of the whole floor into four different areas with groups of rooms is particular to Qaṣr Heneiné and cannot be found in central hall houses.

2. The key function of the vestibule as the main distribution space in Qaṣr Heneiné as opposed to the key function of the central hall as a combined distribution and living space in a central-hall house.

3. The numerous communication ways between the different rooms and groups of rooms: Nearly every room has several doors linking it directly or via corridors and galleries to other rooms and complexes. Hereby every room can be walked through or – which is important – can be avoided in order to reach another room. This is diametrically opposed to the functioning of a central-hall house in terms of communication: since many of the rooms adjoining the central hall normally do not have doors to the neighbouring rooms, one has to pass through the central hall in order to reach another room. The central hall controls virtually all communication within the house. It appears however that in the 1890s this rigid scheme began to be partly dissolved in some new houses through the introduction of doors linking the rooms along the central hall

---

27 For a detailed treatment of the functions, spatial arrangement and furnishing of such rooms (mostly by the example of Paris and France) see for instance: Eleb-Vidal & Debarre-Blanchard, *Architectures*, 266-73; Monique Eleb & Anne Debarre, *L'Invention de l'habitation moderne. Paris 1880-1914*, Paris 1995, chapter III; Ursula Paravicini, *Habitat au féminin*, Lausanne 1990, chapter V.

directly to each other.[28] This innovation hints to a further development in the domestic culture of the Beiruti bourgeoisie, but is only rarely found in surviving houses. Research on the further development and variations of the central-hall plan in Beirut *after* its introduction is still a desideratum and would be very helpful for the understanding of the underlying processes of social change.

The above results are mainly based on a comparison of the plan of Qaṣr Heneiné with the plans of some selected examples of Beiruti central-hall houses on the one hand, and of some Western and Central European bourgeois houses of the late nineteenth century on the other hand. Here the method of *access mapping* serves to identify the typical spatial patterns and to analyse the spatial functioning of a house plan in terms of accessibility, permeability and control of space. Access mapping or access analysis is a method that has mainly been developed and applied by British archaeologists since the 1980s in order to study the spatial organisation as an expression of – and a key to – the social organisation. It generally deals with a larger sample of plans in order to establish typical patterns, and less with individual houses as art objects.[29] In our case we naturally face the problem that this method has hitherto not been applied to the study of houses in Beirut. For my research I therefore had to sketch access maps of a broader sample of Beiruti central-hall houses in order to obtain a more representative picture; for comparison I also sketched access maps for some bourgeois mansions in Paris and Berlin dating from around 1870-1890. It would have been useful to have such access maps for similar houses in St. Petersburg or Moscow as well, but no respective plans were available. But for the time being the results of this comparison – as briefly outlined above – are already very telling.[30]

Whereas the exterior design features of Qaṣr Heneiné and its construction technique are clearly rooted in contemporary local ways of building, the organisation of space inside the house is very different from the plans, which we might find in Beiruti – and more general Levantine or Syrian -

---

28 This was observed by Benoît Boyer, *Conditions hygiéniques actuelles de Beyrouth (Syrie) et de ses environs immédiats*, Lyon 1897, 21.

29 West, *Social Space*, 108. For access analysis as a method for the functional and social analysis of house plans see ibid. (passim); Shane Gould, "Planning, Development and Social Archaeology," in Tarlow & West, *The Familiar Past?*, 140-154; B. Hillier & J. Hanson, *The Social Logic of Space*, Cambridge 1984 (passim); S. Foster, "Analysis of spatial patterns in buildings (access analysis) as an insight into social structure, example from the Scottish Iron Age," *Antiquity* 63 (1989), 40-50 (passim).

30 For reasons of brevity I decided not to present the respective access maps in this paper. They are part of my M.A. thesis.

domestic architecture. The builder of Qaṣr Heneiné must have had needs and expectations from the living space that were very different from that of the local bourgeoisie. This points to a completely different life style and domestic culture of the builder, and leads us to the conclusion that a) the builder of Qaṣr Heneiné must have been a foreigner with a marked European-bourgeois life style, and b) that the domestic culture of the local bourgeoisie was very different from this European-bourgeois domestic culture.

While the latter conclusion strongly challenges the widespread concept of a "westernisation" of daily life in late Ottoman Beirut, we should also be aware of the problem that we actually should not even speak of a "European" domestic culture. What we call Europe is a vast geographic area with sometimes very different cultures depending on the region and the social standing. These cultural differences found expression in the (sometimes slightly) different spatial organisation even of upper-bourgeois mansions in France, England, Germany, and Russia (and even within these countries).[31] In our case we face the additional problem that the Russian nobleman as a builder cannot simply be equated with a "European bourgeois". We may say, however, that the aristocracy in Europe had increasingly adopted a bourgeois life style in the course of the nineteenth century while at the same time the bourgeoisie took over elements of the aristocratic life style, and that this newly developing life style of the West, Central and East-European bourgeoisie had a strong orientation towards the French and English bourgeoisie. [32] This should also hold true for our Russian nobleman who then should at least come from an urban centre like St. Petersburg or Moscow, which were much more attuned to these cultural orientations than the rural areas of Russia. It is in this sense and with these reservations in mind that I will continue to use the term "European bourgeois" in the following.

So far we could see that Qaṣr Heneiné is a thoroughly hybrid structure, with its building techniques and materials being of a very local quality, but its plan being designed to fit the requirements of the European-bourgeois life style of its builder. But the hybridity of Qaṣr Heneiné goes even further and gains a new dimension if we take a look at its orientalizing interior decoration and some additional details in the plan.

---

31 See for instance Peter Thornton, *Innenarchitektur in drei Jahrhunderten. Die Wohnungseinrichtung nach zeitgenössischen Zeugnissen von 1620 bis 1920*, Herford 1985 [revised German translation of the Engl. original edition: P. Thornton, *Authentic Decor*, London 1984].

32 According to Brönner, *Die bürgerliche Villa*, 61-64.

Briefly, there are some arrangements in the plan, which appear to be inspired by the traditional domestic architecture of Syria and Mount Lebanon.

1) The T-shaped great hall with its fountain reminds one very much of the type of T-shaped *qāʿa* (hall) that we can find in Aleppine open-court houses and Damascene palaces.[33] But the similarity does not go very far: the aisles of the great hall are not elevated as the *ṭazars*[34] in a typical *qāʿa* are; the ceiling of the central part is not as high as it would be in a *qāʿa*; the fountain is not in the central part but instead in the northern aisle; there are doors in the end walls of the aisles which we would not find in a *qāʿa*; and the aisles are separated from the central part by arcades instead of having a large arched opening towards it. Hence the plan resembles a *qāʿa* to a certain extent, but the treating of the space is much more closely related to a local central hall. Still there is a stone *dīwān* in the northern aisle and the niches in the walls with *ablaq*[35] design, which are clear references to a *qāʿa* as in Damascus or even in the Lebanese mountains.

2) The northern aisle of the great hall with its two adjoining rooms and the doors between them constitute a spatial arrangement, which strongly reminds us of the plan of a simple vernacular *īwān*-house in the Lebanese mountains.[36] This similarity is enhanced by the small triple arch window in the rear wall of the aisle and the stone *dīwān* running along the walls; they are features, which can similarly be found in the *īwān*s of these vernacular houses. But whereas this group of rooms would already constitute a complete vernacular house, in Qaṣr Heneiné it is inserted into a completely different and more complex architectural context.

3) There are three fountains inside Qaṣr Heneiné: One in the entrance hall, one in the great hall, and one on the western gallery in front of the open loggia. Interior fountains cannot be found in other Beiruti mansions –

---

33 For descriptions of such *qāʿas* see e.g. O. Reuther, "Die Qāʿa," *Jahrbuch der Asiatischen Kunst*, vol. 2 (1925), 205-216; and Dorothea Duda, *Innenarchitektur syrischer Stadthäuser des 16. bis 18. Jahrhunderts. Die Sammlung des Henri Pharaon in Beirut*, (Beiruter Texte und Studien; 12), Beirut 1971, 21-23.

34 A *ṭazar* is the elevated part of a traditional hall. In the case of a T-shaped *qāʿa*, three *ṭazars* would give on a lower central part (the so-called *ʿataba*) from three sides.

35 The term *ablaq* denotes a horizontally striped masonry usually produced by alternating layers of stones in different colours.

36 Compare the examples in Friedrich Ragette, *Architecture in Lebanon. The Lebanese House During the eighteenth and nineteenth Century*, Beirut 1974, and Camille Aboussouan (ed.), *L'architecture libanaise du XVe au XIXe siècle. Le Bonheur de vivre*, Beirut 1985.

apart from interesting exceptions like Qaṣr Pharaon[37] and Qaṣr Ibrahim Sursock (Fig. 4) where the fountains have been added later when the houses were equipped with orientalizing interiors (in Qaṣr Pharaon this happened from the 1920s on; in Qaṣr Sursock the dating is unclear, since the house was subject to at least three alterations or renovations; most of its interior is – for all we can say – not original). The fountains in Qaṣr Heneiné are original and evoke – even without the orientalizing decoration – a very 'Oriental atmosphere' inside the house.

With all these features the interior architecture of the house acquires a second dimension of meaning: the attempt by the builder to give his house a marked 'Oriental flair' by integrating elements of the different regional vernacular architectures into a foreign living space. He appears to have been a connoisseur and an amateur of the traditional regional architecture and wished to enjoy some of its qualities even when living in a modern urban mansion in Beirut.

To this we now have to add the interior decoration: It has not much in common with customary interior decorations of houses in nineteenth-century Greater Syria, where we would rather find a wooden panelling of the walls and a coloured *ʿajamī* decoration of these wall panels and ceilings.[38] And neither does it resemble the interiors of contemporary Beiruti mansions with their European- (or more exactly, Italian) influenced stucco ceilings and wall decorations in Neo-Baroque, Neo-Rococo and other historical styles which are often said to have been made by Italian craftsmen.

Instead the decoration of Qaṣr Heneiné – particularly of the great hall – is mostly designed in the so-called Moorish style. This exotic style was strongly inspired by the Alhambra in Granada and other examples of Muslim architecture in Spain and was *en vogue* all over Europe during the nineteenth century as one of several fashionable exotic styles.[39] Briefly, this origin of the interior decoration of the great hall can be demonstrated with the help of some selected details:

The mesh decoration of the upper parts of the walls and the spandrels of the arcades in the great hall are derivations of such decorations as can be

---

37 See Duda, *Innenarchitektur*, Plate 1.

38 For a selection of such interiors see ibid.

39 For a general treatment of exotic and Moorish style in European architecture see e.g. Nadine Beautheac & François-Xavier Bouchart, *L'Europe exotique*, Paris 1985; Miles Danby, *Moorish Style*, London 1995; Stefan Koppelkamm, *Der imaginäre Orient. Exotische Bauten des achtzehnten und neunzehnten Jahrhunderts in Europa*, Berlin 1987; John MacKenzie, *Orientalism: History, Theory and the Arts*, Manchester 1995; John Sweetman, *The Oriental Obsession. Islamic Inspiration in British and American Art and Architecture 1500-1920*, Cambridge 1988.

found, for instance, on the spandrels of the arcades in the Myrtle Court in the Alhambra (compare Figs. 5 and 6). Here we also find similar multi-foiled arches and similar cubic abutments with *muqarnas* consoles. The rectangular framing of the arched door in the background of the Myrtle Court bears much similarity with the rectangular framing of the triple arch window in the great hall (Fig. 9). However the interior treatment of this frame in Qaṣr Heneiné – especially the cartouches with the calligraphy in *thuluth*-script – is more *mashriqī* than *maghribī* in style. The columns of the arcades in the great hall with cut-in coloured geometric patterns at their lower end, the rings around the shaft, the lotus calyx under the capitals, and the cut-in and originally coloured vegetal motifs and bands on the capitals are very typical examples of the Moorish style. That the columns in Qaṣr Heneiné have bulbous capitals and not the typical square ones can be taken as an instance of free interpretation, which – here as in Europe – was an essential quality of the Moorish style. The copies inspired by the Alhambra and other buildings of medieval Andalusia were rarely faithful copies but rather citations and rearrangements of constituent elements of the originals.[40]

Last but not least there are the coloured stucco ceilings with their over-all star patterns and mirror inlays in Qaṣr Heneiné, which have their coun-terparts in the ceilings of the Wilhelma in Bad Cannstadt in Germany, as well as in the Çirağan Palace in Istanbul and many other buildings of this style.[41] The overall Moorish impression of this decoration is attested by the U.S. inspection report from 1922, where the great hall is described as "a copy of a famous court in the Alhambra Palace in Granada."
But this comparison does not take into account some very peculiar features of this interior: in addition to decorative elements which can clearly be traced back to European orientalism in art and architecture, the builder of Qaṣr Heneiné also integrated some decorative elements of local and re-gional origin: the *ablaq*-facing of the walls of the northern aisle of the great hall and the slim relief frieze running along the upper edge of the *ablaq* are a very common feature of local and regional vernacular architec-ture and can be found in Lebanon and Syria (compare Figs. 7 and 8). The

---

40 Timothy Mitchell called this the "citationary character" of Orientalism; Timothy Mitchell, *Colonising Egypt*, Cambridge 1988, 31.

41 The Wilhelma was built in the 1840s by the architect Ludwig Zandt and had a strong impact on other architects, even in Istanbul where the Balyan brothers took it as a source of inspiration for the Beylerbey and Çirağan palaces in the 1860s (see Turgut Saner, *19. Yüzyıl İstanbul Mimarlığında „Oryantalizm,"* Istanbul 1998, 58-59 and 153, and also Diana Badillari & Ezio Godoli, *Istanbul 1900. Art Nouveau Architecture and Interiors*, New York 1996, 36).

same holds true for the niches with their segmental arches, which are very similar to windows and niches of vernacular houses in the region. The difference is that in vernacular architecture the *ablaq* would be made of stone of different colours, not of a painted plaster facing as it is in Qaṣr Heneiné. Even the twin-arched window motif above the segmental arched doors (Fig. 10) appears to be inspired by similar windows above doors in traditional regional architecture, yet it is treated in a slightly different, i.e. Moorish manner. It is most interesting to see that these 'regionalizing' elements of the decoration are mainly to be found in the northern aisle of the great hall, which in itself is structurally inspired by a traditional *īwān* house. Hence this decoration serves to enhance the deliberate regional character of this part.

Mirror-Games of 'Westernization'

The decoration of Qaṣr Heneiné is as hybrid as its architecture. The builder of Qaṣr Heneiné did not simply import the more or less established set of decorative features of the Moorish style from Europe, which is already hybrid as such, but he blended it with selected elements taken from the traditional regional and local architecture – elements which were mostly out of use in the contemporary local architecture. He created an "Orient" that did not exist either in Beirut or elsewhere. Just like every piece of Moorish architecture in nineteenth century Europe, Qaṣr Heneiné was a private and very personal vision of the "Orient" as imagined, produced by assembling a multitude of elements taken from or inspired by original Andalusian, Near and Middle Eastern architecture, publications on this art, nineteenth century architecture in Moorish style and, again, publication of examples of it. Qaṣr Heneiné is a direct offspring of this international architectural discourse of the nineteenth century, which on the one hand brought an image of the 'Orient' to modern Europe and on the other hand reimported this image to the countries of the Near and Middle East. Qaṣr Heneiné reflects this ongoing intercultural exchange in its own hybridity. And it appears to have played a crucial role in the spreading of the Moorish style – or more generally the exotic-oriental style – in Beirut. Whereas Moorish and orientalizing architecture and interiors could already be found in larger urban centres like Istanbul and Cairo from the 1860s onwards (take for instance the buildings of the Balyan brothers in Istanbul or of Carl von Diebitsch in Cairo), Qaṣr Heneiné is – for all I could establish so far – the earliest example of such a style in Beirut. It must have had a sensational value, as it appears from the fact that the interior of the great hall was considered worthy of being photographed and published as a postcard for public sale just for the sake of its decoration and furnishing around the turn of the century (Fig. 3).[42] This postcard surely has contributed to the fame of the interior decoration at that time. Moreover, the role of Qaṣr Heneiné in the spreading of this style is proved by the fact that it reportedly served as model for another Orientalist interior in Beirut: Nicolas Bustros – a member of a wealthy and influential Beiruti family – had copies of the ceilings of the great hall made for his house in the quarter of Achrafieh around the beginning of the 20th century.[43] If we compare another orientalist interior, the one of the above-mentioned Qaṣr Ibrahim Sursock, with that of Qaṣr Heneiné, we find an identical frieze pattern and very similar *muqarnas* motifs. It is therefore possible that Qaṣr Heneiné served as a model in this case as well, or that the same pattern books were used, or that the same craftsmen made both interiors. It is clear that the decoration of Qaṣr Heneiné must have been made by craftsmen who mastered the relevant repertoire of designs and techniques and who were experienced in such decorations. If we accept that this orientalist decoration is the earliest of its kind in Beirut, the craftsmen who made it can hardly have been locals, as local craftsmen – until then – hardly had an opportunity to get acquainted with this style. In fact the decoration of Qaṣr Heneiné is reported to be a work of Italian craftsmen.[44] This could mean that the house was built by local craftsmen, but its interior decorated by Italians. The later orientalist interiors of other houses, however, can also be the work of locals who learned their craft or at least some techniques from Italian craftsmen. The role of foreign and local craftsmen in the development of Beiruti (and not only Beiruti) architecture in the second half of the nineteenth century is an issue that still needs a lot of research.

The anonymous Russian nobleman who had Qaṣr Heneiné built as his residence must have been a dazzling and extravagant figure. We do not know why he came to Beirut. But from the way he decorated and probably also furnished his house we can conclude that he had an oriental spleen. Maybe he was an anti-modern romantic, "sick of progress and civilisa-

---

42 According to a personal remark by Fouad Debbas, the postcard showing the "Intérieur de la maison du Docteur Calmette" must have been published at the latest in 1905 because of the design of its obverse side. However it cannot have been published before 1903, which is the year when Dr. Calmette came to Beirut. The photo itself may already have been taken some years before, though.

43 I owe this information to Claire Paget, the author of the recently published book *Murs et plafonds peints. Liban XIXe siècle*, Beirut 1998. Unfortunately the house in question was demolished some years ago before the interior could be documented.

44 This at least was reported by one member of the Heneiné family, but was immediately rejected by other family members.

tion"[45] as were a number of other Europeans of his time, and tried to make come true his oriental-exotic dreams by means of this interior. By doing so, he in a way 're-imported the Orient' to Beirut. That he did so might appear ironic in view of the Rococo-inspired interiors of the houses of his Beiruti contemporaries, and in view of the complaints of other Europeans about the locals' ever increasing adoption of European customs and taste.[46] Some Europeans appear to have felt a certain uneasiness about the cultural changes triggered by their presence and activities and developed a preservationist attitude in an ambivalent attempt to counterbalance the effects of colonialism and imperialism.[47] The founder of the Russian 'Imperial Orthodox Palestine Society', Vasili N. Khitrovo, wrote in 1890: "For heaven's sake don't introduce European clothes or even the burnous – in our schools they must remain Arab children."[48] We might understand the interior of Qaṣr Heneiné from this perspective, and maybe also in light of the confrontation between slavophiles and Western-Europe oriented modernists in Russia during the nineteenth century, when Russians were facing similar problems with "westernization" and the cultural hegemony of Western-European societies as people in the Ottoman Empire.[49]
But it is exactly by his way of 'going native', that the Russian builder of Qaṣr Heneiné proves to be very European indeed. His orientalism and his domestic culture – as expressed in the plan of his house – indicate quite clearly that he had internalized a lot of the powerful European-bourgeois culture of his time.

On the other hand the comparison of Qaṣr Heneiné with houses built by and lived in by Beirutis shows that the quality and extent of "western" or "European" influence has to be reassessed. It is true that the Beirutis were looking west – and not only the Beirutis, as Stefan Weber shows in

---

45 Words of the traveller and writer Richard Burton, cited after Karl-Heinz Kohl, "Im Gewand des Orients. Sir Richard Francis Burton (1821-1890) – eine biographische Skizze," in *Exotische Welten, europäische Phantasien*, ed. Institut für Auslandsbeziehungen, Stuttgart – Bad Cannstadt 1987, 72-77, here 73.

46 For some quotations see for instance Sehnaoui, *L'occidentalisation*, 123, 144, 145.

47 For a treatment of the phenomenon of exotism under this aspect see Eckhard Nordhofen, "Der greinende Moloch. Philosophische Motive des Exotismus," in *Exotische Welten*, 34-39. The ambivalence of this attitude is also reflected in the French "ideology of preservation" in their North-African colonies; see Zeynep Çelik, *Urban Forms and Colonial Confrontations. Algiers under French Rule*, Los Angeles 1997, 37-39.

48 Cited after Hopwood, *The Russian Presence*, 145, fn. 5.

49 See Andreas Pflitsch, "Der Osten und der Orient – Russischer Kultureinfluß im Libanon in der zweiten Hälfte des 19. Jahrhunderts," *Beiruter Blätter* 6-7 (1998/1999), ed. Orient-Institut der DMG Beirut, 199-204.

his contribution to this volume. The technical, economical, and political developments of this period led to an increasing flow of goods and ideas from Europe and the "West" to other parts of the world. But what local people in the other parts of the world created out of these imported goods was not necessarily "European" or "western".[50] The combination of the newly developed central-hall plan with building materials and decorative features imported from Europe was a very hybrid and at the same time very original creation (as hybrid and original as Qaṣr Heneiné), fulfilling the needs of the locals by means of available techniques, materials and know-how.

The central-hall plan is the spatial expression of the specific life style, customs, social structure and – resulting from them – residential requirements and domestic culture of those Beirutis who could afford to build such houses. And since houses are long-living and stable spatial structures, which are lived in by subsequent generations, they contribute – within certain limits – to the reproduction and preservation of customs and domestic culture. This is demonstrated by the long survival of the central-house plan in Beirut far into the twentieth century[51] – a reproduction of a spatial pattern which is surely not only due to a conservatism of the architects.

In this context it is very telling that the plan of Qaṣr Heneiné – which enabled a European-bourgeois way of domestic life – did not find a successor in Beirut. Against that, its orientalizing interior did find successors in the houses of wealthy Beirutis, but these interiors were set up in central-hall houses. The adoption of such a style by Beirutis has very interesting implications, which we cannot deal with here. In order to understand the hybridization of domestic architecture and the underlying change and persistence of domestic culture in Beirut or elsewhere, it is not very helpful to speak of "Western appliqué façades on traditional interiors"[52] and to have recourse to simplifying dichotomies like 'oriental and western' or 'tradition and modernity'. The central-hall house is not traditional, but – as far as Beirut and the Arab provinces of the Ottoman Empire are concerned – a product of the nineteenth century. Its changing combinations with im-

50 For a recent critical discussion of the effects of "westernization" and "Europeanization" see Karl-Heinz Kohl, "Das exotische Europa," *Merkur* 1, Jan. 2000, 24-35.

51 Central-hall plans can still be found at houses built in the 1940s (see Saliba, *Beirut 1920-1940*), in some cases even later.

52 This term was used by Zeynep Celik, *The Remaking of Istanbul. Portrait of an Ottoman City in the Nineteenth Century*, Seattle and London 1986, 137, and was transferred on bourgeois residential buildings in Beirut by Saliba, *Beirut 1920-1940*, 29.

ported or locally developed architectural elements and forms should be studied as a much more complex expression and result of an ongoing process, in which different groups of the local population tried to face in different ways the challenges of a rapidly changing world and of dominant European cultures to their culture and identity – by partly adopting, partly transforming, and partly rejecting what the increased flow of goods and ideas offered them. The Russian nobleman and his Beiruti contemporaries were all affected by this global change, but they (re)acted differently.

– III –

Participating in Empire, Shaping the Surroundings, and Challenging Authority

OTTOMAN PROVINCIAL TOWNS FROM THE EIGHTEENTH TO THE NINETEENTH CENTURY

A Re-Assessment of their Place in the Transformation of the Empire

CHRISTOPH K. NEUMANN

Three Different Narratives

The nineteenth century is today generally regarded as the time of rapid change in the Ottoman Empire. No matter which paradigm scholars use, whether they talk about westernization, modernization, imperialism or integration into the world economic system, everybody agrees that this was an age of deep and swift transformation. Obviously, all of the terms mentioned have their merits; equally obviously, all of them pose serious problems.

This paper does not attempt to compare their validity. But the issue is serious and important. If one wants to say something about the nature of Ottoman transformation one has either to address it, or, as I shall try to do, find a mode of analysis where the difference between these approaches does not matter or is at least of secondary importance.

The term "time of reforms" has recently found its way into the titles of important publications such as the chapter on the nineteenth century in the *Economic and Social History of the Ottoman Empire.*[1] The reintroduction of the term "reform", which has been widely used until the first half of this century, is presumably an attempt to avoid a decision for one of the paradigms mentioned above.

This is true even if one admits that the term is connected to the conceptual framework of modernization theory: a transformation that aims outright for example at turning the tide of modern technology has little chance of being called a "reform". The term is inherently connected to the concepts of the nation-state, administrative rationalization, scientific and tech-

---

[1] Donald Quataert, "The Age of Reforms, 1812-1914," in *Economic and Social History of the Ottoman Empire, 1300-1914,* eds. Halil İnalcık, Donald Quataert, Cambridge 1994, 759-946.

nological progress, market economy and monetarization, bureaucratization, centralization and individualization. These are among the elements of the modernization paradigm, and their diversity is partly responsible for the difficulties the discourse on modernization is currently encountering.[2]

The term "reform" connects easily to any of these and perhaps a few other of their kind, no matter what inconsistencies exist between them. As a result, the concept of reform gains a high degree of flexibility. It becomes applicable to diverse spheres of social life. That it has (re-) gained such popularity may largely be due to the fact that it is so easily applicable.

The term "reform" has moreover the advantage of not predetermining the question of agency. Reforms may be launched by a government or by foreign powers, and different social groups may also instigate them. Another aspect of the concept is that reforms may aim at and lead to very different developments. However, the fact that the concept is so open to differing usage does not enhance its analytical sharpness. This is all too well mirrored by the usage of the paradigm in Ottoman studies.

Taking license to oversimplify grossly for the sake of clarity, I differentiate between three types of reform narratives in Ottoman studies. They coincide broadly with a regional division between southeastern Europe, Turkey, and the Arab world. All of them serve as narratives explaining the emergence of the regional nation states, or to put it more carefully: all of

---

2 In the view of this author, the very attempts at rescuing the paradigm bear the clearest signs of the dilemma to which it is subjected: to be content with either very limited validity or with little applicability. A good example with regard to the (Americanised) Turkish discussion is Reşat Kasaba' s recent article "Kemalist Certainties and Modern Ambiguities," in *Rethinking Modernity and National Identity in Turkey,* eds. Sibel Bozdoğan, Reşat Kasaba, Seattle and London 1997, 15-36. Kasaba seeks to defend modernism apparently on (in my view, very honest) political and moral grounds when he argues that the concept of modernization helps Turkish society to cope with the transformations present and future (p. 32). In order to do so, however, he has to incorporate what he calls the "countermovement of protection" (pp. 19-20) into modernization as its integral part. Consequently not (or no longer) reaction but post-modern relativism becomes the main adversary of modernization. He shares this moral and polemical stance with Ernest Gellner who bases his polemic against postmodernism also more on moral than on methodological grounds – see his *Postmodernism, Reason and Religion,* London 1992.

It would be unfair to conceal that the other paradigms enumerated above share the difficulty of preserving coherence, validity, and applicability. In world-system theory, the notion of "uneven development" may have been introduced in order to make the distinction between centre, semi-periphery, and periphery more flexible. Systematically applied, however, it may well blow apart these categories so central for the paradigm. For a discussion of uneven development cf. *Criteria and Indicators of Backwardness: Essays on Uneven Development in European History,* eds. Miroslav Hroch, Lud'a Klusáková, Prague 1996.

them can be read as an attempt to explain that nation states emerged out of the Ottoman empire.

In southeastern Europe, great weight is given to local elites and an emerging bourgeoisie.[3] Figures like the state-building Balkan merchant,[4] the small to middle-scale craftsman and entrepreneur,[5] the schoolteacher and the journalist play a vital rôle in these narratives. Reforms launched by agents of the Ottoman administration are generally assigned only secondary importance. Influential Muslim leaders, even such influential ones as Pazvand-oğlı ʿOsmān and Tepe-delenli ʿAlī, are rarely assigned an active and constructive rôle in the transformation of these societies.[6] The impact of churches and foreign powers belong to the debates that have not yet been settled.

The historiography focusing its view on the Ottoman Empire in Istanbul consists mainly of Turkish and Western contributions. The time of the *Tanẓīmāt* appears in this context often as one of reforms from the top down. Local administration is a consequence of central governmental reform. İlber Ortaylı, the historian of Ottoman local governments, titles a chapter of his pertinent monograph "the city administration that fails to institutionalize" ("*örgütlenemeyen belediye*").[7] Ortaylı includes cities such

3 Slavka Draganova, "Changements dans les rapports agraires des peuples Balkaniques depuis la fin du XVIIIe siècle jusqu'en 1878," in *Histoire économique et sociale de l'Empire ottoman et de la Turquie, 1326-1960: Actes du sixième congrès international tenu à Aix-en-Provence du 1er au 4 juillet 1992,* ed. Daniel Panzac, Paris 1995, 145-64.

4 This phrase is borrowed from the title of Troian Stojanovich's "The Conquering Balkan Orthodox Merchant," *Journal of Economic History*, 20 (1960), 243-313.

5 Nikolai Todorov, *The Balkan City, 1400-1900,* Seattle, London 1983, 238-64 discusses the case of the very successful (and therefore no longer middle-scale) textile producer Gergi Gümüshgerdan. Todorov's book was first published in Bulgarian in 1972.

6 On the institutionalization of the *ʿayānlıḳ* primarily on the Balkans see also Yuzo Nagata, *Muhsin-zâde Mehmed Paşa ve Ayânlık Müessesesi,* Tokyo 1976.

7 Ilber Ortaylı, *Tanzimattan Cumhuriyete Yerel Yönetim Geleneği,* Ankara 1985, 143. This chapter heading alludes to the title of a monograph on İzmir in the nineteenth and twentieth centuries written by a leading Turkish social scientist: Mübeccel Kıray, *Örgütleşemeyen Kent: İzmir,* 2nd ed., İstanbul 1998. This book whose title can be translated as "The City that failed to institutionalize itself: Smyrna" was first published in 1972. Its main thesis is that İzmir underwent a change from a rather typical preindustrial city to an equally typical "half-developed" regional metropolis. The reason for its underdevelopment is seen in the inability of the economic forces in the city to control the urban space and its hinterland. Because of their failing to take control of the socio-economic development, the state seized the opportunity to impose its own agenda – a picture corresponding to the historical research undertaken by many Ottomanists concentrating on the core of the empire.

as Beirut or Salonica in his evaluation but draws his evidence mainly from the central Ottoman lands, largely coinciding with the area the architectural historian Maurice M. Cerasi defines as that of a culturally defined Ottoman Levantine town.[8]

The Ottoman government is given agency, whether it reacts to Western pressure, or attempts to build up strength to resist it. The main actors are the Ottoman bureaucrat, and, to a lesser degree, the westernized intellectual. A contested issue is the degree of impact the reforms had on Ottoman society and the social reactions to them.

Finally, there is the historiography with which the other contributors to this volume are much more familiar than I am. It concerns the Arab lands. Especially in the remarkable bulk of work that has been done on Syria, urban notables are seen in the key position in the process of transformation.[9] Placed at the interface between an often rather remote (sometimes even abstract) central administration and local society these intermediaries were in the position to exploit their standing by adapting to the changing environment of the age.

In 1990, Philip S. Khoury has reviewed what he calls "the urban notables paradigm"[10] and found it basically valid. He proposed, though, to intensify research on everyday life of the urban notables, on their patronage networks and especially their relations to the countryside and the central administration. Finally, he suggested concentrating on the notables' rôle in the cultural life of the towns. All these efforts combined might open up possibilities of writing a history from the bottom up.

In the decade since Khoury published this agenda, parts of it have been addressed. As far as I can see, recent studies have enriched the picture of

---

8 Maurice M. Cerasi, *Osmanlı Kenti: Osmanlı İmparatorluğu'nda 18. ve 19. Yüzyıllarda Kent Uygarlığı ve Mimarisi,* İstanbul 1999 [La città del Levante, 1986, transl. Aslı Ataöv], 58-59. The concept of core area used here is admittedly a rather fluid one; therefore I prefer to employ a rather unstable terminology that does not distinguish between "central lands", "core area" or "central territory".

9 The concept was first put forward by Albert H. Hourani, "Ottoman Reform and the Politics of Notables," in *Beginnings of Modernization in the Middle East,* eds. William R. Polk, Richard Chambers, Chicago 1968, 41-65. Hourani distinguishes between three sub-groups: members of the local religious establishment, janissary officers and other military commanders who had gone local, and the group of people deriving power from their control of tax-sources or endowments. In a review of the literature published in the decade after Hourani's article, Karl K. Barbir, *Ottoman Rule in Damascus, 1700-1758,* Princeton 1980, 71-74, notes that in the eighteenth century notables seem to have been more powerful in the Balkans than in Syria.

10 Philip S. Khoury, "The Urban Notables Paradigm Revisited," *REMMM*, 55-56, 1-2 (1990), 215-28.

the Arab urban notables as main agents of reform. I am not aware of any attempt to replace it with something else.

In a volume published two years after Khoury's article, Adel Manna presented a detailed picture of the change in the composition of the Palestine elite. Overall, he observed "The balance of power between rural *shaykhs* and urban notables… swung in the favor of the latter".[11] The degree of control Damascus-based representatives of the Ottoman central government exerted on the Palestinian elites, however, determined how influential these latter notables could become in the end. Conversely, the representatives of the central administration in Damascus and Sidon (Ṣaydā) were themselves leading men from local elites. They had been allowed to attain regional power when the Porte was left to choose between connivance to their ascendancy and a risky as well as costly attempt to (re-) institute more direct control.

In the case of the al-ʿAẓm family in Damascus, this worked rather well;[12] in others, it did not. Finally, local power-holders less loyal to the Porte such as Ẓāhir al-ʿUmar and Aḥmad al-Jazzār cut back the Damascene influence in Greater Syria.[13] On the other hand, even if their interests were often at variance with those of the Porte, these men came to represent the state towards the local communities. Their power-bases were outside the imminent reach of the central administration but they used state institutions and state income to enhance their position.[14]

Seen from this angle, the basic nature of capital formation in the Ottoman empire had not changed much from the sixteenth to the early nineteenth century, from Istanbul and Rumeli to Syria: it was a basically political process.[15] What did, albeit slowly, change was the nature of the economy: the eighteenth and the nineteenth century saw a transformation towards the commercialization of agriculture,[16] a higher degree of incorpora-

11 ʿĀdel Mannāʿ, "Continuity and Change in the Socio-Political Elite in Palestine During the Late Ottoman Period," in *The Syrian Land in the 18th and 19th Century: The Common and the Specific in the Historical Experience",* ed. Thomas Philipp, Stuttgart 1992, 69-89, here: 78.

12 Linda Schatkowski-Schilcher, *Families in Politics: Damascene Factions and Estates of the 18th and 19th Centuries,* Stuttgart 1985, 30.

13 Richard van Leeuwen, *Notables and Clergy in Mount Lebanon: The Khāzin Sheikhs and the Maronite Church, 1736-1840,* Leiden 1994, 43-45.

14 Van Leeuwen, *Notables and Clergy,* 49-50.

15 Halil İnalcık, "Capital Formation in the Ottoman Empire," *Journal of Economic History* 29,1 (1969), 97-140.

16 *Landholding and Commercial Agriculture in the Middle East,* eds. Çağlar Keyder, Faruk Tabak, Albany 1991.

tion into world-trade networks,[17] capitalist methods of financing and finally new labor relations as a result of these economic changes. Moreover, this age experienced the influx of new technologies. Those notables who were unable to further or adapt to these changes were doomed to loose much of their position.[18]

Beshara Doumani gives a detailed picture of this process. He concludes:

> Over the course of the eighteenth and nineteenth centuries a new ruling elite and a new type of notable emerged in Jabal Nablus, as did a new political discourse. This elite was composed of the beneficiaries of the changing political economy of Jabal Nablus… Merchants were in the best position to take advantage of the new opportunities, as were those families and individuals of the old political and religious elite who were willing to subordinate their pride and devote their energies to playing an aggressive role in business matters. Over time, the boundaries separating these formerly disparate groups collapsed…[19]

Doumani stresses a continuity that is lasting to our days: The families that constituted this new elite in Palestine have been dominating its politics until today.[20] In Damascus, the elite of the 19th century "lost its hold" only after the Second World War.[21]

Notwithstanding important regional differences, at least in Greater Syria and Mesopotamia[22] urban elites are thus seen at the heart of the socio-political transformation.[23] It was they who negotiated, organized and exploited the partial integration of the regional economies into the world market, the introduction of new rules of law and the rise of new ideologies.

---

17 This is, of course, especially true in the case of port cities. The special issue of the *Review* 16,4 (1993) has been translated as *Doğu Akdeniz'de Liman Kentleri, 1800-1914,* eds. Çağlar Keyder et al., İstanbul 1994.

18 As van Leeuwen, *Notables and Clergy,* 81-242, esp. 236 has shown in his case study of the prominent Maronite family al-Khāzin.

19 Beshara Doumani, *Rediscovering Palestine: Merchants and Peasants in Jabal Nablus, 1700-1900,* Berkeley 1995, 240-41.

20 *Ibid.*, 245.

21 Schatkowski-Schilcher, *Families in Politics,* 221-22.

22 Dina Rizk Khoury, *State and Provincial Society in the Ottoman Empire: Mosul, 1540-1834,* Cambridge 1997, 212.

23 In the Maghrib, one of the margins of the Ottoman empire, things were very different. Cf. Julia A. Clancy-Smith, *Rebel and Saint: Muslim Notables, Populist Protest, Colonial Encounters; Algeria and Tunisia, 1800-1904,* Berkeley 1994.

Seen from this perspective, it becomes understandable that cities were in a key socio-economic position even if the economy remained largely an agrarian one.[24] The differences between the history of various regions of the Ottoman Empire can be related to the different ways the land-code of 1858 was enacted.[25] Indeed, this enactment may serve as an ideal test case for inter-Ottoman comparison, because it mirrors the composition of the local elite along with its overall power vis-à-vis the central administration and global market forces.

Urban Elites, Acting Together

Confronted with the contrasting images of the towns of the central Ottoman lands and the Ottoman towns in Arabia and especially Syria, one has to seek an explanation. Is this difference mainly a difference of perception caused by the need to find the institutional and social origin for the nation states of the twentieth century? Or, if there were categorical divides between the urban notables of different regions, what were their reasons?

This is an open question. The concept of empire certainly allows for a high degree of regional diversity. Why should one expect to encounter the same developments in European, Anatolian, and Syrian cities?

On the other hand, there is something like a shared urban culture in the Ottoman eighteenth century. Certainly, there were dramatic disparities between the social and demographic structure, the architectural appearance and spatial organization of cities such as Salonica, Istanbul, Damascus and Cairo, or towns such as Yeñişehir-i Fenār, Maghnisa, ʿAnteb, ʿAkkā and Nābulus – not to mention the many very special cases with their exceptionality. But after all, all these places hosted societies that were highly differentiated along group and class lines. In all of them religion and especially different forms of Islam played a pivotal rôle in formulating and legitimizing social behavior. Finally they shared a number of institutions instrumental in their public and semi-public life: *waqf, qāḍī, muftī,* janissary garrison, Friday mosque and public bath. Ottoman urban society of the eighteenth century, described in loving detail by Abraham Marcus in his monograph on Aleppo, "was clearly not a society in a state of transition

---

24 In fact, the emerging picture was that of urban elites controlling the agrarian hinterland. Cf. James A. Reilly, "Urban Hegemony in the Hinterland of Ottoman Damascus: Villages, Estates and Farms in the Nineteenth Century," in: *Histoire économique et sociale,* ed. Panzac, 455-70.

25 Haim Gerber, *The Social Origins of the Modern Middle East,* Boulder, London 1987, 180-82.

toward Western-inspired modernity".[26] This transformation took place in the nineteenth century.

Nevertheless, it seems meaningful to look into the period preceding the nineteenth century. How different were the situation and the behavior of the notables in the central lands from that of their Syrian counterparts during the eighteenth century? As a historian of the central lands on both shores of the Aegean See, I can only contribute some observations on the conditions in those parts and try to draw some preliminary conclusions.

I work on a number of towns in the Ottoman central lands in the eighteenth century. One of the main concerns of this research is what one could call "concerted action". In the absence of institutions that organized and expressed common or particular interests, concerted and co-coordinated actions of individuals were the only available means to enact the town's communality on the socio-political level. Such actions are of special significance for an assessment of the rôle of the urban notables.

A first class of examples takes the form of collective petitions (*ʿarż-ı maḥżar*) to the sultan. In principle, everybody had the right to direct a complaint or a wish to the sultan. When groups of people took recourse to this attempt at getting redress, this petition was called a *maḥżar*.[27] The documents in question are signed and sealed by the petitioners who thereby assume a group identity. Unfortunately, the original petitions are often lost. The central administration did not record the names or even number of signatories. For this reason, it is often impossible to ascertain who felt himself authorized to sign not only in his own but also in the name of others. But those who are familiar with registers of the Ottoman central administration know how frequently they speak about "the religious scholars and righteous men" (*ʿulamā' ve ṣulaḥā'*) or even the population (*ahālī*) of a certain settlement having submitted a petition.

Fortunately, a number of these maḥżars still exist. To study the lists of signatures is most revealing with respect to the composition and internal hierarchy of urban elites.

The topic of the petition often determined who was to sign it. A request for general repairs of the sultanic foundations in Maghnisa (Manisa) dated 5-M-1210 (22.VII.1795), for example, was only signed by the *muftī* and those *ʿulamā'* employed by the foundations, though the text introduced the

---

26 Marcus Abraham, *The Middle East on the Eve of Modernity: Aleppo in the Eighteenth Century,* New York 1989, 330.

27 Halil İnalcık, "Şikâyet Hakkı: *ʿarż-ı ḥāl* ve *ʿarż-ı maḥżar'lar,*" *Osmanlı Araştırmaları* 7-8 (1988), 33-54; Mübahat Kütükoğlu, *Osmanlı Belgelerinin Dili: Diplomatik,* İstanbul 1994, 315-21, 580-83.

petitioners as "the religious scholars and righteous men" residing in that town in a much more general sense.[28]

Another *maḥżar* from Ankara dated 1170 (1757) asked for an order to newly appointed governors of Anatolia to stop foraging the district on their way to and from Kütahya. In this case, the signatories were first, the *ʿulamāʾ* residing in the town from the *muftī* down to the *imām*s of the more prominent mosques, second, representatives of some prominent local families with connections to mystical orders, and third, military commanders. Within all these groups, a clear hierarchy determined the precedence of signatories.[29] It is remarkable, however, that Ankara's extremely influential *aʿyān* Müderris-zāde Aḥmed Efendi is not among the signatories.[30]

A third example is a *maḥżar* concerning a state purchase of grain in Salonica, dated 1212 (1797/98). 75 men signed it, among them *aʿyān,* representatives of large foundations and some prominent members of Salonica's society along with *ʿulamāʾ* and military officers and landowners. The Orthodox and Jewish communities, however, were not represented.[31]

These examples should suffice to demonstrate that urban notables in central Ottoman lands were perfectly able to cooperate vis-à-vis the central administration. They were able to voice their demands. They would find stratagems such as choosing the right people to sign to give weight to their cause. Seen from this angle, it may even have proven advantageous at times that the framework of their actions was scarcely institutionalized. It has recently been shown that negotiation was of primary importance in the political process of the empire – notwithstanding that the rhetoric always was one of absolute sultanic authority.[32] It is in this framework that one has to interpret these petitions.

A New Fiscal Sector

One can even go a step further: the local elite was not only able to cooperate; by the end of the eighteenth century they had even a material interest to do so. According to Yavuz Cezar's informed guess, locally collected and locally spent taxes, the so-called *maṣārif-i vilāyet,* had developed into

---

28 Başbakanlık Osmanlı Arşivi (Istanbul, henceforth BBA-OA), EV.HMH 7235.

29 BBA-OA, C.DAH 4715.

30 On his term in this position, see Yücel Özkaya, *Osmanlı İmparatorluğunda Ayânlık,* Ankara 1977, 259.

31 BBA-OA, C.BEL 3363, fol. 3.

32 Karen Barkey, *Bandits and Bureaucrats: The Ottoman Route to State Centralization,* Ithaca, NY 1994, 189-228.

a significant fiscal sector by the turn of the eighteenth to the nineteenth century. Cezar believes that the amount of money collected compared to that of the imperial treasury.[33] His documentation mostly concerns the central Ottoman lands; hence the phenomenon is relevant to my argument.

The taxes collected this way were mainly customary payments, the so-called *ʿavārıż-ı dīvāniyye* and *tekālif-i ʿörfiyye*. Originally of an extraordinary character, these taxes were soon routinely collected each year in order to finance a variety of items. An important part of this revenue went to the governor or other officials sent from Istanbul, others were used to pay for rents, the post-station *(menzil)*, town officials, and even infrastructural investments. As the central government was not able to control the actual collection and distribution of the money very efficiently, the *maṣārif-i vilāyet* were an opportunity to raise money for all kinds of purposes that were considered illegal by the sultanic government. However, as the elite of a locality was collectively responsible for the collection and appropriate use of the money even such "misuse" had to be agreed upon.

I have studied a set of two such registers from Salonica in some detail.[34] It emerges that the process can again be understood as one of bargaining within the elite of the district, and between the local elite and the administration in Istanbul. The object of the negotiation was not only the amount of money to be paid to meet certain needs but also, to a degree, the community's agenda: What was to be regarded, "a public local affair" (*umūr-ı vilāyet*)? There was no argument, however, about the very existence of public local affairs.

Local and Central: Valid Categories?

Until this point, my observations have shown that eighteenth century urban elites in the central Ottoman lands had gained means to articulate themselves and to cooperate in the face of the central administration. This interpretation rests on the assumption of a dichotomy of center and periphery, of the Istanbul government and provincial society. My third observation may necessitate a modification of this assumption. The observation con-

33 Yavuz Cezar, "18. ve 19. Yüzyıllarda Osmanlı Taşrasında Oluşan Yeni Mali Sektörün Mahiyet ve Büyüklüğü Üzerine," *Toplum ve Ekonomi* 9 (1996), 89-145, N.B. 105-18. See further Evgenij Radusev, "Les dépenses locales dans l'Empire Ottoman au XVIII siècle: Selon les données des registres de cadi des Ruse, Vidin, et Sofia," *Etudes Balkaniques* 16, 3 (1980), 74-94.

34 Christoph K. Neumann, "Selânik'te Onsekizinci Yüzyılın Sonunda Masarif-i Vilâyet Defterleri: Merkezî Hükûmet, Taşra İdaresi ve Şehir Yönetimi Üçgeninde Malî İşlemler," *İÜEF Tarih Enstitüsü Dergisi*, 16 (1998), 69-97.

cerns the role of foundations and the eighteenth century variety of what Amy Singer has called "localizing the center".[35]

The Ottoman eighteenth century experienced a wholly autochthonous trend of centralization: The Ottoman administration tried, with some success, to get tighter control over at least the more important pious endowments throughout the empire. The *neẓāret* over foundations by the *dar el-saʿāde aghası,* the chief black eunuch, the concentration of imperial foundations in the so-called *Ḥamīdiyye* administration, and the growth and systematisation of the *evḳāf-ı Ḥaremeyn-i Şerīfeyn* administration have to be understood in this framework.

An investigation of the endowments made by different members of the famous *aʿyān*-family of Manisa, the Ḳara-ʿOsmān-oghulları, shows that on the one hand they were designed to protect property from confiscation, but were simultaneously left under the supervision of the *Ḥaremeyn* administration.[36] On the other hand, the *maḥżar* on the repairs to be undertaken at the sultanic *evḳāf* in the city cited above demonstrates that such endowments constituted a very long-lasting commitment by the government.

In the case of Seyyid Nuʿmān Pasha who instituted an important *vaḳf* in Salonica, it becomes completely impossible to categorize man and foundation as either "central" or "local": Born into a family of Salonican notables and raised by another, he had become *dāmād* to the sultan and served all over the empire.[37]

Endowments were thus not only one of the key institutions of Ottoman urbanism, they also served to integrate the empire: a process that was not hampered but perhaps enhanced by the centralization attempted at that time. Equally clear should be that this offered opportunities to members of a local elite to participate in the symbolical discourse on the imperial level. When a foundation of a lesser member of the Ḳara-ʿOsmān-oghlı family, Pūlād Meḥmed Agha, was registered in the presence of an ex *şeyh el-islām* to become then part of the *Ḥaremeyn* administration,[38] this must have en-

---

35 Amy Singer: "Localizing the Center: Imperial *evkaf* in the Ottoman Provinces," to be published in: *Small Regions in the Ottoman Empire,* eds. Hans Georg Majer, Christoph K. Neumann, Beirut, İstanbul, forthcoming. I thank A. Singer for the permission to quote this article.

36 Yuzo Nagata, *Tarihte Ayânlar: Karaosmanoğulları Üzerinde bir İnceleme,* Ankara 1997, 146-63. He misses the last aspect.

37 Meḥmed S̱üreyyā, *Sicill-i ʿOs̱mānī yākhūd Teẕkire-i Meşahir-i ʿOs̱māniyye,* vol. 4, İstānbūl s.a., 570-71; Vasiles Dēmētriades, *Topographia tēs Thessalonikēs kata tēn epochē tēs Tourkokratias, 1430-1912,* Thessalonikē 1983, 359-60.

38 Ankara Millî Ktp., MaŞS 231: 1-3. The ex *şeykh el-islām* in question was Ḥamīdī-zāde Muṣṭafā Efendi.

hanced the status of founder and foundation alike. That foundations of this kind were an important element in urbanizing members of a local elite I add just for the sake of completeness.

Conclusion: An Early End of a Normal Development?

In the light of these observations, the *sened-i ittifāḳ,* an agreement signed 1808 between a militarily and politically weakened Maḥmūd II and powerful *aʿyān*s from the central Ottoman lands[39] appears only as a logical consequence of the overall social situation I have just sketched. The notables in the process match their contemporaries in the Arab provinces with regard to power[40] and social standing. (Muḥammad ʿAlī of Egypt, who did not participate in the agreement, should be considered as a special case, of course.) The sultan and the most prominent provincial strongmen guaranteed each other's standing and mutual assistance with the aim to cooperate and reinvigorate Ottoman military strength.

The content of the document does little more than to formalize and systematize a situation as it had prevailed also in the Syrian parts of the empire more or less throughout the eighteenth century. The step towards a formal, mutual understanding is an important breach with time-honored (indeed, centuries old) state practice. The stipulations themselves were far from revolutionary.

As is well known, Maḥmūd II used the relatively stabile international situation after the peace of Bucharest in 1812 to curb the influence of the notables without officially renouncing the *sened-i ittifāḳ.* The process of dismantling the power of the most powerful *aʿyān* and of curtailing that of one of the lesser ones still waits for its historian. Nevertheless, the removal of the *aʿyān*s from power is seen as one of the two preconditions for the centralizing reforms associated with the *Gül-khāne Khaṭṭ-i Şerīf* of 1839 (the other one is the bloody annihilation of the janissary corps in 1826).[41]

---

39 Text: Aḥmed Cevdet, *Taʾrīkh-i Cevdet: Tertīb-i Cedīd,* 2nd ed., Der Seʿādet, 1309, vol. 9, 278-82. Analysis: Halil İnalcık, "Sened-i İttifak ve Gülhane Hatt-ı Hümâyûnu", in: *Osmanlı İmparatorluğu: Toplum ve Ekonomi Üzerinde Arşiv Çalışmaları, İncelemeler,* İstanbul 1993, 343-58, N.B. pp. 344-50 (first published 1964).

40 Cevdet, *Taʾrīkh,* 9: 5, calls them "*mülūk-ı ṭevāʾif ṭarzında istiḳlāl üzere ḥükūmet edenler*" and compares them by that with the Islamic rulers of the middle age who were only nominally subjects of the caliph. The three representatives of the notables signing the agreement were Ḳara-ʿOsmān-zāde ʿÖmer from Manisa, Sīrozī İsmāʿīl from Thrace, and Cabbār-zāde Süleymān from Central Anatolia.

41 In the most recent state-of-the-art handbook treating the political history of the time, Erik J. Zürcher regards the "subjugation of the *ayan*" as the first stage of conscious prepara-

If there was something like a *sonderweg* of the Ottoman core territories, was it then a product of early nineteenth century developments? The answer seems to be "yes", meaning that the *Tanẓīmāt* succeeded only in those regions of the empire more accessible to the central administration.

There is, however, still more than sufficient room for doubt. The *Tanẓīmāt* integrated local notables (both Muslim and Non-Muslim) in regional and local administration. The institution created to this end was that of *meclis*. The *mecālis* were councils of officials appointed by the central administration and local notables elected by the populace. They existed on local, district, and provincial level in a fairly uniform way all over the empire – as far as one can judge, because very little internal paperwork of any of these councils seems to have survived. Our documentation is once more incomplete and uneven.

It is striking that those scholars concerned with the central lands treat the *mecālis* mostly in terms of composition, efficiency, and control executed by the central administration,[42] whereas those specializing on Greater Syria emphasize the options offered by these institutions to the notables: cooperation, obstruction, opposition, infighting.[43]

For the time being, it seems to be premature to draw any final conclusions. All too obvious are the traces the rather recent formation of nation-states has left on the different branches of Ottoman historiography. On the other hand, the diversity of an empire is not reducible to one historiographic feature. There was authentic diversity within Ottoman boundaries, even at the time they were shrinking and while the great transformations of the 19th century led to more uniformity than there had been before.

To my eye, it is time to address the problem of regional difference in a direct way. Studies in this direction may also help to elucidate the degree to which historians have allowed their view of the modern world to shape their treatment of the preceding period.

---

tions for large-scale reforms and the suppression of the janissaries as the "turning point". See his *Turkey: A Modern History,* London, New York 1993, 33, 41 respectively.

42 Ortaylı, *Yerel Yönetim Geleneği,* index; Stanford J. Shaw, "Local Administration in the Tanzimat," in *150. Yılında Tanzimat,* ed. Hakkı Dursun Yıldız, Ankara 1992, 33-49; Thomas Scheben, *Verwaltungsreformen in der frühen Tanzimatzeit: Gesetze, Maßnahmen, Auswirkungen; Von der Verkündigung des Ediktes von Gülhane 1839 bis zum Ausbruch des Krimkrieges 1853,* Frankfurt a.M. et al. 1991, 119-130; Hans Jürgen Kornrumpf, "Zur Rolle des Osmanischen *Meclis* im Reformzeitalter," *Südost-Forschungen* 34 (1975), 241-46.

43 Examples: Schatkowski-Schilcher, *Families in Politics,* 53-56; Doumani, *Rediscovering Palestine,* 219-22.

As somebody who is working on the core area of the empire, I cannot help feeling that we may have seriously underestimated the continuity between the eighteenth and the nineteenth century, and, consequently, the impact of local elites in nineteenth century, making exceptions only for places such as İzmir and Salonica. Here non-muslim groups with a quite different inner organization and social structure would, to an extent, assume the role urban notables played elsewhere. It is Salonica about which Meropi Anastassiadou writes that its transformation was the result of a combination of state efforts at centralization with foreign capital and private enterprise.[44] This is a picture in a way not too different from that of the Arab cities.

But Doumani has shown in his study on Nablus that integration with world-markets was no precondition for the development of a self-conscious, economically and culturally successful elite: Soap from Nablus rarely reached Paris boudoirs. Conversely, the astonishing degree of dedicated solidarity and organized political will demonstrated in Anatolia throughout the War of Independence (1919-23) could be understood better in this framework: maybe their historical roots can be unearthed more fully in a approach more sensitive towards the rôle of local notables in the *Tanẓīmāt* time.

The emergence of nation-states out of the Ottoman Empire was a conflictual, bloody, and traumatic experience. As one of the many consequences, we are confronted with the effects of mutual historiographic otherization between different parts of the empire. Clearly, only an all-Ottoman perspective can help us to achieve a more accurate picture of the past diversity but also the shared history of the region that was once, actually not very long ago, called the Ottoman Empire.

---

44 Meropi Anastassiadou, *Salonique, 1830-1912: Une ville ottomane à l'âge des réformes,* Leiden et al. 1997, 422-23.

IMAGES OF IMAGINED WORLDS

Self-image and Worldview in Late Ottoman Wall Paintings of Damascus

STEFAN WEBER

> Concerning the clothes of state officials, they dress in the European style: tight trousers, a *jākīt*, and upon it a coat... On their heads they wear the red *ṭarbūsh*... And when they put on perfume and walk in the *sūqs*, they have a special way to stroll. When one of them starts to talk with somebody he puffs out his chest and speaks from the corner of his mouth with a special intonation to show that he belongs among the high officials. And when you ask one of them, or one of his friends or relatives, where he works, they will answer arrogantly and full of pride: 'In the Saray'. Usually they use the word *Efendī* or *Bek*... which they add to their real names.[1]

Clothes, titles, and behavior in late Ottoman Damascus, as elsewhere, were signs to distinguish oneself and to present to the public a certain self-image. This image, a reflection of fashion, a custom, a self-definition, or merely a sign of social differentiation, required a medium to bear its symbols. Symbols – like the *ṭarbūsh* (fez) were comprehensible in public life, and they were well understood by Aḥmad Ḥilmī al-ʿAllāf, who wrote the above quoted words about Ottoman officials in Damascus some two decades

I would like to thank Friederike Stolleis, Elisabeth Kendall, and Inci Kuyulu for their suggestions on material and literature. Michael Provence I have to thank for his patient help on the English text and Marianne Boqvist for her critical reading. This material is part of a survey on Ottoman architecture in Damascus, which is financed by the Deutsche Forschungsgemeinschaft (DFG) and the Deutsches Archäologisches Institut (DAI). The project is located at the DAI in Damascus and is supported by the Syrian Service of Antiquities. I would like to express my thanks to these institutions. A photographic documentation of several hundred houses and public buildings of the survey (including the here mentioned wall-paintings) is available in the photographic archive at the Deutsches Archäologisches Institut - Damascus. For a more indepth study of nineteenth-century Damascus, see Stefan Weber, *Zeugnisse kulturellen Wandels: Stadt, Architektur und Gesellschaft des spätosmanischen Damaskus im Umbruch (1808-1918), (Berlin, Ph.D. thesis, 2001).*

1 Aḥmad Ḥilmī al-ʿAllāf, *Dimashq fī Maṭlaʿ al-Qarn al-ʿIshrīn*, Damascus, 1976, 30-31

after the end of Ottoman rule. His description fits an Efendī of the Qabbānī Family, who had himself painted on the back wall of the *īwān* in the courtyard of his house in the city quarter of Mi'dhanat al-Shaḥm (XIII/2-351)[2] (fig. 1). The object of the portrait may have been Adīb Bek al-Qabbānī (d. 1333/1915)[3], who was *muftī* of the Ottoman army. Whoever it was, he placed his image in the most prominent spot in his house; where guests were received and the family sat during warm summer nights. The medium for distinguishing himself explicitly as an Ottoman official was architectural decoration.

I will argue in this article, that architecture by itself, and especially decorations are an important source for historical research. I concentrate here on wall-paintings in late Ottoman Damascus. Wall-paintings are reflections of the world their patrons were living in and thus bear several layers of information about him and his world. But one can use wall-paintings as a source for historical research only in addition to other sources. Wall-paintings do not represent all of society but, just as written material, they express aspects of society. They bear not only information about the person who commissioned the painting, but to a certain degree about its viewer as well. As we noticed with Adīb Bek al-Qabbānī and as we will notice later in several other examples, the motives behind these images were carefully chosen. As in the contribution of Bodenstein and Gonnella, an understanding of principles of shaping private worlds will illuminate some aspects of every day life of Ottoman subjects beyond theories of political thought. Houses are mirrors of the owners' worlds. As Bourdieu expresses in a different context, and with a much more structuralist approach than is applied here: "The house, a microcosm organized by the same oppositions and homologies that order the whole universe, stands in a relation of homology to the rest of the universe."[4]

---

2 For identification of every building the exact registry-number of the site will be given between brackets.

3 For Adīb al-Qabbānī see: Muḥammad Āl Taqqī al-Dīn al-Ḥuṣnī, *Kitāb Muntakhabāt al-Tawārīkh li-Dimashq*, ed. by Kamāl al-Ṣalībī, 3 vols., Beirut 1979 (First edition Damascus 1927-1934), 913; Muḥammad Jamīl al-Shaṭṭī, *Aʿyān Dimashq fī l-Qarn al-Thālith ʿAshar wa-Niṣf al-Qarn al-Rābiʿ ʿAshar,* Damascus 1994, 429. A certain Adīb Bek al-Qabbānī owned 1323/1905 the well known Café al-Junayna al-Kubrā next to the Marja-square. MWT S1275/W126 (1323/1905). The Syrian National Archives (Markaz al-Wathā'iq al-Tārīkhiyya) will be abbreviated as MWT, S for *sijill* and W for *wathīqa*. The Café al-Junayna al-Kubrā is mentioned in some records of 1894, 1896 direct south-east of the Sūq ʿAlī Pasha. MWT S1008/W149 (1312/1894); S1038/W128 (1314/1896).

4 Pierre Bourdieu, *The Logic of Practice*, Appendix: "The Kabyle House or the World Reversed," Oxford 1992, 227.

Damascus: a city in transition

Wall-paintings were a popular decoration technique in Damascus at the turn of the century, but they were only a very small aspect of a changing urban landscape. During the course of the second half of the nineteenth century and the beginning of the twentieth century, the city of Damascus witnessed, parallel to many other Ottoman cities, far reaching changes in the urban texture. Many streets in the old town *intra* and *extra muros* were enlarged and various streets were laid out around the city. Corresponding to the enormous demographic growth (see fig. A)[5] new urban areas were settled and whole quarters of the city founded (like Muhājirīn, ʿAfīf, ʿArnūs, Shuhadā, Ḥijāz, Barāmka and Qaṣāʿ).

Fig. A: Growth of population in Damascus between 1877 and 1899.

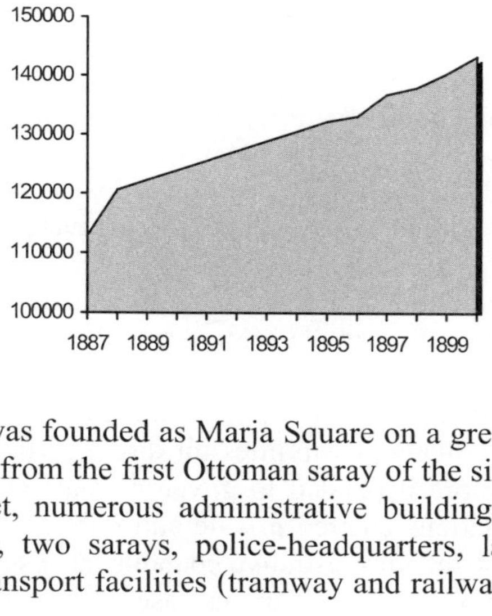

A new public center was founded as Marja Square on a green field outside the city walls. Not far from the first Ottoman saray of the sixteenth century on Darwīshiyya Street, numerous administrative buildings, (such as the municipality building, two sarays, police-headquarters, law court etc.), hotels, and modern transport facilities (tramway and railways) were built.[6]

---

5 These numbers are taken from the yearbook of the Ottoman Province of Syria (Sūriyye Vilāyetiniñ Sāl-nāmesi), that will be abbreviated: Sālnāme [volume] (year *hijrī* / year *mīlādī*) page. See for this figure: Sālnāme [20](1305/1887-88) 137; [21](1306/1888-89) 150; [27](1312-13/1895-96) 250; [29](1315/1897-98) 324; [30](1316/1898-99) 332; [31](1317/1899-1900) 368; [32](1318/1900-01) 364 f. This is not the total population (only adults?) and one has to calculate ca. 20% in addition to the official numbers.

6 See for the Marja Square: Stefan Weber, "Der Marğa-Platz in Damaskus – Die Entstehung eines modernen Stadtzentrums unter den Osmanen als Ausdruck strukturellen Wandels (1808-1918)," *Damaszener Mitteilungen*, 10 (1998), 291-344, Taf. 77-88, and the English summary, Weber, "Ottoman Damascus of the nineteenth century, Artistic and urban development as an expression of changing times," in *Art Turc / Turkish Art, 10th International Congress of Turkish Art*; Genève 1999, 732 ff. For a summery of

Public places like parks, coffeehouses and theatres were located there and provided a space for increasingly lively public life and discussion. In addition, the bazaar (*sūq*) was totally remodelled in the last decades of the nineteenth and the beginning of the twentieth centuries. Starting east of the Marja Square, many new or remodelled *sūqs* were added to the mercantile center inside the walls. Modernized wide bazaar-streets, like the famous Sūq al-Ḥamīdiyya, ran through the commercial heart of the city. The return of Ottoman central power through its enlarged facilities of administration, transportation (new streets, steam boats, and later on railways) and communication (telegraph) had an overwhelming impact on Damascus. Following the efforts of Maḥmūd II (1808-1839) and the celebrated ministers and viziers of the *Tanẓīmāt* period (1839-1876), the urban texture of the city changed rapidly during the decades after the provincial reforms in 1864 until the end of Ottoman rule in Damascus in 1918. The municipality, a modern urban institution, consisting of elected members of the public, was responsible for urban planning, which was based on new principles. Many public buildings, for example some 70 schools, 8 hospitals and sanatoria, many bazaar streets (*sūqs*), railway stations, electric lights, central water supply, a tramway system and dozens of streets, were initiated by the Ottoman administrative councils, by private individuals and in some cases by foreigners.

The enlarged Ottoman bureaucracy provided opportunities for many of Damascenes. The return of the central state did not involve a loss of power for urban notables. Damascene notables were still powerful, but as government officials they now became an integrated part of the political system, which gave many possibilities for direct participation but made them as well much more depended to governmental set of laws. At the same time state regulations entered private and public life in a way they never had before.[7] Several administrative councils gave space for participation in local and state politics as the famous cases of ʿIzzat Pasha al-ʿĀbid (1850-1924) from Damascus or Abū l-Hudā al-Ṣayyādī (1849-1909) from Aleppo illustrate. The potential for integration was enormous and the construction of a new sense of Ottoman citizenship must have had, judging from my work on material culture, a strong impact on the society. This does not

---

developments, see D. Sack, "The Historic Fabric of Damascus and its Changes in the nineteenth and at the Beginning of the twentieth Century," in *The Syrian Land, Processes of Integration and Fragmentation in Bilād al-Shām from the eighteenth to the twentieth Century*, eds. T. Philipp and B. Schaebler, Stuttgart 1998, 185-202.

7 For the integration of societies into a modern state see in another context: Eugen Weber, *Peasants into Frenchman: The Modernization of Rural France, 1870-1914*, Stanford 1976.

Fig. 1: Qabbānī-house (today al-Qaṣṣāṣ, XIII/2- 351), back wall of the *īwān*, detail.

Fig. 2: Mīdānī-house (XXVIII-9), lacquer paintings (*ʿajamī*) dated 1217/1802.

Fig. 3: Niẓām / Khazīna-Kātibī-house, northern *qāʿa*.

Fig. 4: Niẓām / Khazīna-Kātibī-house, southern *qāʿa*, detail.

Fig. 5: Niẓām / Khazīna-Kātibī-house, northern *qāʿa*, detail.

Fig. 6: Atik Valide Camii Istanbul sultan's lounge (*hünkâr mahfeli*).

Fig. 7: Jabrī / Mujallid-house (IX-252), northern *qāʿa*, view of Istanbul.

Fig. 8: Qanbāzū-house (XVIII/2-457), northern *qāʿa*, view of Istanbul.

Fig. 9: Dawajī / Ṣafadī-house (IX-232), Maḍāfa, detail.

mean, that political criticism was excluded or loyalty to the state guaranteed. But, as I will argue in this article, it promoted identification with the Ottoman culture realm.

This reorganization of an entire Arab metropolis, its urban fabric, its architecture and a large part of its social organization, is visible in its most private aspect of urban architecture: houses. First, one has to realize just how often houses were rebuilt in the course of the second half of the nineteenth century and the early twentieth century. More than three quarters of the 600 houses investigated during my survey were substantially rebuilt or entirely new in this period. This observation corresponds to official numbers. The Sālnāme counted 16.832 houses in Damascus in 1900. Three decades earlier, in 1871, only 14.669 dwellings were counted. This suggests an increase of 14,75 % in only 29 years.[8] But not only new residences were built (principally because of the demographic pressure). Reconstructions (mainly because of the very unsteady wood-mud construction) were also numerous. The Sālnāme shows 40 new houses erected and 417 houses rebuilt in the year of 1895. One year later, in 1896, 35 houses were built and 527 houses reconstructed. This means that per year around three percent of the entirely domestic architecture in Damascus underwent reconstruction.[9] The number of new and renewed houses at the beginning of the twentieth century have been similarly high. Unfortunately we do not have any official numbers for the last 18 years of Ottoman rule in Damascus but the new city quarters give evidence for consistently strong building activities.

The successful search for a new style

A new time calls for a new style and the continuous building projects (of new buildings or of reconstruction) allowed an integration of new ideas. During this enormous 'reshaping' of the city, it was possible to rebuild in the latest fashion and to pick up new techniques of construction and decoration.

There were – to simplify – two main lines of a 'modern Ottoman' house form in Damascus. First the traditional, local kind of courtyard-house was adjusted to recent principles of architectural design. They show

---

8 See: Sālnāme [3](1288/1871-72) 129; [32](1318/1900-01) 376. Corresponding Qasāṭilī gives for 1288/1871 14696 houses, contrasting to Sāmī Bek, who mentions in 1890 only 14720 houses. See Nuʿmān Qasāṭilī, *al-Rawḍa al-Ghannā fī Dimashq al-Fayḥā*, Beirut 1982 (first published 1879) 97; ʿAbd ar-Raḥmān Sāmī Bek, *al-Qawl al-Ḥaqq fī Bayrūt wa-Dimashq*, Beirut, 1981, 90.

9 See: Sālnāme [27](1312-13/1895-96) 264; [28](1313-14/1896-97) 243 f.

a clear tendency towards a more regular and geometrical layout of the ground plan and of the façades that are facing the courtyard. Instead of the old-fashioned reception rooms (*qāʿa*), now long halls (*ṣāliya*) were built to provide the appropriate place to receive guests. The house of a branch of the Quwatlī family in the ʿAmāra quarter (XIII/2-412) from around 1870 is a good example (fig. B).

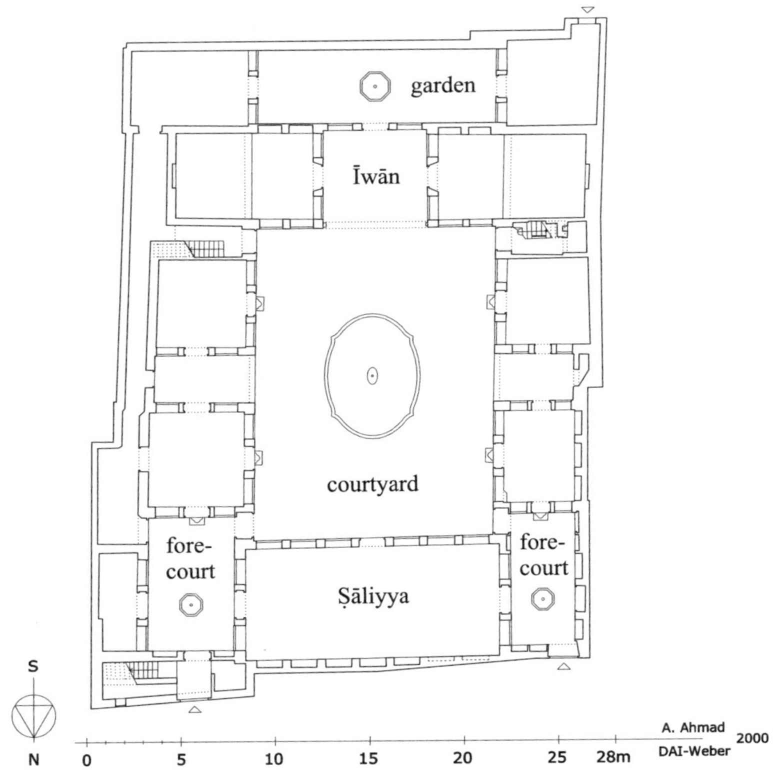

Fig. B: Quwatlī-house (XIII/2-412), ground-floor.

At the same time traditional techniques of decoration such as stone carving filled by color-pastes or wall coverings of wooden panels in lacquer relief work (*ʿajamī*) were replaced by stone and wood carving and stucco-work in the style of Ottoman baroque and wall-paintings. The new emphasis on façades with multiple windows looking over the street, gave the quarters a totally different appearance. This is a characteristic feature for the second house form as well, which was a completely new import to Damascus. The new house organization that appears around 1860 for the first time in Damascus leans heavily on larger houses (*konak*) as we know them from Anatolia and Istanbul.[10]

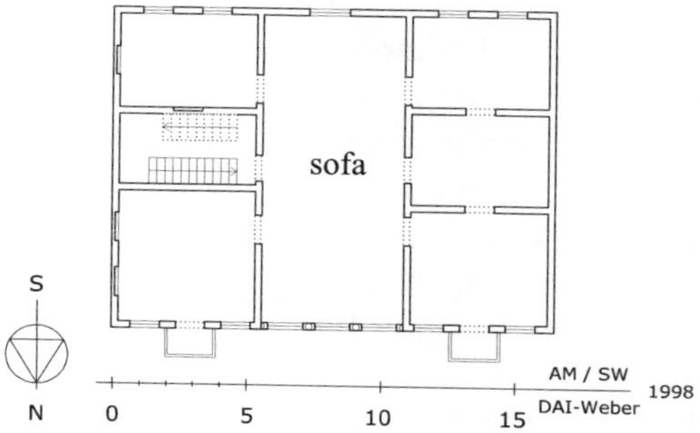

Fig. C: House Ṣāliḥ Khālid al-Jabrī (XXIV/4-814), first floor.

The main feature of the *konak*, besides its elaborate façades, is the central-hall (*sofa*), which as main living room gives access to the other rooms around it (fig. C). One can observe in Damascus the same phenomena as all over the empire. From the 1860s onwards the *konaks* with *sofas* bestow nearly everywhere the space for a modern Ottoman way of housing.[11] One has to explain why this 'global Ottoman' change in domestic architecture took place. This phenomenon was not triggered by any law or public decree.[12] The central-hall layout was a late Ottoman design that marks a modern house to distinguish it from the old and the traditional. Perhaps some *konaks* of high officials – the saray or Ottoman public buildings – originally spread this architectural fashion. But 'trend-setters' cannot be the only reason for this trend. To understand late Ottoman architecture as a reflection of a changing society we have to abandon the concept of Otto-

10 Because of this I call the new model the '*konak*-style', which applies as well for public buildings. For the '*konak*-style' in Damascus, see Weber, "Der Marğa-Platz," 317 ff., and Weber, *Ottoman Damascus*, 733 ff.

11 See the contributions of Yenişehirlioğlu, Mollenhauer and, as 'the exception to prove the rule', Bodenstein.

12 The building code (Ebniye Nizâmnameleri / Qānūn al-Abniyya wa-Qarār al-Istimlāk) for all provinces was issued first in 1864 and was replaced by a new one in 1299/1882. It does not mention the middle-hall. See Amīn ʿAbd al-Nūr, *Tarjama wa-Sharkh Qānūn al-Abniyya wa-Qarār al-Istimlāk*, Beirut 1896.

man society changing only due to Ottoman reform decrees, issued by high officials. Societies in the provinces of the Ottoman Empire were changing and not only being changed. The people of Damascus were searching for a new architectural expression of their experience of life and new principles of shaping private space. Changing private architecture was a clear sign of a new way of life. Throughout the empire a modern Ottoman style developed as an answer to what Çelik called "the search for a style".[13] The *sofa* can be seen as an architectural homology to the Fez.

Wall-paintings played an important role in the search for a new modern Ottoman style starting in the capital in the eighteenth century. Istanbul became, as never before, the model and ideal of 'good taste' in the nineteenth century. Techniques and patterns of embellishment were taken from Istanbul prototypes. The first dated examples were painted in 1193/1779 in the Harem of the Topkapı Sarayı.[14] Judging from the background of portraits of the Sultans, who were sketched in their palaces, or from the paintings in the Kavafyan Kiosk, which was built in the 1750's, wall-paintings in baroque style were already common in the middle of the eighteenth century.[15] The new style of decoration soon spread in the capital and became the most pervasive technique for interior decoration throughout the century.[16] The model of the capital became very popular in the provinces

13 Zeynep Çelik, *The Remaking of Istanbul. Portrait of an Ottoman City at the Beginning of the Nineteenth Century*, Seattle 1986, 126 ff.

14 See for early wall-paintings in the Topkapı Sarayı: Günsel Renda, *Batılılaşma Döneminde Türk Resim Sanatı, 1700-1850*, Ankara 1977, 80 ff., 110, 231 ff.; G. Renda, "Westernisms in Ottoman Art: Wall Paintings in the nineteenth Century Houses," in *The Ottoman House, Papers from the Amasya Symposium, 24-27 September 1996*, eds. St. Ireland, W. Bechhoefer, Ankara 1998, 103, tab. 13.1,2.; Inci Kuyulu, "Wall Paintings from Different Cultures in Anatolia", *Electronic Journal of Oriental Studies*, III, No. 2,1-27 (http://www.let.uu.nl/oosters/EJOS/EJOS-III.2.html). Unfortunately a lot of wall-paintings here were removed during restoration works in the name of stylistic purification.

15 For Sultan-portraits see: Renda, *Türk Resim*, 61, Fig. 30 and for the Kavafyan Kiosk: N. Atasoy, "I. Sultan Mahmud Devrinden bir Abide Ev," *Sanat Tarihi Yıllığı*, 6, (1974-75) 23-43.

16 Numerous examples of palaces and Yalıs in Istanbul are given by: Renda, *Türk Resim*, 79-123, 236 f.; Renda, *Westernisms*, 105. For the wall-paintings in some late Ottoman palaces see: Şule Yum, "Son Dönem Osmanlı Saray Yapılarındaki bazı Tasvirler üzerine Gözlemler," in 9th *International Congress of Turkish Art*, Istanbul 1991, 543-552; Semra Öner, "Tanzimat sonrası Osmanlı Saray Çevresinde Resim Sanatı," in *Milli Saraylar* 1992, ed. by TBMM Milli Saraylar Daire Başkanlığı, Ankara 1992, 76. Some historical photographs with wall-paintings are in the excellent photographic archive of the Deutsches Archäologisches Institut – Istanbul: Yıldız, Seraskeriye reception-hall (Sébah-Joaillier 1090), Beylerbey (DAIR19628). For wall-paintings in Yalıs, see

of the empire. One of the first known and dated houses with wall-paintings outside the capital dates back to 1211/1796. It is the Hadımoğlu Konağı in Bayramiç near Çanakkale in the west of the empire. In the east, in Yozgat, the first known example appeared in 1215/1800-01.[17] The most famous among the provincial houses is the Çağır Ağa Konağı in Birgi with its large scale cityscapes of Istanbul and Izmir.[18] As the *sofa*-style houses (central-hall houses) became popular, all over the empire from the east to the west this new style became the favored decoration. Just as the *sofa* provided a house with a certain late Ottoman character in Greece or in Syria, wall-paintings became the modern Ottoman way of interior design. In Anatolia or the Balkans, houses were more or less decorated in the same manner as in Damascus and Cairo.[19] This tendency towards uniformization" of Ottoman domestic architecture was a very new phenomenon in the

---

Hakki Sedad Eldem, *Köçeoğlu Yalısı Bebek,* Istanbul 1977, 46; Emel Esin: *Sa'dullah Paşa Yalısı – The Yalı (Sea-Side Mansion) of Sa'dullah Paşa*, Istanbul 1977. M. D'Ohsson, *Tableau général de l'Empire Othoman*, Paris 1787-1820, 2nd Vol., Table 83.

17 See: Rüçhan Arık, *Batılılaçma Dönemi Tasvir Sanatı*, Ankara 1976, 27 ff., 40 ff. For further examples see: Renda, *Westernisms*, 104; G. Renda, T. Erol and others, *A History of Turkish Painting*, Seattle, Washington 1988, Fig. 72.

18 See for the Çağır Ağa Konağı: S. E. Eldem and F. Akozan and others, *Birgi, Çağır Ağa Konağı*, Istanbul 1977, 30 f. Inci Kuyulu, "İzmir ve Çevresindeki bir Grup Duvar Resminin İncelenmesi," in *Uluslararası İzmir Sempozyumu*, Izmir 1998, 74 f., figs. 62-64. Further one can find this *konak* in Doğan Kuban, *The Turkish Hayat House*, Istanbul 1995, 59 f.; Godfrey Goodwin, *A History of Ottoman Architecture*, Oxford 1971, 433 f.; Reha Günay, *Türk Ev Geleneği ve Safranbolu Evleri*, Istanbul 1998, 60.

19 For the Şemaki-house in Yenişehir (dated 1836) see: Rüçhan Arık, "Resimli Türk Evlerinden İki Örnek," *Sanat Dünyamız* (May 1975) 15; Johannes Cramer, "Istanbul auf Wandbildern türkischer Wohnhäuser des 19. Jahrhunderts," *Istanbuler Mitteilungen*, 39, (1989), 99. For Izmir, see Inci Kuyulu, *İzmir ve Çevresindeki.* For wall-paintings in Bergama: Serhat Alanyalı, "The Traditional Architecture and Structure of 19th Century Bergama," *Istanbuler Mitteilungen*, 44 (1994), Taf. 72/11. For Safranbolu: Reha Günay, *Geleneksel Safranbolu Evleri ve Oluşumu*, Ankara 1981, Fig. 315; and Günay, *Türk Ev Geleneği*, 336 ff. Numerous examples in Lebanon are given by Claire Paget, *Murs et plafonds peints, Liban XIXe Siècle*, Beirut 1998. In Cairo some wall paintings in palaces and houses remained. From a palace of Muḥammad ʿAlī Renda published one example: Renda, *Westernisms*, pl. 13.9. But as well some older houses do have later added wall-paintings, like the house of ʿAlī Katkhudā: B. Maury, A. Raymond, J. Revault, and M. Zakariya, *Palais et Maisons du Caire. II Eoque Ottomane (XVIe - XVIIIe siècles)*, Paris 1983, 247 ff., fig. 121-22. For wall-paintings of the late 18th century in the Mamluk palace of Qāyt-Bāy: B. Maury, J.-C. Garcin, J. Revault, M. Zakariya, *Palais et Maisons du Caire. I Epoque Mamelouke (XIIIe - XVIe siècles)*, Paris 1982, 207 ff., fig.73. For examples on the Balkans see: Arık, *Tasvir Sanatı* 121 f.; Cramer, *Istanbul auf Wandbildern*, 99 f.; Renda, *Türk Resim*, 165 ff., Catalog-No. 63-71; Renda, *Westernisms*, 104.

late nineteenth century. Of course regional differences were often still very striking and houses continued to differ from place to place. However, techniques and motifs of decoration, the layout and design of rooms, and the techniques and forms of construction became more similar all over the empire than they had been before. New *konak*-style houses in Damascus (on Ṣāliḥiyya Street, for example) are not always easy to distinguish from such examples in Bursa, Plovdiv or Melnik.[20]

The traditional courtyard-houses in Damascus of the eighteenth century were unique in layout and decoration. Traditional techniques of stone-carvings filled by color-pastes or wooden wall coverings of lacquer-work (*ʿajamī*) were more or less specific to Syria or even Damascus where they seem to have had a greater abundance than any other city of the empire. But they disappeared totally during the course of the nineteenth century and were replaced by wall-paintings at the same time as in all other major towns of the empire.

Wall-paintings in Damascus

It is near impossible to trace the development of wall paintings in Damascus. Architectural motifs done in the traditional lacquer-paintings (*ʿajamī*) on wood, like in the Mīdānī-house (XXVIII-9) dated 1217/1802, show a strong resemblance to those paintings that appeared shortly after in cornice-moldings of ceilings or were painted on plaster (fig. 2). Small-scale pictures in cartouches of the *ʿajamī*-paneling appeared in Damascus around 1770 and had already changed the treatment of perspective and style in the course of the eighteenth century. But it is not known when exactly they were first painted on a large scale on the upper part of a wall, which had traditionally remained undecorated. Unfortunately only very few of these paintings are datable and only a small number of such paintings have been discovered. Fifty-eight houses of the 600 surveyed dwellings during this research (out of several thousand still existing houses) provide noteworthy pictures on a larger scale. Many more have paintings on ceilings. The first known dated example belongs to the Ṣārjī-house (IX-43) from 1235/1819-20. Regrettably we do not have any information about the owner.

---

20 See for such houses in the Balkans: Nur Akın, *Balkanlarda Osmanlı Dönemi Konutları*, Istanbul 2001; Bagra Georgieva (and others), *The Old Bulgarian House. Interior, Architecture, Design, and Furnishings*, Sofia 1980; and G. Ryas (ed.), *Architecture traditionelle des pays balkaniques*, Athens 1993. For similar houses in Bursa: Leman Tomsu, *Bursa Evleri*, Istanbul 1950; and Emte Madran (ed.), *Bursa Kale Sokak bir fotogrametrik belgeleme*, Ankara 1985.

This is also true for another early dated example (1238/1822-23) in the north-west room of the house that became known in the seventies of the nineteenth century as the Quwatlī-house (XVIII/2-408) in the Naqqāshīn Quarter.

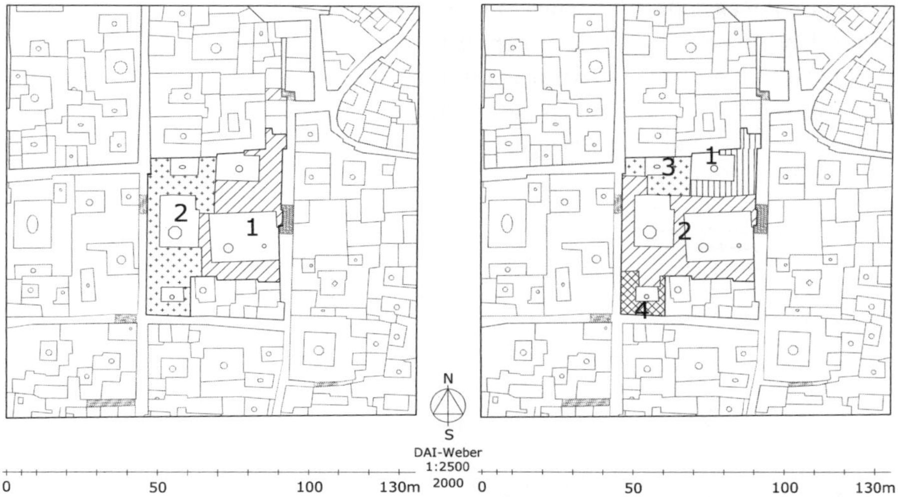

Fig. D: Left: Niẓām-house in 1840; (1) houses of ʿAlī Khazīna-Kātibī (XIII/2-334) and (2) Nuṣūḥ Pasha al-ʿAẓm (XIII/2-314, 315; western part of XIII/2-313).
Right: Niẓām-house, situation after 1927; houses (1) al-Ṣawwān (XIII/2-334 north), (2) Niẓām (XIII/2-314, 334 south), (3) Jawwād and Sulaymān Bek al-ʿAẓm (XIII/2-315); (4) al-Ḥalalī (XIII/2-313 west).

The wall-paintings of the famous Niẓām-house (fig. D, E, 3, 4, 5) are also datable by the history of the building. Through court records we have been able to reconstruct the original ownership of this house.[21] The southern part of the building, which is open to the public today, brought two family-courtyards

---

21 From the private collection of court records of the Dahhān family. I would like to thank the family for letting me study this material. What is today the Niẓām house was constituted in the following stages: In 1334/1916 and 1335/1917 Kāmil and Muḥammad ʿAlī Niẓām rented the southern courtyard of the eastern house (of ʿAlī Āghā Khazīna-Kātibī) and bought in 1927 the southern courtyard of the western house (of Nuṣūḥ Pasha al-ʿAẓm) as well and connected both to the western small *īwān* of the eastern house.

For studies of this house to date, see Irène Laberyie, "Quelques réflexions à propos de la maison Nizam à Damas," in *L'habitat traditionnel dans les pays musulmans autour de la Méditerranée*, ed. Groupe de recherches et d'études sur le Proche-Orient, 3 vols., Cairo 1990, vol. 3, 831-847; Marwān Musilmānī, "al-Buyūt al-Dimashkiyya," al-Qarn 18-19, Damascus 1979, 101-114. A. Rouanet and D. Piponnier, "Etude iconographique et technique d'un Ensemble décoratif: La Maison Niẓām à Damas," *Bulletin D'Etudes Orientales*, 37-38 (1985-86), 127-161; D. Sack, *Damaskus, Entwicklung und Strukturen einer orientalisch-islamischen Stadt*, Mainz 1989, 118; Kamil Sinjab, *Das arabische Wohnhaus des 17. bis 19. Jahrhunderts in Syrien*, Aachen 1965, 48, 154, fig. 46 f.

(*dār al-juwwānī*) of different houses together. The western house was rebuilt in the 60s of the eighteenth century by Nuṣūḥ Pasha al-ʿAẓm (d. 1808), who was exiled at the end of that century to Egypt and became governor there. The house on the eastern side, which is more central to this study, belonged to ʿAlī Āghā Khazīna-Kātibī. Under Ibrāhīm Pasha he became general treasurer for Syria. But he was suspected of conspiracy with the Ottomans, who were on their way back to Syria and was executed in 1255/1839. Shortly before his death ʿAlī Āghā endowed his house as a *waqf* for the Umayyad mosque.

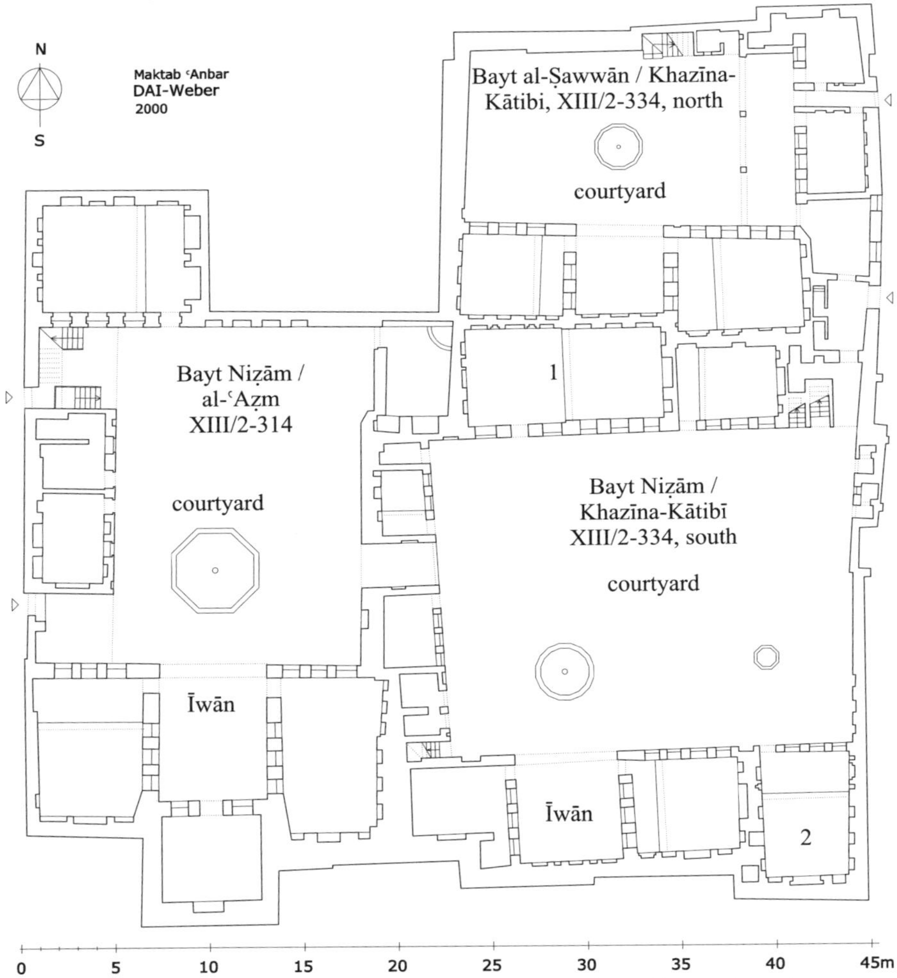

Fig. E: Niẓām-house, today situation (houses al-Ṣawwān XIII/2-334 north, and al-Niẓām XIII/2-314, 334 south). Wall-paintings in northern *qāʿa* (1) and the southern *qāʿat al-ʿaynab* (2).

Addisson observed reconstruction work during his visit to the house of ʿAlī Āghā Khazīna-Kātibī in 1834. This was at a time when ʿAlī Āghā was at the top of his career as the treasurer of Bilād al-Shām under Ibrāhīm Pasha.[22] The decoration of two rooms made in those years is of great importance for our discussion (compare fig. E, northern *qāʿa*, 1, and *qāʿat al-ʿaynab,* 2). They were decorated in a new fashion that Porter described two decades later as follows (fig. 3):

> The grand salon is a noble room. The floor of the first compartment is of the rarest marbles of every hue. The walls to the height of twenty feet are covered with mosaic in panels, in the centre of each of which is a slab of polished granite, porphyry, or finely veined marble. The upper part of the walls is painted in the Italian style. The style of decoration in this mansion may be called the modern Damascene, the painting of the walls and ceilings being a recent innovation. [23]

Wall-paintings became one of the standard techniques of decoration for Damascene craftsmen and they had spread all over the town no later than the 1840s. We do not have many dated examples, but most of them were painted in the 60s and 70s of the nineteenth century, judging from the architectural style of the houses. In these years after the land reform of 1859, the trauma of the 1860 riots and after the provincial reforms of 1864, many large residences were built that give evidence of a pronounced economic and social upturn of many families. Warner wrote in 1875:

> the walls were decorated with painting, usually landscapes and cities. Money had been freely lavished in these dwellings, and whatever the eastern chisel or brush could do to enrich and ornament them had been done. [24]

One only has to mention the extraordinary richly decorated mansions of al-ʿAnbar (XII/2-297), al-Bārūdī (XXIV/2-593, XXIV/2-653), Līsbūnā (XI/1-

---

22 See: Charles G. Addisson, *Damascus and Palmyra. A Journey to the East*, 2 vols., London 1838, vol. 2, 165 f.

23 J. L. Porter, *Five Years in Damascus*, 2 vols., London 1855, vol. 1, 36. This house, in wich Ibrāhīm Pasha himself first stayed, was often visited during the nineteenth century. See also Mikhāyil Mishāqa, *Murder, Mayhem, Pillage and Plunder. The History of Lebanon in the eighteenth and nineteenth century*, translated by W. M. Thackston, Albany, 1988, 201 and Isabel Burton, *The Inner Life of Syria, Palestine and the Holy Land,* London 1884. It was used in the middle of the nineteenth century as hotel, see: John Murray, *Handbook for Travellers in Syria and Palestine,* edited by J. L. Porter, London 1858, 468.

24 Charles D. Warner, *In the Levant*, Boston 1886, 200 f.

494), al-Quwatlī (XIII/2-412, XVIII/1-100), Shāmiyya (X/2-397), and al-Yūsuf (VII/2-1-654, east) to illustrate this point.

Wall-paintings from the turn of the century clearly differed from their predecessors. European style and techniques became standard. The motifs, now often painted in oil-colors (instead of colors on a base of glue and egg), show much attention detail. In the age of photographs and postcards copies were painted from them. A view of the Süleymaniye Camii in Istanbul at the house of Fawzī al-Qabbānī (XXI/2-986, ca. 1913) is certainly painted by a trained hand after a postcard.[25] The same is true for the European cityscapes in the northern part of the Bārūdī-house (XXIV/2-593, fig. 12), that were painted in 1911 by B. Samra, perhaps from postcards that Fakhrī al-Bārūdī, the owner of the house with whom we will deal later, brought back from his travels through Europe in the same year.

Wall-paintings were not only limited to houses. Many public buildings like shops, mosques, synagogues, and especially public baths were decorated with pictures of railways, ships and landscapes.[26] The question is, how did this new technique become so popular in the nineteenth century, and how did it spread so fast, replacing old decoration techniques and requiring trained artists? It is not easy to answer. One may, with a bit of imagination, envisage how this worked, but concrete information is lacking. Almost nothing is known about the painters. The enormous number of wall-paintings suggests, that not only artists from outside Damascus, but also local crafts-

---

25 The artisan of this views must have been travelling around. He was for sure active in the north of Lebanon near Tripoli as well. Compare style and motifs of paintings in the house of Fawzī al-Qabbānī with the house of Marūn ʿAbūd. See Paget, *Murs et plafonds*, 215 ff.

26 For example the shop (XXI/2-227) in Sūq al-Buzūriyya with a painted ceiling of a Bosphorus-like landscape. Further examples are provided by the bathes al-Darb (XXXVI/1-172), al-Jadīd (XXIV/1-2-370), al-Khayyāṭīn (XXI/2-672), and al-Malik al-Ẓāhir (XVIII/1-100). The dome of the Turba in the Sanjaqdār Mosque (VIII/2-1121) was painted in a baroque manner in 1320/1902-03. In the Jewish quarter the Manshā Synagogue (XI/1-525) and the Raqqī Synagogue (XI/2-203) display wall-paintings. For other parts of the Ottoman Empire (mainly Anatolia) the book of Arık, *Tasvir Sanatı*, nearly exclusively deals with wall-paintings in mosques. Further see R. Bozer, "Kula-Emre Köyünde Resimli bir Cami", *Türkiyemiz*, (Ekim 1987) 15-22; Inci Kuyulu, "Geç Dönem Anadolu Tasvir Sanatından Yeni Bir Örnek: Soma Damgacı Camii", *Arkeoloji-Sanat Tarihi Dergisi*, IV, (1988), 67-78; I. Kuyulu, "Kırkağaç Çiftehanlar Camii", *Arkeoloji-Sanat Tarihi Dergisi*, V, (1990), 103-115; I. Kuyulu, "Bademli Kılcızade Mehmet Ağa Camii (Ödemiş) / İzmir," *Vakıflar Dergisi*, 24, (1994), 147-158; Renda, *Türk Resim*, 126 ff., Catalog-No. 26 ff. For wall paintings on fountains and in churches, see Renda, *Türk Resim*, 116 f; On Synagogues, see Kuyulu, *Wall Paintings*, 22 f, and in Mausoleums, see Renda, *Türk Resim*, 121, 135 f., Catalog-No. 28, 52.

men learned how to paint them. Doubtlessly, they were trained by journeymen on the spot rather than in schools. A school of art and crafts in Damascus was only opened during the First World War by Jamāl Pasha.[27] The often mentioned craft school by Midḥat Pasha, founded in 1296/1879, functioned mainly as an orphanage (*maytam*) and reformatory (*iṣlāḥkhāna*), but arts and crafts were taught as well. Unfortunately we only find among its staff in 1881 one teacher of tailoring, blacksmithing and lithography respectively, but no teacher for painting.[28] Qualified artists probably came from Anatolia and Istanbul to Damascus and trained Syrian craftsmen. In Anatolia only three artisans are known by name and in Istanbul several artists were resident.[29] Information concerning these painters is limited. It seems that, as Hanna showed in Ottoman Cairo, painters and their guilds traveled around as they probably had done throughout history.[30]

In Damascus Vogüé talks about a house painter and a group of Italian plasterers who traveled through the city.[31] I identified only two artists by their signatures. The Ḥammām al-Khayyāṭīn (XXI/2-672) bears an inscription stating that the paintings in the dome were done by Aḥmad al-Sīrawān in 1327/1909. The large-scale view of the Place de la Concorde in the *mābayn* of the house of Fakhrī al-Bārūdī is signed by a certain B. Samra in 1911. But their names alone tell us nothing about their training. So far we cannot make any statement about the artists' background. More informa-

---

27 The school of Jamāl Pasha was called Madrasat al-Ṣanā'iʿ and was lead by the German K. Ströckle in the Missionary School of the Sœurs de Charité (X/3-564, 565, 616). See for this school mainly: Hans von Kiesling, *Damaskus. Altes und Neues aus Syrien*, Leipzig 1919, 80; K. Wulzinger and C. Watzinger, *Damaskus, die islamische Stadt*, Berlin 1924, introduction and K/4-1. Further: Engin D. Akarli, "Abdülhamīd II's Attempt to Integrate Arabs into the Ottoman System", in: Palestine in the Late Ottoman Period, Political, Social and Economic Transformation, ed. by David Kushner, Jerusalem and Leiden 1986, 79; Sack, *Stadt intra muros*, 230, 235; Sack, *Entwicklung und Strukturen*, No. 5.35-5.37.

28 See for this building with further literature: Weber, *Marğa-Platz*, No. 12. For its staff see the reports in the Sālnāme, here: [13](1298/1880-81) 128, see further for example [12](1297/1879-80) 355; [25](1310-11/1893-94) 261; [31](1317/1899-1900) 120; [32](1318/1900-01) 239. For its later usage Politisches Archiv des Auswärtigen Amt (R14035, 21.1.1917). See on the Institution of *iṣlāḥkhāna* in general: Hans-Jürgen Kornrumpf, "Islahhaneler," in *Economie et sociétés dans l'Empire ottoman*, eds. J.-P. Bacqué-Grammont and P. DuMont, Paris 1983, 149-156.

29 See summary: Kuyulu, *Wall Paintings,* 12. Further: Renda, *Westernisms*, 105 f.; Renda, *Türk Resim*, 186 ff.

30 Compare: N. Hanna, *Construction Work in Ottoman Cairo*, Cairo 1984, 57-60.

31 Eugène M. de Vogüé, *Syrie, Palestine, Mont Athos. Voyage aux pays du passé*, Paris 1876, 80.

tion is available about the houses, the owners, and the subjects of the paintings. It is to these that we turn our attention now.

Themes of artistic representation

The Bosphorus

By far the most frequently painted motifs were imagined views of the Bosphorus. All over town one can find hundreds of fanciful images of the straits between Asia and Europe (fig. 4, 7, 13). The sheer number of pictures gives evidence that we are dealing with a very special motif.[32] The Bosphorus was perhaps a kind of symbol of an attitude towards life that is comparable with the Golden Gate Bridge or the skyline of Manhattan today. To share or at least to understand aspects of the spirit behind the pictures of those days, one need not have lived in Istanbul. Most peoples today who put posters of New York in their homes or who relate to the skyline of Manhattan as a symbol for the 'American way of life' have never been to the USA. The Bosphorus was the symbol of Istanbul and thus became a symbol for the 'Ottoman way of life'. Of course, it would have been known all over the empire that during the nineteenth century many new palaces were built on the shores of these straits – to mention only Dolmabahçe, Çirağan, Beylerbey, Küçük Su or Yıldız. The 'sweet waters of Asia', the area around the Güzelsu and Küçüksu rivers next to the Bosphorus became quite a catchword for Ottoman high-life among European travelers. In Ottoman literature, life on the Bosphorus was often celebrated in those days.[33] The famous coffeehouses on the banks of the Barada River in Damascus might have played a similar role. But the Barada was never painted. It seems that it did not possess the same symbolic value.

The British Consul in Damascus only saw "... absurd attempts at views of the Bosphorous, forming the admiration of the Damascus housebuilder of to-day."[34] It was not important to give an accurate rendition of the Bosphorus. The images painted on the wall gave an idea of the place that everybody

---

32 Already the first known wall-paintings in the Topkapı Sarayı in Istanbul depict this strait (see the references fn. 15). See for later paintings of the Bosphorus in Istanbul for example: Öner, *Tanzimat Sonrası.*

33 For example: Yakup Kadri, *Flamme und Falter*, München 1986. Pertinent reports from that time one can find in: Klaus Kreiser, *Istanbul, Ein historisch-literarischer Stadtführer*, München 2001, 223 ff., compare as well 168 f.

34 After James A. Reilly, "The Modern Birth of Traditional Damascus," unpublished paper, Toronto 1990.

could recognize and connect to a certain experience in and of time. This vision of an imagined world represents a conception of life which was in some ways shared by most of those inhabitants of Damascus who had the walls in their houses painted. Otherwise it is not possible to explain that in a limited period of time (ca. 1820 to 1915), the same representation of the Ottoman capital prevailed in nearly all wall-paintings in Damascus. Moreover, the Bosphorus was always depicted crowded with ships; and – from the 1830's onwards – with steamboats. Damascus is not a port city, and ships were, of course, not an aspect of the experience of daily life. These hundreds of ships that were painted in Damascus were nearly always flagged with the Ottoman banner. The same was true for military buildings beside the water. A lot of fantasy mosques were painted, but always with distinct Ottoman features. When looking at these paintings one realizes that many people in Damascus did not have any problems with explicit Ottoman symbols. One may add the next question *ex negativo*: Why should they? Ideas of nationalism, identified as they are by researchers today as the prime means of understanding societies, were the exception at that time – limited only to a small intellectual élite in the last two decades of Ottoman rule in Syria. All other aspects of Damascene interior decoration point towards a strong artistic identification with the Ottoman political center. Ottoman baroque, including the half-moon-and-star emblem, was the style of nearly all houses of that particular period.

Istanbul

Many of the paintings depicted the imperial center. Wall-paintings representing views of Istanbul were very common all over the Ottoman Empire. Numerous examples existed in Istanbul and provincial towns. One of the best known examples in the provinces is the large view of Istanbul (next to that of Izmir) in the Çağır Ağa Konağı in Birgi.[35] As in all the other panoramas, the Bosphorus and Golden Horn show landmarks of Istanbul – for example, its hill top mosques and the Kız Kulesi (Leander Tower) at the entry of the Bosphorus.

---

35 Kuyulu, *Wall Paintings,* 7 f; Renda, *Türk Resim*, 146. For views of Istanbul in the empire see: Arık, *Tasvir Sanatı,* 94 f., 120 ff.; Cramer, *Istanbul auf Wandbildern*; Kuyulu, *Çiftehanlar Camii*, fig. 13; Renda, *Türk Resim*, 146 ff., 154, 158 f., 165 f. Views of towns were known before, compare for example manuscripts from the sixteenth century: Arık, *Tasvir Sanatı,* 8 ff. Also one often sees cityscapes in miniature paintings on *ʿajamī*-wood lacquer. Large early views of towns in interior decoration can be found in the Amīr palace near Bayt al-Dīn. Compare also wooden panels in Damascus dated 1189/1775: Dorothee Duda, *Innenarchitektur syrischer Stadthäuser des 16.-18. Jahrhunderts*, Beirut 1971, Tafel 41 ff.

In Damascus the oldest datable panorama of Istanbul is also the most stunning example. It was painted around 1840, in the northern reception room (*qāʿa*) of the Jabrī-house (IX-252, today known as al-Mujallid), and is a large panorama of Istanbul of about 3.50 m^2 on the upper part of the wall facing the entrance (fig. 7).[36] Unfortunately we do not know who arranged the redecoration of the house, but certainly the same craftsmen who were involved in redecorating the house of ʿAlī Āghā Khazīna-Kātibī (Niẓām) in the late 1830s were also active here. The interior decoration in the northern *qāʿa* shows exactly the same features as the famous Qāʿat al-ʿAynab in the house of ʿAlī Āghā. This is true for the paintings as well. In both houses the motifs, colors, and the style of painting were the same.

The details in the painting support the contention that it dates from around 1840 since it portrays the town at the time when the painting was drafted. Only one of what were later two bridges across the Golden Horn is depicted. The bridge between Unkapanı and Azapkapı built in 1836 appears on the wall, while the Galata Bridge, which was erected a few years later in 1845, is not depicted. The panorama of Istanbul gives an impression of the city at that time. The sea is full of large ships, but already one paddle steamer is crossing the Bosphorus (the first steam-boats appeared in the harbors of the Levant shortly after 1830). Buildings that were landmarks in Istanbul from the time of Mahmut II, like his Nusretiye-Mosque (1825), or the palace of Başikitaş, which no longer exists, are visible on the shore.

The delicate treatment of the image of the Ottoman capital in the Jabrī/Mujallid-house gives us some hints about its artist. Most probably he did not copy it from a printed model or something similar since one spots some discrepancies in his view of Istanbul. Yet, he was familiar enough with the topography of the capital that he could produce the most important landmarks of Istanbul accurately. The artist sketched the barracks in Taksim and the Selimiye barracks (rebuilt shortly after 1826) in Üsküdar, the crowded harbor of Kasımpaşa (with the arsenal of the fleet, *tershane*)

---

36 The structure of the house originates from the late eighteenth or very early nineteenth century. It was rebuilt and redecorated around 1840. Other parts of the house (rooms in the upper part of the southern wing) were built or decorated in 1271/1854-55 and the salon to the east around 1870. According to al-Ḥuṣnī the house belonged in the beginning of the twentieth century to a certain Sāmī ibn Saʿīd Jabrī, who was a rich merchant. Oral information in the neighborhood gives Saʿīd Āghā Jabrī, a tax collector (*jābī al-ḍarā'ib*); as the builder of the house. In the case that he was the father of Sāmī ibn Saʿīd only the last building operations in the 1870s could have been undertaken by him. See for this house: al-Ḥuṣnī, *Muntakhabāt al-Tawārīkh*, vol. 2, 895; Musilmānī, *al-Buyūt al-Dimashkiyya*, 71 ff.; Sack, *Stadt intra muros*, 226.

behind the Unkapanı Bridge leading to Sinan's Azapkapı Camii (985/1577). The artist did not give a photographic view of the cityscape. Rather he painted his personal memory of the town. His view of the capital proves that he knew Istanbul well and it seems that he was there for a long time.

Similar paintings are found in Istanbul dating from about 1800 – for example, in the Kadınefendi Odası in the Topkapı Saray, in the Sadullah Paşa Yalı and in a house in Antakiya.[37] More striking are corresponding views in the sultan's lounge (*hünkâr mahfeli*) of Atik Valide Camii in Üsküdar-Toptaşı from the early nineteenth century. They are very close to those in the house of ʿAlī Āghā (compare fig. 5 and fig. 6). One can speculate whether this artist from Istanbul stopped in Antakiya on his way to Damascus, before he worked in the houses of ʿAlī Āgha and the Jabrīs.

During the Damascene building-boom of the 1860s and 1870s many views of Istanbul were painted.[38] The artists of that time were not trained in Europe or in the capital and it is likely that they were local craftsmen basically adapting the techniques of painters who passed through the town. In any case, the artist of these panoramic views painted what they had to paint: an imagined picture that the viewer easily identified as Istanbul. Even though they were far from realistic and faithful copies, the images show a love for details. One example is a wall-painting in the Qanbāzū-house which was highly stylized (fig. 8). But absolute accuracy was not important and it was sufficient to reduce the view of Istanbul to its main landmarks painted in a simple way. The symbols of the city were generally known as they are today and the subjective emphasis of some landmarks was deliberate. Many Damascene pictures displayed a personal experience of the world that reduced the imagery to its main symbols – readily comprehensible for the viewer. The symbol – and with it the picture – gained their importance through the context of their creation. Meaning was assigned to these symbols (like the Bosphorus) by the same historical and cultural experience of viewer, painter, and patron.

The most basic way of presenting symbols and signs refers to the religious and political background of the builder. But only very few examples of wall-paintings had explicit religious themes. The Ṣārjī-house (IX-43)

---

37 See for those in the Sadullah Paşa Yalısı: Arık, *Tasvir Sanatı,* 24 and for the Topkapı Sarayı: Renda, *Türk Resim*, 95. See for the house in Antakiya: Renda, *Türk Resim*, 198; G. Renda, "Painted Decoration in nineteenth Century Ottoman Houses: Damascene Connection," in *Corpus d'archéologie ottomane*, ed. by A. Temimi, Zaghuan 1997, 94.

38 For example the houses Dayrī / Murtaḍa (IX-81), al-Bārūdī (XXIV/2-593), Saʿīd al-Quwatlī (XVIII/1-100) and Qanbāzū (XVIII/2-457) and al-Quwatlī (XIII/2-412).

from 1235/1819-20 shows Christian motifs, such as the Madonna with the child, in an overall Ottoman decoration.[39] Some houses, like Qanbāzū (XVIII/2-457); al-Bārūdī (XXIV/2-593); al-Yūsuf (VII/2-1-654, eastern section) contain views of the city of Mecca and Medina.[40] But these rare religious motifs were the only difference between houses of Muslims, Jews, or Christians. The frequent claim that one finds human figures depicted only in houses of Christians does not hold for Damascus.[41] Only two out of the six houses where I found painted human figures were Christian.[42]

During the second half of the nineteenth century new kinds of social associations emerged. Cultural clubs, political parties and Freemasonry began to influence Damascene society. In some houses symbols of Freemasonry and political sympathies appeared.[43] A new sense of social belonging and new world views and self-images left their imprint on the living-world of Damascenes. These deep-rooted changes, that became visible in urban structures and architecture and its decorations, were much more widespread than normally assumed. It was not only some people in Ottoman service who dressed themselves in a modern Ottoman way, as Aḥmad Ḥilmī al-ʿAllāf suggested, or furnished their houses in the latest style from Istanbul. The new style of decoration often connected with wall-paintings, applies to nearly all houses of that time and gives evidence of a much more fundamental change that influenced huge parts of society.

Topics of new horizons

Perhaps the most important change was that horizons of direct and indirect experience of the world expanded and the world Damascenes lived in be-

---

39 As well in Anatolia religious topics were seldom painted, see for biblical scenes: Arık, *Tasvir Sanatı*, 64; Kuyulu, *Wall Paintings*, 13 ff.

40 Views of Mecca and Medina are well known in Islamic architecture – for example, on a tile of the Rüstem Pasha Mosque in Istanbul (1561) dated 1660 or at the Fountain of ʿAbd al-Raḥmān Katkhudā in Cairo from 1744.

41 For example Cramer, *Istanbul auf Wandbildern*, 98; Renda, *Westernisms*, 104. See for human figures as well: Arık, *Tasvir Sanatı*, 62, 64, 133 f., and G. Renda, "Wall Painting in Turkish Houses," in *Fifth International Congress of Turkish Art*, Budapest 1978, 711.

42 Thus the houses Ṣārjī (IX-43) and al-Shāwī (X/4-788). The houses of Muslim families al-Bārūdī (XXIV/2-593), Jabrī / al-Mujallid (IX-252), al-Qabbānī (XIII/2-351), al-Ṣafadī / al-Dawajī (IX-232) do have painted human figures as well.

43 For symbols of freemasonry: al-Bārūdī (XXIV/2-593), al-Yūsuf (VII/2-1-654) and maybe as well Qanbāzū (XVIII/2-457). Several houses do have a Ṭughrā: al-Shāwī (X/4-788); Fawzī al-Qabbānī (XXI/2-986) and al-Khānjī / al-ʿAẓma (IX-272).

Fig. 10: ʿUlabī-house (XXIV/1-1-149), ceiling of the *maḍāfa*, detail.

Fig. 11: Bārūdī-house, southern part (XXIV/2-653), *ṣāliya*, detail.

Fig. 12: Bārūdī-house, northern part (XXIV/2-593), painting in the *mā-bayn* of the first floor.

Fig. 13: Qabbānī-house (XXI/2-986), Ottoman flagged steamboats.

Fig. 14: Bārūdī-house, southern part (XXIV/2-653), *ṣāliya*, detail.

Fig. 15: House of Fawzī al-Qabbānī (XXI/2-986), back wall of the *īwān*, detail.

Fig. 16: Qandalfat-house (X/3-399), *qāʿa*, detail.

Fig. 17: Ḥammām al-Khayyāṭīn (XXI/2- 672), dome of the *mashlaḥ*, detail.

came larger. Newspapers, school books, and telegraphed news gave an idea of the world outside peoples' daily sphere of activities.

> Although printing brought a new literary form, its chief significance lay in conveying the ideas of authors from distant cultural, historical, and geographical settings. Egyptian newspapers carried articles about Europe and Arabic translations of works in European languages, thus giving Syrians access to ideas from culturally distant societies.[44]

This is true for political affairs as well. Information spread quickly and the overall scheme of events was well known and a topic of daily talk. Things that occupied peoples' minds were often painted on the walls of Damascene houses. The events of the Commune of Paris in 1871 after the collapse of Napoleon III's Second Empire, for example, were certainly discussed in Damascus. During the bloody ending of the Commune some public buildings in Paris were burned, among them the Hôtel de Ville. One of the protagonists of the time was Adolphe Thiers (1797-1877). He crushed the Commune of Paris before becoming president of the French Republic between 1871 and 1873. Apparently, these events had their effects in Damascus as Vogüé reported after he visited a house in 1874:

> [N]ous prenant à témoin de ses sentiments français, il nous montre sur le mur, entre un railway et un steamboat... la maison de M. Thiers! Le bon Damasquin était à Paris pour son négoce à l'époque de la Commune; justement indigné de la destruction de l'hôtel du président, il l'a fait reproduire dans sa galerie.[45]

I was unable to identify the house Vogüé visited, but in the Dawajī-house (today al-Ṣafadī, IX-232) a wall-painting looks very similar to his description (fig. 9): a Parisian cityscape with buildings resembling the Hôtel de Ville topped by a French flag.

People chose the motifs they wanted to have painted and most of the wall-paintings dealt with issues prominent at the time. News of events were available in newspapers and then passed through the town by word of mouth. For example, volcanoes appear as painted motifs on Damascene walls and cornices. News of volcanic eruptions reached Damascus as well – for example, the great eruptions of Mt. Vesuvius in 1872 and 1906 or the

---

44 David Dean Commins, *Islamic reform, Politics and Social Change in Late Ottoman Syria,* New York / Oxford 1990, 18.

45 Vogüé, *Syrie, Palestine*, 80.

catastrophe of Krakatoa in 1883.[46] The most devastating eruption happened in Martinique. In 1902 the eruption of Mont Pelée destroyed the entire port town of Saint-Pierre and killed 30, 000 people. Arabic newspapers of the time reported extensively on the disaster and printed pictures of the island.[47] Intense momentary social concerns for the inhabitants of Martinique were eternalised in the ʿUlabī-house in Qanawāt / Taʿdīl (XXIV/1-1-149) where an island volcano is painted with dramatic effect which shows a town on the shore during an enormous eruption (fig. 10).

Venice was another topic in the artistic imagination of Damascus. In the 60s or 70s of the nineteenth century, Muḥammad Ḥasan Āghā al-Bārūdī (d. 1307/1889-90) – member of the municipal council in 1871 and the head (*ra'is*) of this council between 1877 and 1879 – rebuilt his house in the city quarter of Qanawāt and decorated it with large wall-paintings.[48] Next to pictures of Istanbul, which he visited twice, and of Mecca and Medina, he had depicted a landscape of Venice (fig. 11). The form of a typical Venetian clocktower (or campanile) is clearly visible. The main part of the picture shows the Miramare castle in Trieste, which was built for the Archduke Maximilian between 1856 and 1860.[49] Ferdinand Maximilian (1832 – 1867) rose to political prominence in the 1860s. As the younger brother of Emperor Franz Joseph, he served as governor-general of the Lombardo-Venetian kingdom. In 1863 he accepted the offer of the Mexican throne but lost the war against the Mexican liberal government in 1867. Even though Victor Hugo, Giuseppe Garibaldi, and many monarchs

---

46 An eruption of the Mt. Vesuvius one can also find in the Selamlık of the Dolmabahçe Sarayı (1842-1856). See: Yum, *Osmanlı Saray Yapılarındaki*, 543 f., 549, fig. 2. In the Ṭawīl-house, Damascus, Mt. Vesuvius is painted with Naples (X/3-577). Volcano eruptions were also represented in Lebanese houses; compare Paget, *Murs et plafonds*, 67, 294 (with Naples) or in a house in İzmir; compare Kuyulu, *İzmir'de*.

47 See the newspaper *al-Ḍiyā'* (31. May 1902) 556-560; (30. June 1902) 620-623; (1. November 1902) 78-79.

48 See on Muḥammad Ḥasan Āghā al-Bārūdī: al-Ḥuṣnī, *Muntakhabāt al-Tawārīkh*, 2. vol., 863; Sālnāme [3](1287-88/1870-72) 57; [9](1293/1877) 68 f.; [10](1295/1878) 60; [11](1296/1878-79) 62; Linda Schatkowski Schilcher, *Families in Politics, Damascene Factions and Estates of the eighteenth and nineteenth Centuries*, Stuttgart 1985, 147; al-Shaṭṭī, *Aʿyān Dimashq*, 343; J. Zwiedinek von Südenhorst, *Syrien und seine Bedeutung für den Welthandel*, Wien 1873, 25. Today the house of Muḥammad Ḥasan Āghā al-Bārūdī is divided into a northern (XXIV/2-593) and southern part (XXIV/2-653). The northern part, which is known today as the house of his famous grandson, Fakhrī al-Bārūdī (1887-1966), and which I will deal with a further on, was redecorated in the early twentieth century when its original decoration was over-painted; compare fn. 54.

49 See for the castle among others: Richard Zürcher, *Friaula, Istrien*, München 1982, 212-216.

of Europe petitioned to save Maximilian's life, he was executed one month later. The story of his life and his famous Miramare castle in Trieste, which he left only to lose his life trying to become Kaiser of Mexico, was the talk of his time. Even if Muḥammad Ḥasan Āghā al-Bārūdī had never been in Trieste, he must have known the famous story of the Miramare castle and its owner.

European towns were one of the main focal points of nineteenth century Damascene life as reflected in wall-paintings. Urban centers, like Paris and London, were the very model of modern towns and societies. "In nineteenth-century Syria, European ideas about society and politics possessed an intrinsic authority because of Europe's military and economic superiority, which Syrians wanted to understand by discovering the causes of Europe's progress through reading European history."[50] Events in Europe were very well known in Damascus and became topics of conversation as well as wall-paintings. Not only newspapers played an important role. Increasing international travel in terms of tourism, trade and intellectual exchange, established more than ever before direct contacts between people from Europe and Damascus. The Thomas Cook & Son travel agency started organizing group travels to Palestine and Egypt in 1867 and many tourists came to Damascus in the process.[51] The British consul estimated that around 1100 visitors left a total of 5000 Pounds Sterling in the town in 1905 alone.[52] Much more important were accounts of Syrians who traveled to Europe. One lively account is given by Fakhrī al-Bārūdī, who traveled to Paris in spring 1911 via Alexandria, Naples, and Marseille and visited Munich, Vienna, Budapest and Istanbul on his way back to Damascus.[53] Shortly after he returned, he had several European cityscapes painted in the most prominent rooms in his house and replaced older panoramas of the Bosphorus from the time of his grandfather (but he left the paintings of Mecca and Medina and a view of Istanbul).[54] The view of the Place de la

---

50 Commins, *Islamic Reform*, 18.

51 See Thomas Cook and Son, *Programmes and Itineraries of Cook's Arrangements*, London 1896, 4 f.

52 Compare: Public Record Office, Foreign Office 618-3 / 1.7.1905.

53 An account on his travel can be found in: Daʿd al-Ḥakīm (ed.), *Awrāk wa-Mudhakkarāt Fakhrī al-Bārūdī, 1887-1966,* 2 vols., Damascus 1999, vol. 1, 141-246. His autobiography was first published as: Fakhrī al-Bārūdī, *Mudhakkarāt al-Bārūdī, Sittūn Sana tatakallum*, 1. vol. Beirut - Damascus 1951, 2. vol. Damascus 1952; and Fakhrī al-Bārūdī, *Tārīkh yatakallam*, Damascus 1960.

54 This house has a long history. It is first mentioned in the *waqfiyya* of the governor Muḥammad Pasha Kurd Bayram (reg. 1114/1702-03 and 1117/1705-06). The Bārūdīs rented it since the middle of the 19th century from the *waqf* (in a court-record of

Concorde in Paris, signed by B. Samra in 1911, is the most detailed example (fig. 12). Views of Rome (the Vatican and St. Peter's) in the house of the Jewish family Saysūn (XII/2-293), or Naples in the house of the Christian Ṭawīl family (X/3-577), from around 1870 and 1860, might have a similar origin.

Symbols of modern times

Direct contacts and travels, oral news, books, postcards, newspapers, new curricula in schools all gave an idea of the world in which Damascus and the Ottoman Empire existed. Wall-paintings show that people from Damascus saw themselves as an integral part of the modern world. This world had its symbols: steam boats, factories, railways, and later on, airplanes. These symbols dominated all houses that were decorated by wall-paintings. Imagined views of the Bosphorus are shown with one or several Ottoman flagged steamboats (fig. 13). Modernization and the experience of modernity came to Damascus mainly via Istanbul and the 'modern Damascene mind' was oriented towards that direction. The Ottoman capital was the center of inspiration and all symbols of modernization, like the steamboats, became ottoman flagged i.e. imbued with a sense of Ottoman agency. In order to connect the modern world to one's own city, in the 1870s an artist painted onto the walls of the southern part of the Bārūdī-house (XXIV/2-653) a train running through a fanciful European cityscape (possibly Paris). To convey its destination (literally and metaphorically), the artist wrote "*Shām-i Sherīf*", on the front of the locomotive (fig. 14).

The people depicted what occupied their minds. Symbols of modernization and manifestations of the experience of modernity were manifold.

1303/1886 it is still mentioned as a *waqf*). The most important steps in rebuilding the house were undertaken in the 1860s or more likely in the 1870s by Muḥammad Ḥasan Āghā al-Bārūdī (d. 1307/1889-90). In this period the house was first decorated with wall-paintings. The governor Ḥusayn Nāẓim Pasha occupied the house in 1895 (until 1902) and expected here the visit of the German Kaiser Wilhelm II in 1898. Photographs sent to ᶜAbdülḥamīd to show him the preparations for the visit, shows the *qāʿa* in the northern part of the house before it was painted over. For court-records of the house, see MWT S815/W16 (1303/1886); S1293/W97 (1322/1904). Further: al-Ḥakīm, *Mudhakkarāt Fakhrī al-Bārūdī,* 33, Philip S. Khoury, *Urban notables and Arab nationalism, The politics of Damascus 1860-1920*, Cambridge 1983, 43; Khalīl Sarkīs, *al-Shām qabla Mi'at ʿĀm, Riḥlat al-Imbirāṭūr Ghiliyūm al-Thānī, Imbirāṭūr Almāniya wa-Qarīnatihi ilā Filisṭīn wa-Sūriya, ʿĀm 1316 h. / 1898 m*, Damascus 1997, 138, 178 (first published in 1898); Schatkowski Schilcher, *Families in Politics*, 146 f., Qutayba al-Shihābī, *Dimashq, Tārīkh wa-Ṣuwar*, Damascus 1990, 163 f. For photos, see IRCICA 90483/36-39; compare fn. 48. In the last years the Faculty of Architecture of the University of Damascus started to renovate the house.

Some of the pictures contain telegraph lines or factories with high smoke stacks like in the Qanbāzū-house (XVIII/2-457). It comes as no surprise that in the early twentieth century representations of airplanes appear on the walls of Damascene houses. In 1330/1912 the first airplane landed in Damascus in the meadows next to the Takiyya al-Sulaymāniyya. A wall painting of this period in the house of Fawzī al-Qabbānī (XXI/2-986) recalls this event explicitly (fig. 15). Later the First World War was illustrated in the Qabbānī-house (XIII/2-351) – replete with a warship and a biplane.

Times were changing and so was the perception of time. First of all, time became measurable matter in Europe and in the provinces of the Ottoman Empire alike. The erection of clocktowers in the center of nearly all large towns of the empire was the most conspciuous sign of this – again, it was also reflected in wall paintings in Damascus. For instance, in the Qandalfat-house several clocks were painted on the walls (X/3-399, dated 1863 and 1281/1864-65, fig. 16).

Second, wall-paintings evinced an awareness of the global simultaneity of time. Time was not only experienced differently from previous epochs, temporal perception also changed the relation to one's own history. The more or less conscious identification with a new age required (and generated) a perception of the past through the definition of tradition. This concept of the past as a monolithic period of a bygone time and as contrasted to a modern present, brought about the phenomena of historicism in architecture, which blossomed in *fin de siècle* Damascus. For example, a wall painting in the Ḥammām al-Khayyāṭīn, composed by Aḥmad al-Sīrawān in 1327/1909, depicted roman ruins – a motif that had never been chosen before (fig. 17). Historicity became a value judgement of the epoch in literature and art alike. Another example of this phenomenon of defining and thus fixing tradition was the Encyclopedia of Damascene Arts and Crafts (*Qāmūs al-Ṣināʿāt al-Shāmiyya*).[55] Here further research on the link between literature and art will yield a more nuanced understanding of the emerging role of historical expression in the construction of social identities along essentialist and/or epochalist lines.

55 The encyclopedia was started by Muḥammad Saʿīd al-Qāsimī around 1890, who finished the first part before his death in 1900. The second part was written by Jamāl al-Dīn al-Qāsimī (1283/1866 – 1332/1914) and Khalīl al-ʿAẓm (1286/1870 – 1926).

Conclusion

The discussion of a single aspect of private architecture as a material expression of self-image and worldview provides a phenomenological insight into a 'provincial' society in the age of Ottoman reform and global simultaneity. Ottoman reform was not limited to a small elite of state officials, and did touch those in the periphery. The dynamics of transition of urban societies captured vast parts of the public. Shaping of private worlds in late Ottoman Damascus gives evidence of a deep-rooted cultural change, which was – as always in history when we are dealing with social actions – a process of reciprocal communication and effect.

If we look at the relationship between the periphery and the center, the different cities – first Istanbul, then European metropoli – were the point of reference in this period of cultural change to which wall-paintings refered almost exclusively. The production of images of the Bosphorus in Damascene houses was an attempt to connect the center to the province. These pictures as 'world views' expressed the realm people of Damascus felt themselves to be living in. The Ottomanization of urban and social organization, clothing and architecture as well as the Ottoman symbols in decoration, evinced an internalization of the center by provincial societies on a cultural but not necessarily political level. Here it comes to the discussion as to whether the Ottoman Empire was "*an imperial power like all the others*".[56] It is a tricky undertaking to render precisely the point from which on the relation between Istanbul and Bursa, Izmir, Damascus, Baghdad or Sana'a could be characterized by imperialist power relations. One way to analyze the qualities of this relationship is to investigate shifting cultural identities. Wall paintings can help us in this undertaking.

Regarding material culture, it seems that many Damascenes considered themselves an integral part of the Ottoman Culture and as members of the modern world. Noticeable renderings of exotic places like Martinique were signs of perceiving oneself as unmitigated citizens of the world. That distant events stirred the local emotions, expressed a sense of 'we are part of this world.' But modernity and Ottomanism were closely connected, as we can see in wall-paintings. Damascene inhabitants were not only building modern public spaces through new parks, coffeehouses, and theaters. They also adapted their homes, the most private element of architecture, to correspond to their self-image and world view. Architecture then became, like

---

56 Selim Deringil, *The Well-Protected Domains. Ideology and the Legitimation of Power in the Late Ottoman Empire 1876-1909*, London 1998, 148. See also contributions of Kühn and Makdisi to this volume.

clothes, a medium of self-representation, which was comprehensible in public. Maybe the young al-ʿAllāf met a certain Adīb Efendi al-Qabbānī strolling in the new *sūqs* of Damascus, noticed him stalking around from shop to shop and got his impression of Ottoman bureaucrats from watching him. Maybe he was once a guest in the house where Adīb Efendi al-Qabbānī had had himself painted on the back wall of the *īwān*, representing himself as a modern Ottoman citizen.

THE CAIRO CAB DRIVERS AND THE STRIKE OF 1907

JOHN CHALCRAFT

Introduction

It has become increasingly clear that the historiography of the nineteenth century Middle East has often measured economic transformation by rather narrow models of Westernization. A considerable amount of economic change has been defined out of the frame by a focus on the large-scale, the highly mechanized, the scientific, the apparently European, and the élite-managed. We hear of railways, trams, harbors, modern banks, industrial imports, European merchants, and modern factories,[1] but little of the small-scale, the workshop-based, the unscientific, the family-run, the hand-powered, the local subject and the sub-altern. Hardly anything is known about numerous tailors, shoemakers, carters, cab drivers, barbers, carpenters, builders, small workshops, and vendors in the cities and towns of the Middle East. These crafts and trades have an undeserved reputation

---

1 Charles Issawi, *Egypt in Revolution: An Economic Analysis*, London 1963. (See especially p. 13-19); Charles Issawi, "Asymmetrical Development and Transport in Egypt, 1800-1914," in *Beginnings of Modernization in the Middle East: The Nineteenth Century,* Ed. William R. Polk and Richard L. Chambers (eds.), Chicago 1968, 383-401; Jacques Berque, *Egypt: Imperialism and Revolution*, New York 1972, 97; Peter Gran, "Political Economy as a Paradigm for the Study of Islamic History," *IJMES* 11 (1980), 511-526; Roger Owen, *Cotton and the Egyptian Economy 1820-1914: A Study in Trade and Development*, Oxford 1969; Roger Owen, *The Middle East in the World Economy: 1800-1914*, London 1981; David S. Landes, *Bankers and Pashas: International Finance and Economic Imperialism in Egypt*, Cambridge 1958, (See especially p. 79); Eric Davis, *Challenging Colonialism: Bank Misr and Egyptian Industrialization 1920-1941*, Princeton 1983; Eric Davis, "Political Development of Political Economy?" *Review of Middle Eastern Studies*, 1 (1975), 41-61. Also, until recently, those interested in labor history situated their subject matter almost exclusively inside large-scale and European-owned businesses. Here the small-scale is either invisible or treated as a paternalistic obstacle to the rise of a Marxian proletariat. Ra'uf ʿAbbas, *Al-Ḥaraka al-ʿummāliyya fi Miṣr 1899-1952*, Cairo, 1967; Zachary Lockman and Joel Beinin, *Workers on the Nile: Nationalism, Communism, Islam, and the Egyptian Working Class, 1882-1954*, Princeton 1987.

as the decaying remnants of a traditional past, unable or unwilling to adapt, and ready to collapse in the face of progress.[2] Only recently has this view started to look one-sided, according to re-evaluations of the industrial revolution in the West on the one hand,[3] and, on the other, the idea that small enterprise might be a dynamic force in the advanced economies and developing world alike. Debates have been joined, albeit slowly in the case of the nineteenth century Middle East,[4] about small business – its contribution to the economy and its political and social significance. This article is a case study of just one of Egypt's small-scale, urban trades in the decades leading up to the First World War. I trace the expansion of the one and two horse cab drivers of Cairo, a trade which, although more or less unknown in the historiography, became one of the most numerous and visible occupations in Cairo before 1914. I make special reference to a little known cab strike of 1907, a protest in which cabbies forcefully asserted their claims to and role within the changing city. I argue that the adaptation and multiplication of a small-scale, low profit, and family-run trade was an integral part of colonial, urban modernization in nineteenth century Egypt.

Context

Whereas historians argue about whether Egypt's economy was contracting, holding its own, or expanding at least to some degree and in certain areas in the seventeenth and eighteenth centuries, few dispute that the nineteenth century witnessed considerable economic growth.[5] This expansion was largely based on the wealth generated by the exchange of cotton for the

---

2 André Raymond, "Les Porteurs d'Eau du Caire," *Bulletin de l'Institut Francais d'Archéologie Orientale* No. 57 (1958), 183-203; Gabriel Baer, *Egyptian Guilds in Modern Times*, Jerusalem 1964; ʿAbd al-Salām ʿAbd al-Halīm ʿAmīr, *Al-Ṭawā'if al-ḥiraf fī Miṣr 1805-1914*, Cairo 1993 (especially p. 212-214).

3 Raphael Samuel, "Workshop of the World: Steam Power and Hand Technology in Mid-Victorian Britain," *History Workshop*, (1977) No. 3, 1-74; Maxine Berg, *The Age of Manufactures: Industry, Innovation and Work in Britain 1700-1820*, Totowa NJ 1985.

4 Roger Owen, "The Cairo Building Industry and the Building Boom of 1897-1907," *Colloque International sur l'Histoire du Caire*, DDR, Ministry of Culture of ARE, 1969, 337-350. Roger Owen, "The Study of Middle Eastern Industrial History: Notes on the interrelationship between factories and small-scale manufacturing with special references to Lebanese silk and Egyptian sugar, 1900-1930," *IJMES*, 16 (1984), 475-487. Donald Quataert, *Ottoman Manufacturing in the Age of the Industrial Revolution*, Cambridge 1993.

5 Although they might characterise this growth as 'dependent', 'lop-sided' or fatally reliant on cotton alone.

manufactures and capital goods of Europe.[6] The exchange was underpinned by the century-long development of the agricultural and communications infrastructure, especially under Muḥammad ʿAlī (1805-1848), Ismāʿīl (1863-1879) and the British after 1882. In the last quarter of the nineteenth century, further, private capital was increasingly attracted to land, banking, commerce, transport and municipal infrastructure, especially as confidence in the stability and permanence of the British occupation increased in the late 1890s and after the Anglo-French agreement of 1904.[7] The resulting prosperity – mostly amongst a narrow elite of landowners, bankers, merchants, concessionary capitalists and a rising technical class – led some to dub Egypt "an El Dorado, the fabulous prosperity of which was truly something supernatural."[8]

But what of small business? Which trades failed, which adapted and expanded, where exactly, and how was this possible under colonial conditions? Did not small enterprises rapidly become mere decoration atop an economy based on cotton exports and industrial imports, or did they remain an important source of consumer goods, trade and service provision, and even provide cheaply for the new demands of both consumers and large-scale industry? Were the crafts and trades efficient, dynamic and innovative, or merely an impecunious stopgap, an inefficient form of employment for a swelling, subsistence-seeking population? In what ways did small enterprises articulate their interests to the local and colonial regime? Did they stand apolitically on the sidelines as Ismāʿīlian reform, colonialism, nationalism, and workers' strike action came and went, or did they

---

6 Egypt's external trade increased quite markedly in the first half of the century, roughly quadrupled in nominal value during the cotton boom of 1861-4, then in general held its own until the early 1890s, before almost tripling in nominal value terms by the outbreak of the First World War. (External Trade Statistics: *al-Nashra al-sanawiyya al-tijāra al-Khārijiyya*: al-Qāhira: al-maktaba al-ʿāmma 1876-1914.) Mehmed ʿAlī's successful interventions in the agricultural infrastructure, and high cotton prices during the American Civil War in the early 1860s set the scene for a rapid expansion in the cultivated area devoted to this lucrative crop (as well as the arrival of large-scale, mechanised cotton ginning and pressing). Favourable movements in the 'cotton terms of trade' thereafter only increased the real levels of wealth that cotton could bring. Owen, *World Economy*, 1981, 135-148.

7 While less than 7 million LE was held in capital in banking, commerce and industry in 1883, this figure had doubled by 1897, doubled again by 1902, then tripled before the slump of 1907, before adding a few more million to attain about 100 million LE in 1914. Owen, *World Economy*, 234. The Societé des Eaux started to pipe water around Cairo after 1863, the urban tram appeared in 1896, the Baron d'Empain constructed Heliopolis, the 'city in the desert' during the early years of the twentieth century.

8 Pierre Arminjon, *La Situation Economique et Financière de l'Egypte*, Paris 1911, 590-1.

mobilize in defense of trade concerns? And finally, what was it like to work in such crafts? Was it a refuge from intense capitalist exploitation, a last bastion of hereditary craftsmanship and social solidarity, or was it monotonous, toilsome, poverty stricken and exploitative? Clearly these questions cannot be answered all at once. They can probably only be addressed by the gradual build-up of scholarship, by studies of particular cases, and the slow discovery of new sources.[9]

The Cab Drivers: Tracing Expansion

In the 1880s, one and two horse carriages for public hire were a fairly common sight in Cairo, especially in the newly constructed streets between the Ottoman city and the Nile. ʿAlī Mubārak recorded 486 such vehicles in 1887.[10] It was said that "the usual shape [of the public cabs followed] that

---

9 This study makes use of: (I) Petitions to the government: the Ministries, police, Governorate and Khedivial Diwān – from cab drivers and others. These are to found under (1) *Dār al-Wathā'iq al-Qawmiyya* (hereafter DWQ) *Ḍabṭiyyat Miṣr, Wārid al-ʿArḍḥālāt* 1274-1287 AH.; (2) DWQ *Niẓārat al-Dākhiliyya* (ND) *Mukātabāt ʿArabiyya* (MA) *Maḥfaẓa* 1-40 [Cole first discovered these rich sources and used them, I have reread certain petitions on the one hand, and found new ones on the other]; (3) DWQ *Sijillāt ʿAbdīn ʿArabī wa-Turkī: Qaid al-ʿArḍḥālāt al-Wārida* 27/5/Seen 1893-4 and *Qaid al-ʿArḍḥālāt* 32/5/Seen 1902-1914; and, relating to the same series of petitions DWQ *ʿĀbdīn: Diwān Khidīwī ʿArḍḥālāt* Nos. 612-618 1892-1912; (4) DWQ *Sijillāt Muḥāfaẓat Miṣr: Wārid al-ʿArḍḥālāt* 31/1/lam 1275-1296 AH. (II) Ministerial documentation: there are too many boxes to list here, but a large set of Ministerial records are grouped within DWQ *Majlis al-Wuzarā'*; I have used materials from DWQ *Majlis al-Wuzarā': Niẓārat al-Māliyya* [Finance], *Niẓārat al-Dākhiliyya* [Interior], *Niẓārat al-Ashghāl* [Public Works], *Majlis al-Nuẓẓār* [Council of Ministers]; I have also used other series in DWQ such as *Muḥāfiẓ al-Abḥāth* [Research Files] and *Biṭāqāt Mawāḍīʿa al-Dār* [Archive Card Index]. (III) British sources: Foreign Office and Embassy correspondence and reports including the Consular Court Records (PRO, London): PRO FO141, FO841, FO633, FO848, FO371. (IV) Other material: newspapers, journals, censuses (including a relatively unused 70 volume census of Cairo Governorate of 1868: DWQ *Sijillāt Muḥāfaẓat Miṣr. Taʿdād nufūs* 1285 84/1/lam); published government legislation and statistical compendia *al-Nashra al-sanawiyya al-tijāra al-Khārijiyya*. Cairo: *al-Maktaba al-ʿāmma*, yearly; and pre-First World War accounts. These sources are useful, largely new, but patchy, especially in comparison to those available to historians of Europe.

10 ʿAlī Mubārak, *Al-Khiṭāṭ al-Tawfīqiyya*, Vol 1, 95. ʿAlī Mubārak was using local authority records. I have seen a few petitions from passenger coachmen (*ʿarbajiyya al-rukūb*) to the government dating from the 1870s. The Cairo Governorate census of 1868, furthermore, lists 1,470 coachmen and carters (*ʿarbajiyya wa qamāshajiyya*). This category likely included a certain number of cabs for hire, but how many is unclear. Coachmen selling rides to the public were probably slower to appear in provincial towns. A relatively comprehensive list of the trades of Mansura from the early

of the private carriages, viz., a one-horse or pair victoria with hood. Both classes are built for two persons, with a small let down seat capable of holding, with some discomfort, two more passengers."[11] Their drivers were variously called *ʿarbajiyya* (sing. *ʿarbajī*) - coachmen or cab men;[12] *ʿarbajiyya al-rukūb* - passenger coachmen;[13] *hūdhiyyūn* - coachmen;[14] *hūdhiyyāt al-markabāt*;[15] and *sā'iqū al-markabāt* - drivers of coaches.[16]

Carriages for public hire probably appeared in these numbers only in the nineteenth century, for the coachmen and stable boys (French: palefreniers, Arabic: sing. *sā'is*, pl. *suyyās/suwwās*) of Raymond's eighteenth century were mostly in private service. Consumption patterns were changing – more and more wealthy individuals lived in Cairo who did not own private carriages themselves, and sumptuary laws restricting non-elites from carriages and horses[17] were less and less observed. By the 1880s, numbers of private and public carriages were roughly equivalent.[18] However, a more popular way of getting round the city was still the donkey: there were over 3,000 donkey-boys in Cairo in the 1860s.[19]

From the 1880s, however, and for at least twenty-five years thereafter, cab driving appears to have undergone rapid expansion, leaving donkey boys and private coachmen in the shade, and competing successfully against various newer forms of urban transportation. No less than 6,156 Cairean cab drivers are listed in the census of 1917. I take these figures not as the literal truth, but as an indication (taken together with other evidence) that some fairly substantial expansion of cabbies took place during these years. Probably the key to this expansion – over and above the increasing scale and population of the city – was that the coachmen, more so than their competitors, tapped the pockets of Cairo's wealthy classes, the beneficiaries of Egypt's 'El Dorado'. Colonial memoirs and other evidence

---

1860s, for example, does not include such a category: DWQ MA MM 118 *amwāl* 1863. Mansura, however, had 238 public coachmen in 1917 according to the census.

11 *Egyptian Gazette*, January 4, 1907.

12 This was the most frequently used term in censuses, newspapers, and petitions.

13 This term was sometimes used in government communication. Eg. DWQ ND MA M33 No. 477 Cairo Local Authority/Ministry of the Interior 27 Dhū al-Qaʿda 1296.

14 Newspapers; 1917 census.

15 *Al-Ahrām*, April 22, 1907.

16 Used in the 1917 census to refer to public coachmen.

17 For example, Raymond, *Artisans et Commercants*, Damascus 1973-74, vol. 2, 597.

18 400 strong in 1887, ʿAlī Mubārak, *Al-Khiṭāṭ*, vol. 1, 95.

19 To be (over)precise, 3,176. Census of Cairo Governorate 1868: DWQ *Sijillāt muḥāfaẓat Miṣr. Taʿdād nufūs* 1285 84/1/lam.

indicate the quotidian usage of these cabs by rich foreign subjects in Egypt.[20] Relatively transient foreign residents were also less likely than local, established landowners, say, to employ private stablemen. Private coach men lost out in relative terms as more and more of the local elite took to the convenience of the public carriage.[21] Cabbies also benefited from ever-increasing tourist demand.[22] Donkey boys could not compete with cabbies and their numbers appear to have diminished rapidly from over 3,000 in 1868 to 417 in 1917.[23]

After about 1890, however, cabbies found themselves competing with various new forms of urban transport: horse-drawn omnibuses, the tram, and the motor car, whose owners were attracted to the market Cairo offered. Two and three horse 'omnibuses' for public hire with space for six to ten passengers appeared in Cairo in the 1890s and 1900s (*suwwāq al-awmnibūs*)[24]. Although moderately successful – there were 1,839 'tramway and omnibus drivers and men engaged in this kind of transport' in 1917 –

---

20 Eg. Cecil, *The Leisure of an Egyptian Official*, London 1921, 130-140.

21 Therefore, even though numbers of private coachmen perhaps doubled between the late 1880s and the First World War, public cabbies outnumbered then five or six to one in 1917. This was the case even though the figure given in the 1917 census for 'private coachmen, stable boys (*sā'is*), and chauffeurs' (*sawwāq al-markabāt al-khuṣūṣiyya* and *suwwās al-khuṣūṣiyyīn*) included the growing numbers of private chauffeurs driving motor cars who appeared after 1900 and multiplied as the century progressed.

22 An idea of the considerable expansion in numbers of tourists in mid to late nineteenth century Egypt is given in Al-Sayyid Aḥmad Tawfīq Diyyab, *Al-ṣiyyāḥa fī Miṣr khilāl al-qarn al-tāsiʿ ʿashr*, Cairo 1994. Cabs were the transport of choice for tourists seeing the sights in Cairo, or getting to their hotels on arrival at the Gare Centrale from both Alexandria and Upper Egypt. Useful material in this regard was found in Karl Baedeker, *Egypt: Handbook for Travellers*, Leipzig: Baedeker, 1978, 11-12, 229-231; Karl Baedeker, *Egypt and the Sudan: Handbook for Travellers*, Leipzig: Baedeker, 1908, XXI-XVIII, 30-35; E. A. Wallis Budge, Cooks, *Handbook for Egypt and the Sudan*, London: Thos. Cook & Son, 1905, 3-4; A. O. Lamplough, *Egypt and How to See it*, London: Ballantyne & Co, 1908, 12, 36.

23 Donkey boys were in the market for neither upper class nor so much for tourist transportation in Cairo. See for example, John MacGregor, "A Donkey-Boy of Cairo," in *Sons of the Empire*, London 1903, 83-92. Many tourists favoured cabs. See, for example, Douglas Sladen, *Oriental Cairo: the City of the Arabian Nights*, London 1911, 1-10. Another reason for the attractiveness of cab over donkey was that new urban infrastructure increased the relative speed of larger, less manoeuvrable, and wheeled cabs compared to donkeys. Consider, for example, the effect of Muḥammad ʿAlī Street, which cut straight through the old quarters between Azbakiyya and the Citadel. Martin argued that petty traders and artisans started to use buses and trams to get to work rather than mules in the early 1900s: Germain Martin, *Les bazars et les petits metiers arabes*, Paris 1910, 74.

24 This term appears in the 1917 census.

such buses did not become anything like as numerous as cabbies. For one thing, it seems to have been less desirable to drive such vehicles – if the petitions from 1907 of a certain driver – Muḥammad Ḥasan – are to be believed.[25] Also, buses were likely less convenient for single fares: they did not leave as quickly, and made inconvenient stops. The elite were well able to afford the privacy, status and convenience given (to some extent) by the cab, and by and large did not need to trouble themselves to exchange one or two Piastres for the inconveniences of the bus.[26]

The first tramline appeared in Cairo in 1896, and connected Būlāq via the Gare Centrale to ʿAtaba al-Khaḍra Square.[27] By 1914, four additional routes converged on ʿAtaba al-Khaḍra, leading from the Citadel, from Ismāʿīliyya Square via Bāb al-Lūq, from the mouth of the Khalīj, and from Heliopolis via ʿAbbāsiyya. The advent of the tram must have meant that at least to some extent cabbies lost out on the main routes.[28] Nonetheless, the era of the tram also coincided with the fastest multiplication in the numbers of cabbies. On the one hand, demand outpaced what the tram could offer. The tram was not particularly fast, it only moved at certain times, it did not run all night, it did not serve closely all parts of the expanding town. On the other hand, and more importantly, trams probably catered more to lower income passengers (but not the majority of the population, who went on foot). Hotels sent victorias to the Gare Centrale to pick up their wealthy patrons; they did not recommend the crowded tramway. Tourists overwhelmingly used cabs not trams, as did colonial officials and highly placed civil servants. Cabs were controllable, fast and customized. Something of the status of their genesis as the preserve of the rich and powerful (coachmen in private service) must have made their use attractive. There was probably, in short, a class dimension to the consumption of cab rides, which worked in the cabbies favor. Furthermore, the appearance

---

25 DWQ *ʿĀbdīn: Diwān Khidīwī ʿArḍḥālāt* 615 1906-7, no. 386, April 2, 1907. And for other petitions, see below.

26 Omnibuses probably took passengers from donkey boys more than from coachmen.

27 A veritable 'downtown' destination, hard by the newly constructed hotels, banks, the General Post Office, the shopping of ʿAtaba and the Muskī, and serving the entertainment district of Azbakiyya, which offered anything from 'low, Levantine dancing booths' to Ismāʿīl's Opera.

28 It is likely that the smashing of the trams (and the assault on their passengers) by cabbies which took place in April 1907 during the strike resulted in part from resentment about this. Cabbies may have been expressing in particular indignation at the unfavourable comparison made in the press between the 'civilisation' of the tram and the backwardness of the cabbies. Smashing trams was also, however, probably an attempt to make the strike more effective.

of the tram on certain main routes did not necessarily crush out competing coachmen. For example, a government order had to be issued in 1901 banning cabbies from the filled-in canal bed of the old Khalīj, the site of a major tramline since 1898.[29] Finally, the mass flow of passengers generated by the tram actually served the cabbies, who clustered in ʿAtaba to pick up those who disembarked.[30]

The greatest threat to the cabby's livelihood was not the tram, but the motorcar, whose presence was minimal before 1907, but growing thereafter. This new form of passenger transport, supplemented later by the minibus, was destined to take over where the cabbies left off – but this was a story for later years. Before the First World War, the cabbies were only slightly threatened by automobiles, which remained few.[31]

Thus, during just twenty-five years public coach driving became one of the commonest occupations in the city. Cabbies became the preferred mode (if often grudgingly) of intra-city transport for an expanding upper-middle and upper class of bankers, Pashas, landowners, colonial officials, politicians, civil servants, merchants, efendiyya, tourists and others. By 1917 the coachmen were even more numerous than Cairo's ubiquitous tailors (5,880 strong), shoemakers (5,682 persons), carters of goods (5,195 persons), and bakers (4,449 persons). According to the 1917 census, they were only outnumbered by such inclusive categories as of 'public administration' (9,451 persons) and 'trades in alimentary products' (17,598 persons), for example.[32] Thus, whereas public coachmen were probably only present in small numbers in the early 1800s, if they existed at all, by 1917 they were one of the commonest (and most visible) trades in the city. In the 1900s, cabbies were kings of the road in Cairo.

Location, Guild and Structure

During the fifty years before the First World War, cabbies were generally most active in the newly constructed streets between the Ottoman city and the Nile to the West (the Ismāʿīliyya Quarter), and plying the roads, which

---

29 GP QM 1900, 198: No carts, cabs, camels etc. on Khalīj Street in Cairo, March 1900.

30 It is tempting to argue that the tram stole market share mostly from donkey boys who catered to similar middling and lower income customers. See, for example, Martin, *Les Bazars*, 74.

31 Cabbies were even able to successfully lobby the government to restrict numbers of licences granted to motor taxis in the latter half of 1907, as we shall see.

32 1917 Census.

linked Būlāq and Old Cairo (Miṣr al-Qadīma) to the central districts.[33] 'Concentrations of animals' for omnibuses and cabs were noted at Qaṣr al-Nīl bridge and ʿAtaba al-Khaḍra Square, at the convergence of the trams.[34] Cabs waited on promenaders and entertainment seekers in the Azbakiyya; they attended the Gare Centrale for tourists, businessmen and government officials arriving by train from Alexandria; and they plied the streets surrounding the major 'downtown' hotels. They also spilled over the Nile towards Giza, into the Ottoman city down Muḥammad ʿAlī Street towards the citadel, and in the early 1900s, appeared on routes headed towards Wāyilī, Shubrā, ʿAbbāsiyya and Heliopolis.[35]

Most if not all of the drivers were men, and they were largely local subjects born in Egypt. For example, of the 1,470 persons listed in the 1868 census of Cairo Governorate under 'coachmen and carters' (*ʿarbajiyya wa qamāshajiyya*), 1,162 were from the capital (*min al-maḥrūsa*) and 290 from the provinces (*min al-aqālīm*). There were 15 Turks (atrāk), 2 Syrians (*shawwām*) and 1 North African (pl. *mughārib*). The profession was not exclusively Muslim. Certainly of the few cabdrivers' names I have seen, there are examples of Copts.[36]

How were cab drivers, owners, and owner-drivers linked together as a profession? What was the legacy of the abrogation of the guild in 1890? Was there some form of guild or guild-like collective organization, which bound members together in some social or economic sense? Even in the two or three decades preceding 1890 (when the guilds were tacitly abrogated), it is unlikely that the 'guild of coachmen' represented much more than a unit of taxation and regulation. Baer and Raymond tend to agree that guilds generally were no longer the site of 'para-religious' activity by even the eighteenth century.[37] Further, Baer saw the guild more as an administrative link to the government and a unit of urban taxation than a bastion of corporate solidarity which mobilized members' interests before the state

---

33 Prior to 1900, many lived in Old Cairo and Būlāq (1897 census). Būlāq was also one of the centres of unrest during the strike of April 1907.

34 *Egyptian Gazette*, April 7, 1908. Such animals may have been grazing, waiting for rides or both.

35 In 1897, numbers of drivers living in Shubrā, Wāyilī and ʿAbbāsiyya were quite low. However, this distribution had substantially changed by 1917, by which time more cabbies lived in Wāyilī than anywhere else (over a sixth of all those listed).

36 For example, Ḥannā al-Qubṭī. DWQ ND MA M33 No. 477 Cairo Local Authority/Ministry of the Interior 27 Dhū al-Qaʿda 1296. The 1897 census suggests that very few numbers of foreign subjects participated in the trade. Only 73 are listed out the 7,773 under 'driver, carter' (*cocher*, *charretier*).

37 Baer, *Egyptian Guilds*, 9-11. Raymond, *Artisans et Commercants*, 529-544.

and others. Raymond largely concurred. It is still not clear that Cole's evidence of vigorous mobilization by guild members in defense of their interests actually indicates that the guild itself was an interest group or unit of social mobilization, which actively promoted members' conçerns. But, his argument does show that government control over trades was far more decentralized and contested than Baer made out.[38] Mobilizations in the 1870s and 1880s do indicate that groups of craftsmen – factions within guilds (whether allied to a guild hierarchy or not), or whether forming links to those outside the trade such as merchants or not – were practiced at banding together, petitioning and even protesting violently to voice their demands. It is not necessary to see this as a manifestation of guild mobilization per se.

In 1890, the profession, like the other urban crafts and trades, was declared free, in the sense that anyone was permitted to take up the trade, as long as they registered various details with the governorate and obtained a license and number. Thus after this date, there was no official reason for any cab driver to interact with a guild *shaykh* or his deputies. The *shaykh* had lost his powers to tax and regulate traders in 1890. Moreover, the profession was expanding, apparently quite rapidly. New cabbies were obtaining licenses all over the city, which itself had grown to over three quarters of a million souls by 1917. It is unlikely that even rudimentary links were maintained between most in the profession. Yet, coffeehouses in certain areas, various popular hackney stands, ʿAtaba al-Khaḍra and other places probably supported localized social interaction. Although newspapers occasionally spoke of the *ṭā'ifa* (or 'guild') of coach men, this word most likely signified little more than the group of all those occupied in that profession. It does not seem to have implied anything specific about collective organization. Still, the *shaykh* and other senior members of the profession had not been suppressed in 1890, and retained a certain status in the trade. A '*shaykh*', for example, was present amongst one of the deputations sent by the strikers to the governorate in April 1907.

It is difficult to determine how many drivers owned their own cabs, how many hired their carriages, and how many were waged laborers for cab owners (who may or may not have driven themselves), not to mention how these relations changed over time. An example of a driver who owned his own cab was one ʿAbd Allāh Faqr, who purchased a victoria with the

38 Juan Cole, *Colonialism and Revolution*, Princeton 1993, 164-189. A host of others have persuasively made the same point – for Egypt and for previous times in the Ottoman Empire. For example, Haim Gerber, *Economy and Society in an Ottoman City, Bursa: 1600-1700*, Jerusalem 1988, 33-60; Ehud Toledano, *State and Society in mid-Nineteenth Century Egypt*, Cambridge 1990, 226f.

help of his niece, and improved its condition until it became "the best of cabs," whereupon "they [he and his niece] both profited from it".[39] There are several examples of cab drivers who – along with their families – owned or purchased horses.[40] On other occasions horses might have been hired from dealers.[41] At a time when the carriages themselves were quite expensive (relative to the fixed capitals owned by, say, a tailor or a weaver) plenty of cabbies did not own their carriages, but drove for wages. A certain ʿAlī Zayyid declared himself to be a coachman "at the Hackney stand by the side of the Azbakiyya Gardens opposite the New Hotel". He said, "The carriage is not my property," "my wages are PT [Piastres Tariff] 5 per diem" and "I do not pocket any portion of the hire [fare] paid me [by passengers] for my master."[42] Various government departments also paid wages to cabbies. For example, a coachman working for a government hospital was paid 10-13 Piastres per day for his services in 1919.[43] During the strike of April 1907, all the newspapers mention both owners (*aṣḥāb*) and workers (*ʿummāl*). Other wage-earning cabbies probably included those working for the big hotels, many of which controlled carriages for patrons.

Cab drivers and owners, on the face of it, were rather efficiently and cheaply provided with credit, equipment and other forms of working and fixed capital by a combination of local and foreign, large and small business. The finished cab was generally manufactured locally either in one workshop or in several. The British Chamber of Commerce lamented that imported British cabs could not compete with local makers, most likely because of a combination of transport costs and the cheapness of the product made by local craftsmen, who worked for low profits and low wages. Wheels, axles, lamps, springs and varnish, however, were usually imported from Europe, whereas the blacksmithery, saddlery and carpentry were local.[44] Most cabs were fitted with iron tyres, although a few used India rubber. Little is known about how the owners of cabs accessed credit. One can assume that such money was unlikely to have come from a modern

---

39 DWQ *ʿĀbdīn: Dīwān Khidīwī ʿArḍḥālāt* 615, 1906-7; January 28, 1907.

40 In this case, Muḥammad Sulaymān's son purchased two horses to pull his cab. DWQ *ʿĀbdīn: Dīwān Khidīwī ʿArḍḥālāt* 615, 1906-7, no. 46; January 10, 1906.

41 It is possible that some drivers hired their cabs from owners and pocketed the fares paid by the passenger, but I have not seen any evidence to confirm or deny this.

42 PRO FO 841/55 Case No. 3, May 19, 1893.

43 PRO FO 848/17 *Government Budget 1919,* 121-181.

44 *Egyptian Gazette* January 4, 1907, 4. *Al-Muqtaṭaf* (1909), 1007: The author mentions carriage-making as an industry which had grown in Egypt over the last few decades.

financial sector geared to the needs of land and merchants. In the one example I have seen, ʿAbd Allāh Faqr purchased his cab with family money. The supply of other fixed and working capital was abundant. Whips were sold on principal thoroughfares. In the Azbakiyya, whip makers and sellers made cheap use of the trees (planted by westernizing town planners) on which they plaited and hung their wares.[45] Indeed, saddlers, harness-makers, whip and lash makers in Cairo increased their numbers by half between 1897 and 1907.[46] A stream of camels and donkeys whose presence was especially noted on the new Qaṣr al-Nīl bridge supplied fodder for the horses.[47] Piles of fodder were observed in ʿAtaba al-Khaḍra. The 1903 abolition of the octroi duty on goods entering Cairo probably had a favorable impact on this particular supply line.[48] Horses were probably both owned and rented from dealers,[49] shod by local blacksmiths, and housed in stables (probably rented)[50] and in the open air around the city. The cabbies themselves ate from pavement restaurants and bread sellers, or slaked their thirst from *zīrs* set up on public thoroughfares. There is little reason to doubt that Egypt's economy in the late nineteenth century was quick to provide the fixed and working capital necessary to support the rapid expansion of the coach trade.

Whether or not cabbies were recognized implicitly as being indispensable to the functioning of the city – as evidenced by complaints during the strike (as we shall see) – they were generally held in low regard amongst their clientele and by literate opinion. They were considered ruffianly, boorish, incompetent, cruel, and backward. A writer in the Egyptian Gazette wrote "it might be asked why they [the police] do not, when issuing licenses to *arbajis*, insist on some test of driving and topography. The local

45 Sladen, *Oriental Cairo*, 58.

46 Censuses of 1897 and 1907.

47 Again one observes how modern urban infrastructure benefitted those using older technologies.

48 That prices increased in Cairo after the abolition of the octroi was probably unrelated to this measure – contrary to Cromer's claims. It probably had more to do with constraints on the food supply and other inflationary pressures. See Arminjon, *La situation economique*, Paris 1911, 399-415.

49 There were 793 dealers and hirers of donkeys, horses, and camels in Cairo in 1907 according to the census.

50 A certain Aḥmad ʿAlī was renting a stable from Ismāʿīl Darwīsh. In this case, the latter (the owner of the stable) was supposedly responsible – at least according to Aḥmad ʿAlī for the upkeep and hygiene of the stable, a responsibility which may have included the supply of fodder for Aḥmad's horse. DWQ *ʿĀbdīn: Dīwān Khidīwī* 613, 1902-3, March 3, 1902.

Jehu has no idea of either, and having also no 'hands', plies the whip savagely and ceaselessly to cover his defects." The writer continued: "[a] s the *ʿarbaji*, so is the donkey boy a class ...composed chiefly now of hulking loutish men who form a public nuisance to pedestrians and a menace to any defenseless or nervous client".[51] Another wrote "I have no hesitation in saying that the reckless way in which the Cairo *ʿarbajis* drive, their insolent manners, and the condition of their horses, is a disgrace to civilization."[52] At some point, in popular idiom at least, the word *ʿarbaji* became an insult, carrying the meaning 'low life' or 'scum'. Such attitudes were probably nothing new. An eighteenth century enumeration of the "basse classe" (*al-nās al-dūn*) included stablemen (*suyyās*).[53] However, for local elites, the cabbies were not only low and callous, they were also backward, especially in comparison with the modern tram, that wonder of science and progress. This attitude was new. Consider the following:

> The tram was the end of a chapter in the history of Cairean society, which was transported through it from the stage of nomadism and backwardness which is represented by the use of the donkey and the mule to the stage of urban civilization (*al-ḥaḍāra al-madaniyya*) which is represented in the use of electric power ...the terrible difficulties in transport [stemming] from the tyranny (*istibdād*) of the donkey drivers and coachmen and their power over people, and the cursing that they make people endure.[54]

In an age of progress, the cabbies and their horses, which lacked science or mechanization, were thought of as belonging to a bygone age.[55]

Wages and profits amongst the *ʿarbajiyya* were low – even in comparison with other urban crafts and trades. The 5 Piastres paid to ʿAlī Zayyid in 1893, the 10-13 Piastres paid to government coachmen in 1919,[56] the fact

---

51 *Egyptian Gazette*, February 27, 1907.

52 *Egyptian Gazette,* October 18, 1907.

53 Raymond, *Artisans et commercants*, vol. 2, 381.

54 Jamāl al-Badawī, "*ʿAfrīt*" in *Miṣr min nāfidhat al-tārīkh*, Cairo 1994, 196-198. Al-Badawī is here summarising Kitānī's account from the early 1900s.

55 Such a notion owed little to their multiplying numbers, or the fact that their prominent public presence was probably only recent and grew out of the modern landscape of the city in many ways, as well as owing to distinctively modern social relations and consumption patterns.

56 Government coachmen other than the one cited above were also paid the same wage. For example a driver working for the Ministry of Interior was also paid 10-13 Piastres per day in 1919 according to the budget records. *Government Budget 1919*, FO 848/17, 121-181.

that the twenty new recruits to the deputyship of Būlāq in the late 1870s were all in the lowest tax bracket for the crafts and trades (*arbāb al-kārāt*)[57] all argue that the coach men were at the low end of male urban incomes.[58]

Enter the SPCA

Just when numbers in the profession were increasing as never before, and when economic expansion was at its height – in the boom times leading up to the slump of the second half of 1907 – a threat emerged. In the early 1900s, the recently established British-run Society for the Prevention of Cruelty for Animals turned its attention to the health and safety of cab drivers' horses (as well as other livestock) in the city. The SPCA lamented the lameness, emaciation, and beating of 'dumb animals', which in its view resulted from the cruel and wanton behavior of cab drivers and others. They spoke of "animals with sore backs, shoulders, legs," "sores and swellings" and of "overloading, underfeeding, cruelty, [and] beating".[59] The Society combined favorable opinion[60] and a certain political clout[61] to enforce existing regulations relating to the health and well being of horses.[62] They worked with police and even secured the appointment of

57 From a statement compiled by the guild in 1879. DWQ ND MA M33 No. 477 Cairo Local Authority/Ministry of the Interior 27 Dhū al-Qaʿda 1296.

58 Although evidence from tax returns is highly problematic – as the return often reflected guild politics rather than actual levels of profit. I have not seen evidence relating to tips.

59 FO 371/450 enclosure to a PQ 12378, April 10, 1908.

60 Writers in the *Egyptian Gazette*, for example, would passionately swear allegiance to the cause. *Egyptian Gazette,* July 6, 1907.

61 It provoked questions in parliament in England, and secured letters from the Foreign Office to Gorst, who found himself nudged to do something about cruelty to animals in Cairo. FO 371/450 PQ 12378, April 10, 1908; FO 371/450 43520 Malet/Gorst, December 15, 1908.

62 The Society appealed to regulations which had already been issued. Quite comprehensive rules affecting cabbies up and down Egypt had been promulgated in the early 1890s – probably in view of the public and visible nature of the trade, and especially in that it was patronised by the elite. Licences were to be issued by the governorate or provincial offices in return for the registration of the applicant's name, title, nationality, address, and description of his cab. Livestock were to be kept healthy, able and adequately fed. Cabs were only allowed to tout for rides in certain areas of town and to stop in certain locations. Comprehensive tariff lists were drawn up for all major points in Cairo as well as for Egypt's other main towns. The SPCA was interested in enforcing the few provisions relating to the health and well-being of the horses. From Gharbiyya province in the Delta, to Assiut in Upper Egypt the regulations were broadly

one of their own – a certain Major Jarvis – as a special inspector with powers to arrest animals and offenders himself. Hence, in the early 1900s, thousands of arrests were made, licenses withdrawn, animals ordered rest or forcibly hospitalized, prosecutions pursued and convictions obtained. The SPCA celebrated over 5,000 convictions in 1906, which was declared a record year.[63]

The First Response: Petitions

Cab drivers and owners protested in a string of petitions. To them the enforcement was not a noble crusade, but a heavy handed and unjust intervention. Often they felt they were being punished for no reason at all. Or they argued that the regulations on lameness and ill health were far too severe. Punishments were also thought unreasonably harsh. Horses were confiscated, and either put down or treated at the owner's expense; licenses were suspended or withdrawn completely; offenders were fined heavily and regularly sent to prison for weeks at a time. Others argued that punishments were arbitrary and unfair seeing as most cabdrivers were in contravention of the new regulations most of the time, and therefore being punished was just a matter of bad luck. Others complained that the interaction with the police involved large bribes, not to mention police brutality, which in one case allegedly lead to death. All such difficulties were encountered by cabmen who often claimed to be and were poverty stricken, disabled, and trying to support a family.[64]

---

similar: GP QM 1893 194-197: Daqhaliyya Province: April 1893. GP QM 1893, 275-295: Gharbiyya, Sharqiyya, Assiut, May-June 1893. GP QM 1894, 166: Cairo Governorate. GP QM 1894, 400-5: Alex and Suez Governorate and elsewhere. GP QM 1901: 170-3: Passenger cabs regulations tightened.

63 The SPCA claimed that "5,699 animals were arrested during the past year [1906], as against 4,661 in 1905... . 1,858 were ordered rest, their owners being prosecuted, as compared with 1,831 in the previous year. 3,013 animals were admitted to the Infirmary in 1906, as against 2,423 in 1905." Convictions obtained amounted to 4,533 in 1905 and 5,315 in 1906. "In addition to the above 3,491 persons were punished administratively for furious driving, over-loading, etc." Major Jarvis himself, the special Inspector, arrested more than 400 animals in 6 months in 1906. "To sum up... work performed by the Society with the help of the police, during 1906, constituted a record." See *Egyptian Gazette,* September 5, 1907. Considering that in Cairo governorate there were around 11,000 cart and cab drivers (according to the 1907 census), it would appear that a substantial proportion of cab drivers were directly affected.

64 Examples of family budgets from Martin's work show the intense poverty in which the urban poor lived. Martin, *Les Bazars*, 78-81.

In the initial stages, the cabmen are found blaming each other rather than the strictness of the regulations. For example, when Aḥmad ʿAlī lost his license because of the ill health of his horse he blamed the owner of the stable, Ismāʿīl Darwīsh for failing to 'follow healthy practices'.[65] As the enforcement was intensified, however, cab men started to blame the police and the regulations themselves. Muḥammad Sulaymān, who had been dismissed from government service owing to paralysis, had a son who bought a pair of horses so that the family could subsist on income from cab driving. Then the Azbakiyya police (*qism*) took one of the horses on December 2, 1905 and the second on the 16th "and on the first there was a slight injury and on the second a minor lameness". The family only discovered later that the vet had put the horses down. The father requested an investigation and the price of the horses, because he was "very poor and needy". The petition enclosed a 'certificate' from four cabmen stating that the condition of the horses in question had been good for years.[66]

In November 1906, a petition without seals or signatures was sent complaining about the "tyranny (*istibdād*) and injustice (*ẓulm*)" inflicted by the police on the cabmen and the "extraction of large sums of money from them" and the "beating of whoever refuses to cooperate with them," "beating which sometimes leads to the death of who is beaten... after the doctor's statement that the reason for death was drunkenness." The petition also cited police opposition to "selling [touting for lifts] in the street," and "whoever does not pay what is demanded from him is taken to the station" and the police ensure an unfavorable verdict if the case goes to court.[67] In January 1907, another petition was summarized as follows:

> ʿAbd Allāh Faqr of Cairo, after finishing his military service, wanted to work as a cabdriver due to his poverty and the size of his family. So his niece bought a cart to be used [for this] by him. They both benefited from it. After that he spent a sum on repairing it… until it became the best of cabs… [but] the inspector of traffic (*mufattish al-murūr*) stopped it's working without giving a reason. Therefore he petitioned twice about this to the interior adviser (*mustashār al-dākhiliyya*) and requested an order [to return the cab to work].[68]

65 DWQ *ʿĀbdīn: Dīwān Khidīwī* 613, 1902-3, March 3, 1902.

66 DWQ *ʿĀbdīn: Dīwān Khidīwī ʿArḍḥālāt* 615, 1906-7, no. 46, January 10, 1906.

67 DWQ *ʿĀbdīn: Dīwān Khidīwī ʿArḍḥālāt* 615, 1906-7, November 24, 1906.

68 DWQ *ʿĀbdīn: Dīwān Khidīwī ʿArḍḥālāt* 615, 1906-7, January 28, 1907.

Sometimes women petitioned on behalf of husbands or sons. Perhaps this was thought to be a more effective way of gaining clemency from the authorities (*wilāyāt al-umūr*). For example, Umm ʿAbd al-Raḥman, the wife of Ṣāliḥ Jawhar, a master cab driver, petitioned the Khedivial Diwan to forgive her husband from a prison sentence he had received.[69] Another petition on March 17, 1907 was summarized thus:

> Muḥammad Ḥasan Abū Sitta of Cairo deposes that his trade (*kār*) has been that of cabman since old times. He has been in his trade for around 30 years. [But] the government withdrew the license from him and from some persons on the pretext that they had no permission to work on account of the injuries [of their horses]. However, there are many present like them still in work. And... with this family [he is] in the greatest need (*ashadd al-iḥtiyāj*) and requests an investigation and their return to their work and that he is prepared to bring the guarantee, which is demanded of him.[70]

Yet another petition arrived on March 21, 1907. Muḥammad Ḥasan, previously a cabman in Cairo, deposed that the governorate took away his license (*rukhṣa*) without reason. He was then living off 'generosity' for three years until his condition deteriorated, partly because of an illness. His complaints, he said, did not bear any fruit, until finally the governorate permitted him to drive a Suarès coach. But Muḥammad thought this made little sense, given that such coaches involved being in charge of three horses, whereas working on his own account, which was what he wanted, only meant being in charge of two horses. He requested permission for work on his own account, and was ready to offer a guarantee.[71] A few weeks later Ḥasan continued to press his case: "why is it possible for him to run three horses, but it is not possible for him to run two?" Ḥasan claimed this was 'tyranny' which "prevented him from making a living," while "he is poor and disabled and has no [criminal] record in the least," and "seeks permission to work his trade directly".[72]

The Question of Nationalism

It is difficult to establish to what extent anti-English sentiment or even nationalism was either generated by or fed into the sense of grievance felt

---

69 *Sijillāt ʿĀbdīn: Qaid al-ʿArḍḥālāt al-Wārida 1/27/5/S* 1893-4, March 16, 1893.

70 DWQ *ʿĀbdīn: Dīwān Khidīwī ʿArḍḥālāt* 615, 1906-7, no. 288, March 17, 1907.

71 DWQ *ʿĀbdīn: Dīwān Khidīwī ʿArḍḥālāt* 615, 1906-7, no. 309, March 21, 1907.

72 DWQ *ʿĀbdīn: Dīwān Khidīwī ʿArḍḥālāt* 615, 1906-7, no. 386, April 2, 1907.

by cab drivers in respect of the heavy regulations under which they labored. It was likely that most cab drivers knew the English S.P.C.A. was behind the enforcement. The petitions make only one or two references to English involvement, but this may well have been a judicious strategy by cabbies who thought it wiser not to express anti-English sentiment. But I have seen no evidence, which linked cab drivers systematically to organized nationalism prior to the strike of April 1907 – although after the strike things changed, as we shall see. One might suggest, somewhat speculatively, that cabbies expressed their grievances in part by their manners, and by small acts of non-cooperation. Certainly such practices would have fed into the English opinion (which mistook politics for nature), that cabbies were naturally boorish. At times, indeed, bad manners became actual aggression – behind which may well have lain the politics of trade regulation as well as more widespread anti-imperial sentiment. Consider the following account by an English resident of Cairo:

> He [the cab driver] is… a sportsman in his way, and his chief recreation consists in endeavoring to 'run down' well dressed Europeans. It soothes his racial antipathies and even if he can't bag his man he can splash him with mud or cover him with dust according to local atmospheric conditions, or, if he has a clear street before him and the khawagah does not look like a 'sprinter', he can slash him over the face with his whip. … A month ago an arbaghi came up behind me along the Sharia Kamel and with the whole road to spare hugged the right side and without a word of warning I felt his off horse's shoulder cannon into mine; he had plenty of space but having some experience in 'riding off' I got clear of his hoofs and the wheels, but still it was not a bad attempt.[73]

It is possible to posit some relation between such incidents and the situation with the S.P.C.A., especially in view of the timing of the above encounter – early 1907.

In spite of the depth of grievance on enforcement, no accommodations were forthcoming. Indeed, punishments for offenders were actually increased in the early spring of 1907.[74] Rising prices, especially after 1900, can only have heightened cabbies' discontent. Those at the bottom end of the adult male wage scale must have been particularly badly affected. The end of the tourist season in early April must have added to their immediate woes. Where, then, could the cab drivers turn? Or, to put it another way,

---

73 *Egyptian Gazette*, February 27, 1907, 3.

74 It was decreed that if an emaciated horse was arrested then its owner would be imprisoned for 7 days and fined 100 Piastres. *Al-Jarīda*, April 18, 1907, 3.

what else informed their sense of injustice? First, the urban trades could look back on a tradition of fairly direct forms of protest (beyond petitioning): of shutting shops, occupying slaughterhouses, marching in the streets, of withholding their services and goods.[75] Second, cab drivers must have known about foreign and local strike action of various kinds.[76] Third, the cab drivers probably hoped for the favor of ever more vocal nationalist opinion[77] – particularly if they were making the connection between the English SPCA and their grievances.

The Strike

My research has not been able to uncover how the cabbies actually organized in the days before the protest, nor have I been able to determine precisely the nature of the spark that lit the tinder. Nonetheless, on April 18, 1907, in a development which took all the newspapers by surprise, between two and five thousand Cairean cab drivers and owners joined a near total strike (*aḍrabū ʿan al-ʿamal*). Al-Jarīda reported that "the streets were empty of cabs". The Egyptian Gazette concurred: "not a single cab is to be found in the streets".[78] In Al-Ahrām it was stated that "a total strike prevailed".[79] In the words of one newspaper:

---

75 Cole, *Colonialism*, 1993, 164-189. Raymond, *Artisans*, 1973, 592.

76 Walk outs and protests at Port Saʿīd had rumbled on since 1882 and were well reported in the press. As was the strike of the cigarette rollers of 1899 and the tram workers action of 1906. Foreign strikes – in Iran, Turkey and Europe – sometimes made front page news in al-Ahrām and elsewhere. Beinin, Lockman, *Workers on the Nile,* 48-82. Donald Quataert, *Social Disintegration and Popular Resistance in the Ottoman Empire, 1881-1908: Reactions to European Economic Penetration*, New York 1983 *passim.* in Egypt were not illegal on the one hand, but nor were they specifically legislated as a legal form of protest on the other. In other words, demonstrators would probably face arrest in practice. Thus the law did not pave the way for the cabbies' strike by generating a certain category of legal action into which they could slot themselves.

77 Amongst many others, Bassam Tibi, *Arab Nationalism: Between Islam and the Nation State*, London 1997, 178-190.

78 *Egyptian Gazette*, April 18, 1907.

79 *Al-Ahrām* April 18, 1907. *Al-Jarīda* estimated that there were more than 2,000 strikers, and that the number at work under police supervision remained very small *Al-Jarīda*, April, 18, 1907, 3. Al-Ahrām estimated that as many as 12,000 cab men had struck work – surely an exaggeration. Whatever the exact figure, the strike was probably near total.

> The coachmen went this morning in groups to the police stations and the governorate building... they did not see one of them driving a cab without getting him down [ejecting the passenger] ... in order that their colleague participate with them in the strike against the police and the traffic bureau (*qalam al-murūr*).[80]

According to Al-Jarīda, the chief of the police, on the arrival of a deputation from the cabmen, "promised them orally that the owners of horses found to be sick would not be imprisoned but a fine would be paid".[81] Some were satisfied, most were not. Therefore, along with their leaders they wrote their complaints and demands down and sent them to the Minister of Justice, with a copy to the chief of police, and then returned to the governorate building to await developments.

During this time the workers held a number of meetings in their coffeehouses in areas of the capital and its outskirts and they decided on a general strike until the governorate changed the traffic regulations. They delegated their *shaykh* and some of their senior people to talk with the authorities on the subject.[82]

As the morning wore on, tensions began to rise. "Some joined demonstrations but were arrested and taken forcibly to prison".[83] Large numbers of cabmen, according to Al-Jarīda, then "called out all of those in sympathy with them to fight to assist them against the injustice (*ʿaṣf*) of the police." Then "they met in groups and set about striking private cabs and omnibuses and the tram. Then they surrounded the police stations, clamoring and menacing trouble if those who had been imprisoned were not released."[84]

There was a large gathering in ʿAbd al-ʿAzīz street close to Muskī police station:

> where they waited for the arrival of the tram cars... and prevented the passengers from boarding... . After that they smashed it [a tram car] to pieces and beat the driver and the passengers, young and old, women and children, as if the strike was directed at everyone and not [simply the] police.[85]

---

80 *Al-Jarīda*, April 18, 1907.

81 *Ibid.*

82 *Ibid.*

83 *Ibid.*

84 *Al-Jarīda*, April 24, 1907.

85 *Ibid.*

There were other desperate scenes. Near the Azbakiyya police station, close to the Abu ʿAlā bridge "they smashed the windows of around 20 cars and omnibuses carrying school-children". Al-Jarīda reported that:

> they were assisted... by a group of rabble and riff-raff (*al-sūqā wa al-rāʿāʿ*) who have no work until most of the coffeehouses in ʿAbd al-ʿAzīz street as well as [those in] the nearest [streets] of Fajjala were closed, and some people hurried to their homes.[86]

Al-Ahrām wrote that "mixed in with these [the cabmen] were fanatics who are considered [mere] street clamorers and who strike one another with cudgels".[87] Such 'street clamorers' may well have had more political considerations in mind. Anti-imperialist sentiment was apparently abroad during the strike. Consider the following letter written by an Englishman after the strike:

> When the cab strike was on I... noticed a European driving in a cab pursued by a number of low class natives... . Several shawishes were in the immediate vicinity making a feeble pretence of protecting the cab and a patrol of mounted police with two officers were galloping to the cab's assistance and at that moment were about eighty yards from the cab. An Arab just then hurled a heavy lump of stone, which narrowly missed the head of the European in the cab. It was so big that if it had hit him the blow might easily have proved fatal. Any of the foot police could easily have arrested the man. But on the contrary they flagrantly allowed him to escape up a side street so as to avoid the mounted policemen, who, be it noted, had European officers with them... . Ten minutes afterwards when the crowd had dispersed, the man, who had thrown the stone, was talking and laughing with the two shawishes on the very spot where he had committed the outrage.[88]

Meanwhile, back amongst the strikers themselves:

> [T]he tumult at the [police] stations continued until 8 pm, whereupon they attacked the commissioner (*ma'mūr*) of Azbakiyya police station and wrestled him to the ground, and he was only saved from their hands by the force of the mounted police.

---

86 *Ibid.*

87 *Al-Ahrām,* April 19, 1907.

88 *Egyptian Gazette*, April 26, 1907.

But, al-Jarīda continued,

> the government did not seek to treat them with severity, rather it released those imprisoned in the police stations and then called their leaders and their *shaykhs* to the Governorate to agree with his honor the Governor to break up the demonstrations.[89]

After negotiations in the Governorate building, four major concessions were made. First, some of the officials about whom complaints had been repeatedly raised were to be sacked. Second, small injuries to horses and livestock were not to be forcibly hospitalized but treated by the owner. Third, serious lameness would lead to hospitalization but not the arrest of the driver or the imprisonment of the owner. Fourth, infractions in traffic regulations would not result in the loss of license, but a fine of 15 Piastres. By the following morning, (Friday) many cabmen had returned to work.[90]

If the cabmen had suspected that they would find some support amongst nationalists, they guessed right. This does not mean that any newspaper supported the actual violence – but partly because they saw it as undermining the cause of self-government. As al-Ahrām wrote, "we regard [the attacks of the cabmen on people] with sorrow, and perhaps [this] affirmed to us that the powers that be... wished for chaos. They take it as a pretext for English government over Egyptians."[91] Nonetheless, both al-Ahrām, and most of all Al-Jarīda were ready to detail what they viewed as the legitimate grievances of the cab drivers. Here is the latter:

> They [the coachmen] have a great many complaints about the police... . Scarcely can one of them leave the stable before he is taken by surprise by a policeman and he demands his license and number [saying] that he has too many passengers or some other trivial complaint. [The policemen is then] not satisfied with less than 10 Piastres [as a fine/bribe] and [so] withdraws his license and number and takes him to the traffic bureau. This is called 'the tomb' from which no license returns.

Al-Jarīda went on to say that it would take bribery and 'weeks and months' to get the license back, during which time "they and their families do not

---

89 *Al-Jarīda*, May 1, 1907.

90 23 cabmen were ultimately accused of attacking police, tramway workers or passengers during the strike. 18 of these went to prison for between 7 and 31 days. *Al-Jarīda*, May 1, 1907.

91 *Al-Ahrām*, April 20, 1907.

know how they can eat."[92] The cab drivers, it seems, had found allies amongst those who – at least temporarily – found their nationalism stronger than their ideas about boorish and backward cab drivers.[93]

Success

It may have come as a surprise to even the cabbies themselves, however, that their strike was something of a success. Not only were reprisals – in terms of fines, prison terms and police action – relatively mild (as far as one can tell from the relative brevity of the few prison terms meted out), but, more importantly, the concessions made on the evening of the 18th April were real and became law. Changes corresponding to the promises given were made to the regulations. Major Jarvis resigned in disgust. Witness the subsequent complaints of one SPCA supporter:

> [f]or a year past... since Major Jarvis left, cruelty has become worse, the police do nothing to check it... .The police used to examine the backs and look under the collars of animals. They are not allowed to do so anymore. The order was issued last year because a strike of cabmen... was feared by reason of their vigilance. When the order was issued, Jarvis resigned.[94]

Subsequent pressure from the SPCA, and the British Foreign Minister himself to tighten the regulations did not alter Gorst's post-strike policy of non-interference. Gorst had to justify the changes to the regulations as 'satisfactory' to Grey (following a parliamentary question) in April 1908.[95] And he seems to have quietly ignored a letter from Malet in December

---

92 *Al-Jarīda*, April 18, 1907.

93 The colonial press, on the other hand, tended to dismiss the cabmen as mere brutes, or as an urban rabble without purpose or legitimate cause. In the most extreme cases, a clearance was recommended. Here is the *Journal du Caire*: "These recent events clearly show that at the present time there is a large number of people in Cairo without any occupation, whose pleasure it is to utilise their leisure in the refined amusement of maltreating the passengers and the staff of the tramways. In such a case the police in every country in the world sweeps them away and clears the town of this disagreeable class. When are we to have a clearance at Cairo?" Quoted in the *Egyptian Gazette*, April 22, 1907. Other papers, such as *Les Pyramides*, hinted that "the whole affair was engineered for a political object by the Anglo-Egyptian authorities". Quoted in the *Egyptian Gazette*, April 23, 1907.

94 FO 371/450 12378, April 10, 1908. This letter enclosed in a Parliamentary Question from John Robertson.

95 FO 371/450 no. 14076, April 18, 1908 Gorst/Sir Edward Grey.

1908 urging him – in the wake of another parliamentary question – to take action on the matter.[96]

In an important sense, the cabmen had scared the English, and won a major victory. The key to the cabbies' success was probably the connection to nationalist politics. It was not that nationalists had engineered the strike action – although no one could be absolutely sure of this and certainly some of the more hysterical elements in the colonial press claimed that they had. But, the seriousness with which the major Arabic dailies took the demands of the strikers was a warning to the occupiers that alliances might be quick in the making. Links between nationalists and popular forces – in particular the unpredictable urban 'rabble' – were better avoided.[97]

Conclusion

This study is intended to show that at least in the case of the coachmen, economic modernization in Egypt was more complicated than the historiography would have us believe. The cabbies of Cairo were not merely the decaying remnants of a traditional past. Nor were they simply replaced by large-scale infrastructure and a modern proletariat. Instead, these family businesses expanded their numbers quite rapidly – possibly by more than ten times between the late 1880s and 1914, especially as the pace of modernization quickened. They quickly became one of the most multitudinous and visible of Cairo's trades. The cabbies' expansion owed most to their success in tapping the pockets of Egypt's increasingly wealthy upper classes, most markedly in the decades before the First World War. It also owed something to their own quite dramatic mobilization of April 1907, one of the largest pre-1919 popular protests, which secured the relatively unmolested passage of their livestock through the streets of Cairo. Both factors were deeply bound up with colonial conditions. The first because the colonial invasion did nothing to hinder the accumulation of wealth amongst Egypt's upper classes. In fact, in continuing a legacy of political stability and intervention in the agricultural infrastructure the British did much to secure this accumulation. The second because the very nervous-

96 FO 371/450 no. 43520 PQ John Robertson MP.

97 It may have looked to some as if the urban masses were starting to rise up towards the end of April 1907. I have had to completely leave out the wave of strike action amongst various urban crafts and trades which followed the protests of the cab men. The next to come out on strike were the carters (the following Saturday) whose activities provoked the arrival of the military and something approaching hysteria in various parts of the colonial press.

ness of a colonial regime before a nationalist threat was an impetus to capitulation over strict trade regulation.

The small, unmechanised, unscientific, low profit and family-run businesses of the cab drivers were part and parcel of the modernizing city in other ways. Their expansion owed very much to the rapid extension of its population and street plan – whether because of sheer weight of traffic, increasing scale, or wider, paved and straightened roads. Cab owners and drivers even benefited from the modern Qaṣr al-Nīl bridge in as much as it facilitated the supply of fodder for their horses, or modern town planning in as much as it supplied roomy pavements for fodder storage and trees for improvised whipstalls. From another angle, cheap industrial imports brought wheels, axles, and varnish, and inexpensive local craft skills provided saddlery, carpentry and ironwork. Both low cost inputs were hallmarks of a developing nineteenth century world economy. They made use of high technology on the one hand and low cost labor and dexterity on the other. Strong kinship structures were probably a good source of credit. Colonial tax policy, as we have seen, was also beneficial to small-scale urban trades like coachmen. Beyond this, the consumption of cab rides was now unavailable to most because of a lack of cash rather than because of what amounted to traditional sumptuary laws on the privilege of riding in a carriage or on a horse. Thus, a key (but not universal or uncomplicated) principle of modern economy was at work in the success of public cab driving. Further, cab drivers did not stand apathetically aside from the political mobilizations of the time, but engaged energetically with the regulations and interest group politics of the centralized, colonial state, bringing old-established notions of injustice and taking inspiration from newer forms of strike action and nationalism. Their engagement actually helped construct the new regulative regime. Only during the inter-war period and after did small operators running taxis, motorcars, and eventually minibuses take over the mantle of kings of the road in Cairo.

What contribution, though, did the cab drivers make to the economy? It would perhaps be pitching it too high, when much remains obscure, to trumpet the cabs as a dynamic, flexible small business which drove wealth creation and economic expansion. Levels of accumulation and innovation were low where hands were cheap and abundant and conditions competitive. On the other hand, it would surely be mistaken, in the light of the foregoing, to dismiss the coach drivers as a mere repository of inefficient employment for a swelling, impoverished populace. It is not easy, for instance, to specify how exactly cabbies could have improved the speed or efficiency of their service. They seem to have squeezed what they could from their horses. They worked seven days a week themselves for low wages. ʿAbd Allāh Faqr, we recall, improved his carriage 'until it became the best of cabs'. Cabbies also went to considerable lengths to successfully roll back unwanted regulations. Finally, the coachmen catered to real demand on the part of Cairo's wealthier inhabitants for rapid and customized transportation. Indeed, by the early 1900s, the cabbies – for all their bad reputation, low wages, and baladī clothes – were indispensable to the functioning of the city, as the disruption of April 18, 1907 amply demonstrated.

One suspects, therefore, that as more is known about small-scale enterprise in Egypt, there will be an adjustment to the standard view that Egypt's nineteenth century economy was almost entirely based on an exchange of local raw materials for foreign manufactured and capital goods. As research continues, the majority of the urban population and their crafts and trades will start to appear as agents in the economic transformations of these years. This article is but a nod in this general direction.

– IV –

Urban Institutions Between Centralization and Autonomy

WAQF ONLY IN NAME, NOT IN ESSENCE

Early Tanẓīmāt Waqf Reforms in the Province of Damascus

ASTRID MEIER

In the *Hatt-i Şerif* of Gülhane of 1839, the Ottoman state committed itself to safeguard the lives, the honour and the property of all its subjects, Muslims and non-Muslims alike. The guarantee of these fundamental rights was considered a prerequisite to spur in Ottoman subjects "devotion and love for their state". After a long period of decline and weakness, caused by the neglect of the *sharīʿa*, the edict declared, a new era of a rule of law was about to start, as "it is evident that countries not governed by the *sharīʿa* cannot prevail".[1]

The edict, the opening statement of the *Tanẓīmāt* reform era (1839-1876), was seen as a new departure – the novelty of the commitment being above all that the state was publicly undertaking to honour these promises. The new, however, came in the guise of the old: the time-honoured rules of the religious law. But the reference to the *sharīʿa,* though legitimating change as a return to the origins, was not a reference to a set of fixed and unchangeable rules, as the law itself proved to be an important field of reform – a process which Derengil calls the "Ottomanization of the *sharīʿa*".[2]

In this article, I shall trace some aspects of this process focusing on shifting notions of property. The attempts of the Ottoman state to establish direct control over its whole territory resulted in a new relationship between the central government and its subjects. Strategies of modernisation, centralisation and bureaucratisation transformed the old imperial relationships that bound the centre and its peripheries and led to a new ideology of power relations seen as a separation of a "supposedly secular subjecthood

---

1 Translated in J. C. Hurewitz, *The Middle East and North Africa in World Politics, A Documentary Record*, New Haven 1975, vol. 1, 269-271.

2 Selim Deringil, *The Well-Protected Domains: Ideology and the Legitimation of Power in the Ottoman Empire, 1876-1909*, London 1998, 9.

from a modern secular state".[3] A similar bifocal perspective came to dominate property relations: property had to belong either to subjects (private) or to the state as the representative of common interests (public). In the long term, therefore, the reshaping of imperial relations led to decisive shifts in the interpretation of the *sharīʿa* regarding the legitimacy of different categories of property. Many discussions centred on a type that defied an easy categorisation along the newly emerging line of separation between state and subject, between "public" and "private", namely, the religious endowments (*waqf*).

Not only in the Ottoman Empire, but also in many other parts of the Islamic world, the institution of *waqf* became one of the battlefields of the advocates of reform in the name of progress and modernisation. Endowments came to be seen as a traditional stumbling block on the path to modernity and prosperity. Not only were, in this view, large parts of agricultural lands and urban space blocked from profitable use, but endowments also favoured a class of idle rentiers and religious scholars who were seen as desperately trying to protect their privileges and thus considered potent enemies of economic and social progress.[4]

Such views had a profound impact on Ottoman notions of the legitimacy of the *waqf* system. The control of *waqf* assets had always been a field contested by the central administration, its representatives on the provincial and local level, and other social groups. From the second half of the eighteenth century, however, a decisive shift toward increasing state control took place: starting in the imperial capital with the endowments of certain rulers, the state, in its attempt to extract more revenue from the *waqf* system, extended its direct control not only over a growing number of imperial endowments, but over other *waqf* types as well. In 1826, the year of the annihilation of the Janissaries, a further significant step was taken when the Ministry of *Awqāf* was established.

By mid-century, reform attempts reached provincial capitals like Damascus where a new order was introduced between 1843 and 1845. For the implementation of the reform, the newly introduced instruments of the *Tanẓīmāt* were being put into use: new functionaries and the provincial

---

3 See Ussama Makdisi's article in this volume.

4 For a later but very out-spoken example of this tendency see C. H. Becker, "Islam und Wirtschaft," in *Islamstudien: Vom Werden und Wesen der islamischen Welt* I, Hildesheim 1967, 62-63; David S. Powers, "Orientalism, Colonialism, and Legal History: The Attack on Muslim Family Endowments in Algeria and India," *CSSH* (1989), 535-570. For a similar attitude to the guild organisation see John Chalcraft's article in this volume.

advisory council (*majlis al-shūrā*). The proceedings allow insights into the interaction of the central administration with old and new local elites, into the bargaining processes that shaped the new relations between the centre and the peripheries. The *waqf* reform can thus be seen as an example of how new channels of participation opened during the early *Tanẓīmāt* period.[5]

This article will concentrate on the first phase of the *waqf* reforms, initiated in the imperial capital in the second half of the eighteenth century, ending with the changes in the provincial *waqf* administration of Damascus in 1845. Special attention will be paid to the imperial discourse on property, dissecting the category of *waqf* into new types of differing moral, religious, legal and economic legitimacy. I shall start, however, with a short introduction into the significance of endowments in the Ottoman era, concentrating in the second part on how the *waqf* system was controlled. The third part will focus on the introduction of *waqf* reforms into the provincial capital of Damascus.

Waqf, Private Property and the Ottoman State

At the beginning of the nineteenth century, large tracts of agricultural land and a high proportion of urban space throughout the Ottoman Empire were registered as *waqf* property. Contemporary observers estimated that between one half and two thirds of the land had already been endowed.[6] Stating the sheer numbers – which, it should be noted, derive from estimations of often rather unqualified and prejudiced observers – can help to apprehend the importance of the *waqf* institution in Islamic societies, but such a perspective does not give credit to the different religious, legal, social, economic and political aspects of endowments. The reasons why women and men turned their properties into *waqf* and what forms this took, were manifold and could vary from place to place and over the course of time. Apart from the general requirement that an endowment had to be established with the aim to come closer to God (*qurba*),[7] the rules of the dif-

---

5 See Jens Hanssen's article in this volume.

6 John Robert Barnes, *An Introduction to Religious Endowments in the Ottoman Empire*, Leiden 1986, 83; Ömer L. Barkan, "Les problèmes fonciers dans l'Empire ottoman au temps de sa fondation," *Annales d'Histoire Sociale 9* (1939), 237; Gabriel Baer, *Studies on the Social History of Modern Egypt*, Chicago 1969, 79.

7 For a discussion of the concept see J. N. D. Anderson, "The Religious Element in *Waqf* Endowments," *Royal Central Asian Journal* 38 (1951), 292-299.

ferent schools of law left a considerable margin for individual decision making.

The following remarks will focus on the rules concerning *waqf* as they were formulated in Ḥanafī legal thought of the early Ottoman period because they represent the official view of the empire. From this perspective, property was divided into the three main categories of *milk* (absolute property), *mīrī* (state property) and *waqf* (endowed property).[8] If property can be defined as a bundle of rights that determines a set of relationships between people (and the state) with respect to relevant objects,[9] the category of *milk* represented the highest degree of control an individual or a group could exercise over a given object. The most characteristic feature of this category was the liberty to transfer property by buying and selling, by making gifts and by inheritance. The category of *mīrī*, on the other hand, concerned ownership by the state. State property was normally confined to agricultural land outside the perimeter of cities (it is therefore not very significant in an urban context, where properties were either *milk* or *waqf*). Only rights pertaining to its use or to its revenues, but not to the land itself, were to be farmed out. The usufruct rights to the land (*taṣarruf*) came to be passed down the generations along with the rights to revenues from both the old *tīmār* system of land grants to the military and the more recent forms of tax farming (*iltizām, mālikāne*).

Waqf properties share characteristics with both *mīrī* and *milk*. The purpose of endowed properties was to produce an income that could be spent according to the will of the endower. This rather obvious point marks an important difference between *milk* and *waqf*, and sets *waqf* close to state property that also had to be rented out to make profit:

> The difference [between *milk* and *waqf*] is that the proprietor may refrain from farming out his property. He may want to live on it or to sell it or not to use it at all and in this respect his property differs from the *waqf* that is 'reserved to be farmed out' (*muʿadd lil-ījār*). The administrator of the *waqf* must farm it out.[10]

---

8 Leaving aside the two categories of land reserved for special forms of public use (*matrūka)* and unused lands (*mawāt)*, which are not significant in this context.

9 Tosun Aricanli, "Property, Land, and Labor in Nineteenth-Century Anatolia", in *Landholding and Commercial Agriculture in the Middle East*, eds. Caglar Keyder and Faruk Tabak, Albany, N.Y. 1991, 123-133.

10 Muḥammad Amīn Ibn ʿĀbidīn: *Al-ʿuqūd al-dhurriyya fī tanqīḥ al-fatāwā al-Ḥāmidiyya*, 2nd ed., Bulaq 1300 A.H., II 208; transl. Baber Johansen, *The Islamic Law on Land Tax and Rent: The Peasants' Loss of Property Rights as Interpreted in the Hanafite Legal Literature of the Mamluk and Ottoman Periods*, London 1988, 108.

Endowments are often classified as either *khayrī*, when the benefits were to go to a pious institution, or *dhurrī/ahlī* when the beneficiaries were members of the endower's family or his/her manumitted slaves (*mushtarak* if the *waqf* combined the two purposes from the moment of the endowment). *Khayrī* is thereby often translated as public and *dhurrī/ahlī* as private *waqf*.

This classification has been questioned for its inconsistencies on various grounds. Seen from the point of view of eternity and the Ḥanafī legal doctrine, every *waqf* had a *khayrī* purpose, and the *dhurrī* period is only a first stage in the history of an endowment.[11] Both types were equally acknowledged in legal and religious thought as good works or charity *(ṣadaqa)* for which one was to be rewarded in the afterlife. Contrary to views prevailing in the nineteenth and twentieth centuries, the establishment of a family endowment was indeed especially meritorious and earned at the same time both the rewards for carrying out a good deed and for taking care of relations, *ajr al-ṣadaqa* and *ajr al-qarāba*.[12] Furthermore, exactly the same legal rules applied to both forms.

Among the more substantial critics, two tendencies can be made out. Studies from a socio-economic and socio-political perspective, on the one hand, tend to see *waqf* property in general as a kind of private property, even if the controlling power invested in the owner of *milk* was decisively cut back.[13] This tendency focuses on the entitlement of individuals to various forms of income, stemming from different kinds of objects as for example rents from *mīrī* land or *waqf* assets, or the income from posts in mosques, *madrasas* and other institutions. From this perspective, the legally relevant distinctions lose their importance and the definition of private property becomes very broad to include the whole range of rights of individuals and groups to objects.

---

11 Miriam Hoexter, "The Idea of Charity: A Case Study in Continuity and Flexibility of an Islamic Institution," *Wissenschaftskolleg zu Berlin, Jahrbuch 1985/86*, Berlin 1987, 179-189.

12 Muslim, *Ṣaḥīḥ*, *Kitāb al-zakāt*, 45. For the spiritual aspects of *waqf* and *ṣadaqa* see T. H. Weir and A. Zysow, art. "*ṣadaqa*" in *EI²*, *II*, vol. 8, 708-716, and the forthcoming article of Johannes Pahlitzsch, "The Concern for Spiritual Salvation and *memoria* in Islamic Public Endowments in Jerusalem (XII-XVI c.) as Compared to the Concepts of Christendom," in *Egypt and Syria in the Fatimid, Ayyubid and Mamluk Eras III, Proceedings of the 7th International Colloquium organized at the Katholieke Universiteit Leuven in May 1998*, ed. Urbain Vermeulen, Leuven 1999.

13 See for example Zuhair Ghazzal, *L'économie politique de Damas durant le 19e siècle, Structures traditionelles et capitalisme*, Damascus 1993.

Studies of the development of the land law in the Ḥanafī school, on the other hand, stress the assimilation of *waqf* property to state property. Based on a new legal doctrine on rent and taxation, elaborated in the late years of Mamluk domination over Egypt and Bilād al-Shām, *waqf* assets enjoyed legal privileges which, to quote Baber Johansen, come close to a concept of "public law":

> Holding the unauthorised user of *waqf* lands (and state lands) and orphans' lands liable under all circumstances to pay the fair rent is certainly the most important change that the Hanafi jurists of the post-classical period introduced into the Hanafite legal doctrine concerning rent. (...) The new doctrine on rent grants a privileged legal status to all forms of rent-yielding property and makes the *waqf* the rent-yielding property par excellence. (...) This liability in no way depends on the will of the *waqf* administrator or the intention of the user.[14]

Both of these perspectives have brought to light new aspects of the *waqf* system in Ottoman societies. But if we want to focus on the role of the Ottoman state in the control of endowments and how this role changed at the outset of the *Tanẓīmāt* period, both positions need to be modified and other distinctions have to be taken into consideration.

The Ottoman State and Waqf Control

State intervention in *waqf* affairs was not a new phenomenon. The transformation of Ḥanafī legal thought that had brought legal privileges to *waqf* properties had been triggered by the conflicts over state and *waqf* lands that arose in Egypt and Bilād al-Shām during Mamluk rule.[15] A legally fully valid *waqf* (*ṣaḥīḥ)* could only be made from objects that were *milk* of the endower. By endowing it, the Ḥanafī doctrine held it to have become God's property, and it could therefore no longer be entered into the normal circulation of goods by being sold, bought, given or inherited.[16] Many of

---

14 Johansen, *Land Tax*, 110.

15 See Johansen, *Land Tax*; Kenneth M. Cuno, "Was the Land of Ottoman Syria *mīrī* or *milk?* An Examination of Juridical Differences within the Ḥanafī School," *SI* 81.1 (1995), 121-152; Oktay Özel, "Limits of the Almighty, Mehmed II's 'Land Reform' Revisited," *JESHO* 42.2 (1999), 226-246.

16 In practice, the inalienability of *waqf* assets was very difficult to be upheld, and some legal devices helped circumvent that prescription, in the name of the interest of the *waqf*. See Miriam Hoexter, "Adaptation to Changing Circumstances: Perpetual Leases and Exchange Transactions in Waqf Property in Ottoman Algiers," *Islamic Law and*

the smaller endowments in cities and villages were of this type, and although the individual endowment was often of little economic impact, their high number made them a significant factor in the economy of Ottoman societies.

Much more important in economic terms, however, were the foundations that were based on agricultural revenues. They were also more controversial, as they were seen as infringing on the rights of the state: most of them were based on *mīrī* lands that belonged to the state treasury (*bayt al-māl*). Through a formal act acknowledging a transfer of possession (*tamlīk*), the sultan or his representative had to authorise the transformation of agricultural lands and / or revenues into the private property of a future endower. In many cases, the title to the land itself (*raqaba*) probably remained with the treasury.[17] Therefore this *waqf* type, in contradistinction to the former, was called "unsound, extra-legal" (*waqf ghayr ṣaḥīḥ*).[18]

The jurists had difficulties including these endowments in their system, since this type clearly violated the rules. A prerequisite of a fully legal *waqf* was the endowment of the substance (*aṣl, ʿayn*), and not only revenue stemming from it, as in this way the perpetuity of the endowment could not be guaranteed. Some legal experts saw such endowments as temporary because they could be revoked by succeeding rulers.

Nevertheless, the economic and social impact of this extra-legal category could not be denied. Many of the important institutional *waqfs* were established by the sultans themselves or high officials in the early phase of Ottoman rule in Syria. They were based on the revenues of whole villages and agricultural farms and were indicated to the running of mosques, *madrasas,* and other institutions of common interest. An important number of these endowments, although naming a charitable or public institution as main beneficiary, provided also for the descendants of the endowers in various forms. Since the fortune of Ottoman officials was considered to belong to the sultan and the central treasury, endowments were an important means of diverting the impending danger of confiscation after the

---

Society 4.3 (1997), 319-333; Randi Deguilhem-Schoem, "The Loan of Mursad on Waqf Properties," in *A Way Prepared: Essays on Islamic Culture in Honor of Richard Bayly Winder*, eds. Farhad Kazemi and R. D. McChesney, New York 1988, 68-79.

17 Barnes, *Introduction*, 40-42.

18 Or *waqf irṣād*. Barnes, *Introduction,* 45-49; Kenneth Cuno, "Ideology and Juridical Discourse in Ottoman Egypt: The Uses of the Concept of *irṣād,*" *Islamic Law and Society* 6 (1999), 136-163.

death or disgrace of a state functionary.[19] The religious and legal sanction of *waqf* could be used as a protection against claims of the state to safegard the interests of families and other groups of beneficiaries. Endowments, even of the *khayrī* type, were thus often perceived by family members as their exclusive domain. "This is the endowment of my ancestor; I can do with it what I like and nobody can oppose me in this", an obviously incompetent eighteenth century administrator of the famous Darwīshiyya mosque in Damascus is said to have repeated incessantly, insisting that he could not be taken to court neither according to the rules of the *sharīʿa* nor to those of the *siyāsa*.[20]

These two terms are key notions for understanding the role of the state and of the judicial system, represented by the *qāḍī*, in the control of the *waqf* system.[21] In the *waqf* institution diverging and often conflicting interests of individuals, groups and the state and its representatives came together. The legal tradition saw these interests divided into two different spheres of law, the claims of God (*ḥuqūq Allāh)* and those of human beings *(ḥuqūq al-ʿibād).* Whereas the *sharīʿa* ruled the sphere of transactions between individuals, the rights of God, identified as the common interests of the Muslims, were to be safeguarded by the political authorities. This role of the Islamic ruler was formulated in the principle of *siyāsa,* later incorporated into the *sharīʿa* as *siyāsa sharʿiyya.*[22] From this perspective, the *waqf* institution has to be seen as a complex combination of claims of God and of men and therefore enters both the realms of *sharīʿa* and *siyāsa.*

Long before Ottoman times, aspects of both legal spheres came to be administrated by the *qāḍīs.* Already in Māwardī's (d. 450/1058) "*Aḥkām al-sulṭāniyya*", the competence of the judges in matters of *waqf* was differentiated according to whether it concerned the *ḥuqūq Allāh* or the *ḥuqūq*

---

19 Klaus Röhrborn, "Konfiskation und intermediäre Gewalten im Osmanischen Reich," *Der Islam* 55 (1978), 345-351.

20 ʿAbd al-Ghanī al-Nābulusī, "Taḥqīq al-naẓar fī taḥqīq al-naẓar," Ms. Damascus, Asad Library, Ẓāhiriyya collection, no. 5316, 299-306.

21 For the following see Miriam Hoexter, "*Ḥuqūq Allāh* and *Ḥuqūq al-ʿibād* as Reflected in the *Waqf* Institution," *Jerusalem Studies in Arabic and Islam* 19 (1995), 133-156; Baber Johansen, "Secular and Religious Elements in Hanafite Law: Function and Limits of the Absolute Character of Government Authority," in *Islam et politique au Maghreb*, eds. J.C. Vatin and E. Gellner, Paris 1981, 281-303; and "Eigentum, Familie und Obrigkeit im hanafitischen Strafrecht: Das Verhältnis der privaten Rechte zu den Forderungen der Allgemeinheit in hanafitischen Rechtskommentaren," *WI* 19 (1979), 1-73.

22 See F.E. Vogel, art. "*siyāsa*", in: *EI*^{2}, vol. 9, 694-696.

al-ʿibād. Māwardī distinguished between two types of *waqf*, according to beneficiaries: if they were charitable and religious institutions, endowments were called "general" (*ʿāmm*), and "specific" (*khāṣṣ*) if the profits were to go to individuals, family members or others.[23] In Ḥanafī legal thought, the endowed properties themselves belonged to the sphere of *siyāsa* as a claim of God. The relevant distinctions concerning the *qāḍī*'s authority depended on whether a person or an institution was to benefit from an endowment: *khāṣṣ* meant that with regard to the beneficiaries an endowment was within the claims of men and the *sharīʿa* rules applied. The Ottoman *qāḍī* as the representative of both spheres of law was the general supervisor of all endowments, though in the case of *khāṣṣ* he could only act if a dispute was referred to him by an interested party. In the case of endowments of general interest and in cases where the assets themselves were concerned he could initiate steps of his own to protect the interests of an endowment without following the rules of legal actions under the *sharīʿa*.[24]

The safeguard of the rights of God (or of the law), however, was not a primary aim of the legal system. Public interest was limited by the claims of individuals, and the authority of the government was relatively restricted.[25] The experts on law held that since God cannot suffer loss or damage, such claims were secondary; in the words of the Damascene jurist Ibn ʿĀbidīn (1784-1836): "This is not so because we are treating the claims of the law lightly, but because the human being is in need and the law is not."[26]

The supervision of the *qāḍī* only proved nominal in many cases. In practice, it was the actual administrators of the various endowments who controlled the performance of endowments themselves and secured the *waqf*'s interests.[27] The legal privileges and protection which were accorded to the institution as a whole depended on these persons, as there was no administrative body that was able to control the totality of endowed assets. The notion of a "public law" governing the *waqf* institution is, at least for the period under study, confined to the theoretical deliberations of the law experts.

---

23 ʿAlī ibn Muḥammad al-Māwardī, *Aḥkām al-sulṭāniyya,* ed. Maximilian Enger, Bonn 1853, 118, 139-140.

24 See also *ibid.*, 139.

25 Johansen, "Religious Elements," 299-301.

26 Muḥammad Amīn Ibn ʿĀbidīn, *Radd al-muḥtār ʿalā l-durr al-mukhtār*, Cairo 1307, II 156; transl. Johansen, "Religious Elements," 300.

27 See Randi Deguilhem's article in this volume.

The ineffective control by the legal system can be corroborated by many lawsuits that were presented in the courts. The judges would invariably, as prescribed in legal doctrine, defend the *waqf's* claims to outstanding payments. In these instances, the protection of *waqf* properties by the legal doctrine can be seen most clearly. But these cases also make it very clear that this protection could only work if somebody was there to demand it. Although the *qāḍī* was supposed to oversee the management of all kinds of *waqf*, this rather formal duty was far from being an effective control.

The *waqf* system was therefore actually controlled to a large extent by members of the social group who were also the main beneficiaries of the system: the *ʿulamāʾ*. They not only held the teaching and administrative posts in institutional endowments, but in their function as judges were also in charge of the general supervision of the whole system. They were also prominent as founders of family endowments.[28] The considerable wealth that was invested in endowments provided the *ʿulamāʾ* "with an extensive economic base that made them largely independent of Muslim rulers".[29]

The independence of the local *ʿulamāʾ*, however, was not absolute. The appointment of *waqf* personnel by the local judges had to be confirmed by Istanbul. Posts were gained and lost through personal contacts in the capital. The central administration was also involved in the administration of some of the most important foundations, like the local endowments for the two holy cities of Mecca and Medina (*waqf al-Ḥaramayn*) or for the major mosques where many supervisors came out of the ranks of the military or of Ottoman officials. The revenues of such institutional endowments were often used for other than the designed beneficiaries, allowing local needs and other more imperial interests to be coped with.[30] In the administration of the imperial endowments, the local and the imperial spheres had always been intertwined.[31]

The reforms affecting the control of the *waqf* system in the late eighteenth and early nineteenth centuries reflect the old lines of conflict, but also introduced new elements. In a time when the central administration was in desperate need of money and new sources of income, the claims of the state finally took precedence over the rights of individuals and social

---

28 Yediyildiz, Bahaeddin, *Institution du vaqf au XVIIIe siècle en Turquie: Etude socio-historique*, Ankara 1985, 163, 169-170.

29 Powers, "Orientalism, Colonialism, and Legal History," 538.

30 Hoexter, "*Ḥuqūq Allāh,*" 152-153.

31 Jane Hathaway, *The Politics of Households in Ottoman Egypt: The Rise of the Qazdağlıs*, Cambridge 1997, esp. 139-164.

groups: in a reversal of the old order, the *ḥuqūq Allāh* came to prevail over the *ḥuqūq al-ʿibād*. In the name of the common good and claiming to be the rightful owner of the lands made into "unsound" endowments, the state was able to secure the control of both the administration and the revenues of an increasing number of endowments from all over the empire and to reduce the claims of individuals and families to a mere salary paid by the state.[32]

A small but significant step initiated the change in the system of imperial *waqf* administration. In 1775 Sultan ʿAbd al-Ḥamīd I (1774-1789) placed his own endowments under the supervision of a newly created agency, and not as had been customary under the control of the Chief Black Eunuch of the Imperial Harem *(Dârüssaade Ağası)*. Up to that point, the different sultanic and imperial endowments had been under the supervision of certain high state officials in the capital. From the nucleus of Hamidian endowments, the new agency grew slowly as other important foundations of former sultans and Ottoman officials were put under its control. In 1826, after the destruction of the Janissaries, Sultan Maḥmūd II (1808-1839) added the vast foundations of the corps to the charge of the administrative body which then became the Ministry of Sultanic Endowments (*Evkaf-i Hümayûn Nezareti*).[33] After 1826 the five separate *nezarets* of the imperial endowments which had been in the hands of the highest officials of the empire were also incorporated, and by 1835 all important imperial *waqfs* except the *waqf al-Ḥaramayn* had been put under the control of this agency. In 1838, finally, the *Ḥaramayn* ministry was also annexed to the *Evkaf-i Hümayûn*. At that time, the reform began to take root in the provinces as well.

Waqf Reform in the Province: Damascus 1843-45

In the early 1840s, the *Tanẓīmāt* were beginning to take effect on different levels in the political, economic and social life of the province of Damascus. From 1843 to 1845, the provincial *waqf* administration for example underwent substantial changes, initiated by new orders from Istanbul. Exactly how and by what steps the reform was implemented is not easy to understand because of the lacunas in the source material of this period.

---

32 For the following: Barnes, *Introduction*, 68-86.

33 *Ibid.*, 73-76.

The following remarks can therefore only be of a preliminary and tentative nature, and further research both in the provincial and the central archives might bring to light new aspects. Fortunately, an imperial *firmān* which the provincial advisory council of Damascus[34] discussed in Jumādā II 1261/ July 1845 and a few related documents offer valuable insights into at least the planning stage of the new system of *waqf* administration and how it was met in the province itself.[35]

At the time the decisive reforms were undertaken in the imperial capital during the 1830s, Damascus was under Egyptian occupation. Certain measures carried out by the administration under Muḥammad ʿAlī and his son Ibrahīm had dealt with the supervision of the *waqf* system, but their impact is not clear.[36] By the time the Ottomans had re-established their control over the Syrian provinces in 1840, a new official had been introduced into the imperial *waqf* administration, called the *nāẓir muʿajjalāt al-awqāf* or simply *nāẓir al-awqāf*.[37] This office had been created in 1837 or 1838 to check the decision making power of the *qāḍīs* after an alarming report from Izmir had reached the capital. The important function of ap-

---

34 The provincial council was itself a product of the reforms: see Elizabeth Thompson, "Ottoman Political Reform in the Provinces: The Damascus Advisory Council in 1844-45," *IJMES* 25 (1993); Ghazzal, *Economie politique*, 47-67.

35 Damascus, *Markaz al-Wathā'iq al-Tārīkhiyya* (Centre of Historial documents), series *Awāmir sulṭāniyya*, vol. 5 (in the following AS 5), Minutes of the *majlis wilāyat al-Shām* 1844-45, pp. 296-308, 28 Jumādā II 1261/ 4 July 1845 (Ottoman-Turkish text and Arab translation); the document has already been used by Abdulkarim Rafeq, "Land Tenure Problems and Their Social Impact in Syria around the Middle of the Nineteenth Century," in *Land Tenure and Social Transformation in the Middle East,* ed. Tarif Khalidi, Beirut 1984, 371-396, esp. 379-380; Randi Deguilhem, "Government Centralization of Waqf Administration and its Opposition: The Syrian Example," in BRISMES Proceedings 1991; and "Ottoman Waqf Administrative Reorganization in the Syrian Provinces: The Case of Damascus," *AHROS* 5-6 (1992), 31-38; and Ghazzal, *Economie politique*, 107-108. I would like to thank Ms Daʿd al-Ḥakīm, the Director of the Markaz, and all her staff for their warm welcome and generous help.

36 See Moshe Ma'oz, "The *ʿulamāʾ* and the Process of Modernization in Syria During the Mid-Nineteenth Century," *AAS* 7 (1971), 80, who mentions a new system of *waqf* supervision as a cause of the deterioration of the economic situation of the *ʿulamāʾ* (no details given).

37 Barnes, *Introduction*, 79 explains the title as follows: "For the purpose of collecting the revenue of these vakıfs which were scattered throughout the empire, a number of local notables in the centers of the provinces of Rumelia and Anatolia were commissioned as salaried evkaf directors with the title Muaccelât Nâzirları. They were given this title because of their main function: they acted as receiver and controller of money paid on the first sales of evkaf property; muaccelât were the sums of money paid at once on the purchase of real property."

pointing the personnel for the endowments was then given to this new functionary who was paid directly by the *waqf* ministry and who was thus considered to be less prone to accepting bribes:

> While it has been the customary procedure to confer on persons the office of administrator (tevliyet), preacher (hitabet), and prayer leader (imamet) by the kadıs and their deputies (şer'iye memurları), since excessive and exorbitant fees have been taken by these şer'iye officials, and whereas posts have been conferred by them upon those who are either unqualified or incompetent, and in view of the fact that contradictory decisions both for and against litigants have been given by the kadıs and their substitutes (naibs), henceforth the issuing of these decisions and the conferral of these offices will be made by officials placed in the sancaks and the eyâlets who are known as muaccelât nâzirları.[38]

The new functionaries were not outsiders sent from Istanbul, but were to be chosen from the local notables. In the case of Damascus, the office was conferred in 1843 to a member of the provincial *majlis,* Aḥmad Efendi al-Mālikī, Ḥanafī scribe at the court of the chief *qāḍī* and descendant of a family of Damascene notables.[39] In the following year, the new *nāẓir* was given his own rooms in the immediate neighbourhood of the Saray, the seat of the Ottoman governor of the province.[40] This was a highly symbolic step illustrating a main feature of the reform: the power to control the *waqf* system was no longer in the hands of the chief *qāḍī* or his substitutes in the different courts of the city, but was now invested in a new bureaucratic agency, directly responsible to the *waqf* ministry in Istanbul, being placed at the centre of the imperial presence in the city.

The impact of centralisation and bureaucratisation increased further, when in 1845, after the fusion of the *Hümayun* and the *Ḥaramayn* ministries, a non-Damascene took charge of the imperial endowments in the province, a certain Muḥammad Saʿīd Efendi, referred to by the title of *mudīr al-awqāf.*[41] At least for a certain time, both offices seem to have

---

38 Decree dated 1253/1837, Cevdet Adliye No. 4933, after Barnes, *Introduction*, 103.

39 Irade Dahiliye No. 3735, 1259/1843, after Barnes, *Introduction*, 106; for a biography see Muḥammad Jamīl al-Shaṭṭī, *Aʿyān Dimashq fī-l-qarn al-thālith ʿashar wa-niṣf al-qarn al-rābiʿ ʿashar, 1201-1350H*, Beirut 1972, 51.

40 AS 5, pp. 45-47, d. 68-69, 20 Dhū al-Qaʿda 1260/1 December 1844. I thank Stefan Weber for the information about the location of the rooms.

41 AS 5, 296-308.

existed simultaneously, but the division of charges between the two men is not clear.[42]

According to the imperial *firmān* of 28 Jumāda II 1261/4 July 1845, the decision making of the *mudīr* extended to the endowments of the Sultans Salīm and Sulaymān, the *Ḥaramayn*, and the so-called *mulḥaqāt*. This second group consisted of various foundations dating from different times that did not have a separate supervision (*naẓar*) as in the cases of the foundations of the *amīr* Nūr al-Dīn al-Zankī, the *waqf* of the Egyptians (an important foundation dating probably from Mamluk, but certainly from early Ottoman times), or the endowment of Murād Pasha, a former Ottoman governor of Damascus.[43]

The *firmān* contained 16 regulations concerning the administration of these endowments. In many of these points, the strategy of the central administration becomes manifest: to establish better control over the administration by tighter supervision of the bookkeeping through frequent inspections, to curb the power of individual *waqf* managers (*mutawallī*) by limiting their range of autonomous decision making, to increase the state's share of the income by increasing various fees and taxes for every transaction involving *waqf* assets.

The members of the Damascus *majlis*, clearly comprehending their role not as mere recipients of sultanic orders,[44] discussed every single point of the 16 regulations, adapting them to the local situation, sometimes insisting on the specificity of the Syrian case. Of particular interest are the discussions about the second point: it was ruled that if an endowment was left without a supervisor (*nāzir*) and came therefore under the supervision of the Ministry or if a *waqf* property fell into disuse (*mahlūl*), the assets had to be "sold" to the highest bidder and a down payment (*muʿajjalla*) was due to the state treasury. What was sold in these public auctions were not the assets themselves, but the right to collect the revenue of the foundations. The beneficiaries and people employed by the foundations now received fixed salaries rather than a share of the income.[45] The council

---

42 The sources are not consistent in the use of the titles *mudīr al-awqāf* and *nāẓir al-awqāf*, cf. Rafeq, "Land Tenure Problems," 379.

43 AS 5, 296-308; the regulations of the *firmān* closely follow the memorandum of 1843 concerning the new organization of the provincial *waqf* system in the whole empire: Maliyeden Müdevver No. 9061, 1259/1843, see Barnes, *Introduction*, 104-105.

44 For the *majlis* as a representative of provincial interests see Thompson, "Ottoman Political Reform," and Ghazzal, *Economie politique*, 47-67.

45 See Barnes, *Introduction*, 106-107.

stated that the selling of *waqf* properties in the prescribed form did not exist in their province (with the exception of four specific cases) because "every realm (*mamlaka*) has its own terminology and these terms are not used in Shām province".[46]

The confusion was not only due to the novelty of the procedure, but also to the various contracts that were in use in different parts of the Ottoman empire: the terms used in the *firmān* are those of the *ijarātayn* contract that was widespread in Anatolia and the Balkans, but not in the Syrian provinces where other forms of long-term lease prevailed.[47]

Though starting with the imperial endowments, the reforms also affected the administration of other types. As shown above, the new officials had taken over functions that, earlier on, had been the prerogatives of the *qāḍīs*. The case of Damascus also shows that the old system of control was not replaced all at once, but that the reforms were introduced in small steps that led to a co-existence of different controlling agencies. This feature is evident in the instructions that the chief *qāḍī* of Damascus sent to his deputies in all other courts of the city not long after the promulgation of the *waqf* reform: every document concerning *waqf* transactions with long-term effects (*murṣad, ḥikr, gedik* etc.) had to be sent for inspection to the *nāẓir al-awqāf* before being brought to the chief court for registration. The supervisors of independent endowments had to present their books at the end of every month to the *nāẓir al-awqāf* so that unregistered transactions no longer went undetected, and even the chief *qāḍī*'s registers had to be checked monthly against the books of the *nāẓir al-awqāf*.[48]

The complicated regulations of the provincial *waqf* reform seem to have caused problems not only for the understanding of researchers, but for contemporary people concerned as well. In Damascus, shortly after the promulgation of the *waqf* reform, the *mudīr al-awqāf* Muḥammad Saʿīd Efendi had to make clear once again which kind of endowments were affected by the reform and in what way. On that occasion, he presented a new categorisation of endowments along the following lines:

---

46 AS 5, 301.

47 See Heffening, art. "*Waqf,*" in EI[1], vol.4, 1158-59; Yediyildiz, *Institution du vaqf,* 138-140.

48 See Damascus, *Markaz al-Wathā'iq al-Tārīkhiyya* (Centre of Historical Documents), series *Maḥākim sharʿiyya Dimashq,* vol. 384/1/1, *murāsala* of Shaʿbān 1261/August 1845; for *murāsalāt* in general see the forthcoming article of Brigitte Marino, "Les correspondances (*murāsalāt*) adressées par le Juge de Damas à ses substituts (1750-1860)", in: *Espaces et sociétés dans les villes arabes du Mashreq à l'époque ottomane, Actes de la table ronde en honneur d'André Raymond,* IFEAD, Damascus 2000.

> There are three types of endowments concerning descendants (*dhurriyya*): first, the ones endowed for the common good and pious purposes with stipulations that the surplus income (*faḍla*) should go to the descendants of the endower; secondly, endowments for one's descendants, but including stipulations naming other persons and purposes as beneficiaries; and thirdly, endowments completely dedicated to one's descendants. The new regulations do not concern the last two categories (...), *because they are waqf only in name, not in essence*. They are like absolute property (*milk*) under the aspect of testation (*waṣiyya*), as property is devolved to the heirs, for the males twice the part of a female or otherwise, following the wishes of the endower, to prevent descendants from selling the assets.[49]

These lines constitute an important step towards a new and secularized discourse on the *waqf* institution as a whole. From the perspective of the centralising state, endowments were no longer treated as one legal category. Although the Ottoman functionary in this instance did not question the legitimacy of family endowments and did not interfere with their administration, since (as was explicitly stated) the will of an endower had to be respected like the will of the Divine Lawgiver conforming to an old *sharīʿa* principle,[50] the new dividing line ran clearly along the private/public dichotomy. The state obviously considered itself the only legitimate representative of common interests and the public sphere, hence the new regulations and stricter control of public endowments that could now be seen as deserving that denomination. Established rights of individuals, families or other groups did no longer have a place in this system and had to be cut back.

The redefinition of the family *waqf* as a mere form of private property has to be seen as an early step in the process of delegitimisation of this type of property. From this point of view, it was not far-fetched to conclude that family endowments were only an instrument to circumvent the inheritance laws of the Qur'ān. By defining inheritance and *waqf* as mutually exclusive institutions, family endowments came to be seen as a perversion of so-called charitable foundations, thus reversing the historical record in which family endowments predate other forms of *waqf* and were even seen as especially meritorious. The "attack on family endowments" did not only come from outsiders like the French in Algeria or the British

---

49 AS 5, 389-390, no. 450, 29 Shaʿbān 1261/1 September 1845 (italics mine).

50 See Eyal Ginio, "Violations of Founders' Stipulations in the *Sharīʿa* Court of Jaffa During the British Mandate," *Islamic Law and Society* 4.3 (1997), 389-415.

in India,[51] but also from within a state whose ideology and legitimisation centred around its role as defendant of the *sharīʿa*. The reinterpretation of an old institution in Islamic law culminated in the middle of the twentieth century in new secular legislation that implemented new restrictions and, in the case of Syria, even the complete abolition of the family *waqf*.[52]

Conclusion

> I can speak confidently to the fact that a considerable number of these works (i.e., mosques, bridges, fountains, inns, tekkes, and the like) which are destroyed and useless now, were in a tolerable good state of repair no further back than the year 1820. But the reformers, who are uprooting religion, and a respect for it in every direction, have utterly destroyed the security which the mosque, and the mosque alone, could give to any landed property; they have destroyed the independence of the Turkish Church – if I may so call it; they have laid their greedy hands on nearly all the vakoufs of the empire, and are undertaking to provide out of the common state treasury, for the subsistence of the Ulema, Mollas and college or medresseh students, to keep up the mosques and the medressehs, to repair the bridges, khans, etc., and to do, governmentally, that which the administrators of the vakouf had done or ought to have done. Hence, with very few exceptions, we see the heads of the mosques and the medressehs in abject poverty, the rabble of (religious) students in rags, the most beautiful of the temples and the minarets shamefully neglected and hurrying into decay, the bridges, fountains, and khans in the state I describe. It is notorious that since the vakoufs have been administered by the government nothing has been done to maintain the works of public utility.[53]

When Charles MacFarlane published his diatribe in 1850 against state administration of the public *waqf* system, taking firmly the side of the seemingly dispossessed *ʿulamāʾ,* he enumerated, though completely one-sidedly, many of the problems connected with the changes of the endowment administration

---

51 See Powers, "Orientalism, Colonialism, and legal History," Gregory C. Kozlowski, "The Changing Political and Social Contexts of Muslim Endowments: The Case of Contemporary India," in *Le waqf dans l'espace islamique*, ed. Randi Deguilhem, Damascus 1995, 227-291.

52 Anderson, "The Religious Element;" Randi Deguilhem, "Le *waqf* en Syrie indépendante," in *Le waqf dans le monde musulman contemporain, XIXe-XXe siècles: Factions sociales, économiques et politiques, Actes de la table ronde d'Istanbul, 13-14 mars 1992,* ed. Faruk Bilici, Istanbul 1994, 123-144.

53 Charles MacFarlane, *Turkey and Its Destiny*, London 1850, 396, after Barnes, *Introduction*, 118.

that went under the headings of modernisation and reform. As a consequence of the disempowerment of the *ʿulamāʾ* as independent local administrators and of the pressing needs of a state in search of new sources of income, the important revenues of the *waqf* system came to be a constituent part of the budget of the central state treasury and were redistributed according to its own agenda.[54] Though the autonomy of all intermediary powers was decisively cut back, this process touched most severely the local *qāḍīs* who had lost many of their prerogatives and were – not only in *waqf* affairs – put under close supervision by the central authorities.[55] Even if the *ʿulamāʾ* as a group saw their influence dwindling, new channels of participation had opened for individual members in the newly founded state agencies like the Ministry of Awqāf or the provincial councils.

The increasing influence of the state also affected the *waqf* institution as a whole. In its efforts to secure control over the lucrative institutional endowments (the revenues of which often stemmed from state-owned agricultural lands) the central bureaucracy had laid the foundation for a new categorisation of endowments. As all areas of common interest were being redefined as the exclusive domain of the state, the so-called public endowments came under the supervision of newly created governmental agencies. Family endowments were relegated to the status of private property and thus lost the religious sanction of former *waqf* regulations. The flexibility that had characterised the endowment system and had allowed it to retain its important role in the social fabric of Ottoman cities came under severe censure.[56] The institution as a whole proved difficult to conform to the conceptions of the centralising and bureaucratising imperial mind that characterised many of the attempted reforms.[57] Soon it came to be considered, in the eyes of Ottomans and Europeans alike, not only as pre-modern, but simply as unmodern and anachronistic.

---

54 See Barnes, *Introduction*, 119-127.

55 Halil Inalcik, "Application of the Tanzimat and Its Social Effects," *AO* 5 (1973), 100.

56 For the notion of flexibility see Hoexter, "Idea of Charity," 186-189; for the importance of *waqf* in the urban context see e.g. Richard van Leeuwen, *Waqfs and Urban Structures: The Case of Ottoman Damascus,* Leiden 1999.

57 See Isa Blumi's article in this volume.

CENTRALISED AUTHORITY AND LOCAL DECISIONAL POWER:

Management of the Endowments in Late Ottoman Damascus

RANDI DEGUILHEM

Despite persistent and generalised assertions that the Ottoman Empire was overwhelmingly subject to economic stagnation and overall decline in the nineteenth and early twentieth centuries, assumptions supported even fairly recently regarding *waqf* in this period,[1] the past thirty years of archival research on Ottoman foundations attest, on the contrary, to a certain level of dynamism in market activity, especially on the local level, for *waqf*-held real estate in the Empire during the last Ottoman century.

This study analyses information which reveals that an appreciable extent of decisional power regarding this activity, especially in relation to the administration of the foundations' assets, their revenues and the personnel attached to the endowments continued to remain in local hands during the nineteenth century in Bilād al-Shām despite policies drawn up in Istanbul which, in today's jargon, could be categorized as unification or even globalization measures within the Ottoman territories. The primary material studied for this research indicates that real decisional power over *waqf* was exercised locally in the provincial capital of late Ottoman Damascus and that Istanbul found itself in an almost secondary position of merely adhering and agreeing to actions sent up from Damascus through the chain of command to the Porte. On a larger scale, the present study is part of ongoing research on the pious foundations whose objective is to examine micro-historical data related to *waqf* as a means of quantitatively and qualitatively evaluating and understanding trends, similarities and differences – in

---

1 Such as by John Robert Barnes, *An Introduction to Religious Foundations in the Ottoman Empire*, Leiden, 1986, ix, analysis questioned by Randi Deguilhem in a review of Barnes' book in *Turcica* XX (1998), 285-289, 288.

time and locale – between the different operational modalities of the Ottoman foundations.[2]

From an imperial perspective, as regards the pious foundations, the reorganizational measures which marked the final century of Ottoman rule focused upon channeling the administration of all the endowments through the Istanbul *waqf* offices. More specifically, these measures aimed at strengthening Istanbul's financial control and tax-collecting capacities over the revenue-generating properties in the Ottoman lands which belonged to the endowments. Legislation was not only directed towards intensifying the centralization of the imperial *waqfs* which stretched across the empire and which, by the fifteenth century, had already been the focus of state control,[3] but also in view of extending the imperial hand over the Ḥaramayn *waqf* as well as the public and private foundations in the empire. Offices such as that of the *muʿajjalāt al-awqāf* were created with such a purpose in mind, with the objective of consolidating certain facets of foundation administration throughout the provinces towards a single bureaucracy in the imperial capital. At the present point in research, it is difficult to evaluate with any certainty the complete functions of the *muʿajjalāt al-awqāf* in relation to the question of centralized authority and local decisional power. But, the *awāmir sulṭāniyya*[4] documents consulted for this study show that the description by Redhouse for the *muʿajjalāt al-awqāf* as "the Receiver and Controller of monies paid on the first sales of *waqf* properties"[5] was far from a complete definition in that other activities associated with the endowments, namely, those connected with the three

---

2 A state-of-the-art for Ottoman *waqf* studies is found in Miriam Hoexter, "*Waqf* Studies in the Twentieth Century: The State of the Art," *JESHO* 41, 4 (Nov. 1998), 474-495.

3 Haim Gerber, "The *Waqf* Institution in Early Ottoman Edirne," *AAS* 17/1-3 (November 1983), 29-45.

4 I would like to once again thank Mrs. Daʿd Ḥakīm, director of the Damascus Centre of Historical Documents, for having authorised me to study these documents and for having extended her courtesy to me over the years. This corpus of eleven registers, located in the Damascus archives, contains nearly 1,000 entries which concern various processes related to the administration of different *waqfs*. The corpus of the *awāmir sulṭāniyya* is classified in the Damascus archives as containing twelve registers; however, register n° 5 does not belong to the *awāmir sulṭāniyya* series but rather, it contains the 1260-1261/1844-1845 reports from the Damascene Provincial High Council – this has been pointed out several times, i.e. Elizabeth Thompson, "Ottoman Political Reform in the Provinces: The Damascus Advisory Council in 1844-1845," *IJMES* 25 (1993), 457-476. For this research, the registers spanning from the end of the eighteenth to the twentieth century have been used (1194-1328/1780-1910).

5 James W. Redhouse, *A Turkish and English Lexicon*, Beirut, 1987 (first pr. Constantinople, 1890), 1905.

domains of action discussed below likewise passed through the *muʿajjalāt al-awqāf* office, inextricably tying together the local and central powers.

Notwithstanding a certain success in the centralization policies of the nineteenth century, especially in relation to the widely-flung imperial and Ḥaramayn *waqf*,[6] individual foundation administrators in the Syrian provinces and elsewhere in the Empire continued, as before, to exercise important daily on-the-ground decisional and interventionary control over the imperial and the Ḥaramayn *waqf* in addition to the private (*ahlī/dhurrī*), public (*khayrī*) and mixed (*mushtarak*) foundations. Information registered with the tribunal courts as well as in official documents going to and emanating from Istanbul concerning activities in the provinces such as that contained in the entries recorded in the *awāmir sulṭāniyya* repeatedly demonstrate that important interventionary powers were routinely and regularly exercised by the *nāẓir* and the *mutawallī* (who was officially under the *nāẓir*'s jurisdiction) who were responsible for managing the individual endowments. Yet, these powers were not plenipotentiary. They were palliated in a concrete way by the central authority in Istanbul which issued certificates (*barāts*) to confirm the administrators' local decisions which, in turn, were not really "individual" decisions in that the *nāẓir* or *mutawallī* acted within his or her particular societal matrix, subject to influences by family, community and other groups.[7]

Omnipresence of Waqf and Domains of Action

In the form of individually operational foundations and as part of a more general institutional system, *waqf* was one of the essential infrastructural factors around which many aspects of urban and rural Ottoman society constructed itself not only within the Islamic community but also amongst the Christian and Jewish populations.[8] As a result, the foundations were omnipresent in Ottoman civilisation as they had been in the pre-Ottoman

---

6 Barnes; Miriam Hoexter, *Endowments, Rulers and Community. Waqf al-Haramayn in Ottoman Algiers*, Leiden 1998; Akael Nomeir, *Les fondations pieuses à Alger (étude comparative du waqf)*, unpublished doctoral dissertation, U. Of Provence, 2002.

7 In the way of Norbert Elias, *La société des individus*, repr. Paris 1991; S. Menell, *Norbert Elias. Civilization and the Human Self-Image*, Oxford 1989.

8 Ron Shaham, "Christian and Jewish *Waqf* in Palestine during the late Ottoman Period," *BSOAS* 54/3 (1991), 460-472; Sabine Mouhasseb Saliba, "Une famille, un couvent : Deir Mar Challita Mouqbès," *Chronos* , 3 (2000), 93-138; Richard van Leeuwen, *Notables and clergy in Mount Lebanon: The Khāzin sheikhs and the Maronite church (1736-1840)*, Leiden 1994, especially 129-150.

Mediterranean world.[9] *Waqf*-affiliated public and charitable services, employment opportunities subsidized by the foundations as well as the management of the latter in addition to the many varied types of rent and other contracts associated with *waqf*-owned real-estate literally permeated Ottoman society, reaching deeply and widely into most spheres of life in all socio-economic levels.[10] A consequence of this ubiquitous and intertwined character of the foundations within the political, social, cultural, religious, administrative, fiscal and economic spheres of Ottoman life meant that *waqf* almost invariably concerned every individual living within the Ottoman lands at some point in his or her life.

In generic terms, administrative control over an endowment signified interventionary powers for the *nāẓir* or *mutawallī* in three principal domains of action:[11]

- over the real-estate, sums of money (*waqf al-nuqūd*)[12] and other assets possessed by the foundation,
- over the personnel working for the foundation both in the administrative sphere of the particular waqf in question as well as those persons employed in the institutions subsidized by that endowment,
- over the distribution of funds generated from the foundation's assets that were allocated to the beneficiaries named or indicated by the founder of that endowment.

---

9 Sylvie Denoix, "Fondations pieuses, fondations économiques, le *waqf*, un mode d'intervention sur la ville mamelouke," in *Le Khan al-Khalili et ses environs, un centre commercial et artisanal du Caire (XIIIe-XXe siècles)*, ed. Sylvie Denoix, Jean-Charles Depaule and Michel Tuchscherer, Cairo 1999, 19-26; Moshe Gil, *Documents of the Jewish Pious Foundations from the Cairo Geniza*, Leiden 1976.

10 For a concise overview of Ottoman *waqf* with bibliographical orientation, see Randi Deguilhem, "Ottoman Wakf up to 1914," *Encyclopaedia of Islam*, 2000, fascicule 179-180, 87-92.

11 In the manner of Louis Pinto, *Pierre Bourdieu et la théorie du monde social*, Paris 1998, 90-99 who critiques and incorporates Bourdieu's concept of power fields or domains of action within more flexible frameworks for the purpose of understanding the nuanced and multi-leveled duality of the domination/dominated theoretical framework as related to the individual and his or her changing adherences to different groups within society.

12 Faruk Bilici, "Les *waqfs* monétaires à la fin de l'Empire ottoman et au début de l'époque républicaine en Turquie : des caisses de solidarité vers un système bancaire moderne," in Faruk Bilici, ed., *Le waqf dans le monde musulman contemporain (XIXe-XXe siècles)*, Istanbul 1994, 51-59; Murat Çizakça, "Cash *Waqfs* of Bursa, 1555-1823," *JESHO* 38/3 (Aug 1995) 247-61; Jon Mandaville, "Usurious Piety: The Cash *Waqf* Controversy in the Ottoman Empire," *IJMES* 10/3 (1979), 289-308.

Despite Istanbul's efforts in the nineteenth century to increasingly exert direct control over *waqf* administration in the provinces, the *awāmir sulṭāniyya* registers demonstrate that there was not any discernible bureaucratic difference in administrative procedures with regard to the local management of *waqf* within the Damascus area during this one hundred and thirty year period. Taken from the perspective of the *longue durée* in relation to the three domains of action listed above which may be perceived during this "long nineteenth century,"[13] that is, from 1780 – the date of the first document in the registers under study which falls during Abdülhamid I's reign – to 1910, the date of the last document of this corpus under study which belongs to the Young Turk period, the information ostensibly shows that virtually all administrative decisions were initially taken by the local *nāẓir* or *mutawallī* of a *waqf*. However, once the decisions were taken, they were then sent up to the Ottoman imperial capital for confirmation with the request for a *barāt* to certify the specific action that was taken locally. In principle, decisions were only final when the interested parties received the *barāt* issued by the Porte.

Yet, despite the almost seemingly rubber-stamp quality of the *barāt*, the necessity of requesting and obtaining this certificate represented one of the major recurrent procedural features in the registers under study and was essential for the ratification of decisions taken within the context of the local administration of *waqf* (as well as for the management of activities that concerned non-*waqf* properties). The *barāt* also functioned as a guarantee which served to accredit subsequent actions regarding both endowment and non-endowment affairs. *Ḥujja* documents, which register a specific action taken subsequently in relation to another, almost always cite a previous *barāt* as proof of the former action. In other words, a *barāt* was the final step in the bureaucratic process necessary for validating, for example, a rent contract on *waqf* and non-*waqf* properties alike, for the appointment to a position as *mudarris*, *imām*, *khaṭīb*, *mu'adhdhin* or another such function within the teaching or religious hierarchy in a mosque, a *madrasa*, etc. or amongst the maintenance personnel (*bawwāb*, *farrāsh*, *kannās*, *saqqā'*) of religious or educational complexes, tombs, etc.

Yet, although the *barāt* was the final phase in the bureaucratic process for certifying an action, it often signified, in reality, a culmination of a

13 In the sense that one may comprehend the nineteenth century Tanẓīmāt reforms as having already begun in the late eighteenth century with the *Niẓām al-Jadīd* (The New Order) of Salīm III (1789-1807) and with Maḥmūd II's (1808-1839) centralizing programmes. The long nineteenth Ottoman century as an opposite example in the manner of Eric Hobsbawm, *Age of Extremes: the Short Twentieth Century, 1914-1991*, London 1994.

series of steps in a bid for power by different individuals whose interests were usually represented in the imperial center either by a *wakīl* who was present in Istanbul or else by the interested person himself or herself who journeyed to the capital to lobby for a particular function. In most cases, however, details concerning behind-the-scene jockeying for a position remain unknown except for occasional references in memoirs or chronicles which sometimes elucidate such actions. It is therefore virtually impossible to ascertain, in the majority of cases, whether a decision was, in fact, predetermined in Istanbul before the actual decision was taken locally by the *waqf* administrator or whether that specific decision depended upon different forces at play in Istanbul. Whatever the specific case may be, the regular bureaucratic process of seeking *barāts* to confirm local decisions meant that many aspects of provincial administration of the above sort routinely passed through Istanbul; records were kept of the *barāts* in both the imperial and provincial offices as well as by the interested parties of a particular transaction as a warranty for any future contestation of the decisions. Indeed, as mentioned above, documents which later registered subsequent activity regarding a specific action (i.e. modification of an existing rent contract; change in personnel relative to the management of an endowment, change in teaching and other appointments in a *madrasa*, mosque or other locale, etc.) consistently mentioned the respective *barāt* as a given invariable, as the set point of departure.

The objectives of *Tanẓīmāt* (1839-1878) and pre-*Tanẓīmāt* programs regarding the administration of the foundations distinctly reveal the power tensions at stake between the political authority of Istanbul which strove to centralize real authority within the imperial apparatus in opposition to localized decisional centers in the empire, whether situated within the provinces or within the imperial capital itself. This included, for example, relations between the Porte and institutionalized power clusters in the provinces such as the Provincial Councils[14] which, in some cases, arbitrated *waqf*-related matters. This context of power opposition in relation to the management of the endowments also refers to other institutionalized state functions such as those of the *shaykh al-islam*, the chief *qāḍīs* of Damascus or Cairo, the Chief of the Eunuchs as well as other government posts

---

14 Thompson, "Ottoman Political Reform"; Zouheir Ghazzal, *L'Economie politique de Damas durant le XIXe siècle. Structures traditionnelles et capitalisme*, Damascus 1993, 47-59, both of whom detail the parameters of power wielded by the Provincial Council for the province of Damascus, the *Majlis al-Shūrā bi-wilāyat al-Shām*. A recent study of power relations in regard to *waqf* has been published by Richard van Leeuwen, *Waqfs and Urban Structures. The Case of Ottoman Damascus*, Leiden, Brill 1999.

whereby the individuals who held these positions apparently exercised autonomous decision-making power in the running of specific foundations associated with their particular state-appointed office.

On a more local level, neighborhood *imāms* in the Ottoman cities also assumed an intermediary position or, to be more accurate, they often played an obstructionist role between the imperial Department of *Waqfs* (re-established by Maḥmūd II after the 1826 abolition of the Janissaries and re-organized at regular intervals during the *Tanẓīmāt*) and the management of foundations in the cities and towns since, along with their other functions, many neighborhood *imāms* supervised local endowments (whether at the express demand of the *wāqif/a* or when the designated line of managers died out), including the collection of taxes on *waqf* properties and the distribution of their revenues. Finally, as far as regards the level of management that was closest to the quotidian operational administration of the individual endowments, the *waqf* administrators – the *nāẓir*s and the *mutawallī*s – personified, so to speak, individualized decisional autonomy regarding the veritable on-site daily management of the endowments in the three domains enumerated above. Nonetheless, these different power centres that were inter-connected as well as often being antagonistic with one another resulted in a multi-leveled and complex set of relations pertaining to the running of *waqf* and to the authority and control over the foundations.

Centralising and channeling the collection of endowment revenues throughout the Ottoman realm toward the Department of *Waqf* in Istanbul and then distributing the funds to the designated beneficiaries was the major objective of *Tanẓīmāt waqf* policy, a policy which had already been articulated – but not realised – within the goals of the reform project for the endowments planned by Maḥmūd II in the 1820's. Nor, in reality, despite limited success with the foundations whose management was directly assumed by the imperial Department of *Waqf* offices in the capital (aside from the imperial *waqfs*, this essentially pertained to the *waqf mulḥaq* whose administration, at the expiration of the line of *waqf* administrators nominally or generically appointed by the endowment founder, legally devolved upon the state), the *Tanẓīmāt waqf* projects were also largely left on paper, bereft, as it were, of enough real power by the Porte to enforce the aims of the reform program in relation to the endowments.

Thus, by the end of the *Tanẓīmāt* period, Istanbul still found itself pursuing the same objective of centralising *waqf* administration. In the 1860's and 1870's, Istanbul again established regulations pertaining to the administrations of *waqfs*. Especially aimed at the non-imperial *dhurrī* and *khayrī* endowments, these regulations required that administrators of all the endowments in all the provinces of the empire submit financial reports to the Department of *Waqfs* in Istanbul on a quarterly basis, detailing the receipts and expenditures of each foundation for which they were responsible.[15] In this way, the central political authority attempted (mostly without success) to supervise or, at least, to contain the influence of individual foundation administrators who controlled an important amount of wealth in the Ottoman lands.

The three domains of action mentioned above, which fall within the foundation administrators' power spheres, are situated within the primary, secondary and tertiary sectors of Ottoman society, a fact which signifies that the institution of the *waqf* – and the corresponding reach of the administrators – touched almost every aspect of economic life. Schematically speaking, the first responsibility of a *waqf* manager, namely, the management of endowment property (to ensure a profit for the foundation), falls within the primary sector in the Ottoman Empire since foundation assets included agricultural land which produced crops not only for the Ottoman economy but also beyond the confines of the Ottoman world through export, tying the *waqf* thereby to the Mediterranean and international markets. Second, the manufacture of finished items, the realm of the secondary sector, was also part of an endowment's business that was supervised by the *nāẓir* and *mutawallī* in that *waqf* properties also included, for example, workshops and stores where wood, brass and other articles were produced for sale on the market. And, third, the endowments occupied a place within the tertiary structure, the service sector of society, in view of the fact that properties owned by *waqfs* such as boutiques sold finished items to the public or *ḥammāms* which provided bath service to the population. This sector would also include the distribution of *waqf* profits (*istihqāq*) to the foundation beneficiaries, one of the domains of action supervised by the endowment managers.

The activities associated with these three sectors, all of which fell within the *waqf* administrators' domains of action, comprised both the affairs of the most wealthy endowments as well as a myriad of small-sized foundations consisting of rather modest property. It was for this very reason that *waqf* penetrated so deeply into Ottoman society, touching many different levels of local and centralized power.

---

15 Anis Kaylānī, *al-Mawsū'a al-qānūniyya: al-anẓima al-'aqāriyya*, Damascus 1981, 89-90.

Centralized Authority and Local Decisional Power

Possessing both administrative and financial access to the endowment assets which he or she managed, the *waqf* manager was part of a power play, whether explicit or implicit, between three forces: the state which disputed access to endowment wealth through taxes, the legitimate beneficiaries who demanded their part of the revenues (not always dispensed on time nor in accordance with the specified amount) and the administrator's own network, including the extended family, which usually benefited in overt as well as discrete ways from the largesse of the foundation's resources (e.g. receiving salaried jobs in institutions subsidized by the *waqf*).

Property

The correct management of *waqf* assets, i.e. keeping them in a proper condition to ensure that they produce revenues for the endowment was the primary responsibility of *waqf* administrators. Over and above all, endowment managers were to guarantee that the properties owned by the *waqf* for which they worked and from which they received a salary, turned a profit in order to generate revenues for the foundation, more specifically, in order to distribute those revenues to the beneficiaries named or indicated by the endowment founder which, after all, was the very *raison d'être* for the *waqf*'s existence. Generating revenues for the *waqf* was usually brought about through different types of contracts negotiated by the endowment administrator who arranged for both short-term (such as the *ijāra wāḥida*) and long-term (such as the *ijāra tawīla*, the *ijāratayn* and *ḥikr* on buildings or other constructed property owned by the foundations or the *musāqāh* and the *mashshad masaka* on agricultural land) rent contracts on the endowment assets.

And therein lies one of the most important sources of power for the administrators since it was the *nāẓir*s or, in their stead, the *mutawallī*s who allocated these contracts, seemingly to whom they wished.[16] At times, the relationship between administrator and renter is obvious such as when an administrator accorded a contract to a member of his or her family; such ties are sometimes identifiable when the family name is used or if the per-

---

16 Examples of rent contracts for the Damascene area are discussed in James Reilly, "Rural *Waqfs* of Ottoman Damascus: Rights of Ownership, Possession, and Tenancy," *Acta Orientalia* 51 (1990), 27-46; Randi Deguilhem, "*Waqf* documents: a multi-purpose historical sources – the case of 19th century Damascus," in *Les villes dans l'Empire ottoman : Activités et sociétés*, vol. t. 1, dir. Daniel Panzac, Paris 1991, 67-95, 191-203, esp. 76-94.

sons in question are known since rent contracts were always nominative. In some cases, information is available from an exterior source such as from a chronicle, a biographical dictionary, a memoir, etc., which may give a few details about the relationship between an administrator and a renter of property which belonged to the concerned *waqf*. There were, in fact, several levels of potential relationships since rented properties were commonly subcontracted to a second or even a third party in nineteenth century Damascus, traces of which are found in the documents. For example, an administrator may be interested in constructing links with individuals from influential political or wealthy families and the conferral of a rent contract would be a means of building such ties. However, in most instances, relationships between *waqf* administrators and renters remain unknown.

Whatever the association between *waqf* manager and renter of endowment properties – whether this concerned buildings, land or cash owned by the foundation – administrators were essentially free to choose the individual to whom they rented the properties belonging to the *waqf* under their command. In reality, however, this choice was not really "free" in that it was often consciously or unconsciously mediated by social and cultural circumstances (such as family or communal affinities),[17] and, as mentioned, pressure was no doubt exerted from above in specific cases when Istanbul decided that a particular individual was to receive a certain rent contract or position amongst the employment opportunities subsidized by the *waqfs*.

As for the rent that was to be paid to the endowment for the use of the foundation properties, the length of the contracts was usually calculated upon the basis of a three-year unit with the logic being that, at the expiry of every three years, the sum was to be reconsidered in light of market demands. However, some rent contracts ran for long periods of time, for up to 12, 15, 45 or even more years without being renegotiated. In several instances, long-term contracts led to a form of ownership of the *waqf* properties, for example, in the case where a contract ran for 45 years and passed within a deceased's estate to his or her heirs. However, since most rent contracts on *waqf* properties were for fairly short periods, this meant that there was a rather high turn-over as regards the different persons who rented the endowment properties, contributing thereby to the activity of the real-estate market.

---

17 Nicolas Journet, "La construction sociale des idées," *Sciences Humaines* 104 (April 2000), pp. 48-49.

Cases taken from the corpus under study which runs from the late eighteenth to the early twentieth century,[18] shows an important uniformity as far as concerns the registration of rent contracts. The initial administrative step was taken by the *waqf*'s *nāẓir* or *mutawallī* who, as mentioned above, registered the name of the renter of a piece of property belonging to the *waqf* for which he or she was responsible along with the amount of rent, in cash or in kind, to be paid to the endowment (usually on an annual basis). The administrator then registered the transaction with the local religious court (the *maḥkama*). A copy of the document was subsequently sent through the administrative channels to Istanbul through the auspices of the *muʿajjalāt al-awqāf* to the Porte whereupon a *barāt* would be issued. As mentioned above, all rent contracts were only officially ratified once an imperial *barāt* was issued from Istanbul without which neither the administrator nor the renter would have recourse in the event of further action on the property.

Personnel

Similar to the bureaucratic steps followed in the registration of rent contracts on foundation properties, a *waqf* administrator was also responsible for registering new members of the personnel who either worked directly for the endowment itself (such as accountants) or as employees in institutions subsidized by the endowment (such as *imām*, *mudarris*, *bawwāb* or other functions exercised in a *madrasa*, a *dār al-ḥadīth* or other establishments financed by a foundation).

Here, once more, the endowment administrator possessed a certain decisional power owing to the fact that it was the manager's responsibility to register the new member of the personnel that was paid by the *waqf*. However, as pointed out above, the choice was not solely that of the administrator's since appointments were obviously made in concert with neighborhood notables and other personalities. A decision regarding an appointment was, in fact, often a collective one, taking local sensibilities into account, as demonstrated in a document from 1820 that was recorded within the Damascene *awāmir sulṭāniyya* registers.[19] In this case, there was a

---

18 The ensemble of the entries concerning *waqf* in these registers constitute part of the empirical basis for a study in progress. The present article treats but one dimension of the documents, namely the relationship between the administrators and their powers of decision concerning several aspects of managing the endowments.

19 *Awāmir Sulṭāniyya, wilāyat Dimashq al-Shām*, register n° 1, p. 12, case 23, dated 25 Shawwāl 1236.

vacancy for a position of *khaṭīb* at the Jāmiʿ Muʿallaq, located in the northern section of the al-ʿAmāra quarter of Damascus next to the citadel. According to the document, the official process of filling the vacancy for the *khaṭīb* position was the following: the *mukhtār* of the quarter (*ḥayy*) contacted the local *qāḍī*, Āl Katkhudā Muḥammad Ṣādiq bey Asīzāda, about this vacancy, both in terms of verifying the salary and in relation to the individual who was to fulfill the position. The document notes that the *qāḍī*, on the basis of *ḥujjas* that had been recorded in the daybook of receipts and expenditures (*ʿaskarī rūznāmja darkanār*) that were shown to him and in agreement with the accountant of the Muʿallaq Mosque as well as the accountant of the imperial *waqf* office, concurred that the salary of the *khaṭīb* should continue to be fixed at 6 *uqja* per day which was the same sum previously given to the former *khaṭīb* of that mosque. As for the appointment of the new *khaṭīb*, the document specifies that three witnesses (Sayyid ʿAbd al-Ḥalīm, Sayyid ʿAbd al-Raḥmān, and Sayyid Muḥammad, all of them sons of Sayyid Asʿad) testified that no one had come forth with a *barāt*, claiming appointment to the position, in the absence of which the candidate for the job, Shaykh Aḥmad Khalīfa, was to be considered. The document then states that the candidate was to be appointed *khaṭīb* of the Muʿallaq Mosque, as his father had been before him. A request for a *barāt* would then have been sent to Istanbul for official confirmation of the nomination. In return for his salary, the document notes that the new *khaṭīb* was henceforth to pronounce the weekly Friday sermon at the mosque.

This is but one of many examples from the corpus which illustrate the complex social and political dynamics involved in the nomination of personnel in the mosques, the *madrasas* and other sites that were subsidized by the foundations in nineteenth century Damascus. As referred to in the above document registered in 1820, whose modalities regarding personnel nomination were similar to those throughout the sample under study, decisions concerning local personnel were indeed a state affair before the *Tanẓīmāt* era. Decisions and even details concerning salary specifications were formulated between the centralized political authority in the Ottoman Empire and on-site decisional power groups composed of the foundation administrators as well as local *qāḍīs*, neighborhood *mukhtārs* and other notables who exercised power within local and regional networks.

For instance, the daily salary that was to be paid to the newly nominated *khaṭīb* in the Damascene Muʿallaq mosque was agreed upon not only by the accountant of that mosque but also by the state-appointed accountant of the imperial *waqf* office as well as by the endowment administrator who was responsible for the finances of the *waqf*. The document also shows that, in the above case, the *khaṭīb* position passed from father to son; this hereditary aspect is, in fact, commonly noted throughout the 130 years represented by the corpus under study. However, it is also noted in the documents that the "heir" to such learned positions as *khaṭīb*, *mudarris*, *imām*, etc., had to possess the necessary qualifications in order to be nominated to the position. In the event where a son did not qualify for a particular position, it would then often pass to a nephew, a cousin or an uncle who had the necessary training. There were, of course, also many cases where positions would pass outside of the family sphere due either to other individuals who had better access to power circles or simply for a lack of qualified heirs.

As far as centralized authority and local decisional power is concerned in relation to the nomination of personnel paid by the endowments, it is interesting to note that the above document refers to the absence of a *barāt* in which case a decision would be taken locally *vis-à-vis* the new *khaṭīb*. This shows that a *barāt* could function both "from the top down" or the inverse; in other words, a nomination may officially emanate from Istanbul and be ratified locally or just the opposite. However, in most of the cases examined in the corpus, including the 1820 document looked at here, such decisions were usually taken locally and then ratified by an imperial *barāt*.

Beneficiaries

In relation to the third domain of action listed above, *waqf* administrators also exercised a certain amount of personal decisional power in the distribution of endowment revenues. Although they were, on the whole, legally bound to respect the distribution schema of *waqf* funds as allocated to beneficiaries named or indicated by the *wāqif/a*, the administrators did have quite a bit of flexibility in specific circumstances as recognised by *sharī'a*.

For example, in the case of a *waqf dhurrī* or *mushtarak*, when a beneficiary died, his or her part of the revenues would not automatically be given to the deceased's heirs unless the entire level (*daraja*) of beneficiaries had also died out. If the deceased had living siblings who were beneficiaries of that *waqf*, then the deceased's portion of the revenues would be distributed among the beneficiaries of that generation. Although, in principle, the deceased's part should have been allocated according to the *waqfiyya*'s stipulations (e.g. all beneficiaries received equitable parts or, as was often the case, male beneficiaries received the double of female ones – following Quranic precepts), the administrators were in fact often able to distribute the extra revenues as they saw fit according to a formula known as *ziyāda wa-nuqṣān*. Endowment administrators also had a certain latitude in distributing extra revenues if one of the beneficiaries had committed a major crime such as apostasy or murder and had subsequently been removed from the list of those receiving revenues from the *waqf* or if the endowment's assets produced more revenue than had been foreseen, the administrator was free to distribute those extra profits as he or she wanted. Finally, a foundation manager was able to withhold revenue from a beneficiary if those funds were needed to repair property belonging to the *waqf*.[20]

Three documents recorded between 1886 and 1888 from the corpus of the Damascene *awāmir sulṭāniyya* registers serve to illustrate a concrete example concerning the death of one of the endowment's beneficiaries and the subsequent request by his children to inherit their father's benefits.[21] The documents in question concern the Ayūbī *waqf*, one of the oldest *waqfs* in Bilād al-Shām. The first two documents confirmed the death of one of the beneficiaries, Sayyid Aḥmad Afandī Ibn Sayyid Muḥammad Najīb Ayūb al-Anṣārī who died on 23 Safar 1303 (1885). His death was officially noted by a certified copy of a *firmān 'alī* which verified his demise. The deceased's heirs then presented a protocol, which had been registered with the *maḥkama*, and which endorsed their rights to their father's portion of the *waqf* revenues. According to the third document registered in 1888, these revenues came from a shop located in the Sūq al-Quṭn section of Damascus. The heirs' claim to their father's portion of the endowment benefits was proclaimed to be justified and they were enrolled on the beneficiary lists of the Ayūbī *waqf*. This process was overseen by the administrator of the *waqf* who presumably served to relay the information between the concerned individuals. The decision to register the new beneficiaries was sealed with an imperial *firmān* from Istanbul.

Waqf Administrative Power and Gender Blindness

All the above decisions exercised by endowment administrators were gender blind – whether this involved the management of *waqf* capital, the personnel associated with the endowment or the distribution of foundation revenues. There was no "feminine" *waqf* in Islam nor was there an arche-

---

20 Muḥammad Qadrī Bāshā, *Qānūn al-'adl wa-l-inṣāf li-l-qaḍā' 'alā mushkilāt al-awqāf*, Cairo 1928, 54-61; Muḥammad Abū Zahra, *Muḥāḍarāt fī 'l-waqf*, Damascus 1959, 170-174.

21 *Awāmir Sulṭāniyya, wilāyat Dimashq al-Shām*, register n° 9, p. 79, case 217, dated Ḥuzayrān 1304; *ibid.*, p. 79, case 217 bis, dated 16 Shawwāl 1305; *ibid.*, p. 79, case 218, dated 25 Rabī' I 1306.

typal "feminine" founder of *waqf* or a "feminine" endowment administrator. No difference between genders is ever expressed in either *sharī'a* or the *fatwās*, nor in Ottoman state regulations. Furthermore, on-the-ground research has shown that there is no textual difference in the documents registered in the *awāmir sulṭāniyya* nor in the Ottoman tribunal records as concerns transactions, litigation or other documentation on *waqf* which passed through the Ottoman bureaucratic instances. Nevertheless, on a sociological level, there is little doubt that decisions, both in naming beneficiaries of foundations and in the daily administration of *waqf*, were conditioned by gender,[22] but certainly not in relation to Istanbul as the central authority.

Conclusion

A straightforward reading of the documents would lead one to surmise that decisions concerning the rent of *waqf* properties, the appointment of personnel to run the institutions endowed by the foundations and the distribution of foundation wealth to beneficiaries were largely the business of local *waqf* administrators. To a considerable extent, this was true in that the individual *nāẓir*s and *mutawallī*s of the endowments did exercise a large amount of power regarding the activities in the above sectors and domains of action. But, as mentioned above, in view of the fact that the administrators acted within a complex bureaucratic system of checks and balances whose intricacies are being sifted through and analysed,[23] it is highly unlikely that the imperial offices in Istanbul merely assumed a passive role

---

22 Among the published material specifically concerning the relationship between women and *waqf* is found in Stephen Humphreys, "Women as Patrons of Religious Architecture in Ayyubid Damascus," *Muqarnas* 11 (1994), 35-54; Mary Ann Fay, "Women and *Waqf*: Toward a Reconsideration of Women's Place in the Mamluk's Household," *IJMES* 29, (1997), 33-51; Beshara Doumani. "Endowing Family: *Waqf*, Property Devolution, and Gender in Greater Syria, 1800 to 1860," *CSSH* 40/1 (Jan 1998), 3-41, esp. 29; Randi Deguilhem, "Self-Consciousness: The Muslim Woman as Creator and Manager of *Waqf* Foundations in Late Ottoman Damascus," *Dirassat Insania,* Revue d'Histoire de la Faculté des Sciences Humaines de l'Université d'Alger, Algiers, 1 (2001), pp 3-19.

23 For example, recently studied and summarised by Donald Quataert, "The Age of Reforms, 1812-1914," in *An Economic and Social History of the Ottoman Empire*, v. 2 (1600-1914), ed. S. Faroqhi, B. McGowan, D. Quataert and S. Pamuk, Cambridge 1994, 759-943; Paul Dumont, "La période des Tanzīmāt (1839-1878)," in *Histoire de l'Empire ottoman*, Paris 1989, dir. Robert Mantran, 459-522; François Georgeon, "Le dernier sursaut (1878-1909)," in *ibid.*, 523-576, and together by François Georgeon and Paul Dumont, "La mort d'un empire (1908-1923)," in *ibid.*, 577-647.

in ratifying actions taken by *waqf nāẓir*s and *mutawallī*s. As far as concerns the *waqf*, decisional control of the endowment administrators was partially mitigated by the *barāt* issued from Istanbul which endorsed decisions taken locally by *waqf* managers and without which local actions were essentially invalid since any future change depended upon the presentation of the *barāt*. The example of the *barāt* demonstrates the dependency of different bureaucratic levels in the Empire.

Furthermore, although endowment managers incontestably exercised a huge range of operational action extending both horizontally and vertically throughout the society, they were nevertheless naturally subject to the influence of their familial, social and communal surroundings. However much endowment administrators exercised decisional powers, these powers were rooted and influenced by the socio-cultural and political matrix of which they were part: e.g. an administrator was more likely to accord a coveted rent contract to a member of his or her family or an acquaintance rather than to an unknown person in the same way that the administrator would most likely ensure that revenues went towards a beneficiary which was important to his or her family such as a particular mosque or *madrasa*. The administrators' decisions, individually taken according to the documents, were, in fact, anchored within societal concerns.[24] These social forces acted as a means of palliating individual actions or, in the words of Nicolas Journet: "*les individus ne peuvent prendre de grandes décisions que dans le cadre des institutions qu'ils construisent*".[25]

---

24 Journet, commenting upon Mary Douglas, *Comment pensent les institutions*, Paris 1999 (tr. from Mary Douglas, *How Institutions Think*).

25 Journet, "La construction sociale des idées".

– V –

Portraying a New Ottoman Presence

OTTOMAN PHOTOGRAPHY: RECORDING AND CONTRIBUTING TO MODERNITY.

WOLF-DIETER LEMKE

In the last decades of the nineteenth century photography made its appearance even in the remotest parts of the Ottoman Empire. Photographic images are important sources for the study of imperial history. To make the best use of them, they should be read and analyzed in combination with written sources. But even when taken alone, photographs may contribute to a better understanding of the processes of modernization and centralization in the late Ottoman Empire. There are two ways to approach them:

Photographs may be studied at 'face value' in order to visualize historical locations now changed or vanished: landscapes, towns, villages, buildings, people in their public and private lives. Photography cannot be a true and objective mirror of reality – a view widely held in the nineteenth century – but read with caution, photographs possess evident documentary value. They show newly opened buildings and institutions, trace transformations of infrastructure, or portray public events and ceremonies. Some of these buildings, though occasionally disfigured, still exist. Photographs give an idea of their original appearance. Other photographs show public works which still today form the basis of urban structure or of long distance communication networks. Quite often photographs are the only visual witness of an Ottoman presence no longer visible today.

But to study photographs only for their 'face value' is to ignore their intrinsic value. Photography is more than mere representation of objects. There is intent and a characteristic point of view at work: in the choice of subject and in the way objects, persons and events are arranged for the camera's gaze. It has been argued that Ottoman photography had its own special style.[1] It must be seen whether the same characteristics apply to Ottoman photography in the Arab provinces. Furthermore, the introduction of photography, its use even in remote regions like Yemen, was in itself an act of technological modernization. As a side effect, photography created

---

1 Gilbert Beaugé, Engin Çizgen (Özendes), *Images d'Empire. Aux origines de la photographie en Turquie. Collection Pierre de Gigord*, Istanbul 1993, 230-240.

new possibilities of long-distance control, enabling the center to visualize through images what was actually achieved.

History of Ottoman Photography

To understand the distinctive role of photography in the Arab provinces a look at its Middle Eastern history is helpful. Who were the first photographers and what was their aim? What is the state of collecting, publication and research? And what type of material is at our disposal?

There is no reliable history of Ottoman photography, but much progress has been made.[2] The first photographs of the Middle East date from 1839, taken only months after the official presentation of this 'revolutionary' equipment in Europe. They were intended for a public, which had no personal experience of the countries, depicted. Photography was to satisfy European curiosity, to answer the quest for biblical and exotic landscapes, to reproduce the eternal unchanging Orient.

Photographs were published and distributed in Europe and the United States. They were marketed either commercially to a general public, or they were studied for academic and artistic purposes. They presented an Orient through European eyes. Actual Oriental scenery was retouched through the lens of an imagined Orient. European photography included occasional encounters with contemporary efforts at modernization. But documenting them was not their main interest.

The pioneers were almost exclusively western travelers who were later joined by long-term residents in the Middle East. The situation changed with the rise of organized tourism. To answer increased demand, non-Ottoman and soon Ottoman photographers opened studios in Istanbul, in major towns of the empire and in tourist centers. These studios catered for the needs of tourists, enabling them to buy photographic pictures as the most modern type of souvenir. But they also began to serve an emerging urban clientele by providing portrait photography to local and foreign residents alike.

Ottoman photography combined the shared heritage of travel photographers, foreign and Ottoman commercial photographers and Ottoman military photographers. It is to the newly emerging group of local commercial photographers, working from centers like Aleppo, Baghdad, Beirut, Damascus, Jerusalem and Ṣanʿāʾ, that we owe the majority of nineteenth century photographs of the Arab provinces, including manifestations of a new Ottoman presence. This group deserves to be studied with

2 Engin Çizgen (Özendes), *Photography in the Ottoman Empire 1839-1919*, Istanbul 1987.

the same interest reserved until now for the foreign pioneers of Middle Eastern photography.

The preference for centers of tourism and commerce has led to a geographical imbalance in photographic coverage. Some of the Arab areas of the Empire were extensively photographed, for others there exist no early pictures at all. Palestine as a main tourist destination was well covered, especially Jerusalem. Damascus and Beirut were often part of a Middle East tour. Aleppo was not a tourist destination, neither was Baghdad, while Ṣanʿāʾ was out of reach. Smaller towns, especially those far away from a center, were photographed for the first time only years later.

Research on Middle Eastern photography reflects the uneven distribution of material. There has been an immense interest in early travel and studio photography, leading to numerous publications. A good general introduction can be found in "Focus East: Early Photography in the Near East (1839-1885)"[3], supplemented by the more recent "Voyage en Orient".[4] Less satisfying is the research situation for later years. Photographers had now been at work all over the Ottoman Empire. But even most basic cataloguing work needs still to be done. Nonetheless, a new attempt at a synthesis has been tried. The exhibition catalogue "Images d`Empire" deals with favored themes of Ottoman photography and seeks to analyze its stylistic peculiarities.[5]

Historical photographs have increasingly been published in recent years, with the main focus on Turkey. Most books are overtly nostalgic, demonstrating only what a bygone world looked like without providing a critical commentary. Ambitious Turkish and Greek collectors seem determined to cover not only old Istanbul and its many suburbs, but all major towns of Asia Minor and the Aegean.[6] In addition, the output of some local photographers has been reproduced.[7] Some of them are of interest for the

---

3 Nissan N. Perez, *Focus East: Early Photography in the Near East (1839-1885)*, New York 1988.

4 Sylvie Aubenas, Jacques Lacarrière, *Voyage en Orient*, Paris 1999.

5 See footnote no. 1.

6 Engin Özendes, *Osmanlı'nın Son Başkenti İstanbul*, Istanbul 1999. Özer Kangür, *Geçmiş Zaman Fotoğraflarında Büyükada*, Istanbul ca. 1999. Engin Özendes, *The First Ottoman Capital Bursa*, Istanbul 1999. Haşim Karpuz (ed.), *Fotoğraflarla Geçmişte Konya*, Istanbul 1996. *Smyrna. The City before the Destruction*, Athens 1991. Nicholas P. Stavroulakis, *Salonika. Jews and Dervishes*, Athens 1993.

7 Bahattin Öztuncay, *James Robertson. Pioneer of Photography in the Ottoman Empire*, Istanbul 1992. Engin Özendes, *Abdullah Frères. Osmanlı Sarayının Fotoğrafçıları*, Istanbul 1998. Engin Özendes, *From Sébah & Joaillier to Foto Sabah. Orientalism in*

Arab world, as they offer pictures from Arab provinces and cities. Publications on Palestine and Egypt tend to combine more serious research with picture reproduction.[8] The same can be said about the more recent publications on photography in Lebanon[9], Syria[10] and Saudi Arabia[11], while material on Iraq and Yemen is less researched and documented.

Simplifying the matter a bit, two types of photographic print must be distinguished: real photography, printed directly from a negative and reproductions, printed with the help of a cliché. For historical research all forms of printing are important, though real photography will be preferred here due to clarity and detail. Problems of authenticity do not arise, as forging barely existed.

At the beginning the process of taking photographs was complicated and time consuming. Subjects were chosen carefully. Deliberate choice and the preference for large formats, combined with the considerable time of exposure are at the basis of the excellent documentary value found in early photography. As a rule professional photographers were in charge. Private snapshot photography only appears at the end of the century. Prints were acquired in loose form or already mounted on cardboard. They were collected in bulky folders and albums.

The number of early direct prints was limited and not all survived. Copies became abundant only after the establishment of a market for tourists and locals. Progress in photographic technique and picture printing accelerated the spread of photography. Stereoscopic cards became very popular for some decades, picture postcards followed. Photographs were also increasingly used to illustrate journals and books.

It is with the introduction of picture postcards that the small amount of printed photographs grew to unprecedented dimensions. Parallel to this development the number of objects photographed grew too. Some aspects

---

Photography, Istanbul 1999. Bahattin Öztuncay, *Vassilaki Kargopoulo. Photographer to His Majesty the Sultan*, Istanbul 2000.

8 *Revealing the Holy Land. The Photographic Exploration of Palestine,* Santa Barbara 1997. Jean-Claude Simoën, *Egypte éternelle. Les voyageurs photographes au siècle dernier*, Paris 1993. *Excursions along the Nile. The Photographic Discovery of Ancient Egypt,* Santa Barbara 1994.

9 Michel Fani, *Liban 1880-1914. L'Atelier photographique de Ghazir*, Beyrouth 1995. Michel Fani, *L'Atelier de Beyrouth. Liban 1848-1914*, Beyrouth 1996. Fouad Debbas, *Des photographes à Beyrouth 1840-1918*, Paris 2001.

10 Badr El-Hage, *Des photographes à Damas 1840-1918*, Paris 2000.

11 William Facey, *Saudi Arabia by the First Photographers*, London 1996. Badr al-Ḥāǧǧ, *al-Mamlaka al-ʿarabīya as-saʿūdīya. Ṣuwar min al-māḍī 1861-1939*, London 1997. L'Institut du monde arabe, *Photographies d'Arabie. Hedjaz 1907-1917,* Paris 1999.

of the last decades of the Ottoman Empire can best be illustrated or documented by postcards. Picture postcards sometimes provide the only historical views existing, an observation especially valid for regions not covered by tourist photography.

Research into the history of Middle Eastern photography has traditionally dealt with early photography. Intensive publishing of postcards – important for their detailed and wider geographical coverage – only began in the last two decades. Again Turkish and Greek researchers and collectors are at the forefront of this activity. There are numerous publications on regions and towns of Asia Minor, the Aegean and on recent Ottoman history.[12] They could serve as a model for a much needed investigation into the output of leading Arab postcard publishers: Abdullahy Bros. (Baghdad), A. J. Svoboda (Baghdad), Saraffian Bros. (Beirut), D. Tarazi & Fils (Beirut, Damascus, Jerusalem), A. Terzis & Fils (Beirut, Jerusalem), B. Asfar (Damascus), F.Vester (Jerusalem), L. Tzambaz (Ḥudayda).

Even less research has been done on the huge amount of photographic illustrations published in Ottoman illustrated journals. Following French models, this type had become popular at the end of the century. The political and cultural magazine *Servet-i Fünun* is an especially good pictorial source for modernization efforts undertaken in all parts of the Empire. It heavily draws on photographic material provided by commercial, military and amateur photographers.[13]

A study of the Ottoman-Arab photographic heritage making use of all this divergent material has still to be undertaken. Researchers can draw on public and private collections and on picture archives. Most of them are still to be found in Europe and the United States, but new efforts are undertaken in the Middle East. Venerable institutions like the Bibliothèque nationale de France with its very old and excellent stock are joined by new institutions like the Getty Museum which houses one of the best

---

12 Turgut Çeviker, *İbret Albümü 1908*, Istanbul 1991. Ahmet Eken, *Kartpostallarda İstanbul*, Istanbul 1992. Perihan Sarıöz, *Bir Zamanlar İstanbul*, Istanbul 1996. Mert Sandalcı, *The Postcards of Max Fruchtermann*, 3 vols., Istanbul 2000. Ozan Sağdiç *Ankara Posta Kartları ve Belge Fotoğrafları Arşivi Kataloğu,* Ankara 1994. Perihan Sarıöz, *Bir Zamanlar Eskişehir*, Istanbul 1997. Costis Copsidas, *Les juifs de Thessalonique à travers les cartes-postales, 1886-1917*, Thessaloniki 1992. Vangellis Karagiannis, Stratis Molinos, *Mytilini 1912*, o.O. ca 1993. Antonis S. Maillis, *The Coastline of Asia Minor from Pontus to the Mediterranean. Postcards 1880-1920*, Rhodes ca. 2000.

13 Paul Dumont, *Propagande, positivisme et pédagogie. Le rôle de la photographie dans la presse illustrée ottomane. L`exemple du <Servet-i Fünun>*, (unpublished conference paper. Conference: *Image. Functions and Languages,* Istanbul 1999).

collections of Ottoman photography, and the Semitic Museum at Harvard. In the Middle East, the original Yıldız collection is of primary importance, but systematic collecting and archiving is going on in many countries like Lebanon, Syria, Israel, Qatar, Turkey and Saudi Arabia. For the last there exists an extensively researched and well indexed catalogue.[14]

Picturing Ottoman Rule

What do these photographs show that can be identified as characteristic for the late Ottoman period? There are mainly three areas, where the new Ottoman presence, the policy of centralization and modernization, can be demonstrated and illustrated: 1. the areas of architecture and of urban and inter-urban infrastructure; 2. the area of public and official life and 3. the area of private life. Owing to limited space only some examples can be quoted and even less will be reproduced. All images of towns and buildings mentioned in this text exist in my collection.

The will to strengthen central control by modernizing the military infrastructure and improving the civil administration found its architectural expression in newly constructed military and public buildings. Provincial towns were separated from each other by hundreds of miles and were even further away from the Ottoman capital. Nevertheless these buildings bear a striking similarity in their architectural outlines. This observation is especially true for military barracks, for civil and military hospitals, for railway stations, for postal buildings, for schools and to a lesser degree for government buildings and governors' residences. Many of these buildings have been photographed and a lot of them appear on postcards or were chosen to illustrate journals, underlining the model character attributed to them.

The barracks of Aleppo and Damascus resemble for instance those of Istanbul in Harbiye or Gümüşsuyu, and they are close in appearance even to the barracks of a Balkan town as far away as Mostar (fig. 1).[15] A similar observation can be made for numerous hospitals (Aleppo, fig. 2[16], Baghdad, Beirut, Damascus) and school buildings (fig. 3)[17]. Even government buildings and governors' residences seem to follow a common scheme,

---

14 Maktabat al-malik Fahd al-waṭanīya, *Kashshāf al-ṣuwar al-tārīkhīya lil-Mamlaka al-ʿArabīya al-Saʿūdīya,* Riyāḍ 1999.

15 Postcard: "Damas. La Caserne." André Terzis & Fils, Beirut - Jerusalem (Collection W.-D. Lemke, Beirut [= Coll. WDL])

16 Postcard: "Alep. L'Hôpital Civil." K. Missirlian. (Coll. WDL).

17 Postcard: "Alep. Lycée Impérial." Cl. Thévenet & Fils, Alep. (Coll. WDL).

incorporating local architectural vernaculars in Baghdad, Ḥudayda, Aleppo and elsewhere.

Modernizing efforts in architecture were not limited to areas of direct state control. Impressive Belle Epoque department stores like the Orosdi building in Beirut could also have done business on the Grande Rue de Péra in Istanbul (fig. 4).[18] On the other hand, even unspectacular private villas displayed a distinct Ottoman character, like those on Ṣāliḥiyya street in Damascus. Again a picture postcard enables the historian to visualize an architectural ensemble that stood in stark contrast to previous street layouts (fig. 5).[19]

Even in parts of the old town a new grid pattern of streets was laid out. New bazaar buildings with standardized shops, following the model of nineteenth century European shopping galleries were erected. An aerial view of the main road unveils a monumental straightness, which contrasted with the maze of unplanned alleys (fig. 6).[20] Clearly, the straightness combined with the architectural uniformity was part and parcel of the efforts to establish order and control. In other Arab towns less ambitious bazaar buildings or market halls were built, but they all denoted typical features of late Ottoman urban development projects.

Even more ambitious was the creation of new town quarters with a regular street pattern and urban public space, something unprecedented in the Arab provinces of the Ottoman Empire. Public places, marked by memorial columns such as the Marja Square in Damascus and the railway station in Jaffa or by clock towers (in Aleppo, Beirut, Jaffa, Tripoli and elsewhere) became distinctive ingredients of late Ottoman town planning. Public gardens were also laid out. Quite often the Ottoman coat of arms would be displayed on entrance gates, pedestals etc., visually underlining the manifest will to enforce relations between the center and the provinces. Again these modernizing and centralizing efforts can be demonstrated by pictures. There are for instance dozens of photographs and postcards depicting Marja Square (fig. 7)[21] or showing Naṣr street in

---

18 Postcard: "Beirut. Orosdi Bek." Sarrafian Bros., Beirut, No. 301 (Coll. WDL).

19 Postcard: "Damas. Rue de Salhieh." Soubhi S. & Mounir Aïta, Damas (Coll. WDL).

20 Postcard: "Damas. Vue générale." André Terzis & Fils, Beirut - Jerusalem (Coll. WDL).

21 Postcard: "Damas. Place El-Chouhada." Photographie Bonfils, A. Guiragossian, Beyrouth, No. 154. (Coll. WDL). See for the Marja Square: S. Weber, "Der Marğa-Platz in Damaskus – Die Entstehung eines modernen Stadtzentrums unter den Osmanen als Ausdruck strukturellen Wandels (1808-1918)," *Damaszener Mitteilungen*, 10 (1998), 291-344, Taf. 77-88.

Damascus in different stages of early twentieth century construction (fig. 8).[22]

Traveling the Roads to Modernity

To modernize urban structures also meant to improve transport. Besides facilitating private vehicle traffic by planned street systems, public transport was installed by introducing tramways. The example of Istanbul was followed in major cities like Baghdad (fig. 9)[23], Beirut and Damascus, but also in a small town like Tripoli. The modern way of transport was promptly photographed and made widely known by postcards.

More ambitious and of obvious importance for imperial control over the Arab provinces were projects to improve long distance communication lines. A telegraphic network was established, railway lines were built and sea and river shipping was improved. The opening of the Hedjaz telegraph line was marked by the memorial column in Marja Square. Designed by the innovative architect Raimondo d´Aronco in Istanbul, it symbolically underlined the reduction of distance between the capital and the provinces.

Projects to regularize long distance transportation promised visible results. Pictures of railways, stations, and ports were very common. Judging by the amount of material still available, photographing railway construction seems especially to have become an obsession. There are numerous photographs, single postcards, postcard series and journal illustrations showing track laying, viaducts, railway stations and trains. Albums with railway photography regularly turn up in Istanbul auctions.[24] Railway constructions were celebrated as something modern. Staging photographs of work-in-progress and of inaugural ceremonies blended local pride with Hamidian notions of progress and development.

---

22 Postcard: "Damas. Boulevard de Hedjoy[!]." Photographie Bonfils, A. Guiragossian, Beyrouth, No. 180 (Coll. WDL).

23 Postcard: "Bagdad. La seule ligne de tramway à Bagdad." A. J. Svoboda, Bagdad (Turquie) (Coll. WDL).

24 Burak Filateli, Istanbul, auction 7.2.1999, lot 398.

Fig. 1: "Damas. La Caserne." Published by André Terzis & Fils, Beirut Jerusalem.

Fig. 2: "Alep. L'Hôpital Civil." Published by K. Missirlian.

Fig. 3: “Alep. Lycée Impérial.” Published by Cl. Thévenet & Fils, Alep.

Fig. 4: “Beirut. Orosdi Bek.” Published by Sarrafian Bros., Beirut.

Fig. 5: "Damas. Rue de Salhieh." Published by Soubhi S. & Mounir Aïta, Damas.

Fig. 6: "Damas. Vue générale." Published by André Terzis & Fils, Beirut Jerusalem.

Fig. 7: "Damas. Place El-Chouhada." Photographie Bonfils, A. Guiragossian, Beyrouth.

Fig. 8: "Damas. Boulevard de Hedjoy[!]." Photographie Bonfils, A. Guiragossian, Beyrouth.

Fig. 9: "La seule ligne de tramway à Bagdad."
Published by A. J. Svoboda, Bagdad.

Fig. 10: "Damas. Départ des pélerins pour la Mecque."
Published by Dimitri Tarazi & Fils, Beyrouth, Damas, Jérusalem.

Fig. 11: Iraq: "Opening of a Canal." Photo, ca. 1900.
Photographer: Z. G. Donatossian, Baghdad.

Fig. 12: Ṣanʿāʾ: "Inauguration of an official building [barracks?]."
Glass negative.

Fig. 13: "Imp. Ottoman Soldiers Practice Beirut.
Exercises des soldats Imp. Ottomans, Beyrouth."

Fig. 14: "Einweihung der Stadtuhr in Jaffa (Palästina)."
Jaffa, Published by J. A. Mitri.

Fig. 15: "Unknown officer ". Studio portrait. David Gazala, Photographe Baghdad."

Fig. 16: Glass negative: "Ottoman official", ca. 1900 [Ṣanʿāʾ?], most probably of Hilmi Paşa Hüseyin (1855- 1920)

Memories of the Modern

While the value of photographs for outlining the Ottoman impact on architecture and town planning is evident, their documentary value is even more convincing for transitory manifestations of Ottoman power. For ceremonial and other events there are usually various written sources at hand, but at the end of the century it became a habit to take photographs as well. The historical moment of ritual power display was recorded and handed down in picture form.

The use of ceremonial rituals, especially of those connected to religion, constituted one of the most significant ways the Ottoman state employed to underline its legitimacy. The most famous performances are the ceremonies surrounding Friday prayer in Istanbul. They have been extensively captured by photography. Similar rituals were staged by provincial authorities. A major religious event such as the departure of the annual pilgrimage caravan to Mecca was carefully orchestrated with many officials attending (fig. 10).[25] But even at ceremonies without an obvious religious character, the presence of state officials and religious leaders seemed to be the norm. There were many occasions for a public display of Ottoman civil and military power: the inauguration of a building, the implementation of larger projects like new communication lines or irrigation schemes (fig. 11)[26], the public reading of a firman, the visit of a foreign dignitary or military exercises and parades.

Ottoman photographs of extraordinary events are valuable for several reasons. They not only preserved for posterity what was previously only recorded in writing or, rarely, in drawings and, typically only at the center of power. Now photographs were taken in all parts of the empire. Under Abdülhamid II photography became a means of exercising power for the government precisely because of its claim to accurate real-life representation and its coverage of even remote areas like Iraq and Yemen (fig. 12).[27] As there was no tourist photography photographs must be interpreted as genuinely Ottoman in production, even if photographers accidentally chose motifs which in touristic areas served to satisfy the thirst for the exotic and the picturesque.

---

25 Postcard: "Damas. Départ des pélerins pour la Mecque." Dimitri Tarazi & Fils, Beyrouth, Damas, Jérusalem, No. 88 (Coll. WDL).

26 Iraq: "Opening of a Canal." Photo, ca. 1900. Photographer: Z. G. Donatossian, Baghdad (Coll. WDL).

27 Ṣanʿāʾ: "Inauguration of an official building [barracks?]." Glass negative (Coll. WDL).

Pictorial preservation of memorable events is of evident value for the historian. But events were meant to impress. They were photographed for the private or public memory of the living. Photographs, printed as postcards or reproduced in illustrated journals, made official acts and ceremonies that took place in the provinces or the capital known throughout the empire. Government achievements and public power display could now be documented and propagated in an unprecedented, impressive way. Especially postcards, which were cheap to produce and were increasingly used and even collected, must have intensified the effects of Ottoman simultaneity and territorial integration.

Usually it is not recorded by whose order these pictures were taken. Quite often even the photographer is unknown. But photographs covering official acts should be regarded at least as semiofficial records, even if background information is lacking. One possibility to identify them is to look for common themes, another to look for styles, political as well as cultural, which could be called Ottoman. Taking into account the diversity of material, the insufficient state of its collection and publication and the lack of investigation into what may have motivated photographers, this certainly involves some extrapolation. But if there was a special character to Ottoman photography, it would have manifested itself most clearly in semiofficial photography from the Arab provinces.

Framing the Provinces

Fortunately, there is one set of photographs, which is without doubt official. It can serve as a guideline. In 1893/1894 Abdülhamid had a set of photographs assembled and sent to the British Museum and the Library of Congress.[28] These pictures were considered representative enough to propagate Ottoman efforts of modernization to the outside world. The albums demonstrate which role was given to the photographic eye in the discourse of modernization. Much self-assurance was displayed, as many of the photographs were also reprinted as postcards. Their style had obviously found official approval. Some of the photographers were officially recognized court photographers.

As one might expect, efforts at modernization are demonstrated by a range of photographic themes emphasizing improvements in state admini-

---

[28] See: Carney S. Gavin, *Imperial Self-Portrait: The Ottoman Empire as revealed in the Sultan Abdul Hamid II's photographic albums presented to the Library of Congress (1893) and the British Museum (1894). A pictorial selection with catalogue, concordance, indices, and brief essays*, Cambridge, MA, 1988 [JTS 12 (1988)].

stration, educational projects and investment in infrastructure all around the empire. Technological manifestations of Ottoman modernity received high priority. But there were also pictures of troops parading and civil defense forces exercising. In particular those pictures depicting people show a striking symmetry, and a tendency to arrange subjects in clear geometrical patterns is noticeable (fig. 13).[29] The overall impression is one of rigid discipline and a desire for order. Here the Ottoman world was not photographed with an eye for the exotic – a military or administrative eye is at work.

One must assume that there were commonly accepted rules for photographing public events quite apart from requirements of photographic technique. This is not snapshot photography. The individuals present are usually arranged in a slightly curved half circle, with high-ranking officials, officers, Muslim ʿulamāʾ and occasionally Christian priests in the center. The groups look frozen, they resemble statues, bestowing on the composition the overall quality of a memorial monument – an impression underlined by the fact that some photographs were made public through postcards or illustrated journals. Photographs worked as pictorial memoriae, coinciding with the emergence of the official markers in stone erected all over the Ottoman empire during the reign of Abdülhamid. Often they portrayed the official inauguration of such a monumental marker as the Jaffa clock tower (fig. 14).[30]

Photography is employed with two aims in mind, a general one and a more specific. Its extensive use is part and testimony of the modernization project. But there is also a dialogue without words, an unarticulated agreement between the rigid composition and the predilection for orderliness and geometry.

The growing popularity of photography in all its forms, and especially the staggering amount of picture production, reflected another aspect of cultural change: the incursion of the image into Ottoman society.

Pictures of imagined landscapes, towns and human beings had been part of miniature painting. Reproductions of existing towns and real people were less common. They could appear in records of military campaigns or court festivities, but these were only accessible to a very limited number of people. For the majority, standardized views of the holy cities and painted

---

29 Postcard: “Imp. Ottoman Soldiers Practice Beirut. Exercises des soldats Imp. Ottomans, Beyrouth. No. 283” (Coll. WDL). See also: Beaugé, Çizgen: *Images,* 230-240.

30 Postcard: “Einweihung der Stadtuhr in Jaffa (Palästina).” Jaffa, J. A. Mitri (Coll. WDL).

murals with idealized landscapes would be the norm. Compared to European 'image culture', pictures in Ottoman society were very rare.

This started to change even before the introduction of photography, but was accelerated by its spread. Photographic studios and firms had established themselves quickly, postcard publishers followed suit. To issue series of views, portraying whole towns or daily life in detail was a new phenomenon copying well established European practice. The new fascination with pictures and photography is illustrated by a farewell gift presented to a certain Hilmy-Bey around 1865. It is a photograph album containing 48 views from Syria and neighboring countries.[31]

Due to its rising popularity at that time, photography provides a rich source for our study of the private spheres of the Ottoman elites. Ottoman officials and officers were frequently transferred from one province to another. Quite often they had their portraits taken by local photographers (fig. 15).[32] Studio photographs, mounted on cardboard with promotional imprints, made the individual career of an Ottoman official visible and could be dispatched to relatives at home. Studio portraits were collected in albums. Replenished by portraits of distant relatives they mirror widely-branched Ottoman families.[33]

Pictures of individuals and groups were made for private use. They are not the result of a tourist interest in the exotic. We have here evidence for the material culture of late Ottoman-Arab society, especially for its dress code and ways of self-expression (fig. 16).[34] Interpreted with subtlety, these pictures can teach us much about individual behavior and social relations. To my knowledge not much research has been done on the style of

---

31 *Syrie. Souvenir a Hilmy-Bey* (Coll. WDL) – There is no mention of the photographer. He is with great certainty Charlièr-Béziès. On him, see Perez, *Focus East,* 148.

32 "Unknown officer." Studio portrait. David Gazala, Photographe Baghdad, (Coll. WDL). See also the portrait of Midhat Pasha by "G. Saboungi, photographe de S.A. Midhat Pacha (Beyrouth)", (Coll. WDL). Published in El-Hage, *Des photographes à Damas*, 38 and in Debbas, *Des photographes à Beyrouth*, 50.

33 Unfortunately as a rule intact albums have been broken up by dealers. As unique historical documents, Ottoman-Arab family albums deserve to be archived.

34 Glass negative: "Ottoman official", ca. 1900 [Ṣan'ā'?] (Coll. WDL). This is a remarkable portrait (self-portrait?), most probably of Hilmi Paşa Hüseyin (1855-1920), later twice Grand Vizier and last Ottoman ambassador to Austria. He served in Yemen between 1989 and 1902. While in Vienna he had himself and his wife photographed by a leading studio (d'Ora) thus revealing a continued interest in high quality portrait photography (Coll.WDL). Compare: Fritz Kempe, *Nicola Perscheid, Arthur Benda, Madame d'Ora.* Bearb. von Odette Appel-Heyne, Marburg 1980.

Ottoman portrait photography or family photography.[35] An unprecedented interest in the individual was emerging. In earlier times portraits had been the privilege of the imperial court. Now everybody could have his or her individual picture taken. Detailed research would certainly contribute to a better understanding of a new phenomenon in nineteenth century Ottoman society that Faroqhi has called the "Culture of the Intimate".[36]

But it is the invention of snapshot photography at the end of the century, which fundamentally changed the use and the contents of photography. Formal and artificial arrangements were no longer necessary. Daily personal life could be captured that contrasted sharply with staged portrayals of Ottoman rule in the Arab provinces. Photography was on its way to become a popular pastime, soon favored even in remote regions of the Empire. There is the case of an Ottoman official, who experimented with photography in Ṣan'ā' around 1900. He had all the necessary photographic equipment sent by mail order from Paris via Aden or Ḥudayda – an extraordinary voyage to participate in the modernization process.[37]

---

35 A notable exception is S. Graham-Brown, *Images of Women. The Portrayal of Women in Photography of the Middle East 1860-1950*, London 1988.

36 See: S. Faroqhi, *Kultur und Alltag im Osmanischen Reich. Vom Mittelalter bis zum Anfang des 20. Jahrhunderts*, München 1995, 314.

37 See invoice of Photo-Hall, 5, Rue Scribe, Paris. Undated (ca. 1900) for "H. Husni Secrètaire à l'Intendance Militaire à Sana," (Coll. WDL). See footnote no. 34.

– VI –

Empire, Patrons and Domestic Architecture

MERSIN: THE FORMATION OF A TANẒĪMĀT CITY IN SOUTHERN TURKEY

FILIZ YENIŞEHIRLIOĞLU

The organization *in* space and the organization *of* space[1] are two concepts that complement each other in studies relating to urban, historic, social and anthropological contents of a city as they are integrated into its urban texture. The organization *in* space

> does not refer to a specific autonomous object having a material form but highlighted by the economic, political and social understanding, is conceived as a reflection, a projection, an effect, an element of the superstructure that identifies itself with the mechanisms which produced it and to the strategies of which it is a support. The second is a dimension of the social which is not abstract, which in fact receives as a background, as a setting or as a frame, the social practices. This dimension is generally accepted as architecture and in its general definition includes all constructed space vernacular or not.[2]

The application of these two approaches might bring one closer to the reconstruction of used, conceived, and perceived spaces, within a given moment in space and time. Thus, organization *in* space as well as organization *of* space reveal the existing norms and values relevant to a given urban society.

While binding urban planning regulations were applied to Mersin as elsewhere in the Ottoman Empire after the *Tanẓīmāt*, a new type of middle-class house types was introduced by trends emerging not from the capital of the Empire, but from other provincial trading cities such as Beirut. Mersin was formed by a plural population from other parts of the Empire, who imported tastes and styles that made up the domestic architecture of Mersin. As an urban settlement of the *Tanẓīmāt*, Mersin constitutes a stimulating case study for the (trans-)formation of Ottoman cities during nineteenth century.

---

1 For the elaboration of these concepts see: J. Castex, J.L. Cohen et Jean – Charles Depaule, *Histoire urbaine, anthropologie de l'espace,* Paris 1995.

2 Depaule, "l'Anthropologie de l'espace," in Depaule (et al. eds) *Histoire urbaine*, 18-19.

Therefore, I would like to elaborate three main points in this paper: First, to show that the plurality of a population and the new regulations of the empire were reflected in the urban formation of the city (organization *in* space). Second, to illustrate more specifically how the organization *of* space in domestic architecture reflects the social and economic background of their owners. Third, to demonstrate how certain physical aspects of this domestic architecture originating from heterogeneous backgrounds merged in Mersin into a new, hybrid style.

Cities of the Ottoman Empire have become a popular subject of research in recent decades. The analysis of Ottoman archival documents have contributed considerably to the historical perspective of research and their relatively recent extensive use for the cities of the Arab provinces have changed the overall understanding of what has been known for a long time as "the Islamic City". These sources, mainly the *sicill*s and the *tahrir defterleri,* have revealed important indices for the historical reconstruction of an Ottoman city during a given period. They serve to determine the administrative, military, economic and social organization of cities and to initiate discussions on the functioning of Ottoman urban institutions.

Historians of art and architecture have also started a series of research projects on the Ottoman cities. Using their research on existing architectural examples of buildings, streets, craftsmanship and other physical aspects, as well as exploring the patronage system, they try to read other sources than those of text-oriented historians, the visual ones. The elaborate program of preservation of cultural and natural heritage undertaken by the Ministry of Culture in Turkey has resulted in a series of research projects on the urban development of cities. Similar projects have also been sponsored by the municipalities of various cities. It is in this latter context that we have become interested in Mersin, a port city on the Mediterranean Sea in the southern part of Turkey, near Adana and Tarsus, and facing Cyprus.[3] (fig.1)

In the Ottoman world, the plurality, which existed at all levels within its political system, leads the researcher towards an analysis of exceptions rather than rules. The versatility of the system encourages, in fact, the reinterpretation and adaptation of diverse elements within a historical and geographical context. Yet values incorporated into a wider organizational system encourage the perception of the dominant factors common to the vari-

---

3 The project was undertaken in 1993-94 by myself, Fatih Müderrisoğlu and Suat Alp, two research assistants from Hacettepe University, Ankara – Turkey, Department of History of Art and by architect Mustafa Akpolat from the same department. The results have been published in Filiz Yenişehirlioğlu, Fatih Müderrisoğlu, Suat Alp, *Mersin Evleri*, Ankara 1995.

ous manifestations of this plurality. Therefore it is essential that Ottoman cities should be studied in a comparative analysis including different cities during the same period. In this way those aspects can be determined which form distinctive parts of a wider unifying system. Such a comparative method helps also to define the specific, local characteristics of a city and helps to see how those local specific elements actualize, reinterpret or reinstate the general rules and regulations of a centralized system emanating from the imperial capital.

The (trans-)formation of settlements and cities was a continuing process in all periods of Ottoman history from the fourteenth up to the twentieth century. Yet, the factors of settlement patterns vary according to historical periods and circumstances. The patronage of urban (trans-)formation in the fourteenth and fifteenth centuries depended mainly on the Ottoman Bey and the Sultan, followed by the *Akıncı Bey*-s in the Balkan Provinces, who were the commanders of the irregular cavalry during the early Ottoman period. In the sixteenth and seventeenth centuries the members of the high administrative class, pashas and grand viziers became initiators of new settlements while in the seventeenth and eighteenth centuries local notables began to become involved in this patronage system. Large architectural complexes built by these patrons and supported by their *waqfs*, included mosques, *medreses*, baths, public kitchens, hospitals, city-centered commercial khans, *tekkes* and *zawiyas*, libraries and bridges, fountains and *sebils*. These constructions epitomized the various Ottoman institutions in their physical expression within an urban texture and formed the core of cities. Commercial and residential areas were formed around these large complexes as early as the fourteenth and fifteenth centuries. Wooden houses from the nineteenth century with their protruding parts and their large eaves covering the narrow streets, too, represent a distinct feature of a historically evolving urban texture still preserved today in almost every town in Anatolia and the Balkans. Remains of a pre-Ottoman medieval castle or city walls generally contribute to the distinct landscape of these settlements.

Placing Mersin

In the southern part of Anatolia, Mersin possesses none of these historical urban landscapes. It had neither a medieval castle nor city walls; no prestigious elite-sponsored architectural complexes reflecting the institutions of the empire; in fact, Mersin eschewed the imposition of a pre-determined public space by the presence of older monumental buildings. No wooden houses or narrow streets preceded the *Tanẓīmāt* period. The urban texture of Mersin and its buildings and houses were completely different from that of established neighboring towns, such as Adana, Tarsus and Antalya.

Contrary to previous periods, in the nineteenth century the structural changes of the *Tanẓīmāt* period and the reintegration of the Mediterranean region into international trade fostered new patterns of settlements where the patronage system and the physical expression of the cities changed dramatically. Mersin on the south coast of Turkey is such an example. Founded probably by Arab merchants coming from Egypt and Beirut in the nineteenth century, it developed as a Mediterranean port city after 1840, following the introduction of British and French capital to the region for the promotion of cotton industry (fig. 2).

Mersin (the Turkish name for the myrthe tree) does not figure as a settlement on the map of Piri Reis, the Ottoman cartographer of the sixteenth century.[4] Neither is it mentioned by Evliya Çelebi, the famous Ottoman traveler of the seventeenth century.[5] He writes about a nomadic tribe, *Mersinoğulları*, which he had encountered when coming from Corycos (Silifke) and after passing the Erdemli village (near latter-day Mersin). The region where the city of Mersin would be founded later might have been already called Mersina since Thomas Dallam in 1599-1600 mentions it as being 30 km to the east of Corycos.[6] Captain Beaufort, in his maritime journal, describes Mersin in 1812 as a small settlement with a few huts and infested with malaria. W. M. Leake and C. Texier both identify the place as ancient Zephyrium.[7] In fact, it is more likely that Zephyrium was the name of the bay in these maps and not the name of a settlement.

Excavation at Yumuktepe which lies several miles to the east of the modern city of Mersin has shown that this specific point has been inhabited since the prehistoric period until the eleventh century. [8] It is likely that in the medieval period, with the development of nearby Tarsus as a fluvial port and a Christian place of pilgrimage, Yumuktepe was abandoned for the benefit of Tarsus. No medieval findings have been either mentioned by travelers or found archaeologically in the area of the nineteenth century modern city. Scarce accounts of some travelers from the nineteenth century that do mention some ancient architectural constructions and equally

---

4 Piri Reis, *Kitab-ı Bahriyye*, 2 vols. Istanbul 1988.

5 Evliya Çeleb, *Seyahatname*, vol.13 (transl.by Zuhuri Danışman) Istanbul 1971, 184-195.

6 J. Covel, *Early Voyages and Travels in the Levant*, New York 1893.

7 W. M. Leake, *Journal of a Tour in Asia Minor,* NewYork 1976, 204; C. Texier, *Asie Mineure,* 1862, 728-29.

8 J. Garstang, *Prehistoric Mersin:Yumuktepe in Southern Turkey*, Oxford 1953. Excavations have restarted under Prof. Veli Sevim since 1993.

scarce and random archeological findings date back to the Greek and Roman periods.

Ottoman archival documentation is an extremely rich source of information for everything in the Empire and in the case of Mersin, the *Sālnāmes* give important historical facts for the formation of modern Mersin.[9] The town was not included in the Ottoman population census of 1831. It seems it had not yet grown much from the times when Captain Beaufort visited the place in 1812. From a small *kariyecik* in 1841 it grew into a *nahiye* in 1852 because " some boats and ships began to moor" there, and in 1864 it became a *kaza* attached to the province of Adana.[10] In 1891, it was a busy port city where 264 steamships and 1.004 sailing boats stopped and where merchandise was transferred by small boats to its seven jetties. The passage of these boats was usually from Marseille via Izmir, Mersin and Beirut to Alexandria.[11] The population of the city, according to Cuinet, was 9.000: 5.000 Muslims, 2.700 Greek Orthodox, 860 Armenians and 260 Latin Catholics. [12]

The Mediterranean Port-City

As a new settlement with a promising economic future Mersin attracted a mixed population from different parts of the Empire. Some became agents of the new capitalist system. Consequently, the merchants and the employees of commercial societies and banks formed the middle-classes of the city, whereas the boatmen and the temporary workers in the fields emerged as the working classes. The major investors in trade and estate were mainly families from Beirut or locals who had amassed their fortunes through trade. Reverend J. Davis remarks in 1879 that Turkish officials and Europeans were few in the city and did not choose to stay because of the extremely humid weather conditions.[13]

---

9 The following *Sālnames* give information on Mersin: *Adana Vilayet Sālnamesi* 1296 / 1880; 1308 / 1892; 1309 /1891; 1319 / 1901.

10 Since the *Sālnames* where not published at the beginning of the 19th century, this information was given in the *Sālname-i Adana* of 1892. For a summary of Sālnames concerning Mersin see: "Mersin" in *Yurt Ansiklopedisi,* vol. 5, Istanbul 1982, 3617-3762.

11 *Yurt Ansiklopedisi*, 3639-3640. One can also find relevant information concerning the names of the ship companies, the quantity and the various types of goods exported and imported to and from Mersin during the Ottoman period.

12 V. Cuinet, *La Turquie d'Asie*, Paris 1891, 50-58.

13 E.J. Davis, *Life in Asiatic Turkey. A Journal of Travel to Alexandria*, Alexandria 1879, 12.

Where did the inhabitants come from? From Lebanon and Beirut, from the mountains of Nusariye, from Latakia in Syria, from Cyprus (especially after British intervention on the island in 1878), from Central Anatolia (probably from Cappadocia and Kayseri region since certain architectural details can be traced to that region), from Egypt and from Crete. From Egypt came mainly the group labeled *fellah*s. These were in fact descendants of families brought to the region of Adana around 1832 by Ibrāhīm Pasha, the son of Muḥammad ʿAlī Pasha who had occupied the region. These *fellah*s were of rural origin, either Muslim or Coptic, and arrived in the region to cultivate cotton.[14] Most of them stayed after the departure of Muḥammad ʿAlī's forces in 1841.

Who were these people and what were their occupations?[15] Between 1880 and 1914 Mersin's Chamber of Commerce registers introduce us to upper middle class families and Beiruti entrepreneurs like Nādir, Naqqāsh, Najjār and Buṭrus, or Mavromati[16], Babūr and Hājj Tūmā who were involved in international trade. The middle classes were represented in either the manufacture of goods (ice or *sucuk*) or they were shop owners: grocers, peddler, perfumers (Eyüp Sabri)[17], money dealers, *Manifatura* (Selim Mayer Sittuni).[18] Employees of banks, insurance companies, maritime offices, railways and post-offices populated Mersin. They were represented in the municipality and the Ottoman administration. Others were workers in factories at the port, representatives of the diplomatic community (by the end of the nineteenth century every European state had a consulate in Mersin), hotel and restaurant staff, representatives of *Regie de Tabac* and of the Public Debt Administration. Together they constituted a range of population that Jacques Berque has splendidly classified as

---

14 *Yurt Ansiklopedisi*, 3645.

15 A comparison of the economic life of Mersin with that of a central Anatolian city just before the Tanẓīmāt (1808-1839) might reveal interesting results in how economic factors have changed. It would also help to understand the changes in social structure, way of life and urban texture. See: Ömer Demirel, *II. Mahmud Döneminde Sivas'ta Esnaf Teşkilatı ve Üretim- Tüketim İlişkileri,* Ankara 1989.

16 Mavromati was a Greek Orthodox. He had sponsored the construction of the Greek Orthodox church in Mersin which was the most monumental building of the town. He had also founded schools and hospitals for the Greek community.

17 Eyüp Sabri is now famous for his Eau de Cologne made from lemon.

18 *Manifatura* was a word derived from the Italian. These shops sold mainly sewing material. Mayer moved later on to Istanbul and opened a shop in Eminönü famous for his good quality clothing.

"*demi-bourgeois du diplome et du boutique*"[19] reinforced constantly by new immigrants (fig. 3).

Two specific conditions seem to coincide and initiate the growth of the city: investment of families coming from Beirut and Egypt in commerce, and the immigration of Greek Orthodox and Maronite families from Lebanon after the civil unrest in Mount Lebanon between 1840 and 1860. The brothers Dimitrī and Ṭannūs Nādir, for example, are known to have moved to Mersin in order to trade timber from the Taurus mountain to Egypt for the construction of the Suez Canal.[20] Such families consequently speculated in land and in real estate in Mersin as they already had similar investments in Beirut and Alexandria.[21] The Nādir brothers also bought land and real estate for other families in Beirut like the Sursock family.[22] British and French investment in the production of cotton in the Çukuova region constituted another element behind the influx of new population.[23] Adana became the capital of the region with Mersin as its port city. As a coastal town, Mersin also became the port city of Central Anatolia, its hinterland. In 1869, the provincial assembly of Konya decided that a new road should be constructed, most probably in order to link the two cities and integrate Konya into the new markets. [24]

---

19 Berque quoted in Olivier Blin, "Le Caire, XIX-XXe siècles. De la *fasaha* à la *sala* comme modèles," *Espace Centré*, no. 20/21, p. 96. note 8.

20 Şinasi Develi, *Mersin*, Mersin 1990.

21 See Leila Tarazi Fawaz, *Merchants and Migrants in Nineteenth Century Beirut*, Cambridge MA 1983, 91-94: "Musa Nadir, left extensive real estate when he died in Beirut in 1890 – residences, warehouses, shops, vacant land in and around Beirut, in Mersin, Tarsus and elsewhere in Southern Turkey and in Alexandria."

22 *Ibid*. "The name originally (probably Sarsak) is Ottoman Turkish; and the family can be traced to Mersine, a town near Adana in Southern Turkey, much of which was built on Sursuq land. In the seventeenth century, or perhaps earlier, the Sursocks became tax farmers for the Ottoman government and in their capacity came to Barbara, a village in the district of Jubay (near Beirut). There they acquired land, probably *mîri* or state property, which was a record for their services to the Ottoman Governement." Leila Fawaz relies on the interviews with the members of the Sursuk family. But, some of this information has to be revised since nothing proves that Mersin, as a settlement, existed in the seventeenth century.

23 For further reading on Ottoman-British trade relations and the integration of the Adana region in international trade see: Mübahat Kütükoğlu, *Osmanlı- İngiliz İktisadi Münasebetleri*, Istanbul 1976; Charles Issawi, *The Economic History of Turkey, 1800-1914,* Chicago 1980.

24 Musa Çadırcı, *Tanzimat Döneminde Anadolu Kentlerinin Sosyal ve Ekonomik Yapıları*, Ankara 1991, 264.

Mersin's new social classes, who were to support the *Tanẓīmāt* reforms, were encouraged by capitalist opportunities in conjunction with international and interregional trade. One can thus trace the emergence of a middle class in Mersin. Open to social mobility, they were members of an inter-communal society – inter-communal because of the plurality of its population (according to the types of religious buildings): the Latin Catholic Church (1853), the Maronite Church (1878), the Arab Greek Orthodox Church (1878), Mosques (1870, 1884, 1898, 1899, 1900), the Greek Orthodox church (1885), the Armenian Orthodox Church (1870), the Catholic Church (1896), the Protestant church at the beginning of the twentieth century and a Synagogue built in 1906.[25] The earliest residents of Mersin seem to have been the priests of the Latin Catholic Church, who probably came to this region for missionary purposes.

The Ottoman Provincial City

The formation of Mersin coincided with the proclamation of the new urban planning regulations introduced by the reformist bureaucrats of the *Tanẓīmāt*. After the regulations had been applied to the provincial cities of the Empire, the urban texture of the city came to reflect these new laws in many respects. The Building Code,[26] promulgated first in l848 for Istanbul, was applied in 1864 to all the major cities of the empire – thus introducing new rules for construction and urban planning. At the same time, the establishment of the provincial council (*vilāyet mecliseri*) and the municipality introduced a new breed of local decision makers.[27] Through the provincial council's equal representation of Muslims and non-Muslims the citizens were directly involved in taking decisions concerning their communities in an ever expanding city. Moreover, it was stipulated that the council have an architect as a member to control the construction activities of city and region.

This brings us to the urban development of Mersin which started out on the "bare shores" of the Mediterranean. The earliest Ottoman inscription, dated 1865, is to be found on a public fountain, which is now adjacent to *Eski Cami* in the *Cami-i Şerif Mahallesi* built in 1870 near the harbor area. The inscription informs the public that the fountain had been con-

---

25 Develi, *Mersin*, 101-103.

26 For the various clauses of this regulation see: Serim Denel, *Batılılaşma Sürecinde İstanbul'da Tasarım ve Dış Mekânlarda Değişim ve Nedenleri*, Ankara 1982, XXXIV-LXXX.

27 İlber Ortaylı, *Tanzimattan Sonra Mahalli İdareler (1840-1878)*, Ankara 1974, 54-65.

Fig. 1: Mersin in 1994.

Fig. 2: Mersin in the early 20th century.

Fig. 3: The Custom's Square
in 1910.

Fig. 4: The city center with a
typical merchant house.

Fig. 5: The cumba of a house.
46th street, no.23.

Fig. 6: The garden side
of Polis Evi.

Fig. 7: Fabrikalar Caddesi.

Fig. 8: The Şaşati House - Atatürk Caddesi.

Fig. 10: Ahmet Karadeniz House - detail from the street side.

Fig. 9: The Christmann House (now Atatürk Muzesi), Atatürk Caddesi.

Fig. 11: 886 Street. no. 8-10.

Fig. 12: Cottage among the citrus trees.

Fig. 13: Evrensel Ajans - 116 Street, no. 11; ceiling of the Cihannûma.

Fig. 14: Detail from a house.

Fig. 15: Brick tiles produced in Marseille - Roux Frères.

structed on "bare shores" probably to provide water to those coming by boat. Both the fountain and the adjacent mosque belonged to the *waqf* of Bezm-i Alem Valide Sultan, the mother of Sultan Abdülmecit – as did most of the domestic architecture in this area. Yet, this does not necessarily imply sultanic patronage of the city of Mersin.[28] The fact that the fountain has the earliest inscription and that it bears the sultan's name does not suggest that its construction was sponsored by royal patronage and that the part of the city built earliest was initiated by royal patronage. The fountain is neither mentioned in the records of the *waqf* of Valide Sultan nor in the additions to the *waqf* until 1851. The reason why it was added to the *waqf* after 1865 was because Mersin had not been included in the *Defter-ī Hakanī* nor in any other *waqf.* In such cases the Ottoman administration incorporated land into a royal *waqf* in order to legalize the ownership of the land which then could be leased for construction or for other use. Most of the houses of the *Cami-i Şerif Mahallesi* were part of Valide Sultan's *waqf* as well. The legalization of the property came through a royal *waqf* but not the actual patronage of buildings, houses, or fountains. In fact, a *firmān* dating from 1855 had been sent in reply to a request of the provincial council of Adana asking if they could rent the land on the coast of Mersin to those who would like to construct shops and houses.[29] Significantly, the reply informed the *Meclis* that this place called Mersin did not figure either at the *Defterhane-i Amire* nor among the list of *mîri* lands and therefore should be incorporated into the *waqf* of Bezm-i Alem Valide Sultan before it could it be rented out to individuals. The leasing system of the land through the *waqf* organization was characteristic of the Ottoman economic system. The legalization of these "bare shores" constituted part and parcel of the process of land centralization under the new Land Code of 1858.[30]

The formation of the city continued towards the western and northern parts of the Camii Şerif Mahallesi (which includes the aforementioned fountain, the harbor and the Latin Church) with the Mahmudiye, Nusretiye, Kiremithane and Ihsaniye quarters. The latter was formed with 50 houses and a mosque endowed by the state in 1899 and the houses were

---

28 *Bezm-i Alem Valide Sultan Vakfiyesi*, Ms. Ankara Vakıflar Genel Müdürlüğü, Kasa 11. I would like to thank Mr. Sadi Bayram for providing me with the manuscript's transliteration before he published it.

29 Develi, *Mersin,* 53-54.

30 For the changes in the *wakf* organization during the Tanẓīmāt period see: Bahattin Yediyıldız and Nazif Öztürk, "Tanzimat Dönemi Vakıf Uygulamaları," *150.Yılında Tanzimat,* (prepared for publication by Hakkı Dursun Yıldız), Ankara 1992, 571-598.

given to emigrants from Crete (hence the reference to its name).[31] The main axis of the city ran east-west parallel to the seashore. Another determinant axis was a north-south one going from the seashore to the mountains and to Gözne, a village that developed into a summer resort for Mersin's wealthy.

The streets of Mersin did not have names but they were numbered as were the houses in accordance to the rules of the Building Code. The formation of new neighborhoods was subject to these urban regulations, as were the houses which had to conform to street alignment in height and width. Sanitary regulations and the construction of a new sewage system were also included in the Building Code.

Public buildings in Mersin were not monumental and they were mainly sponsored by local notables. These buildings were modest and integrated into the urban texture of the city as stipulated by the Building Code. City space and the location of public buildings seem to have been controlled first by the provincial council and – after its inception – by the municipality. There were no imposing public spaces in the city that refer to sultanic patronage or the power of a centralized system. The idea of equality of communities was reflected in equal distribution of spatial organization. The appearance of the Greek Orthodox Church, which dominated the landscape of the city center, was an exception. The religious buildings mentioned above were sponsored by members of the respective communities. The same is valid for the mosques. In certain cases the municipality donated the land for their construction. In one case, Mavromati donated his own land for the construction of a mosque.[32] There were other similar cases where land owned by an individual was donated to the city council, for the construction of public buildings.

There is one *medrese* next to the Müftü mosque constructed in 1884 at the extreme western part of the city near a Roman bridge that limited the occidental boundaries of the city. The *mihrab* of the mosque is the most elaborately decorated one in Mersin, showing similarities to some decoration on other buildings in Mersin dating from 1865. In addition to three baths there existed two commercial *khans*: Taş Han by the sea and Azakzade Han. Both were buildings with a courtyard. By the end of the

31 Most cities in Anatolia have new quarters formed by the state at this period for emigrants coming from Crete.

32 Maybe it was a concession he made to the municipality to show what good a citizen he was in order to construct his monumental church. He unsuccessfully asked the government for the concession to build a canal between the Seyhan and Ceyhan rivers that irrigate the Çukurova region.

nineteenth century, western-type office buildings were also constructed near the harbor area.

Schools for girls and boys and hospitals were constructed by the members of the respective non-Muslim communities. The Ottoman state undertook the construction of primary and secondary schools for the Muslim population. The construction of the *Hükümet Konağı* (the government center) included rooms for various administrative functions: justice, finance, agricultural bank etc. Other bank buildings and a post-office cropped up in the center of Mersin towards the end of the nineteenth century.

A railway connecting Mersin to Adana and later to the Baghdad railway was opened in 1886. The financing of the construction is typical of the second half of the nineteenth century.[33] Mehmet Nihat Bey and Kara Todori Pasha bought the concession of the railway for 99 years. They then sold this concession to the Union of Ottoman Railways owned by a certain Baron Evain de Vandeuve. The union sold 8,250 shares in the Mersin Railway: 2,500 were bought by French, 3,500 by British merchants, 1,980 by notables from Istanbul and 270 by *eşraf* from Adana and Mersin. The railway station was built to the east of the city. Very quickly an inner city rail system was developed between the station, the harbor, and the cotton and oil factories to the east of the city founded by the French and English investment.

Public buildings in Mersin attest to the modern ways of living of its inhabitants. It was one of the earliest cities of Anatolia where gas lamps were used for lighting the street. A steady supply of fresh drinking water was routed down from the mountains. Between 1919-1921, various urban developments, like the central market place, were executed in the city.[34] It appears that the residents of Mersin continued to maintain their standard of living during the brief French occupation of the city.

Domestic Architecture in Mersin: an Ottoman-Mediterranean Fusion

Within this general framework, a new type of domestic architecture emerges in Mersin which was inhabited by the middle and upper middle classes in the *Camii Şerif* quarter and around it.

---

33 *Yurt Ansiklopedisi.*

34 The building, rectangular in plan, has a very large courtyard. Shops were constructed both inside and outside the building. Similar type of markets have been constructed in southern France as well (on the Côte d'Azur) and also in Tunisia. The one in the Goulette quarter near Tunis is similar to the one in Mersin.

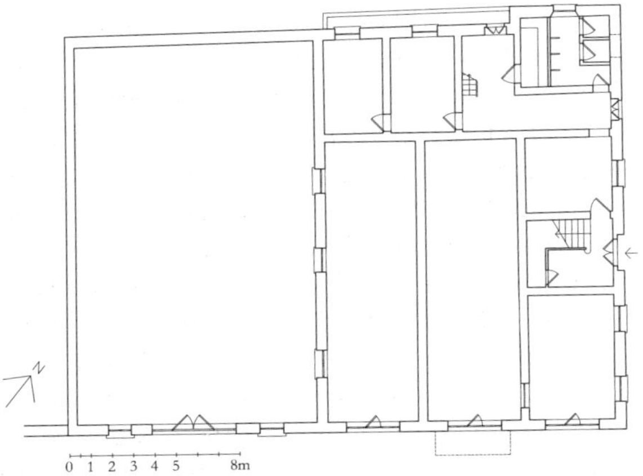

Fig. A: Akdeniz Oteli (Mücahitler Caddesi), ground floor.

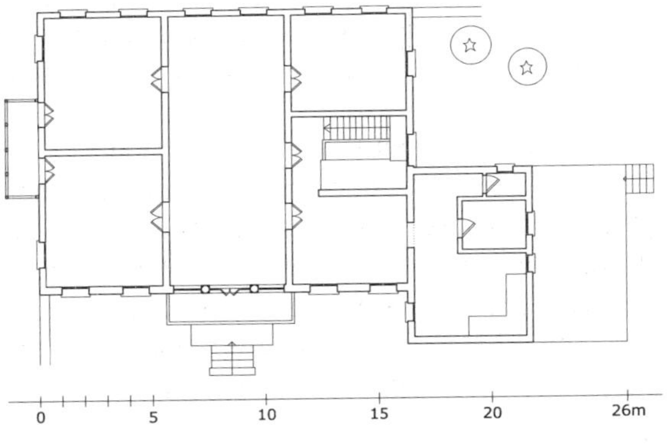

Fig. B: Polis Evi (Atatürk Caddesi no. 123), first floor.

Fig. 4 shows a two-story house constructed in stone with each story independent of the other. The houses generally occupied around 350 square meters and had 150-200 square meters of garden at the back. Shops or storage rooms were on the ground floor (fig. A) and living quarters on the first floor (fig. B). Depots were constructed in the basement of some of them. Inside the house, four or five rooms on both sides of an *iç sofa* (inner hall) were situated either on a vertical or a horizontal axis towards the street. The side of the hall looking towards the street terminated either in form of a *cumba* (structural protrusion, closed balconies with large windows on three sides, fig. 5) or a balcony. The side looking towards the back garden generally had a triple arch or three-bay opening to either a *dış sofa* (exterior hall) or a balcony (fig. 6). The gardens and the exterior *sofas* were oriented towards the east and the north so as to escape exposure to the sun. Where the ground floor was not occupied by shops, it replicated the plan of the first floor. In these cases, the main entrance to the house on the ground floor replaced the structural protrusion of the first floor. In some cases, entry to the first floor was gained from the side – emphasizing the formation of two different apartments in the same block. Two buildings that show this layout in Mersin are dated 1889 and 1908.

In this respect, the plan differs from the traditional Ottoman house[35] where all stories were occupied by the same family. This type of house was not constructed for large family households, nor were they divided into women's (*harem*) and men's quarters (*selamlık)*. There were no fixed architectural elements reminiscent of traditional houses like the wooden cupboards or niches in which beds and other personal belongings were restored. The walls were bare and undecorated. The planning of the sanitary and wet areas are included in the houses whereas traditionally they had been in the garden. Toilet, bath and kitchen were planned side by side and were grouped on both floors on the same side of the house.

All these features suggest that the houses were constructed for small families not necessarily coming from traditional Ottoman-Anatolian backgrounds. Houses could probably be rented by employees residing in Mersin. The fashion for using furniture already seemed common in this period since none of the houses had fixed diwans along the walls of the room. Each room had a special function as defined by its furniture and was used for living, dining or sleeping, in contrast to the flexible use of space in traditional houses. Lack of ornamentation on the walls also suggests that most of these houses were constructed for rent or for short-term residency. In contrast, traditional Ottoman houses, and also modern houses constructed at the same time in nearby cities, were richly ornamented. Wall paintings, wooden ceiling decorations, plaster work and stone reliefs were part of an interior decoration that was conspicuously absent in the houses of Mersin.[36] Dates and inscriptions on the walls established ownership. The dates can be found in a number of houses in Mersin but examples of inscriptions in Latin, Arabic and Armenian are less numerous.

---

35 See: Sedad Hakkı Eldem, *Türk Evi Plan Tipleri,* Istanbul 1968; *Türk Evi: Osmanlı Dönemi*, Istanbul, 1984-87. Metin Sözen-Uğur Tanyeli, *Türk Konut Mimarisi Bibliyografyası*, Istanbul 1984.

36 See Stefan Weber's contribution to this volume.

The hall and the way it is terminated on its short sides as a protrusion or balcony is, however, reminiscent of the established *iç sofa* (inner hall) type houses of the Ottoman Empire. The *sofa* is a place of circulation and gives way to the rooms which do not communicate with each other. It is a typical plan of urban houses both in Istanbul and in the provinces of the eighteenth and nineteenth centuries. In Istanbul, however, the plan of the *konaks* follow the central hall type[37] which emerged in the capital in the eighteenth century and epitomized the planning of domestic architecture patronized by the royals or by the members of the high administrative class.[38] Members of this group when posted by the government to provincial cities preferred to have their houses constructed according to the "Istanbul" examples. Thus the plan and the visual expression of their houses conveyed to the public their administrative status that was directly linked to the political power of the capital. Amasya in Anatolia is a good provincial example: its traditional central hall houses along the riverside referred back to the urban pattern around the Bosphorus. In Mersin, one house has survived with a central hall plan, and its origin probably goes back to Kayseri.

Yet, the conventional inner-hall plan in Mersin was being modified in two important ways: it became strictly axial and generally symmetrical, and a tripartite organization of wet areas were added to the plan. In traditional houses, the hall also determined the axis of the house but the rooms could not be placed in such axiality and symmetry around the *sofa* because the streets had not yet been geometrically arranged. The *Tanẓīmāt* reforms facilitated this process and the fact that Mersin was a clean slate where the architects did not need to adapt their plans to an older urban pattern but could plan freely, must have been a determining factor in the choice of this symmetric grid.

Unlike the tripartite organization of kitchen, toilet and bath in Mersin houses, in traditional Ottoman houses, the kitchen and toilets were never laid out side by side because it was not considered hygienic. The tripartite organization of the wet places was more common in Syria mainly in the new quarters of Aleppo in the late Ottoman period. Even if one considers it

---

37 The central hall differs from the inner hall in that the rooms are placed at the four corners of the central hall that is generally covered by an inner false dome; the rooms protrude out of the façades of the house and iwans are placed in between them. The hall does not give way to a *cumba* or a balcony. In general, spectacular staircases lead from the ground floor to the *iwans* of the first floor and the other two are occupied by *sedirs*.

38 Filiz Yenişehirlioğlu, "l'Architecture domestique Ottomane: évolution historique et étude de deux exemples situés à İstanbul," *L'habitat traditionnel dans les pays musulman au tour de la Mediterranée,* vol.3, Le Caire 1990, 665-715.

as part of the process of technological modernization, this feature was not extensively used in other parts of the Empire.[39]

The structural protrusion with which the inner *sofa* terminated on the street side of the houses was a common and typical element of traditional Ottoman houses. One can find them quite abundantly in Mersin (fig. 7). Similar arrangements can be found in Lefkoşe (Nicosia) in Cyprus during the same period. The use of three arches or the use of twin windows in the termination of the *sofa* on the opposite side were new features that neither existed in traditional Ottoman houses nor in the contemporary domestic architecture in other parts of Anatolia (except in rare cases in Cappadocia) (fig. 6).[40] However, the use of the inner hall together with a triple-arched opening is a much more common feature in late Ottoman houses in Jerusalem (*extra-muros* quarters), Jaffa (*extra-muros*), Haifa (near and around the train station),[41] and Beirut. [42]

It is likely that the inner-hall house with its triple-arches and its tripartite organization of the wet areas and the new building technologies used, was an innovation of an architect with a higher education, rather than that of a mason formed within a guild system. Members of the non-Muslim communities were educated in schools in France and Italy and would come back to work in their original towns or cities. The missionary schools

39 However, an Ottoman building from the seventeenth century, which currently houses the conservation office of post-Byzantine monuments in Rethymno, Crete, has a similar organization. The architectural elements are from the seventeenth-century Ottoman architectural repertory but the tripartite organization of the kitchen, bath and toilets are original features. The encounters between Ottoman and Venetian architecture in Crete has produced local, hybrid styles. The reinterpretation of the same organization in the modern period might refer to the Italian origins of the plan. "Italianization" of Mediterranean architecture in the nineteenth century could have been influential in Ottoman planning as well.

40 But then one needs more specific research on the date of construction of these houses and their patrons. Because in the nineteenth century it was common for people to go and work in other regions and then construct houses back in their own village according to the characteristics of the place where they have worked. It might be a similar case between Cappadocia and Mersin in the second half of the nineteenth century since Mersin was a prosperous city compared with Central Anatolia, attracting many immigrants. The scarce number of these houses in villages in Cappadoccia reinforces this view.

41 A. R. Fuchs, M. Meyer-Brodnitz, "The Emergence of the Central Hall House-Type in the context of Nineteenth Century Palestine," in *Dwellings, Settlements and Traditions* eds. Jean-Paul Bourdier, Nezar Alsayyad, London 1989, 403-425.

42 Friedrich Ragette, *Architecture in Lebanon,* New York 1980.

played a considerable role in educating artists, particularly in Lebanon.[43] It should also be taken into consideration that the Ottoman education system, particularly for engineers and architects, changed under Sultan Abdülhamid II. This triple-arched house type suggests origins from Beirut rather than Anatolia or Istanbul.[44] It can only be found in Mersin where there was considerable emigration from Beirut in the second half of the nineteenth century. There are also other architectural details in various examples that reflect Beiruti origin. The Şaşati house (fig. 8) with its round towers at the corner of the façades is another significant form corresponding to styles in Beirut. A similar house has also been constructed in Adana. Old photographs of Mersin show staircases leading to the first floor over an arch outside the building. Again, this resembles a common pattern in late Ottoman Beirut.

A distinct transfer of patterns from Beirut to Mersin is thus visible. Once the plan would be introduced in Mersin, the houses could consequently be constructed by masons or *kalfas*. The possibility of European architects working in towns and cities is of course another explanatory option. Buca near Izmir in Western Anatolia represents examples of houses from the nineteenth century constructed by European architects for *Levantine* families.[45] But in Mersin, it is difficult to trace a similar phenomenon.

Outside the harbor area and in the *Camii Şerifler* Quarter, the triple-arched house type was also constructed on larger grounds towards the outlying western part of the town. Here, this house type benefited from a thinner urban texture where land plots accommodated large, well-kept gardens at the rear of the houses. Constituting the rich neighborhoods of the town, a conspicuous bourgeois life style emerged in these quarters in the first

---

43 This seems to have been typical in the education of the painters in Lebanon. see: Liban Culture, *Liban – Le regard des peintres – 200 ans de peinture libanaise,* Paris 1989. Armenian painters, sculptures and architects working in Istanbul were also trained in Italy because of their family or community connections. See Filiz Yenişehirlioğlu, "Une source documentaire pour l'histoire de l'art Ottoman: La Patrie, Journal Ottoman publié en Français," in *L'Empire ottoman, La république de Turquie et la France,* eds. Hāmit Batu, Jean Louis Bacqué-Grammont, Varia Turcia III, Istanbul 1986, 359-67.

44 The only name of an architect that we know for Mersin is Mimar Ligor who has constructed in 1908 a house for the Greek İstikoğlu family (now owned by Necati Tüzüner) with depots and shops on the ground floor, an inner *sofa* which ends with a three arched opening to an exterieur *sofa* on the garden side.

45 Levantine families are considered in Turkey to be families with a European background and passport but who have lived in the Ottoman Empire for more than two generations. For the Izmir houses see: Feyyaz Erpi, *Buca'da Konut Mimarisi (1838-1934)*, Ankara 1987.

decades of the twentieth century, with pool facilities, garden parties and tennis matches punctuating the new affluence.

Fig. C: Victoria House (177 Street no. 2).

A variation of the inner hall plan houses so common in Mersin can be found in the Christmann House (today's Atatürk Müzesi).[46] The two-story building (fig. 9) had shops on the ground floor on the main street side and had rooms placed on a corridor in the garden side. The inner *sofa* on the first floor opened onto a balcony on the street side. The rear rooms had the same layout as those on the ground floor but also had a terrace overlooking the garden. The street façade of the building reflected the neo-classical style of houses fashionable in Istanbul, Western Anatolia and in Greece during the nineteenth century. The rear side was noticeably European in its layout of corridors and a terrace. The Christmann house is the only preserved example of domestic architecture with ceiling paintings. The main hall and the front rooms overlooking the street were decorated with neo-classical scrolls and floral compositions. In this respect, it shows similarities with houses both in Istanbul and Beirut.[47] Yet another hybrid example is the so called Victoria house (fig. C). It is unique in Mersin for the composition of its window- and door frames.[48] A single small room with win-

---

46 According to Şinasi Develi, *Mersin*, Christmann was the German Consul in Mersin and also the son in law of Mavromati. The house was constructed around 1897.

47 See Anne Mollenhauer's contribution to this volume.

48 The use of stone blocks that protrude from the façade to form such frames is a French architectural style found on the façades of the insurance and bank buildings in Istanbul

dows all around – called a *Cihannûma* or a *Mehtabiye* – was constructed on the top floor so as to provide the inhabitants with a view over the city and a place to admire the moon at night. This was a popular feature in late nineteenth century houses.

The second most common house type in Mersin has an exterior *sofa* in either one or two-story houses (figs. D, 11). The one-story houses are common especially in the modest *Kiremithane* quarter. In interviews the inhabitants claimed that their fathers' parents were seamen and had moved from Syria. They were mostly employed in boats used for loading and unloading merchandise. Until new facilities and large jettees in concrete were built this family business was under imperial protection. While the interviewees confirm that bricks were produced in their neighborhood, all the roof tiles in Mersin houses had been shipped from Marseille, as the company name figuring on each tile suggests (fig. 15).

Though the seamen claimed to have immigrated directly to Mersin from Syria, the ground plans of houses in *Kiremithane* were not of Syrian origin. The exterior *sofa* plan has been used at all times in the Ottoman Empire mainly in Anatolia and the Balkan provinces. In this case, the rooms, sometimes with *iwāns* in between, open to an exterior *sofa* that ends in an arcade overlooking the garden. It is a characteristic plan in rural areas where owners were mainly involved in agriculture. Elsewhere, the plan was applied to the living quarters on the first floor while the ground floor constituted the service area where kitchen, storage rooms and rooms for the servants were located. Yet, in the houses of *Kiremithane* only the ground floor and the arcades opened directly onto the garden (fig. D). In contrast to the richer houses mentioned above, the kitchen, toilet, and the bath in this quarter were constructed outside the house. The façade overlooking the street had only windows as openings and unlike the merchant houses in the harbor area there was no direct entrance to the house from the street. The windows had wooden lattice work to hide the interior life of the house from the passers-by (fig. 10). Such a disposition suggests a more introverted life style. Houses with this kind of layout can also be seen in Lefke in Cyprus and suggest that the plan has been brought over by immigration at a certain period[49], maybe after the intervention of the British.

---

at the end of the nineteenth century and would be used later on government buildings. It is also a characteristic feature of the railway station that were also planned by the French and German architects.

49 MTV- Hakan Aytekin (director), "Doğu Akdeniz, Karlı Dağların Ardı," video film series *Eski Evler, Eski Ustalar*, nu. VIII, Istanbul 1989.

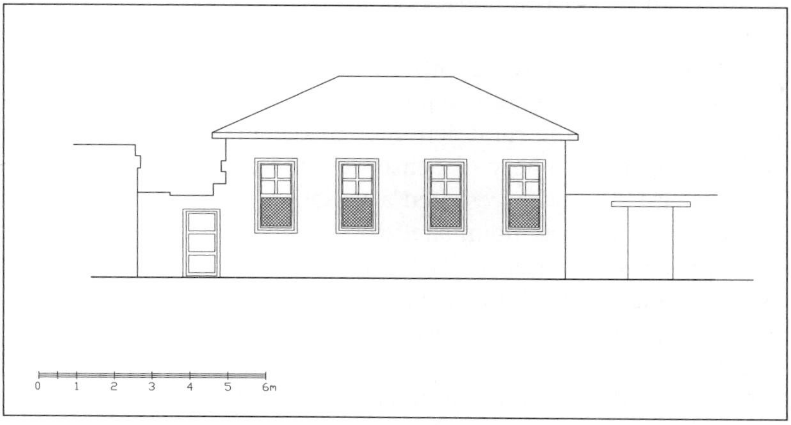

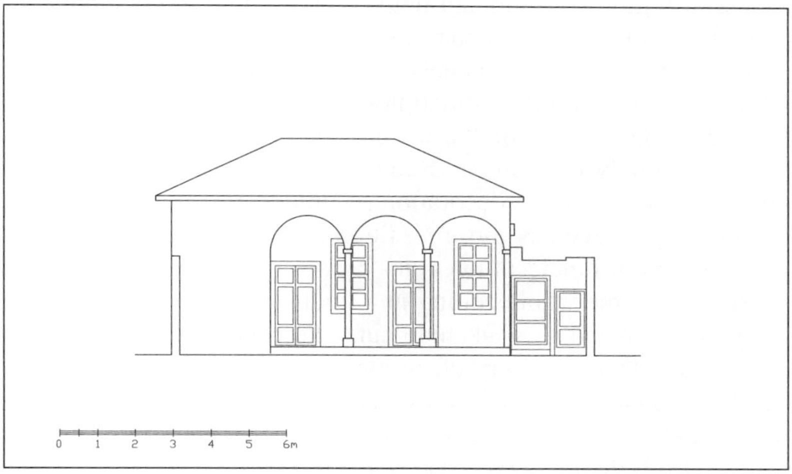

Fig. D: Ahmet Karadeniz House (121 street no. 23), street façade and garden side.

The traditional exterior *sofa* type with one story also appeared in Mersin (fig. 11). In this case, the ground floor is completely closed to the street except the entrance door, and the house is oriented towards the rear garden. The rooms of the living area on the first floor open onto an exterior gallery facing the garden. Here, the main room protruded towards the street. This unique example preserved in Mersin suggests that traditional pre-nineteenth century layouts were also imported to domestic architecture even though they were not abundant. The same layout has been modified over the years in Mersin. They included windows at street level and different versions can be seen in houses dating from the early years of the Republican period.

This third house type represents not only a geographic but also a temporal stylistic hybridity, where architectural styles communicated with past styles. It also reflects the rural activities of their tenants or owners. They were located at the periphery of denser urban areas and were close to the fields or orchards. They represented a variation of the exterior sofa plan. Even though Mersin was dominated by its merchant community and its trade activities, such houses testify to the existence of rural life in the city. Also small, cottage-type houses were constructed in the citrus gardens, which were inhabited by the *fellah*s who took care of the town's arboriculture (fig. 12).

Architectural details in these houses show the plurality of styles and craftsmanship that flourished in Mersin. Woodwork is found but on rare occasions. In traditional Ottoman houses, as in nineteenth century houses in Istanbul and other parts of the empire, the ceilings of the rooms were generally covered with wood panels. Sometimes they were simple, rectangular border-type coverings, sometimes they were more elaborately ornamental and in the middle of the ceiling. In Mersin, these central panels were not elaborately hand-made. Rather, they were machine–cut modules assembled to form a simple decoration. A unique ceiling decoration in one of the houses, however, is more traditional in composition and refers to wood decoration of nineteenth-century houses in Kayseri (fig. 13).[50] Here, the panel covered the whole ceiling in a traditional way and not just a part of it. Again, the wood was machine cut. The central figure represented a bird, a common theme in very elaborate wood decorations of the Kayseri houses. The ground plan is hybrid as well. The central plan is used both for the ground and the first floor. The third floor has a *Mehtabiye* like the Victoria house. Both these characteristics suggest that the owner of the house was probably someone from Kayseri where the traditional central-hall plan enjoyed continued popularity.

One can also observe details of woodwork in neo-classical style (fig. 14). The latter is abundantly used for windows with triangular tympanums crowning them. Stone consoles were used under the balconies, and various decorative arches were used for entrance doors and windows. Stained glass windows can be seen in some of the houses. Colored stone revetments covering the inner hall of the ground floors and wooden rec-

50 Vacit İmamoğlu, *Geleneksel Kayseri Evleri*, Ankara 1992, 170.

tangular shutters for the windows were characteristic elements of all the houses around the Mediterranean in the late Ottoman period.

Concluding by Way of Comparison

In the formation and development of Mersin various elements interacted. The city itself was founded by private initiative and not by sultanic or state patronage. The founders of the city were Arab merchants coming from Beirut and Egypt who imported their house types. Other communities arrived from different parts, mainly Syria, Cyprus and Central Anatolia, and imported to Mersin other types of domestic architecture and craftsmanship. All these differences were unified by the *Tanẓīmāt* reforms under the umbrella of new urban regulations which determined the main outlines of the urban landscape. With time, urban codes and regulations encouraged the formation of rich and poor quarters as well as a town center and residential areas. However, the social life of the residents of Mersin and the way subgroups used one and the same public spaces or the way social differentiation was produced is yet to be researched.[51]

It is difficult to compare Mersin to other cities and especially to the neighboring cities mainly because they were already founded long before the *Tanẓīmāt* period and were organized and functioned according to pre-*Tanẓīmāt* regulations. But even in older towns, the *Tanẓīmāt* regulations, supported by technological innovations created new quarters, new urban landscapes with new institutions and new life styles which supplanted existing habits and customs. This was a common phenomenon in both the Balkan and the Arab provinces of the empire as well as Istanbul itself. The formation of these new quarters took place parallel to the modernization processes introduced by governors, as in Bursa or in Damascus, or it flourished due to the integration of small settlements into the new market economy of the nineteenth century – mainly the port cities like Thessaloniki, Velos, Beirut, Alexandria, Tripoli, Izmir and Samsun.

By way of concluding, the urban plan of Mersin can be compared to two newly founded towns in Greece, Dedeağaç and Velos. Like Mersin, Dedeağaç (Alexandroupolis) was established only in the nineteenth century. An Austrian company that undertook the construction of the railways in the Balkans also agreed to built a port city at Enez near Edirne. How-

51 For intercommunal relations in Anatolia and the Balkans in the nineteenth century, see the relevant articles in François Georgéon et Paul Dumont, *Vivre dans l'Empire ottoman – Sociabilités et relations intercommunautaires (XVIIIe-XXe siècle),* Paris 1997.

ever, due to technical failure the company ended up building a settlement and a railway station in Dedeağaç in 1870.[52] Here, the streets ran parallel to the seashore and the formation of the streets followed the regulations of the Building Code. Unlike Mersin, the core of the city was formed not spontaneously by merchants but it was planned to include the railway station, depots, customs, the company buildings and housing for those working in the company. It was only then that immigrants arrived in large numbers. In the case of Dedeağaç, the sultan was not the direct sponsor of the foundation of the city. Instead, the state gave a concession to an international company, which then raised a new settlement to service the patterns of international economic development.

Velos (Volos) predated the nineteenth century, but was significantly enlarged during the *Tanẓīmāt*. In 1850 Greek merchants living in the town asked the sultan to enlarge the port area.[53] An engineer was sent to the town by the Ottoman government and planned the port area in a grid formation – with large and regular streets running parallel to the seashore facing the old quarters. In both of these examples urban planning resembled that of Mersin and suggests that similar solutions were applied in different parts of the empire during the same period. Yet, even though the organization *in* space evinced similarities due to the general functioning of the *Tanẓīmāt* institutions, Mersin's architecture was different from the other examples. It was formed and developed by physical characteristics and architectural customs introduced by the influx of heterogeneous populations to the city and their considerable empowerment within the social and economic system of the *Tanẓīmāt* period.

Therefore, even though Istanbul was the capital from which the rules of organization *in* space emanated, the organization *of* space in Mersin was based more on architectural models and features coming particularly from Beirut and other developing port cities. What dominated the social and economic life of Beirut and Mersin alike were their merchant families who invested in both of these cities at the same time. There seems to have been an equal distribution of communal use of city space. Since there was a relative equality in decision making by the members of the various councils, the distribution of space in the city reflects a negotiated consensus between the members of the same social class – the resident elites – while design and location of rich and poor quarters differed considerably.

---

52 Alexandra Yerolimpos, "Tanzimat Döneminde Kuzey Yunanistan'da Şehircilik ve Modernleşme (1839'dan 19.yüzyıl Sonuna), *Modernleşme Sürecince Osmanlı Kentleri* (eds. Paul Dumont-François Georgeon), Istanbul 1996, 31-60, fig.9.

53 *Ibid*. fig. 7.

THE CENTRAL HALL HOUSE; REGIONAL COMMONALITIES AND LOCAL SPECIFICITIES:

A Comparison between Beirut and al-Salṭ

ANNE MOLLENHAUER

Lebanon, Beirut, Zokak al-Blat (Zuqāq al-Balāṭ), 1897. After several years of construction the Muslim draper family, the Mukhayyish, who traded in manufactured goods and owned a branch in Manchester, set an inscription into the gabled lintel of their recently completed mansion: A shining triangle with a star at its center (symbol of the freemasons lodge), flanked by a half-moon and star (symbol of the Ottoman Empire) and the date of construction of the house – 1315h. Their vast mansion with its red tiled roof was surrounded by a beautiful garden. The cubic body of the building was interspersed with three large pointed arched windows, which opened toward the seaside. Behind the triple arched window, a covered hall, flanked by several rooms, formed the architectural and social center of the house.

Jordan, al-Salṭ, Sāḥa al-ʿAyn, 1887. The well-known Christian landowning Abū Jābir family decided to build a huge mansion as a home for the extended family. The house consisted of several apartments, each one including a covered hall in the center, flanked by several rooms. The façade contained rows of windows oriented towards the town's main square. The roof was covered with red tiles.

Similar houses like these two examples began to appear all over the province in the nineteenth century and were built by Christians and Muslims alike. How can we explain these resemblances? Did they develop out of local, vernacular architectural traditions or did regional changes influence correspondences? The historical region of Greater Syria (Bilād al-Shām) faced several administrative, political, economical and social changes in the course of the nineteenth century, due to administrative reforms, technical innovation, and modernization and internationalization of trade. They left their imprint on the cities, manifesting themselves in architectural features. Public administrative buildings, hospitals and schools as well as railway stations and telegraph offices were newly built – either by the Ottoman government or by foreign companies and missions.

Many of these changes date back to the reign of Sultan Abdülhamid II (1876-1909). They did not go unnoticed by the British consul in Jaffa who commented:

> When it is remembered further, that such harbor structures as exist in Syria, and the equipment of principal cities like Aleppo, Damascus, Beirut and Jerusalem, with broad ways, electric lighting, tramways, and other convenient apparatus, are also of Abdülhamid's time, one is bound to admit that a good deal of beneficent construction – almost all that make Syria as a whole the most civilized province of Turkey at this day (1920) – stands to the credit of a Sultan whose energies are popularly supposed to have been uniformly destructive and sinister.[1]

New quarters developed in many cities outside the ancient city walls. The land was parceled out, straight roads were built and private houses erected in line with the street and in accordance with the new construction laws of the Ottoman Empire.[2] A new house form appears in the new *extra mural* quarters of Beirut and Damascus as well as in smaller towns such as al-Salṭ (Jordan), Ṣāfītāh (Syria) and in villages. A common feature of all houses was a closed, cubic body, with rows of windows oriented toward the street. A rectangular covered central hall flanked by several rooms characterized the floor plan. All rooms were accessible from the hall, which served as the family's main living room. It is remarkable that apart from these general common features hall houses differed in many regards such as the building material, aspects of construction and details in the arrangement of the floor plan. The houses in the coastal area and Mount Lebanon formed a subgroup among the central hall houses. They were distinguished by an additional feature: a triple arched, pointed window, which marks the setting of the central hall on the façade.

---

1 Foreign Office, 1920, vol.10, no.58, 9-10. Quoted in Ruth Kark, *Jaffa - A City in Evolution. 1799-1917*, Jerusalem 1990, 39-40.

2 The implementation of the new law was under the responsibility of the *valis* and local municipalities. For Beirut see: Jens Hanssen, "'Your Beirut is on my desk;' Ottomanising Beirut under Sultan Abdülhamid II (1876-1909)," in *Projecting Beirut. Episodes of the Construction and Reconstruction of a Modern City*, eds. H. Sarkis and P. Rowe, London 1998, 41-67, for Mersin see: Filiz Yenişehirlioğlu, *Mersin Evleri*, Ankara 1995 and her contribution in this volume, for Damascus see: Stefan Weber, "Der Marğa-Platz in Damaskus. Die Entstehung eines modernen Stadtzentrums unter den Osmanen als Ausdruck eines strukturellen Wandels (1808-1918)," *Damaszener Mitteilungen* 10 (1998), 291-344.

Fig. 1: Today's view on a Beiruti quarter (in the background: the *corps de garde* of Zuqāq al-Blāt),

Fig. 2: Beirut. Corps de Garde,
Photo: R. Bodenstein.

Fig. 3: Beirut, Qaṣr al-Khūrī, façade.

Fig. 4: al-Salṭ, Modern view of al-Salṭ (in the foreground: Qaṣr Abū Jābir).

Fig. 5: al-Salṭ, Bayt Muʿashir, main façade.

Fig. 6: al-Salṭ, Qaṣr Abū Jābir, main façade.

The appearance of the central hall house during the nineteenth century has been widely discussed in recent decades. Since Friedrich Ragette published his extensive documentation on Lebanese architecture in 1980 – describing the central hall house as "the Lebanese house par excellence," which is "rarely found" "in neighboring Syria and Palestine" – a variety of articles have revisited this house form.[3] They argued for their widespread existence all over the province and pointed out general differences in façade shape, floor plan and construction methods.[4] Several authors tried to explain the evolution of the central hall house from an architectural development. May Davie and Levon Nordiguian suggest that the central hall house in Beirut developed from the Beiruti courtyard house, which featured some elements unknown in cities such as Aleppo and Damascus, for example, the number of windows on the outer façade. In doing so, their approach neglected the impact of modernization and administrative reform, which characterized the second half of the nineteenth century in the Syrian provinces:

> Celle-ci [the central hall house] se présente comme une habilitation où les pièces sont disposées en U sur les trois cotés d'un Hall ou salon, appelé *dar* dans le parler libano-syrien et qui sur son quatrième coté s'ouvre par une arcade généralement triple. Ici le Hall Central correspond parfaitement à la cour de l'habitation que nous avons étudié. En d'autres termes, il suffirait de couvrir la cour du Dar Ghaoui pour obtenir une maison à Hall Central.[5]

This analysis, which is derived from the detailed case study of a single courtyard house in Beirut, did not disclose the exact date when the covering of the courtyard was introduced. Consequently, we do not know whether the alteration adapted a general new fashion or formed a specifically Beiruti innovation. Fuchs and Meyer-Brodnitz examine the emergence of the central hall house from an entirely different perspective. The authors have surveyed houses of the nineteenth century in different areas of Palestine and discuss them generally in the context of social change, western impact, new build-

---

3 Ragette, *Architecture in Lebanon*, New York 1980, 92.

4 Aharon Ron Fuchs and Michael Meyer-Brodnitz, "The Emergence of the Central Hall House-Type in the Context of Nineteenth Century Palestine," in *Dwellings Settlements & Tradition*, eds. J.P. Bourdier and N. Al-Sayyad, New York 1989, 403-423; Yenişehirlioğlu, *Mersin Evleri*; 1995, Anne Mollenhauer, "Historical Residential houses in al-Salṭ – Remarks on their shape and function," *Annual of the Department of Antiquities in Jordan* XLI (1997), 415-431.

5 May Davie, Levon Nordiguian, "L'habitat urbain de Bayrut al-qadīma au 19e siècle," *Berytus* XXXV, (1987), 190.

ing material and cultural influences. Acutely aware of the complexity, which affected the transformation of architecture, they concluded:

> The house-type this period (a period of rapid modernization) produced evolved indirectly out of these processes as Ottoman reform, the Industrial Revolution, European imperialism and the Lebanese struggle. The emergence of the central hall house coincides with the 1860s, the period when the impact of these processes began to be felt most significantly.[6]

Both approaches – arguing of the development of the central hall house using a single case study and the general explanation of the emergence out of a major societal transformation process – neglected the building's own, inherent articulation.

The construction of a house is never just a matter of erecting walls. The building implicates the expression of social values of a society and individual aspirations of the house owner.[7] In urban architecture, the most evident and conscious expression of human aspirations is the exterior decoration of the façade, which may refer to a specific architectural model or even bear symbols of affiliation to a family, a social institution or a political system. In his work "Die höfische Gesellschaft" Norbert Elias[8] has argued that the choices of building material, construction methods or ground plans indicate the social status of a family. As an example he demonstrated how a stone house in eighteenth century Paris came to symbolize wealth as well as the owner's affiliation to the aristocracy, as their architectural features were understood by contemporaries.

Is it useful to transfer observations in the specific context of the European societies of the eighteenth century to nineteenth century Bilād al-Shām, under entirely different historical conditions? Even if Elias' starting point may be fruitful, it is problematic to adopt his notions of a "bourgeois" living and "aristocratic" living, as these are strongly linked to a European concept of civilization. It seems that the acceptance of the central hall house in Bilād al-Shām penetrated all social layers which possessed certain wealth and who played a certain role within late Ottoman society.

Considering the remarkable speed with which the structure of private dwellings in Bilād al-Shām underwent transformation, it is the intention of

---

6 Fuchs, Meyer-Brodnitz, "The Emergence of the Central Hall House," 419.

7 An exhaustive analysis on social statements inherent in the interior organization of houses is given by Pierre Bourdieu, *Esquisse d'une théorie de la pratique, trois études d'éthnologie kabyle,* Geneva 1972.

8 Norbert Elias, *Die höfische Gesellschaft*, Frankfurt 1983, 85-91.

this essay to investigate where innovation prevailed and what traditions were preserved. This chapter, which is based on case-studies of individual houses does not intend to establish an architectural typology of the central hall house, but wants to illuminate the process of construction and the factors which influenced the shape of the building. Due to a lack of detailed written documents on private building activities, I examined and documented several houses in Beirut and al-Salṭ in the traditional manner of building research: floor plan, building material, exterior, interior decoration and spatial usage. In addition, I conducted interviews with the inhabitants as well as house owners to collect information on aspects of the historic and actual use of the building, the social status of the house owner's family, the profession of the original owner and the people who were involved in the building process. The careful reading of the architecture itself will help us to understand factors, which determine the deeper meaning of the new buildings, and the significance they had for the people of the period.[9] Allowing for the peculiarity of each building, I will present in the first part descriptions of two particular houses in each city – a middle-class one (*bayt*) and an upper-class one (*qaṣr*).

Dwelling in the Cities of Beirut

In the middle of the nineteenth century, Mount Lebanon was in the grip of economic transformation and sectarian conflicts. As a result of the fights between Druzes and Maronites in Mount Lebanon in the 1840s and the riots in Damascus and the Biqāʿ Valley in 1860, a large number of Christians fled to Beirut. Labor migration and forced migration elsewhere in the region increased. Meanwhile, Beirut prospered because of the increase of Mediterranean trade and its growing political importance. In 1888 it became the capital of the newly established province of Beirut. New quarters developed outside the walled city in place of mulberry plantations.[10] Merchants and traders built large residences there, while keeping their offices inside the old city.[11] The growing foreign relations found expression in the

---

9 The survey on residential houses of al-Salṭ was conducted in autumn 1994 in preparation of my *magister*-thesis at the University of Frankfurt. In 1997 Ralph Bodenstein and I worked on a preliminary study on the history of the Beiruti quarter of Zuqāq al-Balāṭ, which was initiated and supported by the Orient-Institut of the Deutsche Morgenländische Gesellschaft. I would like to thank the director Prof. Dr. Angelika Neuwirth and Jens Hanssen for their support in Beirut.

10 See May Davie, *Beyrouth et ses faubougs*, Beirut 1996.

11 H. Seeden and R.Thorpe, "Beirut from Ottoman Sea Walls and Landfill to a twelfth century B. C. Burial," *Berytus* 43 (1997-1998), 246.

activities of commercial entrepreneurs, Christian missions, and diplomatic representations. By 1890, Austria, Persia, Russia, Great Britain, Italy, Germany and Belgium had established consulates in the burgeoning quarters of Beirut.[12] The need for new housing due to the rapid growth of population as well as the accumulation of wealth and growing international exchange formed the basis for the maturing of a new house form. In contrast to the dense structure of the quarters *intra muros*, the lots *extra muros* were large and each building was free-standing.

General features (fig.1)

The houses in the new quarters were distinguished by their cubic bodies and tiled roofs. Large windows overlooked the city and the sea. They were two or three stories high and the floor plan was structured around a rectangular central hall. Houses of middle-class families and large mansions shared these features. Friedrich Ragette differentiated the use of central hall houses in the countryside and towns: "In towns the ground floor is also used as a dwelling. Each floor is usually an independent apartment, the upper stories being reached by an external stairway."[13] This description fits middle-class houses. In manorial houses both stories belonged to one extended family. Here, a stairway, which connected both floors, was placed inside the building – but away from the living quarters.

Examples:

1. Corps de Garde (figs. A, 2)
As a first example I want to present a complex of buildings grouped around an open courtyard. In a map of the British Water Company of 1908, the compound was identified as an Ottoman police station – a so-called *"Corps de Garde"*. At the end of the nineteenth century police posts were established all over the city. "New spatial regulations were reinforced by police laws and watched over by Ottoman police units – or *Corps de Gardes* – whose posts were strewn strategically across the burgeoning quarters."[14] The *Corps de Garde* complex in the Beiruti quarter of Zuqāq al-Balaṭ, whose structures are still visible today, consisted of two simple houses with tiled roofs at the southern side of the area, and a stable at the eastern side. Further buildings, which are ruined today, ex-

12 Eugen Wirth, "Damaskus - Aleppo - Beirut," (Part I), *Die Erde* 97 (1966), 119.

13 Friedrich Ragette, *Architecture in Lebanon*, 107.

14 Hanssen, "'Your Beirut is on my desk'," 55.

isted at the northern side. A well was situated in the middle of the courtyard. One entered the ground floor of each house through an entrance door at the center of the façade, leading into the central hall. All rooms were accessible from the central hall but unconnected to each other. Living rooms were placed towards the courtyard; kitchen and sanitary units were built at the rear side. A staircase led from the courtyard up to the first floor. Since the two floors were not connected in the interior of the house and every unit had its own entrance, the two houses must have originally consisted of four separate apartments. The simple but neat shape of the façade, the plan with several rooms and plain interior decoration suggests that the apartments were not for official use but served as living quarters – possibly for high-ranking Ottoman officials. It is possible that public buildings existed at the northern side of the compound, but they are not identifiable any more.

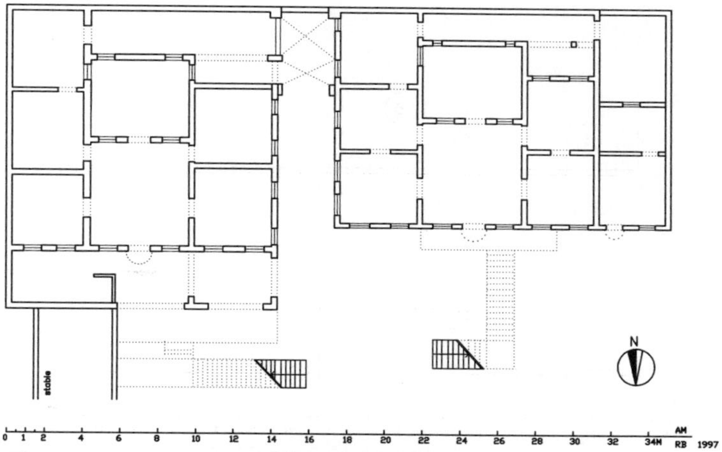

Fig. A: Beirut, Corps de Garde, ground floor plan.

2. Qaṣr al-Khūrī (figs. B, 3)

The Qaṣr al-Khūrī was one of the most ostentatious houses in Zuqāq al-Balāṭ. It was two stories high. A gallery, which was placed along the outer walls, surrounded each floor. In contrast to the majority of Beiruti central hall houses, the triple arched window was hidden by the gallery and did not offer a sea view.

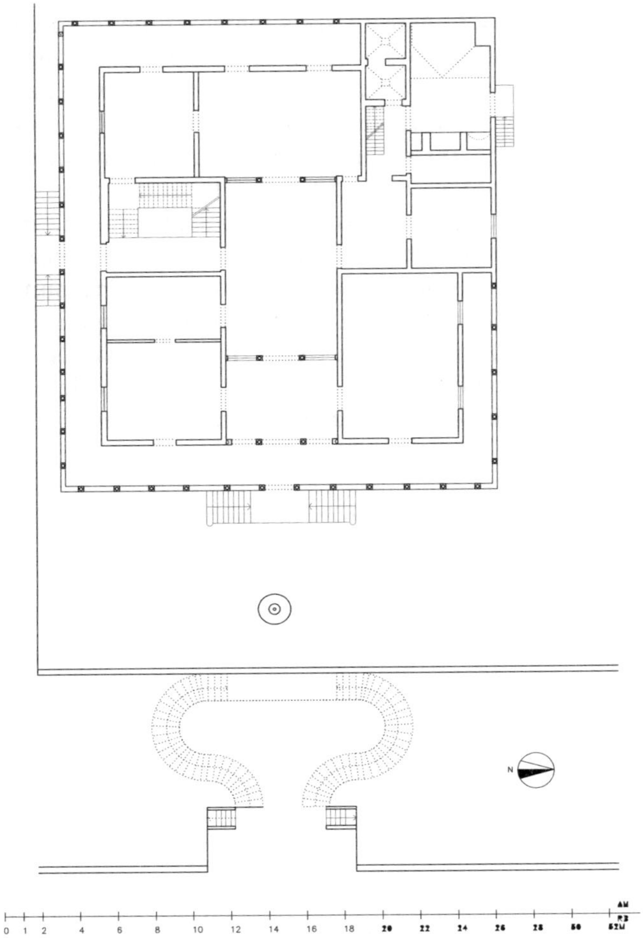

Fig. B: Beirut, Qaṣr al-Khūrī , ground floor plan.

A large ostentatious staircase led onto a terrace, which was located in front of the main façade. A door was placed in the center of the façade, which led the visitor into a small entrance hall. It accessed the larger central hall and connected two rooms placed at the left and right. Both rooms were beautifully decorated with stucco ornaments, depicting birds, garlands and angelic heads in Rọcoco patterns. Probably used as reception rooms, they were also connected with the central hall. The central hall constituted the main living room of the family and each chamber was accessible from here. At its western side, a triple arched window from the central hall, the so-called "*liwān*", partitioned the rooms. Several doors led into the garden at the rear side of the building. Given that the *liwān* was directly connected with the kitchen at the northern side it probably served as a dining room. A large staircase, connecting the two floors, is located at the southern side of the house. The clear separation of the staircase from the living quarters shows that both floors, even if inhabited by one extended family, have to be seen as individual units. The floor plan of the upper floor is similar to that of the ground floor. A typical Beiruti feature of mansions are two small summer chambers placed on the eastern edges of the roof, called *maṣīf* (pl. *maṣyāf*).

Dwelling in the Cities of Salṭ (fig. 4)

The town of al-Salṭ is located in a hilly area 30km northwest of the Jordanian capital Amman, at an altitude of 800m.[15] Owing to its mild climate and fertile soil, settlements have existed there since the Stone Age. During the first centuries of Ottoman rule the area was depopulated and in a state of instability, until the Balqā' was declared as an administrative unit *(qaḍā)* in 1867. The establishment of the post of a *qā'immaqām* (governor of a *qaḍā*) and the installation of governmental troops in the castle provided security. During the following years the town grew continuously and attracted traders from Palestine to settle here. At the end of the nineteenth century new quarters developed outside the historic center. Public and religious buildings were erected: in 1871 a Latin convent opened, whose owners constructed a church nearby in 1890; the Anglican church erected a complex consisting of a mission building (1873); a hospital (1882-1923) and a church (1926); and in 1906 a small mosque was built. In contrast to the old quarters where small houses were packed side by side, each house was freestanding and consisted of several rooms, which created a wide and open atmosphere. The British traveler Lawrence Oliphant commented:

> Besides the dense population which is, as it were, hived on the steep projecting shoulder, there is a quarter of the town built on the opposite side of the gorges which gives it quite a civilized aspect; here are a number of houses boasting of whitewash, with two stories and verandas; here too, is the serail or Government building, and the residence of the caimmakam, and a Greek monastery, and several schools.[16]

---

15 On al-Salṭ in the late Ottoman period, see Eugene Rogan, *Frontiers of the State in the Late Ottoman Empire*, Cambridge 1999.

16 Lawrence Oliphant, *The Land of Gilead with Excursions in the Lebanon*, Edinburgh, London 1880, 200.

Even if the newly built houses differ in shape and ground plan from the traditional dwellings, the construction methods did not change immediately. Until the twentieth century all houses were built of the locally available yellowish limestone and each room was covered by a barrel or cross vault.[17]

General features

Central hall houses in al-Salṭ were one to four stories high and usually contained at least four rooms, placed to the left and the right of the hall. The central hall was commonly of longitudinal shape, which covered the full length of the house. In contrast to Beirut, where the orientation of the hall toward the sea was common, in al-Salṭ the hall opened either toward the valley or was placed alongside the slope. To lighten up the hall, light wells were placed in some houses at the rear part or in the center of the hall, forming a small courtyard. In other houses, the hall was equipped with windows opening towards the adjacent rooms. Built to lighten up those parts of the house, which were situated on the dark slope sides, they accessed each room and made all goings-on in the house visible.

Examples:

1. Bayt Muʿashir (figs. C, 5)
Bayt Muʿashir is a small two-storied house with a sumptuous façade: The ground floor is windowless, while the first floor is dominated by a row of windows flanked by twisted columns. The house is built of well-cut limestones; each room was covered by a cross vault – the central hall, however, by a barrel vault. An inscription dates the building to the year 1330/1911-12, but nothing indicates who the mason was – who designed this unusual façade. The ground floor consisted only of stores, whereas living quarters were located on the first floor. One entered the first floor through a door at the southern side, which led straight into the central hall. A reception room was located at the valley side to the right of the entrance. As in Beirut, it had two doors, one was placed beside the entrance, and the other connected the inner part of the house. This constellation allowed women to leave the room unnoticed when visitors appeared. A large niche located at the southern wall of-

---

[17] On the architecture of al-Salṭ see: Royal Scientific Society (ed.), *Al-turāth al-miʿmārī: madīnat al-Salṭ*, Amman 1990; Ranya Yahya Khatib; Hala Shaker al-Asir, "The Golden Era of as-Salṭ (1870-1950): Urban and Architectural Development," *Studies in the History and Archaeology of Jordan* V (1995), 351-360; Mollenhauer, "Historical Residential houses".

fered space for the customary piling of mattresses. The reception room was the only room decorated with ornamented floor tiles, which were imported from Palestine. This underlines this room's social significance. A multifunctional room was located beside the reception room. Kitchen and storage rooms were situated on the hill side of the building.

In complex mansions the plan described above indicates the existence of independent cells. To create the floor plan of a house, several units were combined according to the specific needs of the families. Thus, one house may contain three or four central halls with adjacent rooms, located either horizontally beside each other (i.e. Qaṣr Abū Jābir) or vertically on different floors (for instance, Qaṣr Sukkār).

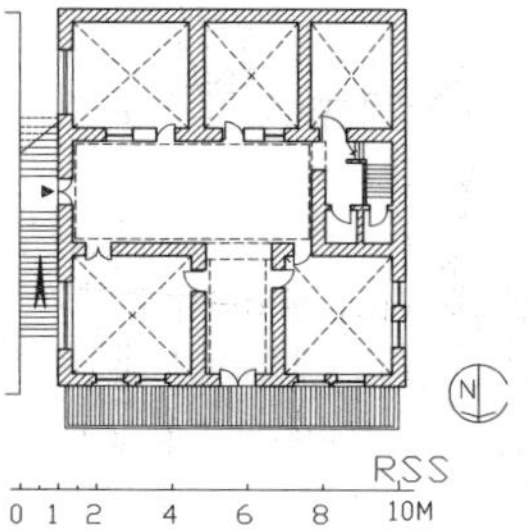

Fig. C: al-Salṭ, Bayt Muʿashir, first floor plan (Source: *Royal Scientific Society, Amman 1990).*

2. Qaṣr Abū Jābir (figs. D, 6)

An extraordinary example of this social and architectural complexity is the Qaṣr Abū Jābir, the largest mansion in the city. The family Abū Jābir, one of the wealthiest and most notable families of the Balqā', settled in al-Salṭ in the mid-nineteenth century. Shortly thereafter, the two brothers Ibrāhīm (born around 1817) and Ṣāliḥ (born around 1819) acquired some wealth and were elected into several communal councils.[18] In the 1860s the brothers obtained agricultural land in al-Yadūda, 12km south of Amman and became a well-respected merchant and landowning family. Around 1887 the Nablusī master builder ʿAbd al-Raḥmān Aqrūq started to build the house by order of Ṣāliḥ Abū Jābir. In 1907 he finished the second floor. After the death of the Ṣāliḥ Abū Jābir in 1897 his three sons inhabited the building with their families. The ground floor accommodated ten narrow cells – used as shops to sell crops – and adjoining stores at the rear. The first and second floors contain apartments to accommodate the families and a guest-wing. The arrangement of rooms follows strictly the specific needs of the owner. Each apartment had a separate entrance from outside as well as a connec-

[18] Raouf Saʿd Abujaber, *Pioneers over Jordan. The Frontier of Settlement in Transjordan 1850-1914*, London 1989, 134-135.

tion to the other units through the inner part of the house. The western part of the first floor was used as a guest-wing (*maḍāfa*).

Fig. D a: al-Salṭ, Qaṣr Abū Jābir, first floor plan (Source: *Royal Scientific Society, Amman 1990*).

Since the Abū Jābir building was the only private house in al-Salṭ where an entire wing is reserved only for the reception of guests, the *maḍāfa* indicates the family's prominent position. The guest section contained a large hall, several rooms and an open terrace directed towards the street, a kitchen and toilets adjacent to the hillside. A second entrance of minor importance was situated at the back of the house. From there, a stairway leads into the *maḍāfa* on the first floor and the apartment on the second floor. This constellation formed a hidden connection, which allowed family members to enter or to leave the *maḍāfa* unnoticed. A technical innovation applied for the first time to a private house was the integration of latrines into the building. Comparing the two residential floors – built between 1896 and 1907 – the dissolution of the traditional symmetric central hall scheme becomes obvious. The first floor plan still strictly followed the vernacular rules with a longitudinal hall and adjacent rooms, while the second floor showed a rather free variation of the traditional plan in each apartment.

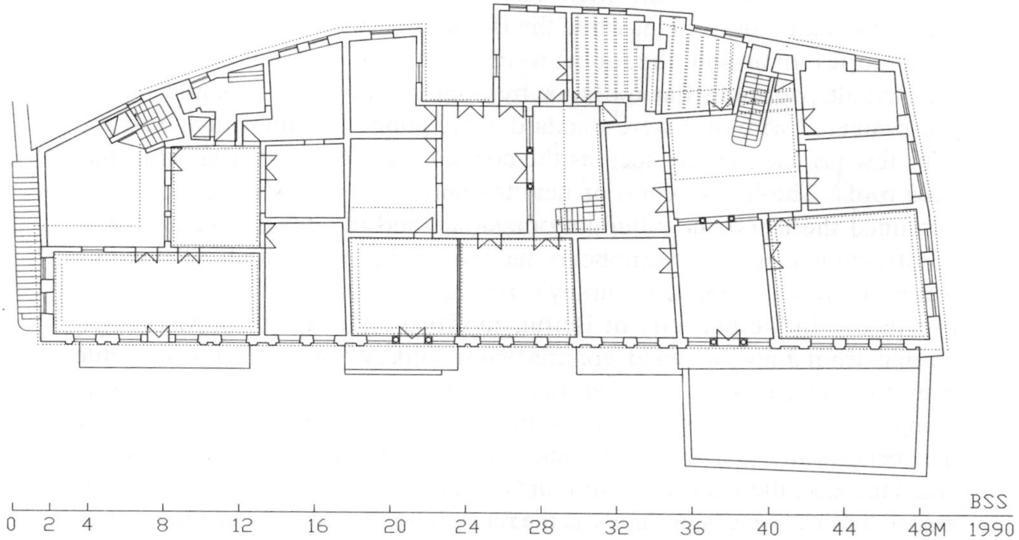

Fig. D b: al-Salṭ, Qaṣr Abū Jābir, second floor plan (Source: *Royal Scientific Society, Amman 1990*).

Comparison

In Beirut and al-Salṭ central hall houses appeared in new quarters whose social structure differed from that of the historic city center. In Beirut, May Davie observes that the city did not respond to a simple concentric zoning model, nor to tight sectorial divisions in terms of urban function, politics or community. Nevertheless, Davie insists that a professional differentiation between the quarters expressed a recent restructuration of society.[19] In al-Salṭ, the first houses were built by notable families linked to the Ottoman administration who settled near the seray. Later on, smaller hoses were erected at shorter intervals on the same hill. The new quarter was clearly distinguishable from the ones of the old city, not only by the shape of the houses, but also by its social structure. The traditional quarters were separated according to the tribal affiliation of the family, while within the new quarter this connection did not influence the location of the house. In both cities, the houses were erected on slopes and built of locally available stone. While in Beirut the walls were usually plastered and painted in a

19 May Davie, *Beyrouth et ses faubourgs*, 62.

reddish or yellowish color, in Salṭ the masonry was visible. Each stone was decoratively scratched with small dots.[20] The central hall houses in al-Salṭ are one to four stories high, while the Beiruti houses commonly had two or three stories. In al-Salṭ, the rooms were usually covered either by barrel or cross vaults, forming flat roofs, or by domes. In Mount Lebanon hipped roofs covered with tiles were standard. Only public buildings in al-Salṭ and very few private houses, such as the above described Qaṣr Abū Jābir, had tiled roofs. The introduction of new transportation facilities attracted and sustained the use of new building materials and the development of new construction methods. Steamboats facilitated the importation of building materials from Europe and Turkey – railways the transportation within the province.[21] In the port city of Beirut, roof tiles imported from Marseilles, marble from Italy or wood coming from Turkey[22] were easily available even for house owners of lesser means.[23] In al-Salṭ, which was not located along a railway line, roof tiles became known only towards the end of the nineteenth century. They were mainly used in communal buildings like the small mosque, the Latin Church or the complex of the Anglican mission. The mansion of the Abū Jābir family is the rare case of a private house covered by a tiled roof. Here, the huge red roof represents a new type of roofing construction, a sign of the social status of the house owner, who was able to defray the costs of the troublesome transport from the port of Haifa to al-Salṭ. The con-

20 The same decoration pattern can be found in Nablus. Both cities are situated in a hilly region, which suggests that the landscape influenced the houseform. But from examining the spread of central hall houses over the province it appears in lowland areas like Damascus and Homs.

21 In 1868 the road between Jaffa and Jerusalem was paved, in 1892 the railway constructed. Between 1861 and 1863 a railroad between Beirut and Damascus was built. Transjordan was connected in the beginning of the twentieth century with Palestine (1905: railway Haifa-Dara'a) and Damascus (1903-07: Hijjāz railway Damascus-Medina). For the construction of railroads and roads in Bilād al-Shām see *The Syrian Land: Processes of Integration and Fragmentation*, eds. Thomas Philipp and Birgit Schaebler, Stuttgart 1998, 19-27.

22 Vitale Cuinet, *Syrie, Liban et Palestine*, Paris 1898, 68, mentions wood for construction imported from Trieste and Turkey and rooftiles imported from Marseille. The factory and place of manufacture is marked on each tile. Several interviewed people confirmed that wood came from Turkey (*qatrani*). This correlates with Fouad el-Khūrī's statement: "The low and rectangular doors... made of a special wood (called cotrani) coming from Turkey," Fouad el-Khūrī, "Domestic Architecture in the Lebanon," *Art and Archaeological Research Papers*, June 1975, 16.

23 The construction of Beirut's modern port was completed in 1895. See Mahmoud Haddad, "The City, the Coast, the Mountain and its Hinterland," in *The Syrian Land*, 129-154.

spicuous roof tiles became a symbol of his contacts and wealth.[24] Likewise the use of cross vaults and barrel vaults did not appear in al-Salṭ before the middle of the nineteenth century. The close trading relations between Palestine and Transjordan and the settlement of several families from Nablus during the nineteenth century suggest architectural influences from Palestine. Since the roofing construction with cross and barrel vaults or domes was a common phenomenon in Palestine, one may assume that this method was brought by masons who had come from there to Transjordan.[25]

One of the main differences between Beiruti and Salṭi houses was in the appearance of the main façade. Even if in both towns the façade shaping was symmetric, the large triple tipped arched window placed in the center dominated the main façade of Beiruti houses. In some cases the façades were encircled on one or more sides by pointed arched galleries, which were supported by marble columns. In al-Salṭ, the shape of the triple arched windows differs from those in Beirut: they are placed regularly in a line without focusing on the location of the central hall.

In both cities the exterior embellishment is limited to the decoration of entrances and windows. Another similarity is the absorption of known regional and exterior ornaments into the decorative vocabulary. First indications of eclecticism, which will grow during the Mandate period, are visible: In Beirut, local characteristics (pointed-arched galleries) are mixed with baroque and classical forms: Doors and windows crowned by triangular gables, terraces surrounded by classical railings, marble columns of the triple arched windows arranged in a classic order (base, shaft and capital) and gothic elements (the wooden lattice of the triple arched windows adopts tracery forms). In al-Salṭ the development of new decorative forms may be traced back to the immigration of Palestinian master builders.[26] Traditional Palestinian biforic windows are introduced in the architectural vocabulary in al-Salṭ. The soft and easy-to-tool limestone facilitated the invention of fine ornaments: straight or twisted columns with fancy capitals, crowned by decorated oculi and flanked entrances. The exterior decoration is characterized by local specificities in each town, according to the particular regional or international contacts of each place. Considering the

---

24 In many places all over the province rooftiles produced by the Guichard-Carvin factory, St.André, Marseille were used, it seems that the trade was dominated by a few factories.

25 Al-Aamiry, Suad Cejka, Jan, "Das palästinensische Haus," *Pracht und Geheimnis*, eds. Gisela Völger, Karin von Welde and Katharina Hackstein, Köln, Berlin 1991, 92-99.

26 Comparing the decoration of entrances in Nablus with those of al-Salṭ, their similarity is apparent. Many master masons came from Nablus to al-Salṭ, e.g. ʿAbd al-Raḥmān Aqrūq.

variety of different forms within each town it seems that the individual background of the house owner or master builder was of major importance for the style of decoration chosen.

As mentioned above in both cities the ground plans of the new middle-class houses were characterized by a covered inner hall which was flanked by several rooms. In both cities a large number of variations in entrances to the building existed. In middle class houses, the ground floor consisted of living quarters. The house was usually entered through a door in the main façade, leading directly into the central hall. The upper floor was commonly accessible through an external staircase. Consequently, the triple-arched window functioned as a door, flanked by windows. In many mansions the ground floor contained shops and stores or stables. Staircases to reach the living rooms in the first floor were located either on one side of the house or in the interior of the house. Ostentatious 'swirling' swung staircases, which were placed in front of the building, were a particular Beiruti feature. Another stairway, which connects the floors, was usually integrated into the building.

The main difference between the two cities was the shape and location of the central hall: in al-Salṭ, it was always located behind the entrance, but could be situated either facing towards the valley or along the slope. In Beirut the central hall was usually oriented towards the sea, even if the entrance was located to the left or right of the main façade. Triple arched windows often divided the interior with marble columns in the rear part (called *liwān*). In al-Salṭ, kitchen and stores were integrated into the cubic body of the building. Located at the windowless hill side, toilets and baths (if existing) were located on a terrace outside the house. In Beirut, instead, a segregation within the plan was prevalent: kitchen, bath and stores (often built as a mezzanine above the kitchen) were located in a corner of the house. Sometimes the kitchen, stores and housemaids' rooms were placed in an annex, separated from the families' living rooms. The plan of Beiruti houses and mansions was characterized by fine elaborations of convenient room arrangements. In large mansions several entrances allowed the segregation of semi-private spaces, private rooms and kitchen and servants' parts. In al-Salṭ, the difficult topographic situation dictated the shape of the house plan. In most cases, the steep slopes determined the entrance of the building and the placement of the central hall, which sometimes caused an awkward use of the space. One of the interviewed people reported that her apartment was entered from the hillside, but the reception room was located on the valley side of the house. Every visitor had to cross the whole apartment before reaching the reception room. This often caused inconveniences to women who had to withdraw to one of the side rooms, since men who did not belong to the family were not allowed to see the women of the family. Only in mansions built on a large piece of land could the rooms be arranged according to the desired shape with an appropriate arrangement of the rooms.

With the introduction of central hall houses in Beirut, niches and recesses for cupboards vanished and the rooms were equipped with furniture inspired by European fashions. The rooms were arranged with diwans, chairs, tables, mirrors and wardrobes, which replaced customary and inherited mobile furniture.[27] The walls were painted with simple rectangular ornaments, structuring the wall into a pedestal zone and a main part. The floor was covered either with limestone, terracotta or marble slabs. The lavish interior decorations of Beiruti mansions were often influenced by European artistic tradition. Some of the stucco decorations of the ceiling corresponded to sumptuous decorations in Istanbul, known as "Ottoman baroque".[28] The interior of the Qaṣr Mukhayyish, was decorated in a classical manner, with a tectonic painting in light green, pink and light blue and stucco ornaments, orthostates and *trompe l'oeil* paintings imitating marble columns and architraves. According to the house owners, an Italian artist who trained local staff, had carried out the decoration. At the same time, neo-oriental patterns were used, like the Moresque decoration of the Qaṣr Hunayna.[29]

The interior decorations of the central hall houses al-Salṭ were very different. In al-Salṭ, the floor was covered with smooth limestone slabs; rooms of major importance were decorated with colored tiles, produced in Palestine or (in mansions like that of Abū Jābir or Sukkār) with marble floor tiles imported from Italy. The walls were usually whitewashed with recesses for storing the traditional pile of mattresses. G. Bell noticed the furnishing of the guest room of Yūsuf Sukkār, one of the rich Christian merchants of the town:

> The floor and the divan were covered with thick carpets, the windows glazed (though many of the panes were broken), a European chiffonier stood against the wall.[30]

In the central hall, large pointed-arched windows opened to the adjoining rooms, structuring the undecorated walls of the hall. The use of vernacular elements as wall niches in al-Salṭ indicates that traditional living patterns

---

27 Ragette, *Architecture*, 117. Fuchs, Meyer-Brodnitz, "The emergence of the Central Hall House," 411. The authors mention the same lack of wall niches and the introduction of westernized furniture in Palestinian central hall houses.

28 See Weber's contribution to this volume.

29 See the contribution of Ralph Bodenstein to this volume.

30 Gertude Bell, *The Desert and the Sown,* London 1909, 19.

were transferred to the new building, while in Beirut the change in the decoration and furnishing of houses signified a change of living patterns, too.

In both cities, the ground floor contained either stables, shops, stores or living-quarters, while the upper floors were only used as living quarters. The central hall was not only the spatial but also the social center of the house. It is the main lounge of the family where children played, people sat and where all movements in the house crossed. The term "*wasaṭ al-dār*" "center of the house" was used in al-Salṭ and illustrates this meaning. In al-Salṭ each house was commonly inhabited by one extended family, while in Beirut the strict separation of the two floors by external stairs supports the idea that in middle-class houses each floor was inhabited by an independent family and mansions belonged to one extended family.

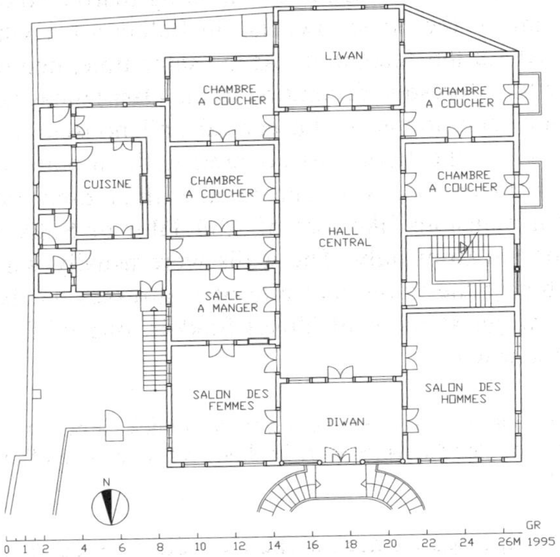

Fig. E: Beirut, Qaṣr Mukhayyish, first floor plan (Source: Ghia Rifai, Beirut).

In Beirut average houses usually did not accommodate stables but had living quarters on each floor. In mansions, stables were situated on the ground floor, and the living quarters were located on one or two floors above. Kitchen, bath and – if existing – servant rooms were located either in one corner of the apartment or in an annex adjacent to the main building. Reception rooms were still used, but covered a rather small area of the house, as the plans of the Qaṣr al-Khūrī and Qaṣr Mukhayyish suggest (fig. E).

The Qaṣr Mukhayyish was built in 1315/1897-98 by Amīn Pasha Mukhayyish. His descendants still inhabit the house. Within his vast palace, a segregation of the plan separated domestic parts and living areas, while the space for the reception of guests was reduced to two rooms next to the large representative staircase, one each for men and women. Both rooms were connected to the entrance hall as well as the central hall itself. According to the house owner, the entrance hall was not closed by glass towards the garden, forming a semi-private zone before entering the house.

In al-Salṭ, the separation of reception rooms and family living rooms was the main element organizing domestic space. In rural communities separate houses were used by the villagers to receive visitors or as meeting places. Now the development of house forms consisting of more than one room fostered the establishment of a specific guest room in each house. The accommodation of foreigners in the private guest-room instead of a tribe's *maḍāfa* signified the rising importance of specific families within the community. Gertrude Bell described in detail how Yūsuf Effendi Sukkār insisted on lodging her when she visited al-Salṭ in 1907. The *maḍāfa* of the Abū Jabīr family formalized this transformation of domestic space by becoming an independent part of the palace.[31]

Comparing the central hall houses in Beirut and al-Salṭ, it can be observed that the appearance of the house type in the new quarters of Beirut suggests a radical transformation of living patterns. Decorative features, the organization of space and the furniture differed from the traditional forms known in the old city. The social status of the different quarters varied. Generally, the closer to the city center and the higher up on the surrounding promontories, the greater the wealth of the owners. As May Davie argues :

> Le modèle de la maison à trois arcades et toiturée de tuiles se repand partout et s'impose dans le paysage par sa taille et ses couleurs. Symbolisant l'époque historique que la ville traverse, elle se présente également comme un trait d'union ente ses different ensembles.[32]

The need for new housing due to the rapid population increase promoted the elaboration of simple and elegant design. In contrast, the change of the house type did not affect fundamentally the living patterns in al-Salṭ. But

---

31 Bell, *The Desert and the Sown*, 19.

32 Davie, *Beyrouth et ses faubourgs*, 65.

even if the plan was unsuitable for accommodating social needs in relation to the topographic situation, the choice of this specific type seems to have had a special meaning for the owners. The house-type demonstrates the affiliation of the house owner with the local elite. Moreover, the social status of individual families within the community was measured by the location and size of the house and by the degree of decoration.

The comparison between both cities has shown that apart from basic similarities, the Salti house in the late nineteenth century presented many varieties of plans, caused by the topography of the town, while the nineteenth century Beiruti house featured more elaborate decoration patterns and façade shaping, often inspired by European features (pointed arched-window patterns with tracery-like lattices and railings) or local characteristics (galleries).

In both cities the houses of Muslims and Christians were indistinguishable and there is no evidence that the organization of space differed much according to religious denomination. In al-Salṭ the traditional living patterns, especially the importance of the reception of guests, continued to dominate the organization of space use.

Dwelling in Bilād al-Shām in the Nineteenth Century

The central hall house appeard in Greater Syria in the mid-nineteenth century. Its rapid spread throughout the provinces and its prompt acceptance by middle and upper classes poses several questions. In contrast to the traditional courtyard houses, which were hidden behind windowless, undecorated facades, the central hall houses built outside the city walls were deliberately exposed to the exterior. The balcony, which was often placed in front of the triple-arched window, symbolized this change: inhabitants wanted to see their surroundings and wanted to be seen by the public. What did they want to demonstrate? Their contemporaries must have easily understood the message in the extroverted design of the central hall houses. People passing by were able to judge at first glance the wealth of a family by the size of the building and its surrounding property. Looking closer at it, one could observe further details: The large mansions had well arranged gardens, fine stone carvings and large windows with colored glass panes, indicating the care which had been taken to decorate one's house. The well-traveled and well-educated members of society were able to read the decorative style as a story: In Beirut, the swung staircase recalled the nineteenth-century palaces in Istanbul (the most prominent example is that of Dolmabahce Serail), the pointed arches with its tracery-like wooden carvings evoked Venetian mansions while the galleries surrounding the facades corresponded to local architecture in Mount Lebanon. In al-Salṭ the decoration of the entrances and treatment of the stone reminded the beholder of similar architecture in Nablus, while the roof titles and colored glass panes were a sign of the trading relations with Beirut and Europe.

But apart from these external and evident features, the most significant changes took place in the floor plan. The conceptual change from a house with a large inner open courtyard to a house with a covered central hall requires an investigation into its social meaning and significance. Some authors have tried to explain the transformation of the central hall plan as a linear architectural development. Davie and Nordiguian see the origin of the central hall in the covered courtyard. This formal analysis neglects the basic difference between the character of an open living space and a closed hall.

Ragette explains the evolution as an enlargement of the traditional "*Līwān-house,*" which is characterized by an open *iwān* hall, flanked on each side by rooms. Even if the similarity of the plan is evident, he did not explain convincingly why a rural house type of minor representative character should have been used as the model for a new urban house type. Urban houses with a covered inner hall (*sofa*), mainly on the first floor, were well-known in Anatolia even before the nineteenth century. A rectangular or cruciform hall characterized the plan, with independent rooms in each corner. In contrast to the block-like central hall stone houses in Bilād al-Shām, the first floor of houses in Anatolia was often built in wood or half-timbered construction, which facilitated the construction of oriels. But this feature, which leads to a different appearance of the building, did not affect the floor plan. Given the different sources of inspiration for the façade's decoration, it seems worthwhile to 'read' the plan like the façade. The similarities between both local architecture and the architecture of Anatolia and Istanbul in particular, seem to be a distinctive feature in the central hall plan in Greater Syria. Geoffrey Goodwin has observed the correspondence between the *sofa*-plan of mansions and the plan of early Ottoman kiosks.[33] The plan of the Çinili kiosk "was a plan which was to remain important in domestic Ottoman architecture in particular, indicating that its symbolism remained meaningful into the nineteenth century."[34] If one reads the central hall plan as a synthesis of the local *liwan*-plan of Bilād al-Shām and the *sofa*-plan, it could be understood as an expression of a self-conscious identification with the Ottoman Empire amongst the newly

---

33 Godfrey Goodwin, *A History of Ottoman Architecture*, London 1971, 136-139, 429-447.

34 *Ibid.* 137.

formed elites in nineteenth century *Bilād al-Shām* – an elite which was recruited from the local population and which had strong ties to the Ottoman administration. [35]

The integration of Ottoman symbols into private residences of urban notables underlined the personal ties of some families with Istanbul. The above-mentioned Amin Bāsha Mūkhayyish, a Beiruti trader, carried an honorary title of the Ottoman government and demonstrated his identification with the Ottoman Empire by carving the symbols of the half-moon and star into the architrave of the main door. Likewise, in al-Salṭ wealthy merchants, landowning families and/or officials of the Ottoman administration built representative central hall houses which were conspicuously located outside the old center near the serail. The vernacular tradition, particular regional and exterior contacts (Beirut – Istanbul/ Europe; al-Salṭ – Palestine) and individual needs of the house owners transformed archetypes into specific regional styles. Both spatial organization and architectural design were hermeneutic carriers of social and political affiliation.

35 Another source of inspiration might have derived from venetian mansion. But this argument needs further investigation.

AS-SAYYID ABŪ 'L-HUDĀ AL-ṢAYYĀDĪ IN ALEPPO

JULIA GONNELLA

The Enigma

Al-Sayyid Abū 'l-Hudā al-Ṣayyādī was one of the most enigmatic figures of the late Ottoman Empire. For someone who was born in a small humble village south of Aleppo (according to his biography he was born in Ramadhān 1266/July 1850) he followed a stunning career. No one knows exactly how it started, but by 1289/1872 he had already become *naqīb al-ashrāf* in Jisr al-Shughūr, by 1290/1873 he was *naqīb al-ashrāf* of Aleppo and around three years later he moved to Istanbul where he eventually ascended to one of the closest advisors of Sultan Abdülhamid II (1876-1909). Amongst other posts he held the office of *Ḳāżī-asker* of Rumeli second in rank only to the *shaykh al-islām* in the *ʿulamā'*-hierarchy. In particular, Abū 'l-Hudā was instrumental in disseminating Abdülhamid's panislamist policies. As head of the Rifāʿiyya brotherhood he strengthened the Sufi-movement, especially in Syria, which was probably a deliberate attempt to counter more liberal and modern tendencies. Abū 'l-Hudā died in Istanbul in 1909, the same year in which Sultan Abdülhamid II. was forced to abdicate.

Apart from two articles by Werner Ende[1] and Butrus Abu-Manneh[2] who recommended twenty years ago that further studies were needed, there has been a dearth of research carried out on this highly intelligent and ambitious shaykh.[3] No doubt this is partly because carrying out research on Abū 'l-Hudā is no easy matter. Contemporary assessments about his per-

---

1 Werner Ende, "Sayyid Abū 'l-Hudā, ein Vertrauter Abdülhamid's II. Notwendigkeit und Probleme einer kritischen Biographie," in *XIX. Deutscher Orientalistentag* 1975 in Freiburg, *ZDMG* Suppl. III., 2 Bde., Bd. III/2, ed. W. Voigt, Wiesbaden 1977, 1143-55.

2 Butrus Abu-Manneh, "Sultan Abdulhamid II and Shaikh Abulhuda Al-Sayyadi," *MES*, 15 (May 1979), 131-53.

3 A dissertation on Abū 'l-Hudā is presently being prepared by Thomas Eich at the university of Bochum/Germany.

son and work are extremely divergent and at times contradictory which make an appraisal of the shaykh very difficult. Abū 'l-Hudā had a large number of adversaries: many political opponents and numerous people who simply envied the shaykh's success. Werner Ende makes a rather drastic summary of the situation of the sources:

> the only reliable information one can draw from the various statements about him is that Abū 'l-Hudā did indeed live, that he became head of the Rifāᶜiyya brotherhood in the Ottoman Empire, that he played an important role in the entourage of Abdülhamid II and that he died in Istanbul in 1909.[4]

There is disagreement about his personal life, his social background, the reasons for his career, his degree of learning and education, about his personal integrity and the integrity of his written work. One of the main sources available to the modern scholar is his biography.[5] The work which was approved by Abū 'l-Hudā himself, has mainly been drawn upon by his supporters or devotees. On the other hand, we find an unusually large body of highly critical and also derogatory accounts by his adversaries such as the articles and pamphlets written by those in the circle around Jamāl al-Dīn al-Afghānī – Abū 'l-Hudā's most prominent enemy at the court of Abdülhamid II.[6] Another group of fierce opponents is to be found among the notable families of Aleppo, many of whom had followed Abū 'l-Hudā's career at the very beginning. The local historian al-Ṭabbākh,[7] for example, contemptuously turned his back on him and denied him the separate biographical entry he provided for most other prominent members of Aleppo's notable society. When he mentioned him at all it was unfavourably. Particularly remarkable is the considerable antipathy towards him, which exists among the descendants of notable families in Aleppo even today – ninety years after his death.

During my fieldwork on saints in Aleppo, I frequently came across highly emotional comments about him.[8] Abū 'l-Hudā has been described to me by all and sundry as a major fraud who forged his mystical and fam-

---

4 Ende, "Sayyid Abū 'l-Hudā," 1144.

5 Ḥasan Ḥusnī al-Tuwayrīnī, *al-Qawl al-faṣl*, Cairo 1313 AH. For further references, see Abu-Manneh, "Shaikh Abulhuda," 148f., fn.1.

6 Ende,"Sayyid Abū 'l-Hudā," 1145.

7 Muḥammad al-Ṭabbākh, *Iᶜlām al-nubalā' bi tārīkh Ḥalab al-shaḥbā' [1341/1923]*, 2nd. ed., 7 vols., Aleppo 1408-9/1988-9.

8 Julia Gonnella, *Islamische Heiligenverehrung im urbanen Kontext am Beispiel von Aleppo (Syrien)*, Berlin 1995.

ily lines of descent. The fact that he held the position of *naqīb al-ashrāf* in Jisr al-Shughūr was considered laughable. It was pointed out to me, that there were no *sharīfs* but only Nuṣayrīs in this little town on the Orontes. That Abū 'l-Hudā managed to pursue such a stunning career in Istanbul is generally attributed to his extraordinary intelligence. At the same time he was described to me as extremely vicious. Someone even designated him as a spy of the Ottoman secret service. Of course, many of these disparaging comments correspond to the ones known from contemporary written sources.[9]

Aleppo – the Launch-Pad of a Local Notable's Career

One thing is sure, Aleppo was an important place for Abū 'l-Hudā. It was here that he made his first contacts outside his village, Khān Shaykhūn, and where he was initiated to the Rifāʿiyya brotherhood. He settled here and was later 'appointed' *naqīb al-ashrāf* of the town. Later in life, when residing in Istanbul, it seems Abū 'l-Hudā remained in contact with his town. At least part of his family, I suppose his parents, continued to live in Aleppo. They also entertained a *zāwiya*. It is here where Abū 'l-Hudā eventually buried his father.

Listening to the comments of the present day descendants, Abū 'l-Hudā could not have found Aleppo the easiest place for launching a career, for notable families here constituted a rather inaccessible, elitist society, closely linked to each other by kinship and marriage.[10] For the past 150 years or more, these families had produced the intellectual and economic upper class of the town. One important way through which they exercised their influence was through the Sufi brotherhoods, and the *zāwiyas* and *takiyyas* were also organized along family lines.[11]

For an outsider without an appropriate family background it must have been difficult to become established. It is not surprising that the family with whom Abū 'l-Hudā came into contact first, was the family al-Khayrallāh,[12] which itself had moved to Aleppo not long before him. They entertained a thriving Rifāʿiyya *zāwiya*. At least in Northern Syria and

---

9 Cf. Ende, "Sayyid Abū 'l-Hudā," 1143f.

10 See Ruth Roded, *Tradition and Change in Syria During the last Decades of Ottoman Rule: The Urban Elite of Damascus, Aleppo, Homs and Hama, 1876-1918*, Ph.D thesis, University of Denver 1984 and Gonnella, *Islamische Heiligenverehrung*, chapters 6, 7, 8.

11 *Ibid.*

12 Ṭabbākh, *Iʿlām al-nubalāʾ*, VII, 159.

certainly also in Aleppo, the Rifāʿiyya brotherhood had been gaining in popularity for reasons not entirely known. Perhaps it was difficult to enter the other orders such as the Qādiriyya which was controlled by the established families and Abū 'l-Hudā's choice was an obvious and well-trodden path for a newcomer.

Abū 'l-Hudā was initiated by shaykh ʿAlī Khayrallāh (d. 1289/1872)[13] who he claimed was his cousin. Another family Abū 'l-Hudā made early contacts with was the al-Rifāʿī family,[14] a rather prominent notable family which entertained several *zāwiyas*. Altogether, the al-Rifāʿī family had a much better standing than that of the al-Khayrallāh family. They were comparatively rich. They also enjoyed close connections to Istanbul, which is most likely to have prompted Abū 'l-Hudā to approach the family in the first place.[15] It is not clear how the contacts between Abū 'l-Hudā and the family were initially established, possibly via his father, supposedly a tradesman with whom the al-Khayrallāhs could have fostered business connections.

Present day descendants in Aleppo comment upon these "Rifāʿī-connections" rather sarcastically. A particularly malicious comment was conveyed to me by a descendant of the al-Kayyālī family[16] – a rather curious fact given that they claim to have Rifāʿī connections, too. Obviously they consider themselves to be of more noble origin. This descendant claimed that when Abū 'l-Hudā came to Aleppo he first turned to the *zāwiya* of the Kayyālīs but was declined by the family because they considered him to be a fraud. Abū 'l-Hudā was forced to move on to the al-Khayrallāh family, which – according to the Kayyālīs – was not very discriminating in accepting newcomers. As for the second shaykh who apparently initiated Abū 'l-Hudā into the Rifāʿī brotherhood, Muḥammad al-Rawwās from Baghdad, he is considered an invention, which is what many written sources say, too.[17] Also the contemporary shaykh of the al-Rifāʿī family, Shaykh Bahā' al-Dīn (d. 1290/1873-4),[18] was similarly frowned upon. Already Ṭabbākh[19] mentioned that he was elected *muftī* but that he did not qualify for the post.

---

13 On shaykh ʿAlī Khayrallāh, *ibid.*, VII, 327-31.

14 On the family al-Rifāʿī and their *zāwiyas*, see Gonnella, *Islamische Heiligenverehrung*, 250-52, 258f., 265.

15 Abu Manneh, "Shaikh Abulhuda," 132.

16 On the family al-Kayyālī, see Gonnella, *Islamische Heiligenverehrung*, 254-56, 265-68.

17 Cf. Ende, "Sayyid Abū 'l-Hudā," 1143f.

18 Cf. Abu Manneh, "Shaikh Abulhuda," 132.

19 Ṭabbākh, *Iʿlām al-nubalāʾ*, VII, 331-35.

Fig. 1: The house and *zāwiya* of Abū 'l-Hudā as seen from the citadel.

Fig. 2: The tomb of Abū 'l-Hudā.

Fig. 3: The *iwān* of the living quarter.

Fig. 4: The southern palais with double-flight staircase, today seat of the *muftī* of Aleppo.

Fig. 5: The eastern representative building.

Fig. 6: The courtyard of the *zāwiya* with the entrance to the *haramlik*.

Fig. 7: The entrance to the mosque.

Fig. 8: The eastern representative building as seen from the *zāwiya* courtyard.

Whether they were right or wrong, the reservations of the contemporary notable families basically forced Abū ’l-Hudā al-Ṣayyādī to justify both his family and his spiritual background for the rest of his life – even after he moved to Istanbul. After all, in Islamic brotherhood circles, both adequate genealogy and spiritual lines of descent are indispensable prerequisites to legitimacy. Accordingly, we find a long list of books and pamphlets which supposedly certify Abū ’l-Hudā’s family and mystical origins. In particular, he was keen to trace his genealogy back to Aḥmad al-Rifāʿī, the founder of the Rifāʿiyya brotherhood which Abū ’l-Hudā was so fervently trying to turn into the most influential brotherhood of the Ottoman Empire. What is novel here is that in Abū ’l-Hudā’s times, Aḥmad al-Rifāʿī was also considered a direct descendant of the prophet Muḥammad, which in turn enabled Abū ’l-Hudā to call himself a “*sharīf*” – a title given to supposed descendants of the prophet. It is only natural that Abū ’l-Hudā portrayed his closer ancestors as ‘shaykhly,’ too. His ‘official’ biography claimed that his grandfather possessed supernatural powers and that his tomb was a place of visitation.[20] Two years before his death Abū ’l-Hudā had the tomb reactivated with a *takiyya*.[21] He also had a large tomb built for his father in their family *zāwiya* in Aleppo. Ṭabbākh[22] mentions this laconically as follows: “When his father died in 1312 (1894-5) he built him a grandiose tomb in the *qiblīya* of their *zāwiya* so that everyone should believe he was a great saint”. Judging from the numerous bottles filled with oil, which are still laid down by his tomb today, Abū ’l-Hudā was quite successful in the end: the grave is still a popular place to visit.

Of course, opinions about the shaykh were not as unanimous during his lifetime as they are today, which could simply reflect the limited circle of informants which I encountered during my fieldwork. One of the closest friends and followers of Abū ’l-Hudā was Abū’l-Qādir al-Qudsī (d. 1309/1891-2) who according to Ṭabbākh did nothing without the shaykh and vice versa.[23] The Qudsīs were an old, distinguished family, albeit not running a *zāwiya*. Like his forefathers, Abū’l-Qādir entertained close connections with the government in Istanbul and occupied several important posts in various parts of the Ottoman Empire. Another eminent family which supported Abū ’l-Hudā was the al-Mudarris family. Muḥammad al-ʿUbaysī was also a committed follower in Aleppo. He was a shaykh originally from Hama, who had been appointed by Abū ’l-Hudā to the post of

---

20 Abu Manneh, “Shaikh Abulhuda,” 131.

21 Heinz Gaube, *Arabische Inschriften aus Syrien*, Beirut 1978, Nr. 224, 225.

22 Ṭabbākh, *Iʿlām al-nubalāʾ*, VII, 330.

23 On Abū’l-Qādir al-Qudsī, *ibid.*, VII, 409-12.

wakīl in his Aleppo *zāwiya* in 1309/1891-92.[24] The shaykh clearly acted as a kind of representative for Abū 'l-Hudā taking on several posts in his name. He was also made supervisor *(mutawallī)* of various *waqfs* in his name. With Abū 'l-Hudā's support Muḥammad al-ʿUbaysī later became *muftī* of Aleppo.

Abu Manneh[25] explains that the split between the supporters and opponents of Abū 'l-Hudā was related to the political polarization in the city. Whereas the supporters of Abū 'l-Hudā seem to have belonged to the conservative faction of the city who sympathized with the sultan, his opponents were recruited from families pushing for reforms. I doubt whether one can really split the Aleppine families along these lines since it was common for various members of one and the same family to support different political factions. Surely, one can say that Abū 'l-Hudā had a strong preference for those with government connections and it is also true that likewise Abū 'l-Hudā enjoyed governmental protection from early on in his career. The only exception to this rule was Abū 'l-Hudā's exile in 1878. He was denounced to the sultan and ordered back to Aleppo – much to the satisfaction of the notable families who asked the governor to dismiss him from the post of *naqīb al-ashrāf*.[26]

The strong antipathy felt towards Abū 'l-Hudā in the past would certainly not provide an adequate explanation as to why he is still not accepted today. One of the reasons is probably connected to a general aversion by Syrians to the late Ottoman sultans and their politics – a sentiment that is evident in much of the literature or oral statements on the topic even today. However, considering that the antipathy has lingered on for so many years and indeed is still so deep, it seems that it is more the result of a powerful resistance of the old established families to newcomers which – and this is fascinating – has been clearly handed down from generation to generation. After all, this mechanism is not so surprising in a society where the question of the family ("*bayt mīn?*") is still today of major importance.

Architectural Patronage and Imperial Politics

Apart from the written and oral material there is yet another intriguing source on Abū 'l-Hudā al-Ṣayyādī which sheds light on how the shaykh perceived himself: The house he built in Aleppo and his *zāwiya*, quite a stately complex in the "Ughul Beg" quarter east of the citadel, not far from

24 *Ibid.*, VIII, 586-89. I would like to thank Thomas Eich for this reference.

25 Abu Manneh, "Shaikh Abulhuda," 134f.

26 *Ibid.*

the Ḥammām Bāb al-Aḥmar (fig. 1).[27] Today, the entire complex is owned by the Awqāf ministry. The former reception wings are used by the Dār al-Iftā' and have recently been renovated.[28]

Abū 'l-Hudā's house consists of three parts: the reception wings (the "*salamlik*"), the *zāwiya* and the private quarters (the "*haramlik*"). The *salamlik* includes two separate buildings that open towards the citadel. The *zāwiya*, a domed mosque, is located in an oblong courtyard, which extends behind the eastern reception wing. It is here where one can find the tombs of Abū 'l-Hudā's father, his brother ʿAbd al-Razzāq, another of his relatives, Aḥmad Khālid, as well as his own (fig. 2). Abū 'l-Hudā's mortal remains were transferred from Istanbul to Aleppo in 1937. Behind the *zāwiya* is the *haramlik* of the complex where members of Abū 'l-Hudā's family used to live (at least his parents): a traditional Aleppine courtyard house with an *iwān* at its southern side and with a separate entrance from the back street. The courtyard of the *zāwiya* could have been entered both from the family quarters and from the official courtyard outside through a passage in the eastern reception wing. There was also direct access to the mosque from the interior of this building.

According to Ghazzī[29] the *zāwiya* was founded by Abū 'l-Hudā in 1295/1878, and finished in 1327/1909. He writes that "it was well visited, had many rooms and pretty sights (*jamīlat al-manāẓir*)". Two inscriptions can be found *in situ* which mention the years 1290/1873-4 and 1295/1878. The early inscription was set above the western entrance door of the *haramlik*, the latter, correlating with Ghazzī's date sits above the door of the mosque. One can, therefore, conclude that Abū 'l-Hudā started to build his complex during his years as *naqīb al-ashrāf* in Aleppo, beginning with his family home. The *zāwiya* he completed while in exile from Istanbul. It was probably the southern building of the *salamlik,* which was the last building to be finished as Ghazzī writes in 1909. An empty cartouche on the staircase might have been meant to include another inscription. In addition, Ṭabbākh[30] noted that the *wakīl* of the *zāwiya*, Shaykh Muḥammad al-ʿUbaysī, had been instructed by Abū 'l-Hudā to buy a number of houses in

---

27 The complex is mentioned by Heinz Gaube and Eugen Wirth, *Aleppo. Historische und geographische Beiträge zur baulichen Gestaltung, zur sozialen Organisation und zur wirtschaftlichen Dynamik einer vorderasiatischen Fernhandelsmetropole*, Wiesbaden 1984, 381, Nr. 333.

28 I would like to thank the *muftī* of Aleppo, Aḥmad Ḥassūn, for showing me around the premises.

29 Kāmil al-Ghazzī, *Kitāb nahr al-dhahab fī tārīkh Ḥalab [1345/1926]*, 2nd. ed., 3 vols, Aleppo 1412/1992, II, 299.

30 Ṭabbākh, *Iʿlām al-nubalā'*, VIII, 588.

the neighborhood to enlarge the complex. Unfortunately we have no precise information about the actual houses to which he referred.[31]

For the old town of Aleppo, Abū 'l-Hudā's house is indeed an extraordinary complex. Whereas the *haramlik* still follows the traditional inward-orientated house style albeit making use of some modern elements such as the neoclassical window frames and the railing half way up the *iwān* (fig. 3), the *salamlik* of the complex is open to the public with window fronts and balconies. Especially the palais like southern building with its sweeping double-flight staircase and the vases on top of the roof is different from anything that had existed in the old town before (fig. 4).

The reception section consists of two separate buildings, which were certainly built one after the other, both conveying a distinct style: the southern palais and the eastern front building. The palais was structured by slender pilasters with Ionic capitals and arched windows with decorative keystones and was much more elegant than the eastern building which in comparison is bolder with arcades, different size windows, rustic pilasters and a broad ledge topped by different types of palmettes-acroteria. There is no internal connection between the two buildings. The southern building was built to touch the eastern building in one corner only – thus creating a kind of front courtyard, which is delimited on its northern side by a neighboring house. It is unclear whether this was the original layout. A wall with posts and a decorative metal railing separates this court from the road on the western side. The entrance to the entire complex was through a two-winged gate in the railing, which again lies on the axis of the entrance to the *zāwiya* on the ground floor of the eastern front building.

The architectural arrangement of the reception wings is not quite as balanced as one might expect in such a stately residence. There was no majestic approach to the building from a distance. Instead, the visitor had to take turns in order to ascend the pompous staircase. Also the facades of the two wings had no semblance of symmetrical arrangement. The staircase of the southern palais is not at the center of the building: the facade was extended to the west by a further set of windows. The facade of the eastern building consists of a regular three-part block with the entrance to the *zāwiya* on the ground floor (fig. 5). This facade was also extended towards the south with two arcades on the ground floor and three large windows on the first floor, which originally belonged to a loggia. The loggia has been closed at a later stage although the *mashrabiyyas* probably belong

---

[31] A survey of the land registry would certainly increase our knowledge of the history of the property conditions.

to the original set up. Incidentally, the plan of the interior of both reception wings is much more regular. Each floor of both buildings is organized around a central hallway (in the case of the ground floor of the eastern building a passageway) from which single rooms branch off on either side symmetrically. The visitors were clearly received in the first floors of the buildings.

Architectonically, the inner courtyard of the *zāwiya* presents itself much more as a unit bound together by a molding, which runs along three sides of the wall (fig. 6). Whereas the facade of the *haramlik* with a central door and five windows was held rather simple, the entrance to the mosque was built more elaborately, accentuated by a portal with a muqarnas cornice topped by palmettes (fig. 7). Similar floral elements also decorate the windows of the mosque next to the central door.

The most conspicuous construction of the courtyard was the inner facade of the eastern front building, again with a double-flight staircase but here there is a small protruding platform at the top (fig. 8). The decoration of the facade is highly eclectic: whereas the frame of entrance was built in the traditional Syrian *ablaq*-style, using alternate layers of different colored stones, the windowed front of the upper floor displays strong Gothic reminiscences. The central door with a large rosette arch and the tripartite windows at the side with columns is even reminiscent of some ecclesiastical motifs. The general arrangement of the facade was inspired by classicism, with four pilasters, cornice and palmette – acroteria in the center and at the sides. They are the same as those on the front side of the house. Altogether the facade has a strong imposing character, which attempts to appeal to visitors of the *zāwiya*. The aforementioned molding of the courtyard that continues on this facade suggests that the *zāwiya* and the eastern front building were constructed at the same time.

The Many Styles of Imperial Architecture in a Provincial Palace

In Aleppo, the building of the house and *zāwiya* of Abū 'l-Hudā must have been quite an exceptional event. Especially for the old town, the two prestigious reception wings were examples of a new style of residential architecture in the Middle East: the buildings were no longer closed for the passers-by as was the custom but were meant to appeal to the public with their richly decorated facades. In particular the southern palais-style building with its double-flight staircase introduced an element of extravagance and luxury into a surrounding accustomed to obfuscating wealth and power behind walls.

In his guide to Aleppo, ʿAbdallāh Ḥajjār[32] has described the house of Abū 'l-Hudā al-Ṣayyādī as the first European building in the old town and indeed, both concept and style of the architecture are ultimately based on European models. For direct influences, however, one has to turn to Ottoman architecture. After all, Abū 'l-Hudā spent most of his active political life in Istanbul close to the sultan where he must have been strongly inspired by the new imperial residences which appeared one after the other along the Bosphoros during the second half of the nineteenth century where each sultan trying to outdo his predecessor by a more luxurious palatial mansion.[33] The southern palais-style building with its double-flight staircase is strongly reminiscent of the new architectural vogues in the capital. Elegant staircases have become very fashionable in Istanbul in both the grand sultanic residences such as Dolmabahçe (1853), Beylerbey (1865), Çirağan (1874) and in examples of the smaller pleasure palaces, such as Ilhamur (1865), Küçüksu (1856) or the Büyük Mabeyn Köşkü in Yıldız (1855) which, of course, exceed Abū 'l-Hudā's house in terms of embellishment and luxury but nevertheless served as basic models.[34]

In the old town of Aleppo, at least, the staircase was something new. The only other example of a nineteenth century grandiose staircase, which I am aware of, is in the so-called "house of the caravan-tradesmen" published by Gangler: a single-flight staircase inside a courtyard not to be seen by passers-by.[35] Another double-flight staircase in the old town exists at the present passport office north of the citadel. It is dated 1344/1925 and

---

32 ʿAbdallāh Ḥajjār, *Maʿālim Ḥalab al-athariyya*, Aleppo 1997, 86.

33 Apparently, Abū 'l-Hudā also had a *zāwiya* built in Istanbul which unfortunately I was unable to locate. In Aleppo, I was told that Abū 'l-Hudā was given a house by the sultan in 1307/1889-90 in Beşiktaş, a quarter which is close to the governmental residences. Unfortunately, I was unable to locate this building. Instead, I identified the Çafer Ağa Mescidi a rather unobstrusive, plain rectangular building with a tiled roof in the traditional Turkish style and one minaret. This mosque was given to Abū 'l-Hudā in 1317/1899-1900 and turned into a Rifāʿiyya *zāwiya*. It was obviously rebuilt at the same time. The Çafer Ağa Mescidi is located in the lower class district of Fatih (Ayık Fırını Sokak) which was very popular with Arabs in the late Ottoman Empire and, therefore, probably very important for Abū 'l-Hudā in serving his clientele. For the mosque see: Emine Naza, "Çafer Ağa Mescidi," in *Istanbul Ansiklopedisi*, II, 1993-94.

34 For illustrations of the Ottoman palaces see Chris Hellier, *Splendours of the Bosphorus. Houses and Palaces of Istanbul*, London 1993. Otherwise: Çelik Gülersöy, *Ilhamur mesiresi*, Istanbul 1983; *Küçücksu: Meadow-Fountain-Palace*, Istanbul 1985 and *Dolmabahçe Palace and Its Environs*, Istanbul 1990.

35 Annette Gangler, *Ein traditionelles Wohnviertel im Nordosten der Altstadt von Aleppo in Nordsyrien*, Tübingen-Berlin 1993, pl. 84.

thus after the period discussed here. In the twenties and thirties, elaborate staircases became very popular, particularly in the modern quarters such as ʿAzīziyya. A good example of a 'French-mandate' staircase can be admired in the famous 'Villa Rose' near the municipal park.

Apart from the staircases, other elements are also reminiscent of late Ottoman palace architecture, such as the vases on top of the roof, replacing the statues seen in Europe. Another conspicuous feature is the decorative metal railing with pillars, which were mainly used to separate the residences from the water in Istanbul. Last, but not least, one should mention that the eclectic use of various styles – "Gothic," "Classical" and "Islamic" – was a feature very much present in late Ottoman architecture, too.[36]

Ottoman palace architecture in turn quite naturally drew from European architecture. The members of the architect family Balyan who were responsible for most late Ottoman palaces and mansions in Istanbul were strongly influenced by eighteenth and nineteenth century European buildings.[37] After all, Nikoghos Balyan (1826-58) and his brothers Agop (1837-75) and Sarkis (1835-99) were all educated at the Ecole des Beaux Arts in Paris and introduced many elements of the *fin de siècle* and classicism. To call Abū 'l-Hudā al-Ṣayyādī's house a European building, however, would be much too superficial. With his *zāwiya* and especially with the stately mansions on the front side, Abū 'l-Hudā tried to evoke the architecture of the Ottoman capital, the palaces and the residences of the sultans – no doubt as an expression of his affiliation with the ruler and as a reference to himself as a person who had left for Istanbul. At the same time, Abū 'l-Hudā involuntarily demonstrates his position as an outsider in Aleppo. We can see through the architecture that the shaykh did not belong to the circles of the old families in town. For sure, quite a number of his contemporaries were anything but happy with Abū 'l-Hudā's pompous new house and the *zāwiya*. Al-Ṭabbākh was scathing:

> he who sees these buildings believes it is a castle of some rich people and not a *takiyya* which was built as a place of refuge for the 'poor' [that is Sufis].[38]

---

36 Numerous examples of this phenomenon can be found in Zeynep Çelik, *The Remaking of Istanbul. Portrait of an Ottoman City in the Nineteenth Century*, Seattle and London 1986.

37 Pars Tuğlacı, *The Role of the Balian Family in Ottoman Architecture*, Istanbul 1990.

38 Ṭabbākh, *Iʿlām al-nubalāʾ*, VIII, 588.

– VII –

The Ottoman Civilizing Mission

NINETEENTH CENTURY BAGHDAD THROUGH OTTOMAN EYES

CHRISTOPH HERZOG

Posing the question of how Baghdad was seen by the Ottomans is methodologically related to the analysis of Ottoman history writing. More generally speaking it is a matter of second-order-historiography dealing not with how things were, but with how things were seen. It should be noted, however, that this second-order-perspective does not enjoy any epistemological privileges over ordinary historiography. If we accept that Ranke's option to describe "how things really were" ("wie es eigentlich gewesen ist") is *not* one that can be possibly accomplished because the very notion of historiography bears in itself the oxymoron of history and writing, i.e. of reality and discourse (as Michel de Certeau has pointed out),[1] then this has to apply in the same way to the historiography of historiography. In other words: the reconstruction of "how things were seen" is not, and cannot possibly be, closer to reality than the reconstruction of "how things were". This applies regardless of the additional differentiation of history-writing into positivist narration and the construction of analytical frameworks.

Yet, I believe that the question of how Baghdad was seen by the Ottomans is important in at least two respects:

First of all, it may be regarded as a first step preceding the analysis of "how things were" as it focuses on the sources themselves rather than trying to assume them to be a mere looking glass which provides historical factuality. By carving out narrative structures and cultural bias inherent in these texts it may be possible to achieve a more precise view of historical facts by making a more critical use of the sources.

Second, it may contribute to a better understanding of the nature of Ottoman government in Iraq. More specifically it may provide arguments to the question if or in how far the Ottoman government in Baghdad (and by implication elsewhere in the Arab world) may be meaningfully interpreted as a colonial one. Much of the outcome of this second issue, of course, depends on the conception of colonialism. Without going too much into

1 Michel de Certeau, *Das Schreiben der Geschichte,* Frankfurt 1991, 9.

detail I would like to refer to the definition of colonialism given by the German historian Jürgen Osterhammel:

> *Colonialism* is a relationship of domination between an indigenous (or forcibly) imported majority and a minority of foreign invaders. The fundamental decisions affecting the lives of the colonized people are made and implemented by the colonial rulers in pursuit of interests that are often defined in a distant metropolis. Rejecting cultural compromises with the colonized population, the colonizers are convinced of their own superiority and of their ordained mandate to rule.[2]

While the Ottoman province of Baghdad (*Bağdad vilayeti*) was surely a colony according to the most general definition given by Osterhammel it is a much more complex question whether one can meaningfully describe the Ottoman rule in Iraq as colonial in the sense proposed by him in terms of illegitimate rule, cultural difference of *rulers* and *ruled* and formation of a colonialist consciousness or ideology as important parameters.[3] While the questions of cultural difference and colonial consciousness or ideology may well be approached on the basis of Ottoman source material, the question of legitimacy or illegitimacy of Ottoman rule in Baghdad must remain excluded from the present consideration.

There is, however, an additional question that has to be touched on before delving into the matter: How do I use the term 'Ottoman' in the present context? Was Baghdad in the nineteenth century Ottoman? The answer can only be that 'Ottoman' here means the perspective from the imperial center to the periphery as represented in the genuine Ottoman terms of *Derseadet* vs. *taşra*. It does not involve any ethnic definition nor does it preclude, as will be seen, the possibility that an offspring of a local family and native of Baghdad could have taken that perspective. In other words the notion of "Ottoman" I employ here describes a cultural cluster whose boundaries necessarily must remain ill defined. This is, however, not to say that the Ottomans themselves, Istanbulis or else, did not perceive Baghdad as belonging to the well-protected domains of the Empire and thereby as being Ottoman.

---

2 Jürgen Osterhammel, *Colonialism. A Theoretical Overview. Translated from German by Shelly L. Fritsch*, Princeton 1997, 16. The German original quotation in idem, *Kolonialismus. Geschichte, Formen, Folgen*, München 1995, 21.

3 *Ibid.*, 19f. Osterhammel in fact seems to deny the colonialist character of Ottoman rule in the Arab provinces of the Empire; cf. ibid. 19 and 42. This view is contradicted, however, by John Ruedy in his review of the English translation of Osterhammel's study in question in *IJMES* 30 (1998), 588-590.

Proverbial Epistemologies

Before I will present several writings on Baghdad and Mesopotamia by Ottoman authors dating from the second half of the nineteenth to the first decade of the twentieth centuries, I want to draw attention to the astonishing fact that Turkish proverbs seem to mention Baghdad more often than any other city including Mekka.[4] Baghdad is used mainly as a metaphor for distance or a distant place as in "to the lover, Baghdad is not far off".[5] However, there is another usage in which Baghdad figures as a metaphor of value like in "oppression ruins even Baghdad" or "there is no love like a mother's, and no city like Baghdad". It is interesting to note, that the same combination of remoteness and the vague notion of greatness, importance or value appears – less frequently – in the case of Egypt.[6] Although it is true that these proverbs do not take as their theme the city of Baghdad as such but merely use it as an exchangeable metaphor[7], the very fact that they mention Baghdad so frequently indicates a strong presence of that city as a cliché in the common mind. It is, of course, impossible to tell exactly whose common mind we are talking about, i.e. who knew and used these proverbs but I can find no reasonable objection to the assumption that they were known in the urban milieu of nineteenth century Istanbul thus forming some kind of popular Ottoman notion of Baghdad or rather a popular connotation which, even if not evoked, may have been stored in the memories of those reading or writing in the Ottoman Turkish language on that latter city.[8]

---

4 Cf. Mustafa Nihat Özön, *Ata Sözleri*, Istanbul 1956, index of places on 320f. He lists 13 proverbs which make mention of Baghdad, Mekka has only 10, Egypt 7, Istanbul 4. This tendency is confirmed by another collection: Metin Yurtbaşı, *Türkisches Sprichwörterlexikon*, Ankara 1993. Baghdad here occurs in 14 proverbs, Mekka in five, Egypt in 3 and Istanbul in two. There are, of course, other places mentioned, but their frequency ranges below Baghdad and Mekka.

5 This has been already observed by Longrigg. Cf. Stephen Hemsley Longrigg, *'Iraq, 1900 to 1950. A Political, Social, And Economic History*, Oxford 1953, 1.

6 E.g.: "Venedik'ten tiryak gelinceye kadar Mısır'da adamı yılan helâk eder" and "Sev seni seveni yer ile yeksan ise – Sevme seni sevmeyen: Mısır'a sultan ise," cf. Özön, *Ata sözleri*, Nos. 7966 and 7171.

7 There are variations in which Baghdad is replaced by some other place, e.g. "You need only to have honey then the flees come from Baghdad" (*Balın olsun tek, sinek Bağdad'dan gelir*) or "If you have honey in your pot the bees come from Yemen" (*Çanakta balın olsun, Yemen'den arı gelir*). Yurtbaşı, *Sprichwörterlexikon*, 273.

8 Many of the proverbs listed by Özön were originally collected by nineteenth century Ottoman intellectuals, e.g. by Şinasi and Ahmed Vefik Paşa. Cf. Özön, *Ata Sözleri*, vff.

Encyclopedic Knowledge

In his six-volume *Ḳāmūs al-aʿlām* the famous lexicographer Şemseddin Sami Fraşeri, (1850-1904)[9] reserved four columns of information on the city of Baghdad.[10] According to him, Baghdad was one of the most famous and one of the biggest cities of Ottoman Asia (*Asya-yı osmaniye*). He estimated the number of its inhabitants between 125.000 and 130.000, mostly Muslim, half of them Sunni the others Shiites. From the ethnical point of view, he described them as being of the Arab, Turkish, Persian and Kurdish race (*cinsiyet*). The local language, he claimed, was in the first instance Turkish and in the second Arabic. As it is hard to believe that the majority of the population of Baghdad actually spoke Turkish as their main language, Şemseddin's statement must be seen as reflecting the claim to prevalence of the official Ottoman language over the local idiom.

The general impression of the city especially along the shores of the Tigris was a beautiful one and the houses made of clay brick were pretty, he wrote, although, as they were mostly surrounded by walls and situated in gardens, their beauty was not visible from outside. He criticized, however, the narrow and dirty streets of Baghdad, which were not a welcome sight. After mentioning the multitude of mosques and listing some the many mausoleums of Islamic Sheikhs and imams Şemseddin Sami did not fail to declare that the palace of the government (*hükumet konağı*) was "among the largest and most beautiful buildings of the city" and to list the achievements of Ottoman modernization in Baghdad: a dock for building ships and a reformatory (*ıslahane*), the "Oman-Ottoman" governmental steamboat company with its twelve ships, the horse-tramway to Kazimayn built by Midhat Pasha, a printing office, several military and civil schools and a hospital. "A large school opened by a rich Jewish merchant" is mentioned, while the ones maintained by Christian missionaries are passed over with silence. Baghdad, wrote Sami, was one of the Ottoman cities that were "most active in commercial matters" with a local production of textiles and metal ware and continuous (*daimi*) connections with India (via Basra), Iran, Mosul, Diyarbekir, Aleppo and Damascus.

---

9 For his biography cf. Agâh Sırrı Levend, *Çemsettin Sami*, Ankara 1969.

10 Ş. Sami, *Ḳāmūs ül-aʿlām. Tārīh ve coğrafya lugatını ve tabir-i essahla kâffe-i esmâ-i hassayı câmi'dir*, vol. 2, Istanbul 1307, 1324-1328. As a comparison, the article on Istanbul in the same volume comprises almost 16, that on Bursa ("one of the biggest and most beautiful cities in Anatolia", *ibid.* p. 1294) somewhat less than four columns.

The Omniscient Ottoman Travel-Writers

Everyone did not share this bright vision of Baghdad as a basically picturesque, modern and industrious Ottoman city. There are striking examples of a marked Ottoman dislike for Baghdad and a sharp criticism of its population. Baghdad, to be sure, was not among the favorite provincial places an Ottoman official was likely to be sent to.[11] In 1862 the *Seyahatname-i hudud* by Mehmed Hurşid (d. 1879) was lithographed in Istanbul.[12] Hurşid had been accompanying Derviş Pasha, who was sent to the Ottoman-Iranian border as the Ottoman commissioner according to the stipulations of the Treaty of Erzurum (1847). He had been instructed by the Ottoman government to collect as much information on the region as possible. The *Seyahatname-i hudud* was a result of this four-year field research and was written down after 1851.[13] It contains detailed information on the regions of Basra, Baghdad, Şehrizor, Mosul, Van and Bayezid.

In a chapter on the population of Baghdad Hurşid Efendi distinguished four classes (*sunûf*): (1) the ʿulamāʾ, (2) the notables and the remaining Mamluks, (3) the merchants and craftsmen and (4) those living of casual work (*aylakçılık*). While he had not much to say about the merchants and craftsmen (to which he added the peasants) except that they were pursuing their work, and not much more on the notables and Mamluks he did not spare some critical remarks on the *ʿulamāʾ* and the casual workers. The *ʿulamāʾ* of Baghdad, according to him, generally lacked religious knowledge and professional seriousness[14] (but he made some exceptions among them the author of the *tafsīr rūḥ al-maʿānī*, Abū-l-Thanāʾ Maḥmūd al-

11 Cf. Yusuf Fehmi, *Paris'te Türkler. Casusluk ve karşıcasusluk.* Yayına Hazırlayan: Ergun Hiçyılmaz. Istanbul, n.y., 11. and Longrigg, *'Iraq, 1900 to 1950*, 2.

12 Mehmed Hurşid Efendi, *Seyahatname-i hudud*, Istanbul 1862. A transliteration by Alâattin Esser (Istanbul 1997); a Russian translation by M.A. Gamazov, *Siyachet-name-i chudud. Opisanic putešestvija po tureckoj-persidskoj granice sostovi' Churšid-Efendi*, Petersburg 1877. The work was extensively used by ʿAbbās al- ʿAzzāwī in the seventh volume of his *Tārīḫ al-ʿIrāq bayn iḥtilālayn*. Cf. *ibid.*, 5 for some biographical information of Mehmed Hurşid. A translation into Arabic was printed in Bagdad 1953; *ibid.*, 6.

13 *Ibid.*, 6.

14 "[...] *bu kısmın hoş sohbetleri çok ve ulema diyecek yokdur.*" Hurşid, *Seyahatname*, 77.

Ālūsī (1802-1854)[15] while the casual workers, he said, were wasting their lifetimes gambling in the coffee houses.[16]
The *Seyahatname-i hudūd* was a rather official report drawn up on governmental instruction and destined for governmental use. But the time for European-style Ottoman travel literature composed for a broader readership in Istanbul was soon to come.

Ottoman Journalism and Imperial Narratives of Development

Ahmed Midhat Efendi (1844-1913), the famous Ottoman writer and intellectual, stayed in Baghdad for more than two years from 1869 while his patron Midhat Pasha was governor of the province. He edited the official provincial newspaper *Zevra*, which was the first newspaper to be printed in Iraq. In his autobiographical book *Menfa* (Exile) he later described Baghdad as a mousetrap for many an Ottoman official:

> If the river Tigris brings the Baghdad-bound voyagers easily down to that place. As it does not so in the opposite direction, Baghdad, in my view, resembles the fisherman's net or the mouse trap, where it is easy to get in but hard to get out. This, my comparison is very apt to reality. Because there have been quite a lot of men who came to Baghdad on behalf of Ottoman affaires or by appointment to a [provincial] position [there] and have been unable to rescue themselves [from there]. [17]

After Ahmed Midhat managed to escape this "mouse trap" and to return to the capital he published a series of articles on Baghdad in the important Istanbul newspaper *Basiret*.[18] After a description of his journey to Baghdad[19] he offered his readers some basic information on the city. The part of Baghdad on the right of the river bank, he told them, was called Rusafe (Ruṣāfa) the part on the left bank Kerh (Karkh), the nearby towns of Aᶜzamiye (Aᶜẓamiyya) and Kazimiye (Kāẓimiyya), he assured them, were

---

15 For him s. *EI*², "al-Ālūsī" (H. Péres), 425. More details offers Muḥammad Bahğat al-Atharī, *Aᶜlām al-ᶜIrāq,* Cairo 1345, 21-43.

16 Hurşid, *Seyahatname*, 77 and 79.

17 Ahmed Midhat, *Menfa*, ed. İsmail Cüneyt Kut, Istanbul 1988; first ed. Istanbul 1293 A.H.], 43.

18 For *Basiret* cf. Īlhan Yerlikaya, *XIX. Yüzyıl Osmanlı Siyasi Hayatında Basiret Gazetesi ve Pancermenizm - Panislamizm - Panslavizm - Osmanlıcılık Fikirleri*, Van 1994. (Yüzüncü Yıl Üniversitesi Fen-Edebiyat Yaınları 14).

19 Ahmed Midhat, "Bağdad'dan avdet", *Basiret* No. 345 (1871).

considered as quarters (*mahalle*) of Baghdad.[20] He added some information on the number of the city's inhabitants (comprising 18.407 *hane*'s and amounting to 63.272 male persons). He pointed out that the city was far less spacious than the number of inhabitants suggested. As the houses were small and close to one another and the streets quite narrow the area of Baghdad did not exceed that of provincial towns in Rumelia as for example Rusçuk (Ruşe) or Vidin. As for the aesthetic impression of the city, he remarked that while the gardens of Baghdad were magnificent the houses looked like buildings spared by a fire because, according to his words, "the people did not quite enjoy the pleasures of civilization and prosperity".[21]

In the next issue of *Basiret*[22] Ahmed Midhat delved deeper into the characterization of the population of Baghdad. His perspective on the Baghdadis was divided into three points of interest: knowledge (*maarif*), craft (*sanat*) "which lie at the origin of economic activity (*ticaret*) and agriculture (*zıraat*)" and morals (*ahlak*). "It is known by everybody that Baghdad was the source of many arts", he declares. But today there was no trace of all this knowledge left, so he contends, nor did the population of Baghdad show any enthusiasm for learning. They regarded "it almost a humiliation to stoop so low as to study" he muses. According to Ahmed Midhat the Baghdadis did not only lack knowledge but also skills in craft (*sanat*). No knowledge no crafts; one could resume his opinion on the reasons hereof. Interestingly he adds another reason: As there were so many industrious (*çalışkan*) Iranians in Baghdad, there was hardly opportunity for the populace of Baghdad to engage in crafts. If now the Baghdadis possessed neither knowledge nor skills in crafts, he continues, one would expect them to starve because, as commonly known, most people lived on knowledge and crafts as well as on commerce and agriculture, the latter two being the fruits of the former two. In fact, he assures, the Baghdadis practiced some kind of agriculture but they did so only as contractors of public revenues (*mültezim*). The farmers as the ones actually working were content, he claims, if they were allowed to keep at least ten percent of the harvest. Ahmed Midhat sees the Baghdadis' occupation with the business of *iltizam* as the main reason why they were but little inclined to study or practice the crafts.

On the morals or manners of the population of Baghdad he tells his readers as follows:

---

20 Ahmed Midhat, "Bağdad seyahatnamesinden maba'd numero 345. Bağdad'da ikamet", *Basiret*, No. 348 (1871).

21 *Ibid.*

22 Ahmed Midhat, "Bağdad seyahatnamesinden maba'd numero 348. Bağdad'da ikamet", *Basiret* 349 (16 Nisan 1287 / 8 Safer 1288) [=29.4.1871]).

> What concerns the general morals of the Baghdadis [...] I must say that I do not know about it. This my word shall not arouse surprise and displeasure. I tell the truth. It is very difficult to know the common morals in Bagdad. I shall give only one example: In the common decency of our lands there is something called modesty (*tevâzuʿ*) and is held in esteem. Thus, if someone who knows how to behave goes somewhere and finds the upper seats (i.e. the seats reserved for persons in high position) [partly] occupied by others, he contents himself with one of the lower places. And if the ones sitting [in the higher places] as friendly people do not regard the place he has taken adequate to his position and by the words "Sir, please come over here" propose him that he might sit down on a more prestigious place the person will articulate that he is satisfied with the place he has taken. This person's behaviour is not artificial, but by nature his mind is in harmony with the way he behaves.
> Instead of this our modesty you will find a completely different tradition in Baghdad. If in Baghdad a man goes somewhere and finds the place that is adequate to his grandeur or a place that is even more prestigious occupied by someone else then he says 'I have this or that position' (*faziletlüyüm*) or 'I am from this or that family' (*falan zadeyim*) und almost forces those sitting there to stand up und he sits down himself. When once a member of the council of the province realized somebody sitting on a seat reserved for a person of high position and the one sitting there did not accept his being told to stand up he immediately came over and sat himself down on the other person's lap so that a major incident was arising.[23]

This depiction of the Baghdadis as people who do not know how to behave is seemingly taken back by Ahmed Midhat with the concluding remark that it would be too difficult to explain the obvious differences in manners. However, it can be easily imagined what his Ottoman readers in Istanbul were thinking of these differences. After his return from Baghdad (at the beginning of 1871), Ahmed Midhat tried to make use of his professional achievements as an editor of two official Ottoman provincial newspapers (*Tuna* in Bulgaria and *Zevra* in Baghdad) in order to establish himself as a successful journalist in the Ottoman capital. It is obvious that his depiction of Baghdad and the peculiarities of its inhabitants were done in a style that today would be termed "edutainment" and was to be taken *cum grano salis* to say the least. However, his verdict of 1871 against the Baghdadis was repeated almost forty years later by a native son of this city, who after

23 *Ibid.*

graduating from the *Mülkiye* school with considerable success embarked on a political career in Istanbul, Babanzade İsmail Hakkı (1876-1913).[24]

The Trope of Return

İsmail Hakkı, descendant from a noble family of Kurdish origin, member of the Ottoman parliament (representing Baghdad) and for a short time minister of public instruction in the cabinet of Hakkı Paşa, came back to Baghdad during a journey from Aleppo to Basra at the beginning of November 1909 after having been away for twenty two years. He wrote on this journey in his "Letters from Iraq" (*Irak mektubları*) that were serialized in an Ottoman newspaper, in parts translated into French[25] and also published as a book.[26]

Coming from Aleppo, İsmail Hakkı, entered Baghdad by horse cart. He describes how the golden dome of Kazimiyya was shining in the bright sunlight like a second sun and how the domes and minarets of hundreds of mosques of this city, which, as he does not fail to mention, was for many centuries the seat of the caliphate, induced religious feelings. While those parts of Karkh situated further off from the river bank with their gardens und huts made of mud resembled an Arab village, the parts of the quarter being closer to the river bank looked much more urban. At the head of the bridge connecting Karkh and Ruṣāfa the passengers had to descend the horse cart and continue on foot as the pontoon bridge was not fit for being crossed by carts – a fact that is hardly acceptable to the Ottoman politician İsmail Hakkı.[27] He also criticizes that the streets of Baghdad were generally too narrow to allow the use of carts and sometimes even for pack animals, and he emphasizes the necessity of broadening the streets regardless of the Baghdadis' complaints against such measures. Assuring that such measures would have to remain strictly within the limits of legal provisions, he depicts a vision of nineteenth century European urbanity applied to Baghdad:

> One may say what one wishes, but it has by now become a most urgent duty (farzül'ayn) to syringe air and oxygen meaning life and health, to the

24 For his biography cf. *Yeni Mülkiye Tarihi*, vol 2, p. 996 and Sabine Prätor, *Der arabische Faktor in der jungtürkischen Politik. Eine Studie zum osmanischen Parlament der II. Konstitution (1908-1918)*, Berlin 1993, 264.

25 "De Stamboul à Bagdad. Notes d'un homme d'état turc," *Revue du Monde Muselman* 14 (1911), 185-296. This translation does not give the entire text of the Ottoman original.

26 Babanzade İsmail Hakkı, *Irak mektubları*, Istanbul, 1329.

27 *Ibid*, 109f.

> two hundred thousand inhabitants of Baghdad, who in these narrow streets suffer without knowing it from a state of continuous suffocation, by the means of wide, clean streets under shadowy trees, embellished here and there by water basins, fountains and parks.[28]

It is noteworthy that the memories of his childhood spent in Baghdad, although important enough for him to deserve mention in his description of the city, do not seem to involve the sort of personal nostalgia that would make him express the wish to preserve the city as it was. The idea of progress is prevalent with him. It is also remarkable that his Baghdadi roots do not prevent him from publicly expressing sharp criticism of the city's populace. One of their main social activities was to gather in cafés. "In no place in the world," he declares, "are the cafés as crowded as in Baghdad. As a matter of fact, the whole of Baghdad is one huge café."[29] The only activity of the Baghdadis, he goes on, was to sit in cafés or to pay and receive visits. But in contrast to the *mecālis* in Abbasid times these gatherings were not, according to İsmail Hakkı, , dedicated to the discussion of literature and science but to evil minded gossip and idle talk.

> In this ancient city that used to be the home of knowledge and arts you cannot hear today any talk on crafts, or commerce, or literature. Because there is no commerce, no craft and no knowledge. Because the population from its highest to its lowest member is idle and ignorant (*boş*). Because they have absolutely no idea of the value of what is called time.[30]

Although İsmail Hakkı's characterization of the Baghdadi population seems hardly less critical than the one given by Ahmed Midhat there is an important difference. Contrary to Ahmed Midhat, İsmail Hakkı, in his representation of the Baghdadis does not exploit any "cultural" difference for the amusement of his readers. It would appear far-fetched to attribute this difference exclusively to assumed inside or outside positions of the two authors vis-à-vis the Baghdadis. But it nevertheless seems important to keep this difference in mind. It is important to note that the chapter on Baghdad and its population is missing in the French translation published in the *Revue du Monde Musulman* and authorized by İsmail Hakkı. One may well speculate that he deemed his utterances on this topic not suitable

---

28 *Ibid.*, 111f. This theme is elaborated in the following chapter "*Bağdad'ın kabiliyet-i umraniyesi*" (ibid, pp. 119-129) which is also available in the French translation as "*Bagdad et ses possibilités d'avenir*" (pp. 217-222).

29 *Ibid.*, 114.

30 *Ibid.*, 115f.

for a European audience. Even so he met with sharp criticism in the Istanbul-based opposition newspaper *Teminat* that saw him unfit to represent Baghdad as a member of the Ottoman parliament.[31]

The existence of different stories for different audiences is a phenomenon often observed with Middle Eastern authors (but of course by no means limited exclusively to them).[32] One may assume that more often than not this was an unconscious process of shifting emphasis rather than a deliberate forging of the story. An interesting example may be found in the different versions Ali Haydar Midhat Bey had published of his father's biography, the famous Ottoman reformer and politician Midhat Pasha. As the history of these texts ("Textgeschichte") is somewhat complicated, I will summarize the explanation given by Ali Haydar: While in exile and under surveillance in Taif, Midhat Pasha clandestinely wrote his memoirs. A part of them he secretly sent to his family, which was then banished to Izmir. When his son Ali Haydar much later (after having escaped to England) published the book *The Life of Midhat Pasha* (London 1903) he made use of this manuscript but adding to it further information from other sources. Midhat Pasha, unable to receive confirmation of whether the copy had duly arrived at its destination, had the other parts of it copied twice while keeping the original. When Sultan Abdülhamid II had him strangled, this text fell into the hands of his executioners and was most probably sent to the Yıldız palace. One of the two copies was lost, the other, however, survived and was removed from its hiding place after the restoration of the constitution in July 1908. Ali Haydar used parts of it in his two-volume Turkish version on *Midhat Pasha*.[33] In addition in 1908 a French version of the biography of Midhat was published.[34] The text given in the three books, however, differs considerably. Thus the story of Midhat's governorship in Baghdad (1869-1873) was treated much more briefly in the English and French versions than in the Ottoman. But this is not the only

---

31 Prätor, *Faktor*, 17.

32 Cf. Fazlur Rahman, "Islamic Modernism: Its Scope, Method and Alternatives," *IJMES* 1 (1970), 317-333.

33 Cf. the introduction "Bir kaç söz" of Ali Haydar Midhat, *Midhat Paşa. Hayat-i siyasiyesi, hidematı, menfa hayatı*, vol. 1, Istanbul: Helal Matbaası, 1325. There are even more versions. Cf. Roderic H. Davison, *Reform in the Ottoman Empire 1856-1876*, Princeton 1963, 449 and EI², "Midḥat Pasha" (R.H. Davison).

34 Ali Haydar Midhat Bey, *Midhat Pacha. Sa vie - son oeuvre*. Préface de Monsieur J.-L. de Lanessan, ancien ministre de la marine. Paris 1908.

difference. In the English version (the French one being practically identical here)[35] one reads:

> (47) Hardly the new Vali [i.e. Midhat Pasha (C.H.)] reached his post, when he found himself confronted with some difficult problems of quite a different order from those he had dealt with on the Danube, but of a not less serious description. The question of recruiting was the most urgent, and called for immediate solution. The Arab tribes, turbulent and independent by nature, had always shown themselves refractory (48) to enlistment, and were now in open revolt against its enforcement. One of the difficulties of the situation consisted in the fact that the military authority in the province was separated from the civil, and was in the hands of the commander of the 6th Army Corps, Samih Pasha, whereas the situation required all authority, military as well as civil, to be concentrated in the hands of a single strong central authority. Midhat did not hesitate at such a crisis to assume the full responsibility of this concentration, and took immediate military steps to suppress the insurrection by force. He ordered the city of Bagdad to be surrounded by cavalry, and sent infantry and artillery to protect the foreign Mission Houses and the non-Mussulman quarters from the fanaticism of the Arabs. At the same time he ordered the bridge over the Tigris to be cut, so as to prevent intercommunication among the rebels; and when these energetic measures had rather intimidated the Arabs, he offered them a general amnesty on condition of immediate surrender. These conditions were now accepted, and the insurrection suddenly collapsed, and no further resistance was offered to the recruiting. [36]

It is remarkable that the offenders are characterized not only as "Arabs" but that hardly any difference is made between the inhabitants of Baghdad and the Arab tribes. While this may be partly justified by the fact that many of the Baghdadis in the nineteenth century were indeed of tribal origin, the argument in the given contexts nevertheless lacks differentiation to the degree that not only the difference between urban und rural but as well between settled and nomadic Arabs is ignored. This means that Baghdad in this depiction is not admitted a genuine urban character. To be sure, Ali Haydar does not deny the great past of the country. When he discusses the measures of his father regarding the restoration of the irrigation system he explicitly mentions that they were designed

---

35 *Ibid.*, 16. In general the French text is much closer to the English version than to the Ottoman.

36 Ali Haydar Midhat Bey: *The Life of Midhat Pasha. A Record of His Services, Political Reforms, Banishment, and Judicial Murder Derived From Private Documents and Reminiscences*. London 1903 [reprint: New York 1973], 47f.

> with a view to gradually restoring the system introduced by the first Arab conquerors, which had converted this country into the Garden of the East, and rendered the Caliphate of Bagdad proverbial for its wealth and prosperity.[37]

The view of the glorious Arabs of the past on one side and the "refractory Arab tribes", as opposed to the "Turkish authorities"[38] of the present times, on the other were two stereotypes co-existing independently from each other in Ottoman as well as in contemporary European minds of the late nineteenth and early twentieth century at a time when the question of Arab and Turkish nationalism was well under way. It is remarkable, however, that the Ottoman version of the story completely avoids any reference to "Arabs" not to speak of "Arab tribes". Instead it is stated that the Turkish regiments that until now had formed the sixth army corps were to be exchanged and should be quite naturally replaced by people from the Iraq. It is further mentioned that it had been not possible until now to recruit soldiers (by casting of lots: *kur'a*) in Baghdad proper and its surroundings.[39] The leaders of the revolt against the recruitment are simply called "leaders of the rebellion" (erbab-i ihtilal) while the cause of the revolt is admitted to have been the fact that the recruitment was against the wishes of the people and that enforcing it created widespread dissatisfaction.[40]

Even if the story described is roughly the same the connotations conveyed by the two texts are completely different. Again it is purely speculative but not entirely meaningless to assume that Ali Haydar while writing in a European language for a European audience used ethnonyms like "Turk" and "Arab" just as a concession to presumed European categories. It is also possible that in the Ottoman version he relied on formulations of his father while those of the English version were his own or that of an English aide. In any case in 1909 when the Turkish version of *Midhat's Life* was published there existed an Arab-Turkish question, which had not been publicly debated during the times of Abdülhamid II. İsmail Hakkı, in his "Letters from Iraq" of that same year, dedicated a whole chapter to the refutation of the authenticity of

---

37 *Ibid*, 51. Here again the French version is identical. Cf. Ali Haydar Midhat Bey, *Midhat-Pacha*, 17.

38 *Ibid*, 52.

39 *Ibid*, 67.

40 *Ibid*, 68.

the said question, representing the official Ottoman point of view in claiming that it was a mere invention of irresponsible elements.[41] Things however, were not that simple.

Imperial Discourses of Civilization

Osman Hamdi (1842-1910),[42] the famous Ottoman archeologist, painter and museologist, son of the important Ottoman modernizer Edhem Pasha, was called in 1869 by Midhat Pasha from Paris to Iraq, where he was supposed to study law but in fact had dedicated himself to the fine arts, in order to serve as the vilayet's director of foreign affaires (*vilayet umur-i ecnebiyye müdiri*). Osman Hamdi accepted and, together with a group that included Ahmed Midhat, travelled via Diyarbekir to Baghdad.[43] From Baghdad he wrote several letters to his father, nine of which were edited by Edhem Eldem.[44] The language he used in his letters was French. An admirer of Midhat Pasha and, to all appearances, seriously dedicated to his job he nevertheless seems to have disliked the city[45] and he was highly critical of its people. In his letter dated 29th August 1869 he wrote:

> Plus calme que la semaine dernière, je vais tâcher aujourd'hui, d`être moins chaleureux et vous faire voir l'affaire sous son vrai jour en essayant de vous décrire d'abord ce peuple arabe, vous initier en un mot à son caractère et à son degré de civilisation : S'il en a une!
> Il ne faut nullement nous occuper des habitants des grandes villes d'ici et principalement de ceux de Bagdad : ceux-là, quoique préferables d'apparence aux peuplades du désert puisqu'ils n'habitent plus la tente et qu'ils ont un cachet quelconque d'homme du XIXe siècle, ceux-là, dis-je, sont mille fois en réalité au dessous du bédouin car si celui-ci mène une vie primitive et patriarchale l'autre en mène une corrompue et infame à tel point que dans tout Bagdad et principalement parmi ceux qui servent le gouvernement vous ne trouverez pas un homme honnête! Quant aux

41 İsmail Hakkı, *Irak mektubları*, 47ff.

42 For his biography cf. Mustafa Cezar, *Sanatta Batı'ya Açılış ve Osman Hamdi*, Istanbul 1971.

43 Ahmed Midhat, *Menfa*, 33.

44 Edhem Eldem, "Quelques lettres d'Osman Hamdi Bey à son père lors de son séjour en Iraq (1869-1870)," *Anatolia Moderna* 1 (1991), 115-136.

45 Thus he applied for a governmental position in Bombay where he hoped to be better off: "Bombay est aujourd'hui une ville Européen[n]e. [...] Ma position sera là plus indépendante mieux payé, et j'y viverai [sic!] mieux que *dans ce diable de Bagdad*." Emphasis is mine, letter dated 20th April 1870; *ibid.*, 134f.

> négociants : celui réputé le plus honorable et le plus honnête serait, en France, [envoyé] tout droit aux galères.[46]

The message is clear – and not very different from what could be expected from contemporary Europeans: A fundamental alterity between observer and indigenes is constructed by dividing the latter into two classes: the (relatively) noble savages and the morally corrupted townspeople. The former are uncivilized because they are "primitive" and the latter because they, despite their outwardly civilized appearance, fail to meet the moral standards to which civilization is implicitly connected. The urban Arabs thus lack authenticity. The real Arab is the Bedouin. For Osman Hamdi – as for Ahmed Midhat[47] – it is the task of the Ottoman government to civilize him. It proves the progressist stance of Osman Hamdi that he frankly admits the failure of the Ottoman provincial administration before Midhat Pasha:

> Cette population donc presque nomade et pour ainsi dire vierge encore n'a le défaut que d'avoir été continuellement persecutée et ecrasée par tous les membres du gouvernement depuis le plus grand jusqu'au plus petit des fonctionnaires. Elle est intelligente, probe courageuse et vaillante. Croyez-vous que l'Arabe ait fait un pas vers la civilisation et le progrès? Non! Car jusqu'ici tous les gouverneurs à la exeption de Rechid Pacha n'ont pensé qu'à augmenter les revenus du trésor non pas en développant l'industrie et le commerce ou bien en portant ici une bonne administration et des institutions capables d'enrichir la population [...].[48]

At the same time this criticism of the Ottoman administration is an expression of the intermediate position of the *mission civilisatrice ottomane*. The standards of civilization that were to be applied in the province of Baghdad were not homegrown ones. The ultimate measure was the European metropolis and Osman Hamdi, newly arrived from Paris, must have been acutely aware of that. He even explicitly acknowledged it: the abovementioned "honest" merchants of Baghdad were in reality dishonest according to the standards of Paris – not of Istanbul.

By education and personality Osman Hamdi may be considered an extraordinary case. Nevertheless his example makes it clear that Muslim Ottoman "ethnic" categorizing vis-à-vis the Arab provinces was not a late

---

46 *Ibid.*, 129f.

47 Cf. eg. his article "Irak'ın esbab-i tedennisi ve vesail-i terakkisi", *Zevra* 3 (Salı 19 Rebiülevvel 1287), 5f.

48 Edhem, *Quelques lettres*, 130.

product of the beginning twentieth century. Yet it may be argued that since he used the French language he automatically used ethnic categories alien to Muslim Ottoman thinking. There is, however, ample evidence that these categories were present in the Middle Eastern discourse since pre-modern times.[49] This does not preclude that they may have changed their significance. In fact they have. When the Ottoman army officer Mehmed Emin [Yurdakul] in 1917 published his poems celebrating the war in Mesopotamia and the Turkish-Arabic brotherhood he spoke of the two different races of Turks and Arabs in a definitely modern way that was unthinkable before the nineteenth century but would possibly not even have met with approval from Ahmed Midhat, Osman Hamdi or İsmail Hakkı Babanzade.[50]

In any case, Baghdad and Mesopotamia remained some kind of unknown and exotic place for most Istanbulī Ottomans of the nineteenth century which fact in turn formed an excellent reason for those having seen it to write about their experiences.

Domesticating the Exotic

Ali Bey (1844-1899),[51] a writer and official of the "Dette Publique" who traveled from Istanbul via Mesopotamia to India in 1884/88 published an illustrated description of the lands he had visited – notably of Iraq and India. In a short notice at the beginning of his book he remarked that:

> The contents of this report consist only of what has been seen. If it has any value it lies in the fact that it gives a concise idea of the circumstances and the customs of far off countries like Iraq and especially of some cities of India which are unkown here.
> Places that were only seen as panoramas while passing and of those that may be assumed to be known by everyone, of course, were deemed sufficient to be mentioned only by name.[52]

---

49 Cf. eg. Ulrich W. Haarmann, "Ideology and History, Identity and Alternity. The Arab Image of the Turk From the Abbasids to Modern Egypt," *IJMES* 20 (1988), 175-196. Of course it is not intented here to pre-date nationalism before the nineteenth century.

50 Mehmed Emin, *Dicle önünde*, Istanbul 1332. Not only the text but also the illustrations of this booklet are instructive. Among other things they show Turkish soldiers in modern uniforms and Arab warriors in traditional garment.

51 For him cf. *Türk Dili ve Edebiyatı Ansiklopedisi*, vol. 1, Istanbul 1977, 109f.

52 Ali Bey, *Seyahat jurnalı. İstanbul'dan Bağdad'a ve Hindistan'a min sene 1300 ilâ sene 1304)*, Istanbul, 1314h, 2.

Obviously Baghdad was not counted by Ali Bey among those places known by everyone as he treated it extensively while for example Izmir and Aleppo were accorded just about one page respectively – roughly the same amount of text that he dedicated to the small town Tikrit on the Tigris.[53]

The fact that Ali Bey traveled to a land unknown and exotic to most of his Istanbuli readers should not lead us to ignore that a kind of Muslim solidarity which easily transgressed ethnic and linguistic borders and contributed to the relatively high spatial mobility of pre-modern Muslim societies was still existent in the nineteenth century: Like İsmail Hakkı three decades later Ali Bey too made his entrance to Baghdad coming from Aleppo. When he reached Aʿẓamiyya, named after Abū Ḥanīfa whose tomb is situated there, it was time for the Friday prayer in which he intended to participate. He describes that he was received hospitably, served with a meal and all means of comfort by the trustee of the *waqf* of the tomb of Abū Ḥanīfa, Numan Efendi, who – as Ali Bey particularly emphasizes – did not even know his name.[54]

Conclusion

It is of course impossible to undertake a reconstruction of the Ottoman discourse on Baghdad on the basis of merely a few texts. Even so, however, it would appear that a monolithic discourse simply did not exist.[55] It is interesting, however, that, by and large, Shiʿism remained excluded from that discourse and that the Ottomans seem to have ignored the fact that a substantial proportion of the population of Baghdad belonged to the Shii community. Thus, İsmail Hakkı did mention the dome of the shrine in Kāẓimayn but did not add any comments on the connection of this building with the Shiite creed although, already in the times of Abdülhamid II, the Ottoman government had begun to show some concern on the spread-

53 Parts of Ali Bey's description of Baghdad was put into modern Turkish by Şemseddin Kutlu and published as "Bağdad'ın Eski Günleri" in *Tarih Mecmuası* 10.2 (Şubat 1974), 26-33.

54 *Ibid.*, 61f.

55 This is much in line with the Dennis Porter's criticism of Edward Said's concept of a monolithic *orientalism* pervading all of Western thought on "the Orient". Cf. Dennis Porter, "Orientalism and its Problems," *Colonial Discourse and Post-Colonial Theory. A Reader*, ed. Patrick Williams and Laura Chrisman, New York 1993, 150-161.

ing of Shi^cism in the province.[56] But apparently this did not make its way into public discourse.

Baghdad was styled as a successful example of Ottoman modernization but at roughly the same time it served the appetites of an Istanbuli readership for exotic worlds. The Ottoman criticism of its inhabitants reflected as much metropolitan arrogance as it indicated the comparative underdevelopment of a provincial capital. Its arguments were, at least partly, informed by the basic social problems of Iraq.[57] But they included patterns that clearly may be termed colonial – if one does not decide to reserve the term "colonialism" exclusively to the European expansion[58] – such as the insistence on the ignorance of the Baghdadis. Not surprisingly this colonialist attitude becomes much more tangible vis-à-vis the tribal population of Iraq.[59] The Ottoman *mission civilisatrice* of the nineteenth century was an intermediate one. It received its standards from Europe but creatively modified their symbolism in accordance with its own needs.[60] The Ottoman perception of Baghdad even if deeply influenced by European concepts remained therefore distinctively Ottoman.

---

56 Cf. Yitzhak Nakash, "The Conversion of Iraq's Tribes to Shi'ism," *IJMES* 26 (1994), 443-463 and Selim Deringil, "The Struggle Against Shiism in Hamidian Iraq. A Study in Ottoman Counter-Progaganda," *WI* 30 (1990), 45-62; Gökhan Çetinsaya, *Ottoman Administration of Iraq, 1890-1908*, unpublished Ph.D. thesis, Manchester 1995.

57 For a recent analysis cf. Samira Haj, *The Making of Iraq 1900-1963. Capital, Power and Ideology*, Albany 1997.

58 A point of view that has been criticized as "one of the more prominent symptoms of the persistence of Wertern-centrism". Cf. Michael Adas, "Imperialism and Colonialism in Comparative Perspective," *IHR* 20.2 (June 1998), 371.

59 A good example is in Ahmed Midhat, "Bağdad seyahatnamesinden maba'd numero 349. Gelelim Irak'ın ahval-i umumiyesine," *Basiret* No. 355 (1871).

60 For a comprehensive account of this process cf. Selim Deringil, *The Well-Protected Domains. Ideology and the Legitimation of Power in the Ottoman Emire 1876-1909*, London etc. 1998 and idem, "The Invention of Tradition as Public Image in the Late Ottoman Empire, 1808-1908," *CSSH* 35.1 (Jan. 1993), 3-29.

ORDERING URBAN SPACE IN OTTOMAN YEMEN, 1872–1914[1]

THOMAS KÜHN

Over the past two decades research on the second period of Ottoman rule in Yemen, from 1849 to 1919, has largely concentrated on the conflict between the Ottoman authorities and the Zaydī Imāms and on the debate within the Ottoman bureaucratic elite around tightening the grip of the central government over this part of the empire.[2] While some of these studies shed light on important aspects of the conceptions that informed Ottoman rule in Yemen,[3] the *practices* of Ottoman rule over the empire's southernmost province have remained virtually unexplored. There is ample

---

1 For comments on earlier versions of this paper I am particularly grateful to Khaled Fahmy, Michael Gilsenan, Bernard Haykel, Zachary Lockman, and Paul Sedra (all at NYU) and to the participants of the symposium "Arab Provincial Capitals in the Late Ottoman Empire" (Beirut, April 26th-May 2nd 1999). Needless to say the responsibility for interpretations and mistakes is entirely my own.

2 See, for instance, Fārūq ʿUthmān Abāẓa, *Al-Ḥukm al-ʿUthmānī fī l-Yaman*, 2nd ed., Beirut 1979; John Baldry, "Al-Yaman and the Turkish Occupation, 1849–1914" *Arabica*, 23 (1976), 156-196; John Baldry, "Imām Yaḥyā and the Yamanī Uprising of 1904-1907," *Abr-Nahrain*, XVIII (1978-1979), 33-73; John Baldry, "Imām Yaḥyā and the Yamanī Uprising of 1911," *Annali dell'Istituto Universitario Orientale di Napoli*, 42 (1982), 425-459; Sayyid Muṣṭafā Sālim, *Takwīn al-Yaman al-Ḥadīth. Al-Yaman wa 'l-Imām Yaḥyā (1904-1948)*, Cairo 1971; Klaus Kreiser, "Abdulgani Seni (1871-1951) comme Observateur de l'Administration Ottomane au Yemen," *Revue d'histoire maghrébine*, 31-32 (1983), 315-319; Klaus Kreiser, "Abdülgani Seni – ein aufgeklärter Imperialist im Jemen (1909-1910)," *Jemen-Report,* 14.1 (1989), 11-15; Klaus Kreiser, "ʿAlī Emīrī (1858-1924) – ein türkischer Bürokrat und Intellektueller im Jemen," in *Studies in Oriental Culture and History. Festschrift für Walter Dostal*, eds. Andre Gingrich, Sylvia Haas, Frankfurt a. Main 1993, 199-221; Jon Mandaville, "Memduh Pasha and Aziz Bey: Ottoman Experience in Yemen," in *Contemporary Yemen: Politics and Historical Background*, ed. B. R. Pridham, London, Sydney 1984, 20-33; Michael Ursinus, "*Ṣanʿā'*. Eine amtliche osmanische Provinzzeitung im Jemen", in *Quellen zur Geschichte des Osmanischen Reiches und ihre Interpretation*, ed. Michael Ursinus, Istanbul 1994, 165-181.

3 See particularly Kreiser, *Observateur*, Kreiser, *Abdülgani*, Brinkley Messick, *The Calligraphic State. Textual Domination and History in a Muslim Society*, Berkeley, Los Angeles 1993; Ursinus, *Provinzzeitung*.

evidence in sources such as government papers, state almanacs (*sāl-nāme*), and the press that in administering the new Province of Yemen (*Yemen vilāyeti*) after 1872 the Ottoman authorities sought to bring to this part of the Arabian Peninsula many of those forms of ordering that are characteristic features of the modern bureaucratic state.[4] It was in this context that the Ottoman government and its representatives introduced in the newly conquered province – very much like in other parts of the empire under the auspices of the *Tanẓīmāt* – new forms of producing and controlling space, both in the urban context and on the provincial level as a whole. At the same time earlier forms of producing space were appropriated and redeployed within the framework and for the purposes of the modern state.[5] To the extent that the transformation of urban space during this particular period has been dealt with, research has almost exclusively focused on Ṣanʿā', the capital of the *Yemen vilāyeti*. The pioneering studies on Ṣanʿā' by Robin Bidwell, Ronald Lewcock, and Robert Bertram Serjeant, and by Horst Kopp and Eugen Wirth merit particular mention in this regard.[6] However, the cases of provincial sub-centers such as Ibb, Taʿizz, and Ḥudayda have remained virtually unexplored.[7]

The work of these scholars allows us to follow the broad trajectory of how the urban fabric of Ṣanʿā' changed under Ottoman rule, particularly

---

4 On these forms of ordering see, for instance, Bernard Cohn, "The Census, Social Structure, and Objectification in South Asia," *An Anthropologist among Historians and Other Essays*, ed. Bernard Cohn, New Delhi 1987, 224-254; Bernard Cohn, *Colonialism and Its Forms of Knowledge. The British in India*, Princeton/New Jersey 1996; Michel Foucault, "On Governmentality," in *The Foucault Effect. Studies in Governmentality*, eds. Graham Burchell, Colin Gordon, and Peter Miller, London 1991, 87-104. For some time since the beginning of the Ottoman re-conquest of south-west Arabia in 1849 the territory that the Ottomans initially held in the coastal region was administered as the Province of Yemen (*eyālet-i Yemen*). A series of campaigns between 1870 and 1873 added large parts of the highlands, including Ṣanʿā', to the Ottoman domains and led to the creation of a new *vilāyet* that included the sub-provinces (*sancaḳs*) of ʿAsīr, Ḥudayda, Ṣanʿā', and Taʿizz.

5 See the contribution of U. Makdisi in this volume.

6 Horst Kopp and Eugen Wirth, *Sanaa. Développement et organisation de l'espace d'une ville arabe*, traduit de l'Allemand par Blandine Blukacz-Louisfert et François Blukacz, Aix-en-Provence, Sanaa 1994, Robert Bertram Serjeant, "The Post-Medieval and Modern History of Ṣanʿā' and the Yemen, ca. 953-1382/1515-1962," *Ṣanʿā'. An Arabian Islamic City*, eds. Robert Bertram Serjeant and Ronald Lewcock, London 1983, 68-107; R. L. Bidwell, "Western Accounts of Ṣanʿā' 1510-1962," in Lewcock and Serjeant, *Ṣanʿā'*, 108-121; Ronald Lewcock, Paolo Costa, Robert Bertram Serjeant, and Robert Wilson, "The Urban Development of Ṣanʿā'", in Lewcock and Serjeant, *Ṣanʿā'*, 122-143.

7 See, however, Blumi's contribution to this volume.

during the three decades between 1872 and the turn of the century. It was in the course of these thirty years that the Ottoman authorities restored and extended the city's fortifications, and in several stages constructed those public buildings that underlined Ṣanʿā's new status as a provincial capital of a bureaucratic state. While some of these buildings were located outside the old city (the military hospital to the west, a large barracks complex to the south) most of them – e.g. the *rüşdiyye* and *i'dādiyye* schools, the customs administration, the post and telegraph services as well as the main government office building (*ḳonaḳ*) – were concentrated in the south-eastern part of the old *intra muros* area, and formed something of a government quarter.[8]

Urban Ruptures and Continuities of the Ottoman Reconquest

But, while these studies provide an account of how urban space changed physically as a result of Ottoman rule, they do not investigate the political dimension of this process. It is precisely on this dimension that I will focus in this paper. Exploring various construction and restoration projects that the new rulers initiated, I will argue that these were part of the broader effort on the part of the authorities to affirm the authority of the Ottoman state over the newly conquered province.[9] Also, it is my contention that public ceremonies, such as military parades and public school examinations were to serve the same purpose. In other words, construction projects and public ceremonies are seen as spatial practices that were aspects of inscribing Ottoman rule in urban space. Further, I will argue that these forms of ordering space were an important component of how administrators conceptualized Ottoman rule in their writings on Yemen as a whole. In this connection, I will attempt to explore what I see as an important shift during the Second Constitutional Period (1908-1918): the way in which some Ottoman officials wrote about organizing city space in the Province of Yemen came to reflect the self conscious notion that the *Yemen vilāyeti* should be run as a

---

8 Kopp and Wirth, *Développement*, 29; Serjeant, *Modern History*, 99.

9 On this issue see Jens Hanssen, "'Your Beirut is on My Desk'; Ottomanizing Beirut under Abdulhamid (1878-1909)," in *Projecting Beirut: Episodes of the Construction and Reconstruction of a Modern City*, eds. H. Sarkis and P. Rowe, London 1998, 41-67, see particularly 57; and Stefan Weber, "Der Marğa-Platz in Damaskus – Die Entstehung eines modernen Stadtzentrums unter den Osmanen als Ausdruck strukturellen Wandels (1808-1918)," *Damaszener Mitteilungen*, 10 (1998), 291-344, Taf. 77-88.

colony *(müstemleke)* like Eritrea or the Anglo-Egyptian Sudan and not as a province on an equal footing with *vilāyets* such as Syria or Bursa.[10]

Probably one of the earliest accounts that provides an Ottoman perspective on the issue of ordering urban space in Ṣanʿā' after the Ottoman conquest can be found in the *Tārīh-i Yemen ve Ṣanʿā'* published in 1875 by Colonel (*mīralāy*) Aḥmed Rāşid who had participated in the campaigns that led to the creation of the *Yemen vilāyeti*. According to Aḥmed Rāşid, Ottoman construction activities started right after the town had been occupied by the expeditionary corps under Aḥmed Muhtār Paşa in April 1872; for one, construction carried out by several infantry units was directed towards providing the essential garrison facilities for the Ottoman troops. The fortifications of the citadel and those around the old city were restored and extended.[11] At the same time, barracks, an arsenal, a military hospital, and kitchen and laundry facilities were built inside the citadel compound which was reconverted into an entirely military space: as Rāşid notes, the Ottoman authorities purchased the private houses that had been constructed there prior to the Ottoman takeover from their owners and turned them over to the military.[12]

However, Ottoman construction neither focused exclusively on the area of the old city nor was it geared entirely to the needs of the military. The construction site for the future military hospital was prepared in the Mutawakkil quarter where one of the palaces of the Qāsimī Imāms was located; this included the setting up of a garden with fountains, water basins and trees which for this purpose had been brought from Ṭā'if.[13] More important, it was the southeastern part of the old city, adjacent to the citadel, that received particular attention on the part of the new rulers. There the authorities renovated the Bekiriyye Mosque and the *ḥammām* that had

---

10 In terms of sources, I am drawing particularly on government papers from the Prime Ministry Archives (*BBA*) in Istanbul, on the official provincial newspaper (*resmī vilāyet gazetesi*) *Ṣanʿā'*, the journal *Mülkīye* and other published accounts, most notably Aḥmed Rāşid's *Tārīh-i Yemen ve Ṣanʿā'*, 2. vols., Istanbul 1875, and travelogues/memoirs from the Second Constitutional Period (1908-1918). The fact that Ṣanʿā' figures prominently in these writings is not surprising, and reflects its importance as the administrative center of the *Yemen vilāyeti*. As we shall see, it seems that it was only during the Second Constitutional Period (1908-1918) that Ottoman officials in newspaper articles and travelogues dealt in greater detail with the ordering of urban space in connection with Ḥudayda, the principal port town of the Province of Yemen.

11 Rāşid, *Tārīh-i Yemen ve Ṣanʿā'*, vol. 2, 243, 245.

12 *Ibid.*, 243.

13 *Ibid.*, 245.

been donated by Ḥasan Paşa, a governor of Yemen during the first period of Ottoman rule (1538-1635). In addition, the *maydān* in front of the mosque and the *ḥammām* was cleared of debris, enlarged and partly planted with trees. At its southwestern end several houses with *lokantas*, cafés, and shops were built.[14] It was this complex formed by the Bekiriyye Mosque, the *ḥammām*, and the *maydān* that later on became the nucleus of the government quarter of Ottoman Ṣanʿā'. Finally, Rāşid states that preparations were made for the construction of a *rüşdiyye* school.[15]

In this part of Rāşid's *Tārīh-i Yemen ve Ṣanʿā'* we come across various aspects of inscribing Ottoman rule in urban space. First, the fact that the several departments of the civil and military administration of the *Yemen vilāyeti* were moving into one of the palaces of the Qāsimī Imāms[16] can be read as a particularly powerful way of marking both the end of the period when the Yemen – due to the resistance mounted by this dynasty – had effectively slipped from the control of the Ottoman state and the advent of the new regime. But apparently, the central agencies of the provincial administrative apparatus did not just take over what at least until the 1860s had been the center of the Imāmic regime. The British journalist Walter Harris noted that the office of the *Yemen vālīsi* in the old Imāmic palace where he was received in 1892 was decorated and furnished in what was an adaptation of French baroque style.[17] This suggests that in decorating their office space the governors-general of the new province had tried to imitate the interiors of the imperial palaces of the *Tanẓīmāt* period, such as the Dolmabahçe Sarayı in Istanbul.

At the same time, the restoration of the architectural complex donated by Ḥasan Paşa at the end of the sixteenth century appears as an attempt to stress the continuity between the previous period of Ottoman rule and the new order that men like Aḥmed Muhtār Paşa were seeking to set up in this part of the Arabian Peninsula. In this context, it is interesting to see that whereas a detailed list is provided of all the "general welfare buildings" (*ebniye-i hayriyye*) – i.e., fountains, *ḥammāms*, and mosques – that had been donated by various Ottoman governors during the sixteenth and early seventeenth centu-

---

14 *Ibid.*, 243-245. On the Bekiriyye Cāmiʿi which was built by Ḥasan Paşa after 1597 see Ronald Lewcock, R. B. Serjeant, and G. Rex Smith, "The Smaller Mosques of Ṣanʿā'," in Serjeant and Lewcock, *Ṣanʿā'*, 351-390, 375-381.

15 Rāşid, *Tārīh*, vol.2, 246.

16 *Ibid.*, 245. Rāşid is probably referring to one of the Imāmic palaces that was located inside a fort near the Ḥudayda gate; see Bidwell, *Western Accounts*, 113.

17 Walter B. Harris, *A Journey Through the Yemen,* Edinburgh, London 1893, 303; see also *ibid.*, the drawing between pages 292 and 293.

ries, Rāşid mentions none of the monuments falling under this category that were built under the Qāsimī Imāms.[18] Thus, a connection is established between the "beneficial" construction activities of the earlier Ottoman rulers of Yemen and those initiated by their successors under the auspices of the *Tanẓīmāt*. More important, Ṣanʿā' is to a considerable degree represented as an Ottoman space. There is evidence that the privileging of the Bekiriyye Mosque complex continued during the following decades. In 1892, Harris noted that the Bekiriyye Mosque was well maintained, whereas the other Ṣanʿānī mosques were in a deplorable state.[19] This suggests that – very much as Selim Deringil has argued in his recent book – maintaining the Bekiriyye Mosque because it was a Sunnī mosque that had been donated by a high Ottoman official has to be considered as an example of the "visual confirmation of sovereignty" of the Sultan-Caliph. The Zaydī mosques, by contrast, were quite obviously regarded as "rival symbols" and therefore denied similar attention from on high.[20]

Ottoman Civilizing Narratives on Ṣanʿā'

In this context, the claim to the caliphate that successive Zaydī Imāms put forward during the second period of Ottoman rule might have played an important role. The special attention that the Bekiriyye Mosque received from the sultan himself is also stressed by an article published in the official provincial newspaper *Ṣanʿā'* in January 1881.[21] The article explained that masons and other artisans had been specially brought in from Istanbul to carry out urgent restoration work at the mosque during the year 1880, while ʿAbdülḥamīd had donated a new candelabra, an act that was commemorated in an inscription near the entrance of the mosque, which the author did not fail to cite in full.[22] This tendency to marginalize the role of the Zaydī Imāms in the history of Yemen is also apparent in the historiographic section of Rāşid's book as well as in other Ottoman accounts of the region's history. In the former, for instance, 275 pages are allocated to the conquest of Yemen under Aḥmed Muhtār Paşa. By contrast, barely 50

---

18 For instance, the mosque and *qubbah* of al-Mutawakkil, the Qubbat al-Mahdī ʿAbbās, or the al-Abhar mosque; see Lewcock, Serjeant, and Smith, *Smaller Mosques*, 382-385.

19 Harris, *Journey*, 315.

20 Selim Deringil, *The Well-Protected Domains. Ideology and the Legitimation of Power in the Ottoman Empire 1876-1909*, London, New York 1998, 28-31.

21 See *Ṣanʿā'*, 21 (28 Kānūn-i evvel 1296/9 January 1881), 1.

22 See *ibid*.

pages are reserved for the history of Zaydism or of the Qāsimī Imāms who drove the Ottomans out of Yemen in 1635 and ruled the country for the next 200 years. Similarly, in the provincial *sālnāme* of 1886-87 both the ancient, early Islamic, and Ottoman periods are dealt with *in extenso*, while the period of the Qāsimī Imāms is covered in a single paragraph, [23] with the reader being referred to Rāşid's *Tārīh*!

As we have seen above, Rāşid mentioned that the authorities made preparations to provide Ṣanʿā' at a later stage with a *rüşdiyye* school, a hospital, and a telegraph station, i.e., many of those key facilities that became the markers of Ottoman provincial cities of the *Tanẓīmāt* period.[24] It is a report drawn up by Nāmıḳ Efendi for the Palace in November 1892 when he was touring the Province of Yemen as a government inspector that illustrates that not only the restoration of existing structures like the Bekiriyye Mosque but also the construction of these new kinds of buildings was to play a crucial role in representing the authority of the Ottoman state in Yemen. In his report Nāmıḳ complained specifically about the almost complete lack of administrative buildings (*ḥükūmet dā'ireleri*) and barracks (*ḳışlalar*) in the *Yemen vilāyeti*: only in Ṣanʿā', he noted, could a government office building (*ḳonaḳ*) be found that befitted the honor of the state. In all the other administrative centers of the province, however, government officials were scattered over several of the local houses. While the same held true of some of the Ottoman troops, most soldiers were living in tents. What was more, even ten years after construction on the new barracks in Ṣanʿā' had begun, these were still only half-completed.[25] It was precisely to this absence of what Mitchell has referred to as "an appearance of order" that Nāmıḳ attributed the fact that the local population had supported the Zaydī Imāms against the authorities.[26] Similarly, Aḥmed Rāşid emphasized that the Ottomans were constructing, renovating, or rebuilding in an "orderly way" (*muntaẓam ṣūretde*) where they had found only ruins and decay.[27] Rāşid also did not fail to mention the procedural orderliness

---

23 See *Yemen Sālnāmesi* 3 (1302 A.Māl./ 1304 A.H./ 1886-87 A.D.), 123. Rāşid, *Tārīh*, vol. 1, 170-187, 253-281; vol. 2, 1-275.

24 See Paul Dumont and François Georgeon (eds.), *Villes ottomanes à la fin de l'empire*, Paris 1992.

25 See figure 12 in Lemke's contribution to this volume.

26 BBA/Şura-yi Devlet 2261-17, doc. 10, Nāmıḳ Efendi to Palace, 17 Teşrīn-i sānī 1308/29 November 1892. Timothy Mitchell, *Colonising Egypt*, 2nd edition, Los Angeles 1991, 78-80.

27 Rāşid, *Tārīh*, vol. 2, 242, 243, 244, 245. While the Colonel was favorably impressed with the solidity and the architectural style of the Ṣanʿānī houses, Rāşid stressed that many of them lay in ruins, stating that since the most prosperous period of the city

with which these projects had been carried out. Apparently, all plots for the construction schemes of the Ottoman authorities had been purchased by the state,[28] while a special commission was appointed to supervise the various construction projects.[29] Thus, what is contrasted are local decline and stagnation on the one hand and Ottoman order and efficiency on the other. In other words, the new rulers portrayed themselves as bringing quite literally order out of the chaos that the crumbling buildings of Ṣanʿā' were meant to represent. Rāşid's description, therefore, brings to mind the attempts on the part of the authorities to order and "modernize" cities (to create an orderly appearance) that – according to Deringil – were characteristic of the *Tanẓīmāt* and Hamidian periods.[30] For instance, the efforts of the Commission for Road Improvement (*Iṣlāḥāt-i ṭuruḳ ḳomisyonı*) to regularize the urban fabric in parts of Istanbul between 1865 and 1869 may well have been at the back of Rāşid's mind.[31]

At the same time, his description is in keeping with the rhetoric of a civilizing mission that from the early 1870s onwards was a prominent feature of the Ottoman discourse on Yemen.[32] In both government papers and the press the population of the newly created province was usually portrayed as backward and stagnant – a state that could be overcome only through intervention from without, through Ottoman rule that would raise the locals to the cultural level of the people of the more "developed" parts of the empire. In other words, the goal was to ottomanize them. Thus, what these bureaucrats meant by civilizing the population of the *Yemen vilāyeti* was forging a loyal population of Ottoman citizens through the disciplining techniques of the modern state. For example, both in government papers of the time and in articles that were published in *Ṣanʿā'*, officials frequently expressed the view that education *à l'ottomane* and service in the locally recruited Ḥamīdiyye units that had been established during the governorship of İsmāʿīl Ḥaḳḳī Paşa (1879-1882) were critical to bring the

---

their number had decreased from roughly 7,000-8,000 to an estimated 5,000; see *ibid.*, 332, 333.

28 *Ibid.*, 243, 245

29 *Ibid.*, 246.

30 Deringil, *Domains*, 31.

31 See Zeynep Çelik, *The Remaking of Istanbul,* Seattle, London 1986, 55-63.

32 See, for instance, BBA/ŞD 2254-5, doc. 3, governor-general of Yemen, Muṣṭafā ʿĀṣım Paşa, to Council of State, May 1878, p. 7.; ʿAbdülganī Senī, "Yemen'in Necāt ve Selāmeti. İḥyā-yi Maʿārif," *Mülkīye*, 12 (1 Kānūn-i sānī 1325/14 January 1910), 45-52, 49, 59. Mustafa Nihat Özön, *Namık Kemal ve İbret Gazetesi*, Istanbul 1997, 67-68, Ursinus, *Provinzzeitung*, 178-179.

local population within the fold of "Ottoman civilization" (*medeniyyet-i ʿosmāniyye*).[33] It was İsmāʿīl Ḥaḳḳī himself who remarked in a memorandum dated 31 Mart 1296/12 April 1880 that in creating the *ʿAsākir-i Ḥamīdiyye* he had made an effort to advance the ordering of the province a step further... "since the people of the land of Yemen are sharing in the exalted military aspect of the enviable Ottoman civilization through an army being organized and established from among the people of the province."[34]

Parading Order

Holding school examinations and drill exercises as well as parades in public were therefore ways of using urban space to put on display the success of the civilizing mission and, hence, to demonstrate the increasing integration of the province into the structures of the empire. Both sets of ceremonies received detailed coverage in *Ṣanʿā'*.[35] On 8 Temmūz 1297/20 July 1881, for instance, the official provincial newspaper reported about drill exercises and a parade that had been held in the provincial capital in celebration of the sultan's birthday. According to the article that appeared on the front page of *Ṣanʿā'*, the ceremony began with a drill exercise that the recently created Ḥamīdiyye artillery unit had performed in the presence of the rest of the Ḥamīdiyye corps, the governor-general, some officials and "thousands of people":

> After the above-mentioned guns had been fired everyone present expressed his good wishes by shouting repeatedly: 'Long live the Sultan!' Thereafter they performed a meticulous and orderly parade with, as order requires, the Ḥamīdiyye band taking the lead, the trumpeters behind them, then the Ḥamīdiyye battalions and the gunners at the far end, while the musicians of the band played alternately at special places, and during this parade the afore-mentioned gunners marched by with extraordinary speed. The overall view of these heroes displayed the form of a most or-

---

33 BBA/Yıldız Arşivi, Hususi Maruzat [hereafter cited as BBA/Y.A.Hus.] 167-74, doc. 5.; İsmāʿīl Ḥaḳḳī Paşa to Palace, 31Mart 1296/12 April 1880; on the role of education see Ursinus, *Provinzzeitung*.

34 BBA/Y.A.Hus. 167-74, doc. 5.; İsmāʿīl Ḥaḳḳī Paşa to Palace, 31Mart 1296/12 April 1880.

35 For drill exercises of the Ḥamīdiyye troops see, for instance, *Ṣanʿā'*, 2 (7 Mayıs 1296/19 May 1880), 2, *Ṣanʿā'*, 21 (28 Kānūn-i evvel 1296/9 January 1881), 2, *Ṣanʿā'*, 41 (8 Temmūz 1297/20 July 1881), 1; for public school examinations see, for instance, *Ṣanʿā'*, 43 (22 Temmūz 1297/3 August 1881), 1-2, *Ṣanʿā'*, 44 (29 Temmūz 1297/10 August 1881), 2, *Ṣanʿā'*, 49 (9 Eylül 1297/21 September 1881), 2.

> derly and perfect unit and the agitation of the banners in various colors in their midst with the exalted line "ʿAsākir-i Ḥamīdiyye' written on them presented another pleasant picture to the eyes of the onlooker.[36]

An article that was published in *Ṣanʿā'* two weeks later on 22 Temmūz 1297/3 August 1881 gives us a sense of how much importance the Ottoman authorities in the provincial capital attached to turning the final examinations at the local *rüşdiyye* school into a public event. As the article explained, the examination ceremonies for the students began with the examinations proper which were held inside the Bekiriyye Mosque in the presence of both the governor and his staff and of some officials, *ʿulamā'*, *sādāt* and *ashrāf*. This was followed by an awards ceremony outside the mosque during which the students received their diploma from the hands of the governor-general while an army band was performing in the background. The event concluded with a parade of the Ḥamīdiyye corps and of *niẓāmiyye* troops.[37]

The Matrix of Provincial Divisions

The connection between the ordering of space and the notion of a civilizing mission *à l'ottomane* was made not only with reference to the urban context. For instance, in 1880 and 1888 the members of the province's administrative council (*meclis-i idāre*) notified the ministry of the interior in Istanbul that they considered necessary the creation of new sub-districts (*nāhiyes*) in the region north of Ṣanʿā', not least because the local population had still not been freed from the state of primitivity in which they were living.[38] What is evoked here is the notion that the production of space – in this case in the form of administrative divisions with their respective personnel – would serve the purpose of civilizing the local population since it allowed the authorities to bring to bear on them more efficiently the disciplining techniques of the modern state. This idea is formulated even more explicitly in connection with several plans concerning the administrative restructuring of the Province of Yemen that were drawn up by Ottoman administrators during the last decade of ʿAbdülḥamīd II's reign (1876-1909). It was against the background of several uprisings led

---

36 *Ṣanʿā'*, 41 (8 Temmūz 1297/20 July 1881), 1.

37 *Ṣanʿā'*, 43 (22 Temmūz 1297/3 August 1881), 1-2.

38 BBA/ŞD 2254-17, p. 4. Yemen vilāyeti, Meclis-i İdāre to Ministry of the Interior (10 Ḥazīrān 1296/22 June 1880); see also BBA/ŞD 2259-2, Yemen vilāyeti, Meclis-i İdāre to Ministry of the Interior (10 Teşrīn-i sānī 1304/22 November 1888).

by the Imāms al-Manṣūr Billāh Muḥammad b. Yaḥyā (d. 1904) and al-Mutawakkil Yaḥyā b. Muḥammad (d. 1948) between 1891 and 1907 that both provincial administrators like İsmāʿīl Raḥmī, a former *ḳā'immaḳām* of Qaʿṭaba, and senior officials like the governor-general of Yemen, Ḥüseyin Ḥilmī Paşa, or Lieutenant-Generals Şākir and Ferīd Paşa were calling for smaller administrative units so as to ensure a more efficient control of the local population by the authorities.[39] For instance, speaking in favor of partitioning the Province of Yemen into two *vilāyets* and an independent *sancaḳ* ʿAsīr, Şākir and Ferīd Paşa in a memorandum dated 24 Şubāṭ 1322/9 March 1907 made it clear that such a measure and, hence, the increasing number of sub-province and district centers (*livā ve ḳażālar merākizi*) would enable the authorities "to pay constant attention to the conditions of the population". Since under these conditions "... police could do their duty with ease, security and public order, the origins of wealth and prosperity, would become properly established."[40]

It is necessary to emphasize that some of the above-mentioned spatial practices pre-dated the emergence of the modern state in the context of the Ottoman Empire from the reign of Maḥmūd II (1808-1839) onward. For instance, the use of architecture and public ceremonies (parades among them) to represent the authority of the Ottoman dynasty was indeed already well established during the sixteenth and seventeenth centuries.[41] A similar argument could be made with regard to the Qāsimī Imāms who ruled parts of Yemen between the 1630s and the mid-nineteenth century.[42] In this regard, the renovation of the Bekiriyye Mosque on the order of ʿAbdülḥamīd II was a way of confirming sovereignty that would have appeared familiar to a seventeenth century observer. However, both Aḥmed Rāşid's emphasis of creating an "orderly image" through construction and renovation, and Nāmıḳ Efendi's remarks about the political implications of

---

39 Cf., for instance, BBA/ŞD 2264-32, which contains an entire file on the issue of partitioning the Province of Yemen into four *vilāyets*. In 1904, İsmāʿīl Raḥmī, called for a restructuring of the province's administrative divisions so as to allow administrators and police to keep constantly a watchful eye on the movements and activities of the Yemenī population since by nature (*ṭabʿan*) they had the tendency to indulge in villainy and brigandage (*şeḳāvet*); see Başbakanlık Arşivi/Yıldız Esas Evrakı [hereafter cited as BBA/YEE] 14-2382-126-11, 3, 4.

40 BBA/YEE 14-294-126-8, doc. 1, Şākir Paşa and Ferīd Paşa to Palace, 24 Şubāṭ 1322/9 March 1907.

41 See, for instance, Suraiya Faroqhi, *Kultur und Alltag im Osmanischen Reich*, München 1995, 158, 161-165.

42 See Bernard A. Haykel, *Order and Righteousness: Muḥammad ʿAlī al-Shawkānī and the Nature of the Islamic State in Yemen*, D. Phil. thesis, Oxford 1997, 54-58.

the lack of "proper" government buildings point to a new concept that Timothy Mitchell has studied with reference to nineteenth century Egypt, namely the notion of "order" as "something pre-existent, non-particular and non-material."[43] Only with this abstract notion of order in mind could the dwellings of Ottoman officials or the unrenovated Bekiriyye Mosque appear to the two officials as disorder.[44] It was in keeping with this concept that Nāmıḳ Efendi would regard it as inappropriate that officials went about their business in "civilian" dwellings. Similarly, the public school examinations presupposed the concept of learning "separated out as 'schooling'." This was as characteristic of Ottoman modernity as military parades that celebrated the creation of disciplined bodies of soldiers that would function like an "artificial machine."[45]

Ḥudayda – Ottomanizing a Peripheral Port City

As has been indicated above, it appears that from around the turn of the century new concepts and ideas about ordering urban space were entering into Ottoman writings on the Province of Yemen. As Klaus Kreiser has noted in a recent article on the bureaucrat and intellectual ʿAlī Emīrī (1858-1924), both Ottoman officials and European travelers who arrived in Ḥudayda during the two decades before the First World War usually drew a gloomy picture about the conditions under which soldiers and administrators in the principal port city of the *Yemen vilāyeti* were living and working.[46] Echoing in a way the disparaging comments Nāmıḳ Efendi had made about the province's administrative sub-centers in general, both the *vilāyet mektūbcusu* (head of the governor-general's chancery) ʿAbdülganī Senī (1871-1951) and Brigadier-General Rüşdī Paşa expressed considerable disappointment at the fact that Ḥudayda lacked those public/government buildings *à l'ottomane* which in provincial centers from Manastir to Mecca symbolized the centralizing authority of the imperial center of the *Tanẓīmāt*: while in Ṣanʿā' – or even in smaller garrison towns such as Manākha[47] – travelers like the Italian geographer Renzo Manzoni or the British journalist Walter Harris were impressed by the local army barracks, the municipal hospital or the building housing the industrial

---

43 Mitchell, *Colonising Egypt*, 79.

44 *Ibid.*, 80.

45 *Ibid.*, 85, 36-37.

46 See Kreiser, *ʿAlī Emīrī*, 200-202.

47 Harris, *Journey*, 336.

school (*mekteb-i ṣanāyīʿ*),[48] nothing of that kind was to be found in the administrative center of the *Ḥudayda sancağı*.[49] Wavell, who visited Ḥudayda in 1910, complemented the picture the two officials had drawn in describing both the government *ḳonaḳ* and the military installations of the city as having been in a deplorable state.[50] The only buildings that visitors like Harris or Wyman Bury found worth mentioning were the houses of the wealthy and their country houses on the outskirts of the town.[51] In other words, Ḥudayda was lacking the architecture that would create the impression of a visible Ottoman imprint on urban space of the kind that is reflected in Harris' description of Manākha or Manzoni's map of Ṣanʿā' (fig. 1). Referring to the small garrison town in the Jabal Ḥarāz region, halfway between Ṣanʿā' and Ḥudayda, the former noted: "The Government offices and the military hospital and barracks give the place quite a European appearance, for they are all built in modern Turkish [sic!] style with glass windows and flat roofs."[52]

However, what is important here is that as positive examples in terms of ordering space in a port city the two officials cited neither Salonica, nor Izmir or Beirut but colonial port cities such as Port Sudan, Maṣṣawʿa or Aden. In his book *Yemen Ḫāṭırası* (*Memoirs of Yemen*) – published in

---

48 For Manzoni's description of Ṣanʿā' see Bidwell, *Western Accounts*, 112.

49 Upon his arrival in Ḥudayda ʿAbdülganī simply could not find anything that resembled an official building and stated flatly that "... Ḥudayda didn't present anything that would catch my eye" ("... *Ḥudeyde hiçde gözümde yer ṭutacaḳ bir şey göstermedi.*"); see ʿAbdülganī Senī, "Yemen Yolunda," *Servet-i Fünūn*, 1002 (5 Ağustos 1326/18 August 1910), 250-252, 251 and idem, "Yemen Yolunda," *Servet-i Fünūn*, 1011 (7 Teşrīn-i evvel 1326/20 October 1910), 395-396, 396. Rüşdī, in turn complained about the absence of barracks and the unfinished hospital; see Rüşdī, *Yemen Ḫāṭırası*, Dersaʿādet 1325/1909-10, 66-67.

50 See A. J. B. Wavell, *A Modern Pilgrim in Mecca and a Siege in Sanaa*, London 1912, 210: "We found the government offices ... to be another unstable-looking erection, situated a hundred yards or so from the Casino, facing the sea." See also *ibid.*, 216-217: "The only defensive work, beside the over-built town wall, is a small fort to the north of the town, so much in need of repair, or rather reconstruction, that when it is necessary to fire a gun for saluting purposes the piece is taken outside for fear that the concussion might cause the whole fort to collapse." In a report dated 31 March 1904 the British Vice-Consul Richardson remarked that "[m]ost buildings are in a dilapidated and crumbling condition giving Hodeida the appearance of a bombarded city," see *Records of Yemen*, 16 vols., eds. Doreen Ingrams and Leila Ingrams, n.p. 1993, vol. 5, xiii, 420; ʿAbdülganī Senī, "Yemen'iñ Ḥayāt-i İstiḳbāli," *Mülkīye*, 5 (1 Ḥazīrān 1325/14 June 1909), 1-7, 4-7; Rüşdī, *Yemen Ḫāṭırası*, 66-67.

51 Harris, *Journey*, 369-370, G. Wyman Bury, *Arabia Infelix or the Turks in Yamen* [sic!], London 1915, 135-136.

52 Harris, *Journey*, 336.

1909 – Rüşdī Paşa could not help remarking that during more than three decades in Ḥudayda the Ottomans had not accomplished what the Italians in Maṣṣawʿa had done within less than thirteen years: ordering the city and building both barracks for the troops and a railway.[53] In his view, the local government buildings in Ḥudayda compared unfavorably to those in Aden and Maṣṣawʿa, which were "of a kind that caused amazement" (*naẓar-i ḥayreti mūcib olacaḳ ṣūretdedir*).[54] In fact, even by 1909 Ḥudayda did not have a real harbor at all but only a half-crumbling pier which – according to ʿAbdülganī – was not worth the money which the Ottoman government had paid a German company for its construction.[55] As a result, ships had to anchor two miles off the coast while men and supplies were ferried to the pier in small boats.[56] Thus for Rüşdī Paşa, Maṣṣawʿa quite clearly represented a model of ordering space in a port city through government sponsored construction of official buildings and transportation facilities which could be emulated in Ḥudayda. ʿAbdülganī, however, proposed a more radical solution. Referring to the example of Port Sudan which had been developed from scratch by the authorities of the Anglo-Egyptian Sudan, the *vilāyet mektūbcusu* suggested that Jabāna, a village a few kilometers north of Ḥudayda which possessed a natural harbor should be developed into the principal port city of the province and at the same time become the terminus of the railway that was supposed to link Ṣanʿāʾ to the coast.[57]

The Ottoman Production of Colonial Difference in Urban Yemen

The way the two authors chose their examples was not accidental. For both of them the ordering of space in port cities through government sponsored construction of official buildings and of port and railway facilities was only one among many examples showing that the way in which European powers like Britain, France, or Italy ran their colonies was to be emulated by the Ottomans if they wished to govern the Province of Yemen successfully.[58] This may in part have been a reaction to mounting local opposition to the Ottoman presence in Yemen, which was perceived as the result of

---

53 Rüşdī, *Yemen Hāṭırası*, 66-67, 69-70.

54 *Ibid.*, 70.

55 See ʿAbdülganī Senī, "Yemen Yolunda," *Servet-i Fünūn*, 1001 (29 Temmūz 1326/11 August 1910), 235-236, 236.

56 Rüşdī, *Yemen Hāṭırası*, 66.

57 ʿAbdülganī Senī, "Yemen Şimendöferiniñ Güzergāhı ve Teʾsīrātı," *Mülkīye*, 11 (1 Kānūn-i evvel 1325/14 December 1909), 23-28, 25.

58 See, for instance, Rüşdī, *Yemen Hāṭırası*, 69-70.

the inability of the imperial authorities to firmly establish Ottoman rule in this part of the empire. In contrast, European imperial projects in the Red Sea region appeared to be successful. Thus, what we are observing here is a shift in points of reference. While for Aḥmed Rāşid Ottoman provincial administration with its characteristic institutions and buildings had provided the model for governing the newly set up *vilāyet*, both Rüşdī and ʿAbdülganī propagated European colonial administration as more promising. At the same time, the fact that both the Brigadier and the *vilāyet mektūbcusu* regarded these projects and not the administration of metropolitan France or Britain as examples worth emulating suggests that they saw the Ottoman authorities in Yemen in a position comparable to that of the British and Italian colonial rulers in the Sudan, Eritrea, Aden or India.

There is evidence that these ideas had a broader basis among Ottoman officials and journalists.[59] However, only a few administrators seem to have gone as far as ʿAbdülganī Senī in suggesting that the *Yemen vilāyeti* be formerly given the status of a colony.[60] The *vilāyet mektūbcusu* subscribed to the idea of a civilizing mission in Yemen, but unlike the authors of previous memoranda and articles on Ottoman Yemen he wanted to formalize the perceived cultural hierarchy between the locals and the officials from outside the province by placing the *Yemen vilāyeti* under a special administrative regime. Put differently, for ʿAbdülganī the term colony implied – to borrow Thomas Metcalf's words – a "demarcation of spaces meant to separate"[61] the local population from the more "developed" people in core provinces of the empire, such as Syria or Bursa. However, it is important to note the ambiguity with which Ottoman officials used the term colony with reference to Yemen. Neither ʿAbdülganī who envisaged a Yemen colony run by a governor with wide-ranging powers nor grand-viziers Kāmil and Saʿīd Paşa who apparently favored a form of indirect rule *à l'anglaise*[62] stated explicitly whether Ottoman colonial rule would

---

59 See, for instance, ʿAbdülganī Senī, *İḥyā-yi Maʿārif,* 50; Mevlānzāde Rifʿat, "Yemen Ḥaḳḳında Dāhilīye Nāẓiri Ṭalʿat Bey Efendi'ye Açiḳ Mektūb," *Yeñi Taṣvīr-i Efkār*, 501 (13 Ṣafer 1329/13 Şubāṭ 1911/13 February 1911), 1; İsmāʿīl Ṣubḥī (ed.), *Sālnāme-i Servet-i Fünūn. Üçinci Sene. 1 Mart 1327'den 28 Şubāṭ 1327'ye ḳadar Vaḳāyiʿi Muḥtevīdir,* Dersaʿādet, n.d., 415; Saʿīd Paşa, *Şaʿīd Paşa 'nıñ Ḥāṭırātı*, 2 vols., Istanbul 1328/1911-12, vol. 1, 154-155.

60 See Kreiser, *Observateur*, 317; Kreiser, *Abdülgani*, 12, 14.

61 Thomas R. Metcalf, *Ideologies of the Raj*, Cambridge 1994, 185.

62 Kreiser, *Abdülgani*, 12; Saʿīd Paşa, *Ḥāṭırāt*, 154-155. According to Baldry, in the winter of 1908/09 the then grand-vizier Kāmil Paşa was prepared to "discuss the possibility of autonomy 'on colonial lines'" for the Zaydī populated regions of the province with a delegation to be sent by Imām Yaḥyā; see Baldry, *Imām Yaḥyā*, 428.

entail denying the local people the status of Ottoman citizens and, hence, viewing them as a subject people. This was however, how critics understood the term. In 1911-12, for instance, a certain İbnülhaṭīb Cemāl el-Dīn vehemently attacked any plans to turn the Province of Yemen into a colony, maintaining that "... the Yemenīs are our fellow-citizens, just as we are the fellow-citizens of the Yemenīs."[63]

While Ḥasan Ḳadrī who appears to have worked for two years as a medical doctor in Yemen did not draw explicitly on specific forms of European colonialist practice, the views he expressed on the ordering of urban space nevertheless bring to mind notions that are often associated with colonial rule in the nineteenth and twentieth centuries. Ḳadrī suggested that soldiers and civil servants should not work or live in buildings that were constructed in the local way. These, he argued, were not spacious enough, allowed for too little air circulation and had, therefore, to be regarded as detrimental to their health.[64] Probably with reference to the Ottoman quarter of Bi'r al-ʿAzab in Ṣanʿā'[65] – where according to Ehiloğlu the Ottoman officials and their families lived in "normal houses with glass windows"[66] – he stressed that there were houses in the provincial capital that, by contrast, could be considered "appropriate to the Turkish way of life", with the same holding true for the local barracks.[67] Here, we are touching upon an important point. It is interesting to note that the notion whereby "local" equaled "unhealthy" or "filthy" was part of the standard repertoire of European colonialist thought. Particularly from the 1890s it served for prominent urban planners as a justification for the idea that in some colonial dependencies the soldiers and administrators from the metropole and the local population should live in separate quarters of a town — the *cité européenne* as opposed to the *cité indigène*.[68] In another part of his book Ḳadrī formulated this view even more explicitly by suggesting that due to the deficient cleanliness and sanitation of their houses the minds of "the locals" were "sick and degenerate" (*marīż ve düşkün*).[69]

---

63 İbnülhaṭīb Cemāl el-Dīn, *Yemen'e İsticlāb-i Naẓar-i Diḳḳat*, Ḳostantīnīye 1327/1911-12, 6.

64 Ḥasan Ḳadrī, *Yemen ve Ḥayātı*, Dersaʿādet 1328/1911-12, 132.

65 See also Zeki Ehiloğlu, *Yemen'de Türkler*, Istanbul 1952, 60.

66 *Ibid.*, 60.

67 Ḳadrī, *Yemen ve Ḥayātı*, 132.

68 See, for instance, Jürgen Osterhammel, *Kolonialismus. Geschichte, Formen, Folger* Munich 1995, 95-96; Anthony D. King, *Urbanism, Colonialism, and the World-Economy,* London, New York 1990, 36-37, 40-41; Metcalf, *Raj*, 180-181.

69 Ḳadrī, *Yemen ve Ḥayātı*, 48.

Thus, while stereotyping borderland people as filthy may well have been a part of earlier Ottoman elite perspectives, Ḳadrī, in drawing on "scientific" knowledge to disparage the local population, clearly adopted self consciously a "modern" attitude.

My reading of Ḳadrī's argument would be that he was using ideas about housing, health and sanitation to dichotomize metropole and periphery, to represent the local population as the "other." It is clear from his account that in recommending better housing for Ottoman officials in Yemen he was referring to officials from outside Yemen whom he addressed with an inclusive "we" (*biz*).[70] Ḳadrī suggested that "we" should avoid living like the locals, not that the locals should be provided with healthier housing so as to enable them to escape what he saw as the environmental causes of their inferiority. It is interesting to note the contrast to a more "inclusive" approach to the issue of urban health which is apparent in a short notice that appeared in *Ṣanʿā'* on 7 Mayıs 1296/19 May 1880. The notice praised plans to establish a "people's park" (*millet bagçesi*) on a plot of open land in the provincial capital, pointing to the positive effect of parks on public health.[71] Very much like ʿAbdülganī's idea to create a colony of Yemen, Ḳadrī's argument reflected a concern with formalizing perceived cultural hierarchies and establishing separation to a degree that was absent from earlier writings on Yemen. While İsmāʿīl Ḥaḳḳī and *Ṣanʿā'* had considered the creation of the *ʿAsākir-i Ḥamīdiyye* as a way to civilize the local people, the provincial newspaper emphasized that both *Ḥamīdiyye* and *niẓāmiyye* soldiers served the fatherland (*vaṭan*). While subscribing to the idea of an Ottoman civilizing mission in Yemen, neither Ḳadrī nor ʿAbdülganī made such explicit references to a concept of Ottoman citizenship that would include the population of the *Yemen vilāyeti*.

Conclusion

I have argued that the way Ottoman officials conceptualized the ordering of space in Yemen reflected their broader views about what Ottoman rule over this outlying province should be like. While for the first three decades after 1872 these ideas appear to have pointed towards ottomanizing the locals, it seems that during the Second Constitutional Period these were supplemented by new ones. In taking forms of European colonial rule as their principal points of reference these new concepts of Ottoman rule in Yemen implied that the local population would be assigned the position of

---

70 *Ibid.*, 131.

71 *Ṣanʿā'*, 2 [?] (7 Mayıs 1296/19 May 1880), 2.

a subject people rather than being recognized as Ottoman citizens. However, as we have seen, these views did not go unopposed. More important, the fact that local troops were organized in their own distinctive units (the ʿAsākir-i Ḥamīdiyye), modeled on colonial troops in British India,[72] reflects the ambiguity of Ottomanization. It raises the question of whether already during the Hamidian period Ottomanism could accomodate those differentiating practices that were so characteristic of colonial rule. The above-mentioned accounts from the Second Constitutional Period leave us under the impression that not least a series of uprisings in Yemen led some Ottoman officials to the conclusion that the population of this province was different from the people living in the more "developed" parts of the empire. As Rüşdī Paşa remarked: "Administratively, the *sancaḳ* of Ḥudayda was organized just like that of Izmid. But its population has not been made to resemble that of Izmid."[73] Selim Deringil has argued that the official discourse of Ottoman bureaucrats of the Hamidian period reflected their conceptualizing of the Ottoman Empire as "an imperial power like all the others."[74] While Yemen was never officially categorized as colony (müstemleke) this paper has shown the need to specify this extremely stimulating argument by asking: "Which kind of imperial power exactly?"

---

72 See, for instance, BBA/YEE 1-5, doc.2, İsmāʿīl Ḥaḳḳī Paşa to Ministry of War. 11 Mart 1296/23 March 1880.

73 Rüşdī, *Yemen Hāṭırası*, 67: "[Ḥudeyde] sancağıñ teşkīlāti İzmidiñ ʿayni yapılmış ḥālbuki ahālīsi İzmid ahālīsine beñzedilmemişdir ..."

74 Deringil, *Domains*, 148.

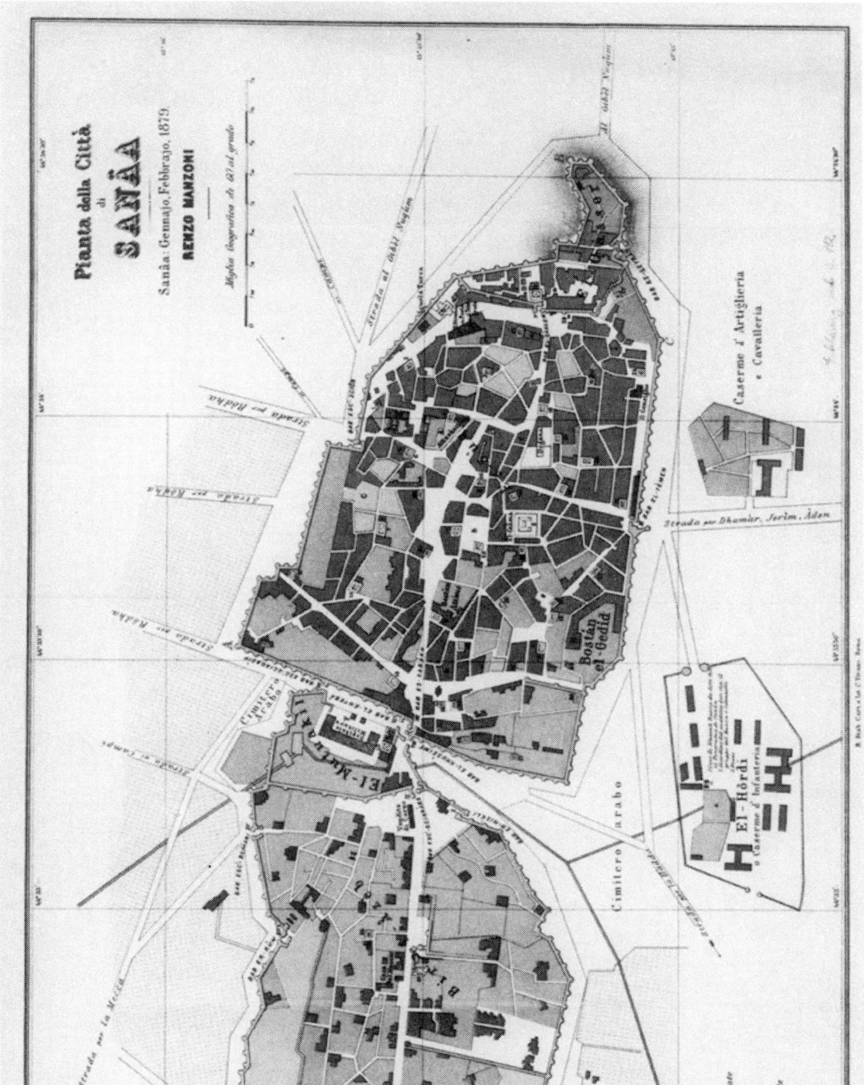

Fig. 1: Map of Ṣanʿāʾ by Renzo Manzoni, 1879; *Jemenreport* 27 (1996),4.

THE OTTOMAN EMPIRE AND YEMENI POLITICS IN THE *SANCAḲ* OF TAʿIZZ, 1911-1918[1]

ISA BLUMI

The impact of the idiom of a nineteenth century romantic idealization of the Islamic world permeates academic and mediatic literature today, often coming at the expense of more substantive coverage of immediate issues. Clichés make great copy and certainly penetrate deep into the audiences' collective unconscious, distorting even the sociologist or historian's perspective. These resilient models have also tainted the study of history in, for instance, Yemeni society as persistent stereotypes are embedded in local mediums of mass communication.[2]

The goals of this paper are to deconstruct the ideal Yemen and the stereotypes that have, attracted many to study Yemen by contesting the concept of the city as a rigidly defined domain of coded interactions between people in history. Far from its transparent and idealized image, Yemen proves to be an important case study of the complexities of daily life in history, even in discursively confined "tribal" areas where ethnographers have attempted to contain variances between the parameters of something called tribal culture and its anomalies and Yemen's relatively unconventional towns and cities. The deployment of symbols and categories that inform these stereotypes of the Middle East is challenged here in order to iterate the need for a far more localized historical focus, one which identifies as its horizon not the overarching comprehensive medium, but

---

1 The author would like to thank the staffs of the Prime Minister's Archives in Istanbul (BBA) and the Public Records office at Kew (PRO) for their assistance and patience. Thanks is also extended to the participants of the round-table discussions held in Beirut who have demonstrated great understanding and humanity. I save special thanks to Jens Hanssen for providing me the opportunity to contribute to this volume. Part of this project has been funded by ARIT's Dissertation fellowship program.

2 I have addressed this problem in an entirely different but relevant context, Isa Blumi, "The Commodification of Otherness and the Ethnic Unit in the Balkans: How to Think About Albanians," *East European Politics and Societies*, 12: 3 (Fall 1998), 527-569; see also Paul Dresch and Bernard Haykel, "Stereotypes and Political Styles: Islamists and Tribesfolk in Yemen," *IJMES* 27 (1995), 405-431.

the no less ambitious aspiration of identifying (as opposed to generalizing) the complexity of daily life in Ottoman Yemen.[3]

Geographical Dimensions of History

The study of the urban social arena in the Middle East rests on a number of assumptions. Imbedded in the historiographical work is an assumption that there exists a rural-urban dichotomy in the Middle East.[4] Prominent Yemeni scholars identify similarly distinctive relationships in Yemeni society, reducing the northern tribes for example, to a unit inherently disengaged from the intellectual/statist tradition situated in Ṣanʿā'. Important figures in Yemeni history are often produced to reinforce such widely-held prejudices, including the nineteenth century jurist Shawkānī, Zaydī Imam Yaḥyā and Muḥammad Idrīsī.[5]

I want to question the utility of rigid polarities around a reading of Ibn Khaldun's urban versus rural cyclicism and those who reproduce such biases in other contexts. I single out Gellner for his reading is strongly reflected on representations of the Ottoman relationship with the region, in particular with its implementing schools, courts and other imperial structures most visible in Ṣanʿā', Taʿizz and Ibb, all, at least nominally cities. I argue what is to be found in the relationship between empire and subject does not reflect such concise breaks between sociologically identifiable

---

3 Many have conceded the inadequacy but ultimately failed to supplant the mechanics of historians and social scientists reliant on typologies of the Middle East. The following aspires to further highlight the gross inability of such retrograde tools of the trade to deal with social realities. These social realities demand a far less doctrinaire approach to representing its humanity, one which is as fluid and flexible as its subject. See innovative work in the field by Lila Abu-Lughod, "The Romance of Resistance: Tracing Transformations of Power Through Bedouin Women," *American Ethnologist*, 17 (1990), 41-55; and Martha Mundy, *Domestic Government: Kinship, Community and Polity in North Yemen*, London 1995.

4 Ernest Gellner for example, attempted to incorporate Evans-Pritchard's segmentary-lineage system within Ibn Khaldun's cyclical model with unsatisfactory results. See his *Muslim Society*, Cambridge 1981. For a specific critique see Talal Asad's, *The Idea of an Anthropology of Islam*, Occasional Paper Series, Washington D.C. 1986. Among others, Richard Tapper stresses that the continuous interaction between countryside and administrative centers are not exceptions but rules to understand societies with large rural populations. Richard Tapper (ed.), *The Conflict of Tribe and State in Iran and Afghanistan*, New York 1983, 4.

5 On Shawkānī, see Ḥussayn al-ʿAmri, *The Yemen in the Eighteenth and Nineteenth Centuries: A Political and Intellectual History*, New York 1985, 122; and ʿAbdullāh b. Muḥammad al-Ḥibshī, (ed.) *Ḥawliyyāt Yamāniyya min Sana 1225 h. ilā Sana 1316 h*, Ṣanʿā' 1980, 4.

units. Life in Yemen during the height of Ottoman rule constituted fused realms that challenge the notion of populations distinguished by productive, ideological or other categories, ultimately limiting the value of dichotomies between the rural/urban, tribesman/scholar, subject/ruler.

Before offering my case study I wish to briefly identify the foundations of what I see as the important sediments of a new way of identifying social history in respect to geography in and beyond the Middle East. In order to do this, one must start with Hegel. Hegel promulgated a powerful spatialist ontology and phenomenology, one which reified and fetishized space in the form of the territorial state, the locus and medium of perfected reason. As Lefebvre argues, and I paraphrase: for Hegel, historical time became frozen and fixed within the imminent rationality of space as state-idea.[6] Time thus became subordinated to space, with history itself being directed by a territorial "spirit", the state. In the case of the Ottoman Empire, it is often forgotten that Istanbul's policies did not enjoy universal sanction nor does the contestation that ensued resonate uniformly in all regions. The cases studied here, in fact, reflect the fluidity of space and social relations engaged within, beyond and between it, thus rendering any narrational attempt to confine Yemen's social history inadequate.

The reason I construct this genealogy is to assert one of the fundamental "codes of culture" identified by Foucault that govern language, schemes of perception, exchanges, techniques, values and the hierarchies of practices in the nineteenth century and for many fields still in the twentieth.[7] In certain intellectual and institutional domains the nineteenth century was also a period of great political transition, which often translated these new principles into systems of domination, terror and set the stage for future totalitarian states.[8] To some, this represented a great positive shift in human development. According to Habermas, the great political revolutions of the eighteenth and nineteenth centuries transformed the conscription of day-to-day life into the democratic public sphere. Here the meaning of public space (in the urban context) was extended to include places of public debate and gatherings where the rational voice of the people could be heard. What was distinctive of post 1789 France, for Habermas (and Landes) was that now public authority had been linked to a system of norms

6 Henri Lefebvre, *La production de l'espace*, Paris 1974, 29-33.

7 Michel Foucault, *The Order of Things: An Archaeology of the Human Science*, New York 1970, xx-xxii, 11, 15-16, 305.

8 William E. Connolly, *Identity Difference: Democratic Negotiations of Political Paradox*, Ithaca 1991, 198-222.

and regulations, and these in turn were publicly known, debated, and discussed until a consensus arose over their legitimate and rational application.[9] While such explorations have been embedded geographically, I suggest such references can be made with Ottoman society as well but only after thorough inspection into the assumed characteristics of social practice.

The interpenetration of the polarities within theories of "structuration" has assumed a place in the literature, and with it has come a return to the concrete, which marks a major renaissance of the interconnections between social relations and spatial structures as a central focus for research.[10] As a result of significant changes introduced in the second half of the twentieth century, space is now seen not merely as an arena in which social life takes place, but rather as a medium through which culture is produced. It is in this sense, perhaps, that human geography and sociology can be said to confront a common "problem of order". In this case, the role of the urban space challenges regressive viewpoints of the classical Arab/Muslim social historical arena.

One should consider Andrew Sayer's still persuasive emphasis on the importance of identifying necessary and contingent relations within social structures in order to establish the "difference that space makes" to concrete research.[11] Sayer's suggestion that we abandon the Kantian dualism between space and society is well received and is partially reflected in this discussion.[12] Peter Saunders reinforces this approach by rejecting attempts to establish "the city" as a distinctive object for an "urban" sociology.[13] Rather than imposing strict terms of engagement around assumed cultural uniformity, Saunders presses the case for what he calls a "non-spatial" but not an "aspatial" urban sociology – in other words, one which is not preoccupied with a supposedly autonomous urban reality but which nevertheless remains sensitive to the wider settings of generic and localized social processes. As will be demonstrated below, Taʿizz as a site for interaction goes through numerous transitions, which require inspection

---

9 Jürgen Habermas, *The Structural Transformation of the Public Sphere*, Trans. by Thomas Berger, Cambridge 1989, 51-59, 67-69 and Joan B. Landes, *Women and the Public Sphere in the Age of the French Revolution*, New York 1988, esp. Chap. 1.

10 Anthony Giddens, *A Contemporary Critique of Historical Materialism, vol. 1: Power, Property and the State*, Berkeley 1981, 25-29.

11 Andrew Sayer, "Abstraction: A Realist Interpretation," *Radical Philosophy*, 28 (1981), 6-15.

12 Andrew Sayer, "Epistemology and Conceptions of People and Nature in Geography," *Geoforum*, vol. 10 (1979), 19-44.

13 Peter Saunders, *Social Theory and the Urban Question*, New York 1981, 77-79, 91-92, 107-109, 256-268.

through numerous transitions, which require inspection beyond the assumed boundaries set in the literature.

To Giddens as well, the traditional representation of both social agents and the organization of those settings in which interaction takes place are inadequate. Giddens suggests "place" cannot be used simply to designate "a point in space" and he introduces the term "locale" to refer to the use of space to provide the settings of social interaction.[14] The properties of these settings are utilized by agents in the constitution of encounters across space and time. Such settings are internally differentiated (regionalized) and this plays an important role in the ordering and regulation of social practices that have become routine and hence in the production and reproduction of power relations, and I would add, culture. For Allan Pred, "place" represents a human product: it always involves a transformation of space inseparable from a transformation of society.[15] The intersection of individual paths and institutions in space and time is embedded in the reproduction and transformation of structures of social relations, and this occurs along with the sedimentation of culture. Pred characterizes this theory of place as "historically contingent process" and indeed we could benefit from incorporating such readings in future research into the changes taking place in Ottoman "cities". For this paper, however, I simply want to set the stage for a viable, comprehensive exploration of the changes and continuities embodied in the, what I consider, fused social unit of the Taʿizz *sancaḳ*. I outline a theoretical constant for underlining what I am going to suggest in specific examples. The following examples do not duplicate the western-biases about traditional cultures and their assumed fixity but demonstrate the complexities of cases such as Taʿizz which requires far more careful and case-specific work in the field of human geography. This presentation acts as a conduit for my future research into human change within the geographic and sociological sphere of the Ottoman urban environment, one which does not conform to notions of social evolution but one which gives new life to so-called traditional societies.

I select the period immediately following the Daʿʿān accords of 1911 until the end of World War I because it enables me to highlight some of the inherent complexities of Yemeni society during a period, which gener-

---

14 Anthony Giddens, *Central Problems in Social Theory: Action, Structure and Contradictions in Social Analysis*, Berkeley 1979, Chaps. 4 and 5.

15 Alan Pred, "Place as Historically Contingent Process: Structuration and the Time-Geography of Becoming Places," *Annals of the Association of American Geographers*, 74 (1984), 279-97.

ally depicts the Ottoman Empire and the Islamic world in a scientifically regulated and generalizable state of stasis.[16] Although the war years have been largely skimmed over in both Arabic and European scholarship, through primary research, I can ascertain that the impact of empire and war was one which inspired a new set of social, political and economic conditions for the population of the Ottoman territory of Yemen. At the same time I am not suggesting this period represented a break from a more predictable and orderly past. On the contrary, the Ottoman period is but a chapter of a continuing process of change, adaptation and contestation. Sociological patterns that have often been glossed over with crude Weberian and Durkheimian typologies simplifying Yemeni (and generally Islamic)[17] society into neatly identifiable units – city, country, peasant, tribes, Zaydī, and Shāfiʿī – prove to be highly fluid in their represented forms. By strategically calling into question the epistemological assumptions such units carry through a historical study of Ottoman Yemen during World War I, it is hoped that highlighting the at times confused and highly "un-conventional" behavior of history's silenced millions can prove to be an attractive narrational alternative to the highly problematic literature of the past.

The Imperial Context

The conventional focus of historians is the imperial context in which Yemen during the First World War is situated. Imperial strategies spanning decades are certainly highlighted as opportunities arise for the imperial actor – Italy, Great Britain and the Ottoman State – in the South Arabian theater. Unfortunately, much of the literature studying imperial rivalries takes a decidedly

---

16 The treaty was signed between representatives of the Yemeni Zaydī community - Imam Yaḥyā in particular - and the Ottoman Imperial state led by Marshall Ahmet ʿIzzet Pasha, ending hostilities which lasted sporadically since 1904. In return for his cooperation, Istanbul conceded significant local powers to the Imam; Fārūq ʿUthmān Abāẓah, *Al-Ḥukm al-ʿUthmānī fī 'l-Yaman*, Beirut 1979, 277-327; and Sayyid Muṣṭafā Sālim, *Takwīn al-Yaman al-Ḥadīth: al-Yaman wa al-Imām Yaḥyā, 1904-1948*, 4th ed., Cairo 1971, 135-161.

17 This in no way suggests Yemen fits an ideal type which can thus simply be "fitted" into other cases, on the contrary, I suggest each case (and the smaller the scope the better) maintains a distinctiveness and complexity that deserves attention. For an important contribution see Brian Turner, *Weber and Islam: A Critical Study*, London 1974.

externalist perspective, ignoring local populations or, at best, portraying them as hapless pawns to the manipulations of the great powers.[18]

As Jon Mandaville has suggested,[19] imperial structures introduced by Istanbul transformed Yemen over the course of some fifty years of nominal rule in the highlands. It is not enough, however, to evoke administrative transformations and imperial intentions.[20] After consultation of both British and Ottoman documents it becomes apparent that the local population proved to be both adaptable and informative to the Ottoman experience, obscuring comfortable sociological boundaries between the tribe and the city. Examples of Ottoman efforts to solidify imperial control of Yemen, implying implements of an urban perspective, proved unsuccessful largely due to the fact that Istanbul's immediate relationship as an imperial power with its subjects did not correspond with realities on the ground.[21] For instance, Sultan Abdülhamid II's efforts to codify a legitimate Islamic orthodoxy around a resurrected caliphate in Istanbul had little resonance in Yemen. A number of widely diverse but not ideologically confined spiritual centers articulated complex interrelationships with imperial centers, frequently, as will be evidenced below, using the fluidity of local political life between city and its surrounding arenas of contestation as its vehicle.

The often cited resistance by locals should serve notice to imperial historians who have attempted to find some generalizable trends in the Ottoman state and its ideological claims.[22] Local resistance and the heightened pious rhetoric certainly had some impact on how Ottoman administrators

---

18 Frederick F. Anscombe, *The Ottoman Gulf: The Creation of Kuwait, Saudi Arabia, and Qatar*, New York 1997; and Fārūq ʿUthmān Abāẓah, *ʿAdin wa'l-Siyāsa al-Brīṭāniyya fī 'l-Baḥr al-Aḥmar, 1839-1918,* Cairo 1987.

19 Jon Mandaville, "Memduh Pasha and Aziz Bey: Ottoman Experience in Yemen," in *Contemperary Yemen: Politics and Historical Background*, ed. B.R. Pridham, London 1984, 20-33.

20 Thomas Kühn explores in this volume the imperial mentality of Ottoman officials in Yemen to assert comparative parallels with Western imperial powers. See also Klaus Kreiser, "Abdülgani Seni-ein aufgeklärter Imperialist im Jemen (1909-1910)," *Jemen-Report*, 1 (1989), 11-15.

21 Nostalgic journalism emerging in Ottoman cities such as Selanik, canvassed the savage back waters of the empire with ethnographic, fact-finding trips to identify the emerging developmental concerns of a modern, at times ethnically-specified center with the external, tribal provinces such as Yemen. See for example, *Zaman* (Selanik), 1 (April 18, 1879), 3.

22 Selim Deringil, *The Well-Protected Domains: Ideology and the Legitimation of Power in the Ottoman Empire, 1876-1909,* London 1998, 16-92; and Cezmi Eraslan, *II. Abdülhamid ve Islam Birliği*, Istanbul 1992.

courted prospective allies in Yemen, but as will be demonstrated below, any steadfast dedication to analytical units based on sectarian identities and the theological positions associated with them fail to fully monitor events on the ground.

Another example of the use of the assumed monolithic Ottoman governmentality and its failure to address Yemen's complex social dynamism is the identification of an administrative vernacular that seemingly borrowed from Europe.[23] Again during the reign of Abdülhamid II, an extensive, ambitious program of indoctrination was carried out with the intention of settling the empire's "tribal" peoples.[24] In an effort which has received some scholarly attention, highly dubious sociological constructions, based on loose translations of an European understanding of tribes in the Islamic world, were the basis of the selection of a large number of Yemeni children to attend *Aşiret Mektebi* in Istanbul between 1892 and 1902.[25] As with the focus on Istanbul's application of ideological constructs centered around Islam, so too did the application of imperial categories, and how an academic interprets these categories, prove untenable when applied in Yemen.

In Yemen, as elsewhere, local groups, families and individuals adjusted to regional conditions transformed by the war. It is all too often the fact that these adjustments render tribal, sectarian and productive characterizations untenable to the careful historian. My primary vehicle in this study are these power struggles between local claimants to fluctuating currents of internal hegemony – in Imam Yaḥyā's Zaydī highlands and the Taʿizz *sancaḳ*-suggesting they offer good examples of how internal relations in Yemen are in a constant state of flux within the imperial context and of how unreliable the tools of the trade actually are in reading these dynamics.

The Struggle for Power in Yemen

Imam Yaḥyā, the spiritual and political claimant to power of a highly fragmented Shiʿi Zaydī community since 1904, and other paramount figures in highland politics, make up a unit constituted in the literature by a

---

23 The most prominent of those are: Carter V. Findley, *Bureaucratic Reform in the Ottoman Empire: The Sublime Porte, 1789-1922*, Princeton 1980, 20-39, 51-57, 131-142, 246 and Roderic Davison, *Reform in the Ottoman Empire, 1856-1876*, Princeton 1963.

24 For the placement of children of so-called tribal families into the Hamidian Tribal School in Istanbul, see The Prime Minister's Archives in Istanbul, hereafter BBA-DH.EUM.VRK 20/102 1/1.

25 See Eugene Rogan "Asiret Mektebi: Abdülhamid II's School for Tribes (1892-1907)," *IJMES*, 28 (1996), 83-107. and Alişan Akpınar, *Osmanlı Devletinde Aşiret Mektebi*, Istanbul 1997.

number of unsubstantiated assumptions about sectarian and socioeconomic relations in highland Yemen. I argue elsewhere that much of Muḥammad Idrīsī's political and economic autonomy enjoyed in the northern highlands after 1911 reflects the growing challenge to Imam Yaḥyā and his Ottoman allies for spiritual, political and economic control of Yemen.[26] The triangular rivalry between the Porte, Idrīsī and Yaḥyā empowered local potentates who played off the tensions and political aspirations of all parties involved and provided key channels of interactive space for a variety of local actors irregardless of their immediate socioeconomic location. These confrontations took place in a highly integrated commercial and social network throughout the Red Sea region, which had an enormous impact on local economic life.

The Taʿizz sancaḳ

In the Taʿizz *sancaḳ*, it is sectarianism, which has been identified as the central animating force in the region's history. Usually framed as Zaydī versus Shāfiʿī, the Ottoman occupation of the highlands in 1872 marked a new era of Taʿizzi politics. In light of these prevailing social categorizations, it may be well to begin this section with a few comments on its framework. Along with tribal categories, sectarian differences are evoked to define (and confine) the analysis of Yemen's history. In the literature, the focus is usually set on the Zaydī community, the dominant voice in local historiography, reflecting both a class and regional bias. This particular sectarian identity carries an association with specific social and productive patterns of interaction, namely the tribe and the urban educated elite (*ʿulamāʾ*).[27] Revealingly, one of the least discussed factors which, nevertheless, complicates Yemeni daily life, is the network of Sufi orders in Yemen, a largely urban phenomenon according to most literature. As Julia Clancy-Smith discovered in the periphery of the Sahara, Sufi orders, despite their categorical rootedness, transcend borders, be they geographical,

---

26 Isa Blumi, "Imam Olarak: I. Dünya Savaşi sirasinda Osmanlı Hakimyeti Altındaki Yemen'de Imparatorluk ve Iktidar Macerasi," in *Osmanlı* vol. 2, ed. Gülen Eren, Istanbul 2000, 609-621. Post-Ottoman historians took exception to Idrīsī's anti-Imamate stand and have thus marginalized his role. ʿAbd al-Wāsiʿ al-Wāsiʿī, *Tārīkh al-Yaman*, Cairo 1928, 338-343.

27 A perfect example is the essentialist representation of tribal structures in Yemen by Faḍīl ʿAlī Aḥmad Abū Ghānim, *al-Qabīla wa-'l-Dawla fī 'l-Yaman*, Ṣanʿāʾ 1990, 258-260.

political, productive or spiritual.[28] Sufism proves to be an ideal indicator of the diversity of constantly changing interests, resulting in a rich variety of sociopolitical scenarios, leaving the chronicles and those historical narratives based on them falsely authoritative. In a case focused on more closely below, Muḥammad Ḥasan of the Shādhiliyya order located in the heart of mercantile Taʿizz, like Muḥammad Idrīsī in the ʿAsīr, proves highly successful in attracting individuals and their retinue from both the major Sunni and Shiʿi communities at various times in the war. While Yemeni Zaydī and Shāfiʿī historians persistently marginalize the impact of Sufi orders, it is clear that the rigid social boundaries local historians and western academics seek to affirm are rendered incompatible with historical realities.[29]

On the surface, the Ottomans enjoyed strong support in the *sancaḳ* of Taʿizz where prominent Shāfiʿī judges and regional landlords existed separately from Zaydī groups located to the North. Such qualified support reflected the impact Ottoman rule had on social conditions and economic links in Yemen's highlands. To some observers, the Ottoman army obstructed Zaydī elements which had periodically invaded the southern highlands in the past.[30] But such simplistic readings of the Ottoman period fail to identify a number of deeper currents taking place. It is clear that Taʿizzī elites who elected to support Ottoman power from the 1870s onwards, embraced alliances with the Porte in recognition of the utility of an Ottoman army, shielding them from rivals both in and around Taʿizz as well as in Zaydī territories.[31]

The Porte encouraged such opportunistic gestures and was rewarded by loyal support from a number of key members of the landed and commercial elite in the Taʿizz and central Tihāma regions. Among other things,

---

28 The Raḥmāniyya of Algeria proved to maintain a fluid relationship with colonial French administrators and communities far beyond the edge of the Sahara. This fluidity is of central concern to me in this paper for it is indicative of the unreliability of the assumptions we carry, and indeed often the rhetoric which attempts to define social and political boundaries on the ground. Julia Clancy-Smith, *Rebel and Saint: Muslim Notables, Populist Protest, Colonial Encounters (Algeria and Tunisia, 1800-1904),* Berkeley 1994.

29 Muḥammad b. Aḥmad Nuʿmān, *al-Aṭrāf al-Maʿniyya fī 'l-Yaman*, Beirut 1965; and Muḥammad b. Yaḥyā al-Ḥaddad, *al-Tārīkh al-ʿAmm li-'l-Yaman*, 5 vols., Beirut 1986, vol. 5, 35.

30 Al-Ḥibshī, *Ḥawliyyāt yamāniyya*, 34, 245-6.

31 We may also benefit by considering Tilly's analogy for the function of the modern state as a protection racket in the Yemeni context. See Charles Tilly, "War Making and State Making as Organized Crime," in *Bringing the State Back In,* Peter B. Evans, et al. (eds.), Cambridge 1985, 169-191.

these allies collected taxes, supplied troops for campaigns against rebellious bands and implemented imperial administrative policies.[32] It must be stressed again that in the Yemen *vilāyet*, as elsewhere, such relationships between the Ottoman state and locals were products of specific, local factors; factors which not only must take Ottoman interests into account, but also the strategies among locals who elected to align with the Porte. Earlier, some interesting negotiations between Shaykh ʿAbdul Wāḥid, a local tax farmer, and the Ottoman state had taken place over the subject of the recruitment and upkeep of the local gendarmerie. This gendarmerie consisted largely of racial minorities and other social outcasts, creating, I would suggest, a dynamic to local politics that animated local relations.[33] The articulation of these interests however, are not inherently attached to one category of Yemenis.

As a direct consequence of the 1911 treaty, the relationship between Imam Yaḥyā and Ṣanaʿāʾ may have (for different reasons) stirred the fires among Shāfiʿīs and Sufi leaders in the South. These new tensions led quite often to armed clashes with both the Imam's men and Ottoman troops.[34] Attempts to shore up revenue collection and military recruitment, as the Porte's attention shifted southwards, towards the border with British Aden, helped create a new generation of local, in particular, urban-based alliances. Those most impacted by this reconfiguration were previously favored rural tax farmers who were immediately identified as barriers to progress in a regime bent on instituting such reforms. The reforms of ʿIzzet Pasha for instance, consolidated power in the regional centers – Taʿizz, Ibb, – introducing a new set of urban-based elites who streamlined

---

32 Abāẓah, *Al-Ḥukm al-ʿUthmānī fī 'l-Yaman*, 350-352, and for conditions in Ibb specifically, see Brinkly Messick, *The Calligraphic State*, Berkeley 1991, 46-53.

33 See BBA DH.ID 16-2/17. In a related event, the Ottoman governor Maḥmūd Nadīm toured Taʿizz in September of 1914 and expressed a desire to raise a "national army" to compliment his gendermarie composed of Akhdām (decendents of African slaves) and other social outcasts. Such an effort suggests a level of coherence in the Taʿizz area which resonated with eager allies such as with Shaykh ʿAbdul Wāḥid. See Political Resident at Aden to L. Robertson, Bombay, 39th Weekly Letter, October 3, 1914 PRO FO 78/69396.

34 ʿAbdullāh al-Ḥibshī, *al-Ṣufiyya wa-'l-Fuqahā' fī 'l-Yaman*, Ṣanaʿā' 1979, 107-109. After the treaty, Zaydī areas already under Imam Yaḥyā's administrative control abandoned Ottoman legal structures in order to follow a strictly Zaydī (Imam dominated) judicial structure. These new legal standards threatened the Sufi orders dependent on the previous dual legal system for protection. According to a British subject travelling in the Yemen at the time, this legal shift also did not go so well with local Zaydīs. Wyman G. Bury, *Arabia Infelix, or the Turks in Yemen,* London 1915, 38-39.

institutional reforms. These reforms were part of an attempt to cut back on the "corruption" of rural tax farmers.[35]

In regards to concerns over territorial aspirations of the Imam, many chroniclers substantiate these fears with a reiteration of a clear cut Zaydī/Shāfiʿī cultural and political divide. Indeed there were a number of instances when violent acts took on the dynamics of a sectarian conflict shaped by urban/rural or tribal distinctions. To the dismay of the Governor Maḥmūd Nadīm, newly appointed from Syria, these fears were reinforced during World War I as many in Lower Yemen felt a shift in the loyalties of the empire. At least in the eyes of some, local security had been greatly compromised by the Porte's larger political interests, and as is often the case in imperial documentation (British, French or Ottoman) the lowest common denominator is identified, in this case sectarianism, as the culprit. A series of documents written by Maḥmūd Nadīm to Imam Yaḥyā demonstrates the governor's concern over the negative effects unruly Zaydī members of the "mujāhidūn", a group formally professing singular allegiance to the Imam, had on relations with the local population in the Taʿizz *sancaḳ*.[36] Other documents show that later in the war, "Zaydī" raids on Taʿizz intensified as it became increasingly evident that the Ottomans were not capable of restraining them.[37] These violent raids stand out, for such incursions had been rare before the Daʿʿān treaty. But I would ask, should we content ourselves with interpretations focusing on sectarian tensions? As noted in the beginning of this paper and by a library of recent critical work on imperial discourse, categories evoked in documentation may not adequately reveal the dynamics of the situation on the ground. These raids, for instance, ultimately were considered criminal acts (I would add they also became highly politicized) precisely because of the number of connotations they carried, which both sides used to their advantage.

---

35 See for instance BBA DH.ID 36/18 documents 3 and 4. Among those most active and responsive to the changes were ʿAbd al-Raḥmān al-Ḥaddād and Ismāʿīl Basālama of Ibb. Their success usually came at the expense of figures such as Muḥammad Ḥasan who (discussed below) resisted accordingly by transcending conventional categories.

36 Telegram from the Governor Maḥmūd Nadīm to Imam Yaḥyā, dated 2 Jimād 'Awal, 1333/April, 1915, private copy.

37 In the Report to General Sir Reginald Wingate, High Commissioner, Cairo from J.H. Stewert, Aden Protectorate, September 7, 1917 in Doreen Ingrams, Leila Ingrams, (eds.) *Records of Yemen,* vol. 6, 178. Concerns over Zaydī subjugation were justified when we note that from the moment when the Ottoman barrier falls in 1918, various Zaydī factions raid Southern areas with impunity. Interview with Lieut.-Colonel Ismāʿīl Efendi, commandant of Taʿizz Garrison, as reported by W. F. Bainbridge, February 19, 1919. ibid., vol. 6, 405.

Local reactions to the Daᶜᶜān accord also did not necessarily reflect the strategies of the Porte correctly. Again, the rhetoric of the victim is often applied with a certain precision in order to evoke the desired administrative response. By playing the category game the imperial regime played, local elites may have elicited a more positive response from the Porte. We must concede that locals were able to read imperial strategies and adapt to currents that would best suite their own needs. The Ottoman administration actively sought to preserve its historical role in the southern highlands, especially during the war when it needed stability on the southern front facing British forces. In an attempt to assuage local fears, therefore, "Zaydī" raids during the war often resulted in clashes between Ottoman troops and groups at least nominally allied with Imam Yaḥyā, ultimately causing strains between the Porte and the Imam.[38] Many cultured Ottoman administrators decried the apparent rural dynamics of Yemen life and actively sought to transform society to fit their largely urban prejudices. As hinted at before, rigidly drawn communal or productive lines fail to capture, however, the complex political dynamic of Yemen. In the Taᶜizz area as in the ᶜAsīr, cultural, productive and "tribal" lines were often muted in spite of Istanbul's imperial categories. These raids in Lower Yemen were certainly a political issue for many to take advantage of, often at the expense of those directly harmed. That said, there are far more nuanced explanations, which reflect more concretely the local politics of the war.

Local Actors and the Strategic Utilization of Imperial Categories of Rule

Specific to Taᶜizz during the war, the process of alliance-building on an individual basis provides helpful insight into the dynamics affecting both local and imperial policy. One particularly visible example is Muḥammad Nāṣir Muqbil. Since 1900, Muḥammad Muqbil, for a number of local reasons, attached his political fortunes to the Ottoman Empire. As a key component to the solidification of Ottoman territorial claims along the border with ᶜAden, Muḥammad Muqbil, in the role of tax collector, is a model example of the Ottoman client. It is easy to follow the logic of Muḥammad Muqbil's intentions during the war when the vigorously contested political environment is taken into consideration. Muḥammad Muqbil and others surfaced during the war for their strategic loyalty to the Porte – Shaykh

[38] For a partisan representation of this issue see Muḥammad b. Aḥmad Nuᶜmān, *al-Aṭrāf al-Maᶜniyya fī 'l-Yaman*, 26-28.

Aḥmad Nuʿmān and ʿAbd al-Raḥmān al-Ḥaddād are also good examples.[39] The task of extracting limited state resources was tied in with Ottoman military concerns as war with Britain loomed. Such concerns provided the opportunity for individuals such as Muḥammad Muqbil, a perennial low-level player, to climb social and political ladders. Such individuals did not hesitate to prove their loyalty to the Ottoman administration by carrying out even the most unsavory of state actions.

Muḥammad Muqbil benefited from the militarization of Taʿizz's social and political environment, countering the influence of several powerful local figures who, historically, monopolized Ottoman attention and were clearly a barrier to his own aspirations. Muḥammad Ḥasan, for instance, due to his religious credentials had been a far more influential figure in the region than Muqbil. During the period under review, however, Muḥammad Ḥasan witnessed a significant deterioration of his relationship with the Ottoman administration. Such a situation provided individuals such as Muqbil the opportunity to prove their loyalty and value as an agent of the state while others, like Muḥammad Ḥasan, became increasingly marginalized.[40]

Muḥammad Ḥasan's story proves a new set of criteria for reading into Taʿizz politics is requisite. It suggests there was a current of transition in the context of the war which resulted, at times, in armed revolt in the southern highlands. Muḥammad Ḥasan displayed an ability, when necessary, to make those intersectarian alliances that are key to understanding Yemeni politics.

Sayyid Muḥammad Ḥasan represented a significant rupture from the past relationship his saintly father had with the Ottoman state. As leader of the most powerful Sufi order in Taʿizz, the Shādhiliyya, the important role his father played throughout the period before the war serves as a model case study of Ottoman imperial policies.[41] The decision by Muḥammad Ḥasan to resist Ottoman reform measures after Daʿʿān and create links with outside opposition figures, particularly with rebellious Zaydī elements who had often demonstrated a certain hostility towards Sufi orders in Lower Yemen, proves emblematic of the dubious value sectarian categories carry.

---

39 Ḥaddād, *al-Tārīkh al-ʿĀmm li-'l-Yaman*, vol. 4, 211-216.

40 The transition period of 1918 is also a fascinating example of what a dramatic shift in local power configurations could do to figures such as Muqbil. See Nuʿmān, *al-Aṭrāf al-Maʿniyya fī 'l-Yaman*, 27-8.

41 See Messick, *The Caligraphic State*, 43 n. 38. See also Report to General Sir Reginald Wingate, High Commissioner, Cairo from J.H. Stewert, Aden Protectorate, September 20, 1917; Ingrams, Ingrams, *Records of Yemen,* vol. 6, 182.

We can speculate why Muḥammad Ḥasan took measures to distance himself from the Porte during the war by focusing our view on the social and political tensions which surrounded him. As noted above, the conditions in Taʿizz changed for the imperial state as World War I erupted – affecting in the process local political relations. In Ḥasan's case, it seems the encroaching hostilities with Britain resulted in mounting tensions between himself and the Ottoman state. While Ḥasan's *tekke*, located in the center of Taʿizz, represented an important cornerstone to the Ottoman governor's pre-war strategies, Ḥasan was being marginalized because of a significant shift in the political relationship between the Ottoman state and its new allies in Taʿizz. The strategic importance of the southern border with the ʿAden protectorate required leaders who could, for instance, recruit loyal forces willing to fight along the southern front.[42] The Shādhiliyya *tekke*'s position in Taʿizz political circles had been slowly overshadowed by the encroaching war which had catapulted figures such as Nuʿmān and Muqbil to prominence. Strategies which resulted in realignments of local power were key to Said Ahmed Pasha's defensive strategy, rendering inactive Sufi shaykhs a liability.[43] There are plenty of examples of local figures who had made the necessary adjustments, protecting their positions locally during the war. It would, therefore, be incorrect to suggest there were universal patterns taking hold. ʿAbd al-Raḥmān al-Ḥaddād, for instance, adapted to the new conditions quite well and effectively performed the Ottoman state's business much like Muqbil.[44] There are always those who fall out of favor, often a necessary sacrifice for the sake of more important local alliances. Muḥammad Ḥasan appears to be one of them.

It is also possible that many like Ḥasan identified potential gains to be had by distancing oneself from the Ottoman administration, especially with the emergence of the southern and northern (Muḥammad Idrīsī's ʿAsīr) fronts in which Britain was the principle adversary. Possibly, Ḥasan

---

42 Abāẓa, *Al-Ḥukm al-ʿUthmānī fī 'l-Yaman*, 346-351. See also the pursuit of Shaykh Abdullāh b. Qāsim by Ottoman officials who blacklisted him despite his past collaboration with the Porte. BBA Dahiliye Nezareti: Hukuk Kalemi Evraki, 59/15 document 6.

43 Said Ahmed Pasha was commander of the 7th Corps, comprised mostly of Syrian troops.

44 See Muḥammad Zabāra, *Nuzhat al-Nazar*, Ṣanaʿā' 1979, 347-48 for a biographical profile of this prominent legal scholar and ally of the Ottomans in Taʿizz. One reason for the alliance may be that Ḥaddād was still mainstream Shāfiʿī and the Sufi element really was being marginalized by the Zaydī alliance in which the Shāfiʿī may have been an indirect partner. For information on Shāfiʿī opposition to Sufi orders in Southern Yemen during the period see, Zabāra, *A'immat al-Yaman*, 1956, 149-57.

and others elected to stake their fortunes on the inevitable fall of the Ottoman army in Yemen and the emergence of a British-dominated peninsula rather than acquiesce to the reconstitution of local politics.[45] There were undoubtedly moments in the war that convinced many of these individuals to take their chances in opposition. In Ḥasan's case, early in the war the Ottomans began to pressure him to pay back taxes. Importantly, they used Shaykhs Muḥammad Aḥmad Nuᶜmān and his uncle ᶜAbd al-Wahhāb to collect these taxes, precisely the two individuals who were rising at the expense of Ḥasan. The imposition of a strict tax policy towards Ḥasan certainly articulates a falling out with the Ottoman administration. Of course, the rise of figures like Nuᶜmān and Muqbil added to his disillusionment by establishing unfamiliar power relations which exposed Ḥasan to abuse and thus hastened his ultimate defection. It may be added that early in the war and indeed as early as 1908, the British demonstrated near military impunity in the area, possibly impressing upon some that the Ottoman's days were numbered in Yemen.[46]

By the time events reached their climax for Ḥasan in 1917, he had amassed a sizable coalition of similarly disaffected leaders from throughout the *vilāyet*. The Shaykhs of ᶜUdayn, for instance, among whom we find the father-in-law of Ḥasan, offered their men to help him against the mobilized Ottoman army.[47] In the whirlwind of events of September 1917, Abbās Narb [sic] and Qāyid Ibn Rājih with their followers of about 1.200 men located on Jabal Baᶜadān added their respective forces to fight on the side of Ḥasan. It is reported that groups from Jabal Ra's, Marᶜrab, Habashī, and Yaḥyā bin Yaḥyā al-Shāyif, a Zaydī notable of great importance in the northern highlands, supported Ḥasan with 1.800 men. Clearly by 1917, local conflicts began to develop across regional links and to transcend urban/rural divides, mostly, I suggest, because of Idrīsī's success, but also because Ḥasan was able to exploit the general impression that the Ottomans were losing the war.

---

45 Shaykh Muḥmmad ibn Qāsim of Taᶜizz for instance, is mentioned in a court case brought against him for commiting dangerous acts, see BBA, *Dahiliye Nezareti: Hukuk Kalemi Evrakı*, 59/15 documents 2 and 3. He is also mentioned in British records for soliciting weapons from Idrīsī to use against the Ottomans. See Report from Major E.R. Reilly, to the First Assistant Resident, Aden, October 26, 1917; in Ingrams, Ingrams, *Records of Yemen,* vol. 6, 130.

46 Rather honest reports stream in from Yemen, depicting the defeats at the hands of the Italians before WWI began. BBA Y.MTV 289/78.

47 Report to General Sir Reginald Wingate, High Commissioner, Cairo from J.H. Stewert, Aden Protectorate, September 20, 1917; in Ingrams, Ingrams, *Records of Yemen,* vol. 6, 186.

The war both fortified and created new alliances within the Ottoman camp and provided opportunities for parties marginalized by the Daʿʿān treaty to seek out alliances which would challenge Imam Yaḥyā and the Ottoman state. In large part, the conditions of war in which a relatively powerful and wealthy outside power like Great Britain contributed to the internal dynamics of Yemen through Muḥammad Idrīsī made these alliances viable.[48] In sum, the war transformed day-to-day political life in the *sancaḳ* of Taʿizz. Often, what was previously a pattern of Ottoman patronage dramatically changed with the shifting needs of the administration. Many groups in the previously favored rural arena were marginalized by the strategic needs of the Ottoman military. With the combination of disrupted patronage patterns, a revitalized Zaydī opposition allied against the Imam and a thriving center of opposition in ʿAsīr, the calculus of revolt greatly changed after 1915. In Taʿizz, these dynamics translated into interesting alliances between disaffected local elites locked into tiny enclaves of support and a broader, essentially anti-Imam Yaḥyā movement in the northern highlands.[49]

Conclusion

The interlacings of social theory and human geography have rarely been developed in any substantial sense. Some paradigms, however, have thankfully been systematically repudiated. Throughout the social sciences, the "social" was traditionally separated from the "spatial" – a profoundly Kantian dualism. In much the same way that Durkheim had tried to secure a niche for sociology by treating its object as the explanation of social structures by intrinsically social processes, so human geography came to be defined in equally exclusive notations: as the explanation of spatial structures by intrinsically spatial processes. Many of these "spatial processes" were described in the terms of formal language systems, especially geometry and probability theory, and this created larger conceptual distances between human geography and the heterogeneous ordinary language systems deployed in social theory. Despite this, for the most part both disciplines

---

48 One only needs to observe the alliances established during the war with Italy in 1911-1912 to understand how the penetration of another imperial power created immediate reconfigurations of power. See John Baldry, "The Turkish-Italian War in the Yemen, 1911-1912," *Arabian Studies* III, 1976, 51-65.

49 See Muḥammad al-Mujāhid, *Madīnat Taʿizz: Ghaṣan Naḍīr fī Ḍuḥa al-Tārīkh al-ʿArabī*, Ṣanʿā' 1997, 191-197.

continued to share a notion of the natural and thus perpetuate notions of positivistic science and the metaphysics of functionalism.

The critique of these positions is by now extensive, and it is not the place to provide a summary of it here. But I do want to signal one of its most important effects, for it identified a break between social theory and human geography which was consummated, ironically enough, by a premature withdrawal from the analysis of spatial structure altogether. Space was seen as somehow epiphenomenal, as a "codification" or a "reflection" of human intentionality or social structure. This meant that any explanation of spatial organization had to be sought within what remained a social theory that was aspatial in nature. Cities were distinctive by design and closed out identifiable extremities. Debates came to pivot around whether social life ought to be conceived in terms of intentionality (the realms of interpretative sociology, constitutive phenomenology and hermeneutics, and of "idealist" and humanistic geography) or of structure (the realms of structural functionalism and structuralism, of systems theory and urban and regional political economy). At best, the problematic of spatial structuring was peripheral to these exchanges; at worst, it was flatly condemned as an irrelevant distraction. The cases noted above demonstrate a fluid transition between categories, suggesting we reconsider previous notions of social order in its relations to geography.

Work to date has failed in answering some of the most basic questions about Yemeni history during the Ottoman period, largely because it does not frame these questions in new ways. In addition to being ignorant of Ottoman archival materials, the literature is oblivious to the theoretical questions raised in other disciplines, most of which would in themselves benefit from contributions in the Yemeni case. I believe Yemen serves as an ideal case to inspire a reassessment of the Ottoman experience in all areas of the empire and challenge the uncritical application of academic conventions. By scrutinizing the imperial context and the effects it has on local political relations, stressing local identifications to, both, challenge the myth of a limited number of cohesive analytical units and identify the components of a multi-tiered social network which exerts a variety of forces, we may begin to be able to make sense of the complexities of local political and imperial power.

It is necessary in Yemen's case to reflect on the dramatic transformations that take place in such administrative areas by expanding the analytical space through which one makes an historical inquiry. This process explicitly seeks to incorporate a notion of an integrated sociological and political unit that will enhance our understanding of these transformations. In the case of Yemen, in particular after the Da‘‘ān accords, the provincial capital, Ṣanʿāʾ, undergoes a modification in respect to its administrative role. I would argue that focusing on Ṣanʿāʾ as a geographical and socio-political unit of analysis obscures its widely complimentary role in the context of transcendent issues. In fact, the urban context – that includes for different reasons Taʿizz, Ṣanʿāʾ and Abha in the ʿAsīr – needs to be studied with a watchful and diligent understanding that Yemeni politics is a far more complex and geographically – and hence culturally – dispersed subject of inquiry.

Throughout I reflect on sectarian relations and their impact on the articulation of imperial and local claims to both political legitimacy and functional efficacy. This inspection has highlighted shortcomings in the literature. The role, for example, of various Sufi orders in the expansion of parties in both Ṣanaʿāʾ and Taʿizz power circles has never been explored and yet proves important. Another example is the fragmentation of Imam Yaḥyā's constituent power base which ultimately led to a redefining of Yemeni urban politics, and as a consequence, tribal composition and trans-regional interaction.

Yemeni social and political life is a complex web of sectarian, racial and productive strata which help shape political decisions. With these strata, ecological, geopolitical and macroeconomic factors all help shape the complexity of the internal dynamics of power. Sectarian, racial and productive differences do animate individual decisions and positions taken by prominent figures. But to attempt to confine the numerous factors which mark each act separate in its basest form, simply seeks to restrict human diversity for the sake of narrational coherence. Once we have rid ourselves of the confining shackles of social categories still actively used in urban sociology we can look into the specific reasons why the son of Imam Yaḥyā joined forces with, of all people, Idrīsī or why the Imam, a Zaydī, formed alliances with Shāfiʿī notables such as Basāmala or even the Ottoman state. Part of the project is finding a new body of evidence; the Ottoman archives in Istanbul prove to be helpful but not a completely satisfying starting point. Access to private papers and the original Ottoman reports, not their summations, can give us an important fragment of daily Yemeni life without the pretenses of an imperial fixation on categories. That requires more assistance from our colleagues in Yemen to open up their accumulated archival resources for all of us to attempt to shed new light onto the Ottoman period specifically and the complexities of human life in general. In the end, however, it is our persistence in challenging accepted norms in our respective fields that will shed new light onto dynamics of politics in places such as Taʿizz.

ABOUT THE AUTHORS

Isa Blumi
Ph.D. cand. in History and Modern Middle Eastern Studies, Kevorkian Center for Middle East Studies, New York University.

Ralph Bodenstein
Ph.D. cand. in Islamic Studies, Department of Oriental Studies, University of Bonn.

John T. Chalcraft
Lecturer in Modern Middle Eastern History, Department of Islamic and Middle Eastern Studies, University of Edinburgh; author of "The Striking Cabbies of Cairo and other stories: crafts and guilds in Egypt, 1863-1914" (State University of New York Press, forthcoming).

Randi Deguilhem
Professor of Modern Middle Eastern History, Centre National de le Recherche Scientifique, Institut de recherches et d'études sur le monde arabe et musulman (IREMAM), University of Provence; editor of *Le waqf dans l'espace islamique outil de pouvoir socio-politique*. Damascus 1995.

Leila Fawaz
Professor of History and Eastern Mediterranean Studies, Director of the Fares Center for Eastern Mediterranean Studies, Tufts University; most recently author of *An Occasion for War; Civil Conflict in Lebanon and Damascus in 1860*. London 1994.

Jens Hanssen
Assistant Professor of Middle Eastern and Mediterranean History, Department of History, University of Toronto; author of *Fin de Siècle Beirut: The Production of Space in an Ottoman Provincial Capital* (in preparation).

Christoph Herzog
Lecturer in Ottoman Studies, Department of Languages and Culture of the Middle East, University of Heidelberg; author of *Geschichte und Ideologie. Mehmed Murad und Celal Nuri über die historischen Ursachen des osmanischen Niedergangs*, Berlin 1996.

Thomas Kühn
Ph.D. cand. in History and Modern Middle Eastern Studies, Kevorkian Center for Middle East Studies, New York University.

Wolf-Dieter Lemke
Librarian-in-chief, Orient-Institute in Beirut and Istanbul; Ph.D. in Islamic Studies.

Ussama Makdisi
Associate Professor of History, Department of History, Rice University; author of *The Culture of Sectarianism, Community, History and Violence in Nineteenth-Century Ottoman Lebanon.* Berkeley 2000.

Astrid Meier
Lecturer in Modern History, Department of History, University of Zürich; author of *Hunger und Herrschaft, Vorkoloniale und frühe koloniale Hungerkrisen in Nordtschad.* Stuttgart 1995.

Anne Mollenhauer
Ph.D. cand., History of Art and Architecture, Department of Archaeology and Cultural History of the Middle East, University of Frankfurt.

Christoph K. Neumann
Lecturer in Ottoman Studies, Istanbul Bilgi University, Department of History; most recently co-editor of *Frauen, Bilder und Gelehrte: Studien zu Gesellschaft und Künsten im Osmanischen Reich; Hans Georg Majer zu Ehren,* Istanbul 2002.

Thomas Philipp
Professor of Politics and Modern History of the Middle East, Department of Modern Middle Eastern Studies, University of Erlangen; most recently author of *Acre, The Rise and Fall of a Palestinian City, 1730-1831.* New York 2001.

Stefan Weber
Postdoctoral research fellow for History and Art History, Orient-Institut Beirut; author of *Zeugnisse Kulturellen Wandels: Stadt, Architektur und Gesellschaft des spätosmanischen Damaskus im Umbruch (1808-1918)* (in preparation).

Filiz Yenişehirlioğlu
Professor of History of Art, Department of History of Art, Hacettepe University Ankara; co-author of *Mersin Evleri.* Ankara 1995.

INDEX